Decades of Crisis

Decades of Crisis

Central and Eastern Europe
before World War II

Ivan T. Berend

UNIVERSITY OF CALIFORNIA PRESS

Berkeley / Los Angeles / London

University of California Press
Berkeley and Los Angeles, California

University of California Press, Ltd.
London, England

© 1998 by
The Regents of the University of California

Library of Congress Cataloging-in-Publication Data

Berend, T. Iván (Tibor Iván), 1930–
    Decades of crisis: Central and Eastern Europe before World War
II / Ivan T. Berend.
        p.   cm.
    Includes bibliographical references and index.
    ISBN 0-520-20617-7 (cloth : alk. paper)
        1. Europe, Eastern—History—20th century.   2. Europe,
Central—History.   I. Title.
    DJK38.B458   1997
    947'.009'04——dc 21   97-39432
                                                                    CIP

Printed in the United States of America
9   8   7   6   5   4   3   2   1

The paper used in this publication meets the minimum requirements
of American National Standards for Information Sciences—
Permanence of Paper for Printed Library Materials, ANSI
Z39.48–1984.

For my teacher and life-long friend,
Paul S. Pach

Contents

Illustrations

Revolutionary Avant-Garde

World War I, Revolutions, and National Revolutions

Life and Society

Authoritarian Regimes and Their Pillars

Dictatorship and Terror

The Arts of Resistance and of the Dictatorships

Acknowledgments

This volume has a long history. Its first version was published in 1982 in Hungary, where in five years it had three editions and
sold forty thousand copies. The English-language edition was derailed
prior to publication when Pergamon Press collapsed in 1991. This
unfortunate situation, however, gave me the opportunity to prepare an
entirely new manuscript in the place of the ten-year-old one.

I should like to express special gratitude to three prestigious institutions. All Souls College, Oxford, elected me visiting fellow in 1980,
and I profited greatly from the college's ideal working conditions and
stimulating intellectual atmosphere. The Codrington and Bodleian
Libraries, and London's splendid museums and exhibitions, enabled me
to complete, with the exception of a single chapter, the first draft of the
first Hungarian version of this book.

I also owe a great deal to the Woodrow Wilson International Center for Scholars in Washington, D.C., which granted me a fellowship
for the academic year of 1982–1983. The center's intellectual environment, seminars, and technical assistance; the unique collection of the
Library of Congress; and the excellent museums of Washington,
Philadelphia, and New York provided a wealth of resources for producing a more advanced, second Hungarian version.

Last, but not least, I am very grateful to the University of California at Los Angeles. I joined the faculty of the history department in 1990,
and the past years have offered an unparalleled working experience. The
rich collection of the University Research Library, the research assis-

tance granted by the Academic Senate and the Center for German and European Studies at Berkeley, and most of all the vivid scholarly life at the university have made the complete rewriting of the book possible. This final English-language version excludes Germany, which was part of the region under discussion in the Hungarian editions, and includes the Baltic countries and the Soviet Union, not handled in the original versions.

Special thanks must be expressed to three great friends of mine. György Ránki, with whom I have coauthored several books in the past, deserves special mention. Our joint research has helped to shape my ideas on economic history. He read the first draft of the first version of my manuscript and made several important suggestions.

Eric Hobsbawm's complex, groundbreaking books, *The Age of Revolution* and *The Age of Capital*, inspired me to write the present work. He and I have discussed these subjects on different occasions in Budapest and in the garden of his house at Hampstead. The final draft of this volume had just been completed when I happily received his new *Age of Extremes*, a monumental work that covers the period of my investigation.

György Lehel, the conductor and my late friend, helped me to understand the music and musicians of the age. Together we heard, enjoyed, and discussed the music connected with my book.

I am also grateful for lengthy discussions with Thomas Balogh, Alec Cairncross, and John Kenneth Galbraith. Barry Supple, a close friend, provided me with new inspiration when he invited me to deliver the Ellen MacArthur Lecture series in Cambridge in 1984. It was in preparation for this series that I rethought the concept of this book. While staying as his guest in the Master's Lodge at St. Catherine's College, I had long talks with him on the topic.

I have profited from the assistance and comments of Daniel Chirot, Norman Stone, Prosser Gifford, James Billington, László Peter, Miklós Lackó, Gyula Juhász, and other fellow historians who were my colleagues at the Institute of History of the Hungarian Academy of Sciences and Department of Economic History of the Budapest University of Economics.

Ellen Wilson deserves special gratitude. Her careful and thorough editing "translated" my English manuscript into English. Without her contribution I could not present this volume to the readers. Last, but not least, I am also grateful to Carolyn Hill, the copy editor of my manuscript, who performed an extremely valuable job in smoothing and clarifying the text of this volume.

In working on a book of this scope, I have accumulated many debts to my family, friends, colleagues, and students. I have discussed the issues raised here with many people in varied circumstances and have received numerous helpful critiques and suggestions. Unfortunately, these debts have been too widely incurred for proper individual thanks to be possible in every case.

Finally, I should like to present my book with the words of the doyen of all historians, Edward Gibbon. I have read with a feeling of déjà vu the last sentence of his eighteenth-century classic, *The Decline and Fall of the Roman Empire*, "which has amused and exercised near twenty years of my life, and which, however inadequate to my own wishes, I finally deliver to the curiosity and candour of the public" (Gibbon 1787).

Los Angeles, April 8, 1995
Ivan T. Berend

Foreword

Central and Eastern Europe is in a state of flux. Only fifty years ago, the establishment of the socialist "ancien régime" was considered revolutionary. Now the world has witnessed its spectacular collapse. Multinational states have dissolved, and independent new states have emerged. Foreign domination has disappeared suddenly from a region that was long controlled by neighboring great powers, and local conflicts, minority issues, and border disputes have emerged in the power vacuum created by the demise of Soviet-controlled state socialism. Some of the newly independent countries of the region have hurriedly adopted Western institutions and are attempting to integrate quickly into the European Union. New hopes, new conflicts, and determination coexist with strong attachments to the old state socialist system.

The present state of this region can be understood only in context of its past. Its legacy derives not only from the burden of the immediate past—the four, or even, in some cases, seven decades of state socialism. Rather, several disparate historical periods have contributed to the creation of a Central and Eastern Europe that differs significantly from the West. One of these determinant periods was the first half of the twentieth century, when, in rebelling against West European modes, the Central and Eastern European region embarked on a historical "detour."

From the turn of the century, a peculiar and complex crisis spurred by a revolution of cultural values began unfolding in Europe. It penetrated not only the economy but also the society and its politics. The nineteenth-century era of capitalism and liberalism was succeeded by a period of convulsions, in which faith in the harmonious working of capitalism wavered or was undermined even in the advanced, industrialized countries.

The less developed countries on the European periphery, among them those of Central and Eastern Europe, faced profound uncertainty: would they successfully follow the example of modernization set by the West and join the Western-dominated world system? The half-century-long attempt before World War I to adopt Western institutions and to imitate Western development had been only partially successful even in the best cases, and in most cases had failed entirely. Because the Central and Eastern European region lagged behind the West and retained agrarian-rural-peasant societies notable for the tenacious survival of feudal and aristocratic forms of organization, it was less wedded to Western capitalism and liberalism and thus more ready to reject the Western system when it began showing signs of weakness and instability.

The bitter disappointment of the unsuccessful peripheral nations, however, was only a part of the European crisis. The atmosphere was filled with a heightened expectation of change. Prophets repeated and scholars attempted to prove that a new twentieth century was coming. Friedrich Nietzsche pronounced that "God is dead!" and thereby suggested that established values were empty and that "the reappraisal of every value" must occur. Looking ahead to the new century, he expected to see the reign of the *Übermensch*, an elite, a new form of superhuman who would lead a rebellion of the courageous, ruthless, and strong against those who were weak, thus transforming all of human society.

Nietzsche was not alone in prophesying a twentieth century characterized by great national wars, upheavals, convulsions, and the politics of force. Marxist scholars from Karl Kautsky and Rosa Luxemburg to Nikolai Bukharin and Vladimir Lenin disclosed their analyses of a transformed capitalism and of the emergence of imperialism. The unfolding era, they said, would be one of wars, of struggle for control and redistribution of regions worldwide, of colonial revolts, and of proletarian revolutions, especially in backward peripheral countries.

Explanations varied and different outcomes were predicted, but no one doubted that the events of the new era would shake the world. This expectation inevitably cast doubt on the validity of the previously dominant Zeitgeist, which was based on an Anglo-French value system associated with liberalism. A product of the advanced West, this system embraced not only laissez-faire capitalism and a free self-regulating market but also specific political and philosophical norms. The rationalism of the Enlightenment, the ideals of individual liberty and parliamentary democracy, free trade, and most of the institutions of nineteenth-century capitalism were challenged. The backward nations, the outcasts, the "lower order," and the "inferior people" now refused to accept their lot in the existing world order as natural and God-given. In the struggle for change, proletarian revolution, nationalist rebellion, and right-wing radicalism functioned as both allies and antagonists. They expressed new ideals and sought to formulate new laws and norms. Great-power domination was attacked by latecomers and subordinated countries, and the traditional ruling elite had to confront the new, rebellious, well-organized social forces of the middle and lower strata of the society. Because vested interests were determinedly defended, open confrontation was unavoidable.

John Kenneth Galbraith states:

People of the World War II generation, my generation will always think of their conflict as the great modern watershed of change. . . . But we should know that, in social terms, a far more decisive change came with World War I. It was then that . . . [countries] centuries in the building, came apart. . . . And others were permanently transformed. It was in World War I that the age-old certainties were lost. . . . The Age of Uncertainty began. World War II continued, enlarged and affirmed this change. In social terms World War II was the last battle of World War I. . . . The Eastern European scene is especially important for us. It was here, not in Western Europe, that the cracks in the old order first appeared. It was here that it dissolved, first in disorder, then in revolution. (Galbraith 1977, 133–34)

Germany and Russia played the leading roles in the twentieth-century rebellion against the West. The nations between these two great powers, especially the countries of Central and Eastern Europe, became supporting actors, and the whole region became a stage for confrontation.

Central and Eastern Europe in the era that led to and emerged from World War I are the focus of investigation in this book. The subject of the analysis is the unique transformation—its causes and interconnections—that penetrated every aspect of politics, economy, society, ideology, and the arts in Central and Eastern Europe.

The book is an historical essay rather than a comprehensive monograph. It does not provide a detailed narrative of politics, economy, society, ideology, and art in the dozen countries of the region—an obviously impossible task. Rather it uses a few dominant historical processes as examples while neglecting others that might be equally interesting. It stresses the interrelationship between economic, political, and artistic trends using the most important countries' examples rather than describing the particulars of each country. It is my hope that my choice of examples suggest the outline of a comprehensive picture of this chaotic period—a picture that will, in turn, lead to a better understanding of the past and, I am convinced, the present of the region.

Map 1. Central and Eastern Europe, 1910.

Map 2. Central and Eastern Europe, 1930.

Map 3. Central and Eastern Europe, 1992.

PART I

The Crisis of Modernization

The Ideologies of Revolts and Their Expression in Art, 1900—1918

I

Catching Up or Lagging Behind?

The Dual Revolution and the Flourishing of Capitalism in Western Europe

In a paradoxical way, the modernization crisis of Central and Eastern Europe was a consequence of the moderate but significant economic and social progress achieved in the second half of the nineteenth century by following the West. The first half of the century had produced an increasing gap between East and West. The British Industrial Revolution transformed the Western European core of the world economy. Conjointly, the French Revolution prepared the ground for major sociopolitical changes. These two revolutions—Eric Hobsbawm's "dual revolution" of the late eighteenth and early nineteenth century—established the Western industrialized, urbanized parliamentary democracies. The subsequent decades saw the triumph of liberal capitalism and of Western colonial powers whose influence extended over all continents.

While Western Europe rode a new express train, most of Central and Eastern Europe still ambled along in an old stagecoach. According to Paul Bairoch's calculations and estimations, the per capita gross national product (GNP) of the Habsburg Empire in 1800 approached that of Western Europe: the latter was 7 percent above, whereas the former was 5 percent below the European average. By 1860, however, the gap had significantly widened. Western Europe's per capita GNP was 150 per-

3

cent higher than that of the European average, whereas that of the empire was 7 percent below. Hungary's level stood at 75 percent of the European average. Countries east of the Habsburg Empire lagged 20 percent behind the European average in 1800, but had fallen to 40 to 50 percent below by 1860. Per capita GNP in Central and Eastern Europe therefore stood at less than one-third of the British GNP (Bairoch 1976).

The prerequisites for the dual revolution that dramatically transformed the West were almost entirely absent in the East. The abolition of the obsolete medieval institutions of noble privilege and serfdom was delayed, as were property rights, personal liberty, the introduction of a self-organizing civic society, and the creation of a modern legal system. The medieval constraints on industry and commerce survived, which prevented the development of modern banking systems, joint stock companies, free access to land, and entrepreneurial freedom.

The Challenge for the Underdeveloped: Temptation and Threat

The speedy rise of the West challenged and demanded a response from those nations in Central and Eastern Europe who lagged behind. The Western pattern provided an attractive model. Intellectuals and even members of the old ruling elite admired the West and argued for change. Pamphlets and books described the alluring transformation of the West and attacked Eastern inertia and backwardness. Influential social groups were mobilized by the fear of lagging behind or of disappearing altogether from the family of European nations—the celebrated early-nineteenth-century Hungarian poet, Mihály Vörösmarty, wrote about a huge mass grave in which the entire nation would be buried.

The formative force with the greatest sociopolitical effect was romantic nationalism. The birth of nations and the recognition of an "imagined community" (Anderson 1983) in the West at the end of the eighteenth century had a tremendous impact in Central and Eastern Europe, sparking imaginations even before political nations were born. National identity, conceived in Western terms, provided a primary impetus for mass mobilization. At the beginning, as Miroslav Hroch convincingly points out, this mobilization was an intellectual phenomenon inspired by a handful of poets, writers, historians, linguists, and artists

(Hroch 1985). The international trend of romanticism arrived in Central and Eastern Europe at the turn of the century and initiated a renewal of national literature, music, theater, and painting that both reflected and created deep, passionate national feelings. National "prophets" bitterly exposed the inner "rottenness" of the ancien régime, denouncing it as a prison for the populace. They worked to stir an awakening of national consciousness. In his 1832 book on the Polish nation and pilgrimage, Adam Mickiewicz equates Poland with freedom and declares that the "crucified Polish nation . . . [which was] laid in its grave . . . did not die." He says that the people, slaves in their own country, would "arise, and free all the people of Europe from slavery" (Davies 1986, 202).

Western industrialization also attracted the interest of Central and Eastern European nobility. By expanding the ability of people in the West to purchase necessities and other goods, Western industrialization extended the market for East European raw materials and agricultural products. During the crucial decades between 1820 and 1880, world trade, which remained primarily intra-European trade, increased ninefold. The landed noble classes, however, could not take advantage of the resulting explosion in export possibilities because they were limited by traditional production methods based on serf labor. The need to modernize agriculture became imminent and evident.

The Western challenge not only provided a tempting model and business opportunities but also posed an economic, political, and frequently serious military threat. The transformation of an expansionist Western Europe into a strong industrial region and efficient democratic system posed an increasing threat to the rest of the continent. Attempting to give an adequate and rapid response to the Western challenge thus became a question of life and death.

Political Responses:
Reforms and Revolutions

Prussia reacted first to the Western threat. Its defeat by Napoleon in 1806 was intensely humiliating and generated an immediate adaptive response. It seemed clear that the feudal economic and political system in Prussia had become outdated and indefensible. The Stein-Hardenberg reforms, imposed from above, had initiated a radical transformation of the economy and society along Western lines. The 1807 emancipation of the serfs, with its provisions for the redemption of feudal services, opened a new path toward modernization that culminated in 1871 in the Prussian-led unification of Germany. The road to rapid transformation was opened, and Germany joined the industrialized core of Europe. The Eastern German states of Prussia, Brandenburg, and Mecklenburg, with economic and social structures resembling those of Central and Eastern Europe, became a part of the West.

The highly industrialized German Reich preserved several "Eastern" elements in its sociopolitical system and, as an ambitious latecomer, played a special role in turn-of-the-century Europe. Since it could not join the "club of colonial empires," the Reich revolted against its Western rivals by producing extremist ideologies and movements. In the stormy history of the first half of the twentieth century, Germany presented a pattern of rebellion against Western values and domination that strongly influenced Central and Eastern European countries. However, despite its pattern of rebellion, Germany shifted into the Western sphere and no longer belonged to the Central-Eastern half of the continent. Consequently the striking story of twentieth-century German history appears here only in references to its strong impact on the region under discussion.

The Russian Empire reacted to Western development much later and more hesitantly. In this respect, the Russian victory over Napoleon amounted paradoxically to a social and political defeat. Victorious, euphoric nineteenth-century Russia remained a sleeping giant. As a stalwart member of the Holy Alliance, Russia staunchly defended the status quo both within and outside its borders, supporting outdated systems, suppressing revolutions, and squelching struggles for independence. Nearly half a century later, Russia finally awoke to the Western challenge. The humiliating defeat in the Crimean War (1853–1856) proved destabilizing, especially in an internal crisis generated by the stagnation of agriculture and by nearly 1,200 local peasant uprisings between 1826 and 1861.

The situation finally moved the tsar to initiate reforms. A tsarist decree, approved on February 19, 1861, abolished serfdom in most parts of the Russian Empire. It guaranteed personal freedom and the right to own private property and granted former serfs the liberty to engage in trade and industry. The manorial justice system was dismantled in 1864 and replaced by a new civil administrative system of justice. Legal and educational reforms were institutionalized as well. In 1870, urban settlements received the limited rights of self-governance, and in 1874, military reforms were introduced in an effort to modernize the army.

All these reforms, however, remained partial and inconsistent in their effects. Although liberated serfs lost about 20 percent of the land previously available to them for cultivation, these lands had been attached to the big estates. Now they worked small plots of land, consisting in most parts of the country of no more than twelve acres. These plots provided only a minimal subsistence for peasants and their families. Free peasants also remained bound to the *obshchina*, the village community, and they could not leave their villages without permission of the ruling council. Until 1906, peasants wishing to exercise their new rights either had to pay about two billion rubles as compensation for the landlord's land they had used that had now become theirs, or to provide "transitional" labor services (a disguised prolongation of feudal services) that might reach forty days per year (Kovalchenko 1971).

Reforms were thus halfhearted. It took yet another military defeat to accomplish the liberation of serfs and the abolition of village communes. In 1905, Japan, a third-rate military power, defeated Russia in a war that revealed the connection between Russian military weakness and the country's social and economic conditions. That defeat stimulated a new era of reforms. Village communities were abolished, compensation was canceled, and the 1906 Stolypin reforms sought to complete the ambivalent steps toward modernization taken by the tsar more than forty years before (Dubrovski 1963).

In the Russian-dominated Baltic territories, reforms from above began much earlier than in Russia itself. Seeking modernization and attempting to follow the German pattern, the Baltic German *Ritterschaften* (landed nobility) emancipated the native peasantry in Estonia and Latvia. Full emancipation was declared in this area earlier than anywhere else in Central and Eastern Europe: 1816 in Estonia, 1817 in Courland, and 1819 in Livonia. More than two-thirds of the Baltic peasantry, however, remained landless. After 1848, a new reform granted tenancies in return for payment of rent. Later reforms, for example in Livonia, altered the political status of peasants, assuring them representation equal to that of the nobility in local administrations.

The Polish Kingdom and Lithuania had more ambitious aspirations. They revolted unsuccessfully in 1794 against Russian rule and the partition of the country, and the next two generations attempted to re-

establish Polish freedom. A November uprising in 1830, although initially successful, was bloodily suppressed; the Polish constitution was
suspended, and eighty thousand people were deported to Siberia. A January 1863 uprising fought bitterly to free the country from the military
government of General Pashkievich, but the following partisan war,
which lasted sixteen months, ended tragically in a new defeat.

The heroic uprisings of the nobility, although militarily unsuccessful and lacking any revolutionary social program, nevertheless resulted
in significant modernization of the country. The tsarist regime not only
dissolved the so-called Congress Kingdom and attempted to incorporate the Polish territories organically into the Russian Empire but also
sought revenge against the Polish-Lithuanian nobility by confiscating
a great part of their land and by distributing it among the former serfs
who had been liberated by a decree of April 1864. The defeated Polish
elite turned thereafter to peaceful actions, to "organic work," that focused on gradual transformation and economic modernization. The result of this long process in the Baltic countries and Poland was reform
more radical than that instituted in Russia (Davies 1986).

If the partially European Russian Empire adjusted to the new Europe with much difficulty, the primarily non-European Ottoman Empire, which occupied the Balkans, experienced even greater problems
adapting to the changes.

The military leaders of the Ottoman Empire, which, since the Treaty
of Karlowitz (1699) had entered a period of defense and decline, realized that the new Europe constituted a threat to the empire. Halil Pasha,
commander in chief, stated in a memorandum to the sultan that "if we
do not follow in Europe's footsteps, we will have nothing left but to
return to Asia." Military defeats at Navarino Bay at the hands of the
united British, French, and Russian navies, and the Russian offensive
that followed, led to Ottoman capitulation and the eventual liberation
of Greece. Together with a series of Serbian uprisings, these events rang
the death knell of the nearly five-hundred-year-old Ottoman rule in
the Balkans. Despite their positive aspects, the *Tanzimat* reforms—the
Hatt-i-sherif (1839) and *Hatt-i-humayun* (1856)—offered too little too
late (Petrosjan 1977). The decline and disintegration of Ottoman control continued, finally leading to the defeats of the First Balkan War. As
a result, in 1913 the Ottoman Turkish Empire was forced back into Asia
Minor, just as Halil Pasha had predicted. A last desperate military attempt by the empire to alter the course of history during World War I
through alliance with Germany ended with the empire's total disinte-

gration; in its place remained a small and poor "third world" country, Turkey.

The gradual decline of the Ottoman Empire and the subsequent rush by other nations to fill the power vacuum in the eastern Mediterranean basin helped to liberate the peoples of the Balkans. From the failed experiment of Alexander Ypsilantis in 1814, to the proclamation of independence of the "Hellenic Republic" in the Peloponnisos, a long road led to the guarantee of Greek independence. The London Protocol of 1830 recognized Greek independence and pledged West European military support, which forced the Sultan to accept the loss of his former territory.

Serbia began its military struggle against Ottoman occupation in 1804. A second insurrection of 1815 led first to a compromise and then to autonomy in 1830. The process of liberation continued with the complete withdrawal of Ottoman troops by 1867 and ended with the Berlin Treaty of 1878, which founded the independent state of Serbia.

The liberation of the remaining Balkan territories and the foundation of independent states was a stormy and bloody process. A series of uprisings in Bulgaria (1876) and in Bosnia (1879), repeated Russian interventions against Ottoman rule, the wars between Serbia and Bulgaria in 1885, and the Bosnian war in 1908 began transforming the Balkans. Finally the two pan-Balkan wars of 1912 and 1913 and the declaration of Albanian independence on the eve of World War I completed the process of creating a post-Ottoman Balkan region of autonomous nations (Jelavich 1977). This development destroyed the Ottoman system of military-bureaucratic-feudal ruling elite. Land that had belonged to the Sultan became the property of the peasantry. This social and political transformation opened the door for modern capitalist change along Western lines. Because the European great powers were deeply involved in the modernization and transformation of the area, and because national independence in each case was guaranteed by international agreements dictated by Western powers, the adoption of Western institutions was predictable. Sometimes reforms were prescribed by the great powers. In the case of Romania, the two principalities that had been under Ottoman domination were united in 1856 as one independent nation by the provision of the Paris Treaty. The United Principalities were also compelled by the Paris Convention of 1858 to emancipate their serfs and to abolish feudal privileges: "All the privileges, exemptions and monopolies," declared the Convention of the great powers, "which certain classes still enjoy shall be abrogated, and the laws which regulate the relations of landlords and peasants shall be revised without delay." The attempt to copy the Western institutions and legal system was crowned by the adoption of the Belgian constitution in Romania in May 1866 (Stavrianos 1963, 352, 357).

Despite the adoption of Western institutions, the economic backwardness in the Balkans, the premodern, traditional societies with their restrictive communal structure, and the existence of wide-spread poverty created genuine obstacles to modernization. Consequently, most of the institutions adopted from the West lacked relevance in the Balkan context and remained formal structures without substance.

Unlike the Russian and Ottoman empires, the Habsburg Empire, which ruled a large part of Central and Eastern Europe, responded more flexibly to the Western challenge. Joseph II, the enlightened absolute ruler of the empire, introduced reforms in the 1780s that emancipated the serfs, secularized the property of the monasteries, created a civil marriage registry, and introduced modern military reform. In the aftermath of the French Revolution and the Napoleonic wars, Prince Metternich instituted a conservative despotic regime that was moderated only by the revolution in Vienna on March 13, 1848. The 1848 revolution created a Constitutional Assembly that introduced social reforms and a modern legal system. Although revolutionary Vienna was reoccupied by the emperor's army in October, its fundamental achievements were guaranteed and opened the road for socioeconomic transformation along British and French lines.

Paradoxically, the Czech hereditary provinces were equally flexible in their response to the Western challenge, although national oppression and the mandatory Germanization of Bohemia-Moravia aimed at assimilating Czech regions into Austria proper.

The Hungarian nobility, unlike the Czech elite, adopted attitudes similar to those of the Polish noble elite. Hungarian nobles revolted against Habsburg domination. On March 15, 1848, two days after the Vienna revolution, a popular uprising began in Pest. The lower nobility, attempting to reintroduce national independence, dethroned the Habsburg dynasty and declared the Hungarian Republic in January 1849. The Holy Alliance, the allied Austrian and Russian armies, defeated the Hungarian revolution in the summer of 1849, but a decree of the emperor renewed the revolutionary laws established by the Hungarian parliament of nobles in April 1848. These laws abolished serfdom (though 60 percent of the peasants were liberated without land), eliminated the nobles' privileges, guaranteed free access to land, and granted personal freedom. A compromise (*Ausgleich*) between the Habsburg court and the Hungarian nobility in 1867 reestablished partial independence for Hungary, setting up an independent government and separate constitutional rights within a reformed dual Austro-Hungarian Empire. Although similar autonomy for the Czech, Slovak, Croatian, Polish, Romanian, and other nationalities of the empire was consistently rejected, the combined impact of (defeated) revolutions and successful compromises paved the road for modern economic-social transformations (May 1968).

Despite these changes in Central and Eastern Europe, remnants of the ancien régimes survived. The old ruling elite preserved their leading positions in the new situation. Big estates were safeguarded, and in most cases, authoritarian, multinational empires were conserved. Institutional and social transformation was thus partial and limited, especially when compared with the West. This situation created severe obstacles for modern capitalist development and for the formation of parliamentary democracies. Central and Eastern Europe, however, sought to follow the West, and the international economic environment fostered the necessary conditions for realizing this goal.

Latecomers in an Internationalized World Economy

In responding to the Western challenge of the dual revolution, Central and Eastern Europe thus adopted the fundamental institutions of modern capitalism and created at least the minimal prerequisites for capitalistic economic development. The turning point occurred in the 1860s. During this period, traditional agricultural methods were replaced by modern cultivation, a new railroad system and modern infrastructure was created, and factories appeared. This process was supported by the increasing cross-border economic activity of the core countries, which helped to integrate backward areas into an internationalized world economy.

The increasing export of capital, which began in the mid-nineteenth century and gained a remarkable impetus during the last third of the century, serves as an example to illustrate the importance of cross-border activity. Until World War I, export of capital amounted to forty-six billion dollars, originating mostly from three core countries. More than a quarter of it was absorbed by European countries. Britain, the leading capital exporter, played a diminishing role in European investments and credit after 1850. Between 1865 and 1914 only 13 percent of her capital exports was channeled to Europe. In contrast, France, the second biggest exporter, whose capital export represented one-fifth of total, developed an increasing interest in Central and Eastern Europe: 40 percent of her capital export went to Austria-Hungary, the Russian Empire, and the Balkans around the turn of the century. From the 1880s on, German capital exports, 13 percent of the European total, became significant. More than half of the German capital exports went to Austria-Hungary, Russia, and the Balkans.

The huge influx of Western capital played a decisive role in financing the economies of Central and Eastern Europe. During the decades around the turn of the century, 60 percent of all capital invested in Russia originated from foreign sources, and in mining and metallurgy, 88 percent of invested capital was in foreign hands. In the Austrian and Czech parts of the Austro-Hungarian Empire in 1900, 35 percent of invested capital came from the West; most of this capital was invested in railroads and state bonds. Banking and industrial activity, especially from the 1880s on, was financed from domestic sources. An increasing part of domestic capital accumulation was also being exported, mostly to the Eastern part of the empire and to the Balkans. This Austrian-Czech capital comprised roughly 80 percent of capital imports in these eastern and southern regions.

Between 1867 and 1914, 40 percent of total investments in Hungary came from outside the country, including from Viennese banks. Railway construction was mostly financed from imported capital, and 55 percent of banking and 36 percent of industrial capital were in non-Hungarian hands.

In the Balkans, capital import was almost the only source of investments in railroads, infrastructure, and raw material extraction. In Romania, 95 percent of oil fields lay in foreign hands, and the copper wealth of Bor, Serbia, was being extracted by foreign companies. A huge part of Western credit, however, was being used to finance enormous budget deficits and to build up the bureaucracies and armies of the newly-established independent states. For this reason Serbia, Bulgaria, and Greece became insolvent around the turn of the century and unable to repay the interest and principal of their foreign debts (Berend and Ránki 1982).

The Role of Railroads and Their Spin-Off Effects

The largest share (about half) of foreign investments was earmarked for railroad building. The economic, political, and military interests of the great powers made the construction of a unified European railway system indispensable. The backbone of the Balkan railroad system was the Serbian and Bulgarian section of the famous German-built Berlin-Baghdad line, which served the expansionist goals of the ambitious German Reich. More than one-third of the existing 360,000-kilometer European railroad network ran through Central and Eastern Europe. The railroad density in the region, calculated on length of rails per one hundred thousand inhabitants and area of land, reached roughly half that of the West. Railroads were thus over-developed when compared with the size of the Central and Eastern European economies. Therefore a great part of the capacity was simply not used. The system—with half the capacity of the Western system—shipped only one-fifth of the cargo and one-tenth of the passengers of the Western railroads.

Railroads were not only a means of transportation in Central and Eastern Europe but also symbols of speed and modernity. Both the King of Naples and the Russian Tsar built short private lines linking their winter and summer palaces; these links underscored their power and status. The railway and the locomotive became a topic of poems and paintings. It is difficult, in fact, to overestimate the significance of railroads in facilitating economic modernization. They played a pivotal role in building a modern economy and accelerated economic and social transformation. They created hundreds of thousands of jobs. They provided not only a major source of income for landless peasants but also mobilized a traditionally immobile population in backward rural areas and served as the main boulevard for internal migration. Railroad construction often offered the first nonagricultural work for peasants and became the first stage on the road toward industrial work and a new working-class status.

Railroads spurred the opening of coal mines and the development of mining, iron, and steel industries. During the first decades of the railway boom in Central and Eastern Europe, construction relied on imports of rails and locomotives. In later decades, an emerging domestic industry produced rails and engineering products. Differences among the countries of the region were significant, however: Hungary's railroads became self-sufficient, whereas railroads in Serbia and Bulgaria remained entirely dependent on imports.

The dense railway network linked remote areas, almost frozen in medieval backwardness, with modern urban centers. The enlarged market and cheap ground transportation they provided, especially for huge land-locked countries, created new opportunities for traditional economic activities such as agriculture. Because of rail transportation, the agricultural Central and Eastern European countries could take advantage of the export opportunities offered by the expanding consumer markets of the West. As a consequence, railways played a decisive role in transforming the agricultural sector of the region (Berend and Ránki 1974).

Agriculture and the Export Sectors

According to Simon Kuznets's calculations, a handful of industrialized countries in Western Europe imported 69 percent of the agricultural products and raw materials produced and sold on the world market in the 1870s. In 1913, they still imported 63 percent of the world's imports. The amount of British imports quadrupled in the first half of the nineteenth century, then increased by eightfold until World War I, increasing overall by thirty-twofold during the long nineteenth century. Western Europe's per capita food imports increased by 133 percent between 1870 and 1913. Food and raw materials represented nearly two-thirds of the world trade.

For the less developed agrarian countries of Europe, this provided a nearly unrestricted market, because non-European economies failed to surpass one-third of the world trade until World War I. Whereas European exports increased by 2.8 percent annually during the fifty years before World War I, Bulgarian exports increased by 5.3 percent, Russian exports increased by 3.8 percent, and Central and Eastern European exports as a whole increased 3 percent annually (Bairoch 1973).

This rate of growth could not be sustained by traditional cultivation. The legal-institutional reforms, introduced after 1848 and mostly in the 1860s, opened the doors for modern agricultural technology. Free access to land, the creation of modern transportation and banking systems, the huge inflow of capital, and the introduction of wage labor, which replaced ineffective serf labor, led to a belated adoption of the major achievements of the eighteenth-century Western agricultural revolution. The elimination of the medieval three-crop rotation system, which left at least one-third of the arable land fallow, and the introduction of scientifically based crop rotation systems (the so-called Norfolk system based on a rotation of seventeen sorts of crops) led to a spectacular increase in cultivated acres. Nonetheless, in the 1860s, even in the more developed countries of the area, 16 percent to 25 percent of the land remained fallow. In Lower Austria the percentage of fallow land was 27 percent, in Bohemia 17 percent, and in Hungary 22 percent. By the beginning of the twentieth century, fallow acreage amounted to only 3 percent to 10 percent of land. In the Balkans, the change in cultivation was even more fundamental; medieval seminomadic animal husbandry, which dominated most parts of the area, was replaced by agriculture during the nineteenth century. In the Romanian Principalities, the area sown with wheat increased tenfold in the 1830s and 1840s, a trend that continued into the second half of the century. Between 1860 and 1900, the wheat-growing area more than doubled. In Serbia and Bulgaria, the same transformation occurred from the 1860s on. In Bulgaria, cultivated land increased from 5.6 to 8 million hectares between 1889 and 1912.

The introduction of the modern crop rotation system went hand in hand with the adoption of other innovations of the agricultural revolution, such as land reclamation, irrigation, extensive water regulation, and the use of manure and artificial fertilizers to improve the soil. Improved types of crops and animals significantly increased yields and meat and milk production. Animal-driven machinery, better ploughs, and a total mechanization of threshing increased production. The total wheat and corn production of Austria-Hungary, the Russian Empire, and the Balkans increased between two and two and a half times from 1900 to World War I. Central and Eastern Europe became one of the world's most important bread baskets, producing 50 percent of the total wheat production of Europe. One-third to one-half of the region's total production was exported. Even Russia, by overtaxing the peasantry and forcing them to sell their products, contributed more than a quarter of the world's total wheat exports. Romania supplied 8 percent of the world's total. Hungary became one of the world's biggest wheat flour exporters, supplying 25 percent of the world's total wheat flour exports.

In Central and Eastern Europe, agriculture was the leading export sector, producing 60 percent to 80 percent of the region's exports. Russian and Romanian oil, Serbian nonferrous metal, and Russian iron and timber became important exports around the turn of the century. The region's economies were closely connected with the highly industrialized Western economy, which provided its market, and followed the typical road of complementary development taken by peripheral countries in the world economic system (Berend and Ránki 1982).

International Division of Labor and Its Impact on the Balkans

The division of labor in Europe offered to each country, advanced or backward, industrialized or not, the possibility of joining the world market and playing a specific role. Moreover, being a part of the world economy and exploiting the export possibilities of an expanding world market ensured a higher rate of growth in production and exports and thus increased income and capital accumulation. Economists from David Ricardo to Milton Friedman spoke about the comparative advantages of free trade, asserting that it is advantageous for all nations, since each country is selling what it can produce in the most productive and competitive way and buying what it could otherwise not produce or could only produce expensively. Several examples support this concept. Some countries—such as the Scandinavian countries and the so-called white-colonies—profited from the expansion of their traditional economies, gradually increasing their income. This was, however, not a general rule, for other examples, probably even more numerous—Portugal, the Balkan countries, and most of the "third world" countries—show unequal exchange and the exploitation and relative decline of less developed nations. Economists and political thinkers of latecoming and relatively less developed countries—among others, Johann Gottlieb Fichte and Friedrich List, who were contemporaries of Adam Smith and David Ricardo—argued against free trade and proposed the introduction of protective tariffs.

In the Balkan countries, as a result of internal economic, social, and political conditions, the increase in exports of traditional products and the resulting capital inflow did not prompt industrialization and restructuring of the traditional economy. The quantitative growth of traditional branches merely reinforced and expanded the obsolete structures of the economy. Processing of agricultural products and raw materials rarely occurred. Romania exported 98 percent of her wheat unprocessed, and the oil industry remained a foreign enclave, almost completely out of reach of the domestic economy. The greatest part of production was delivered for processing abroad, and profit from extraction was not reinvested. Bulgarian tobacco, Serbian prunes, and Greek raisins—some of the most important export articles of these countries—needed almost no processing except drying in the traditional way. Serbian pigs were exported unprocessed. Growth rate was much slower in the Balkans than in other areas of Europe, including the western rim of Central and Eastern Europe. Research calculates "negative growth" in the south Slavic countries, which means a moderate decline during the decades before World War I (Palairet 1995). Structural modernization, building up modern economic sectors and processing industries, had very little effect (Mirković 1968).

The Awakening Giant

The general level of economic development in Russia was not much better than that of the Balkans. Some 92 percent of Russian wheat, the country's most important export item, was shipped abroad unprocessed. Timber, which played a central role in Swedish and Norwegian industrialization, was also exported in unprocessed form. Nevertheless, exports did not remain isolated enclaves from other parts of the economy. The empire's economic system slowly was affected and transformed. In addition, the political and military power of Russia played an important role by generating a massive foreign investment, a situation substantially different from that in the Balkans. Working capital, hardly extant in the latter case, significantly influenced Russian modernization. Foreign investors sank large amounts of capital into the extraction and processing of Russia's vast iron resources. Investments into basic industries were 47 percent foreign around the turn of the century, a fact that played a profound role in creating the modern heavy industrial base of the Don River basin. From the 1880s onward, the government banned imports for railroads and built up a huge engineering industry. Not only did exports of traditional goods increase, but industrialization also received a major impetus, especially from the 1890s on. Between 1900 and 1913, coal, textile, and sugar production doubled, iron and steel production increased by 50 to 60 percent, and agricultural machinery production increased fifteenfold (Crisp 1972).

Russia, a great power, thus did not become a dependent and sub-servient partner of the Western core countries and profited from the in-ternational division of labor. Industrialization promoted structural modernization. Nevertheless, although the "sleeping giant" was awak-ening, its economic transformation remained only partial and limited. Per capita industrial production on the eve of World War I was only one-third that of Austria-Hungary's or Italy's and one-sixth the size of Germany's.

The Polish and Baltic "Miracles"

Against the framework of the slow modernization of Rus-sia, the Western rim of the empire, consisting of the Polish, Baltic, and Finnish territories that had been occupied in the eighteenth century, stand out as examples of progress. These regions had more highly de-veloped social-educational environments and entrepreneurial tradi-tions, and the so-called Polish Kingdom—60 percent of the territory of pre-partitioned Poland—and the Baltic countries profited more from Russian modernization than Russia herself. The introduction of an imperial "common market" through the 1851 abolition of internal tariffs opened the Russian market to Polish exports. Consequently, the Polish Kingdom emerged as the third biggest industrial center of the empire. During the twenty years preceding this development, Polish in-dustry increased its production by only three times. After two more decades, from the 1870s on, the value of industrial production increased by four times. Łodz, the "Polish Manchester," became a center of the textile industry, producing 40 percent of total industrial production. In addition, Poland produced 40 percent of the coal, 23 percent of the steel, and 15 percent of the iron of the Russian Empire at the end of the nineteenth century. Per capita industrial production was twice that in Russia. The driving force behind this impressive industrialization drive was undoubtedly the Russian market, which absorbed 80 percent of the production of the Polish textile industry and 40 percent of the output of the iron industry (Kostrowicka 1966).

The same pattern characterized Baltic industrialization. In the sec-ond half of the nineteenth century, Latvia's industrial growth reached an annual 9 percent increase. This growth was based on the Russian mar-ket, because most of the newly emerging industries—engineering, chemicals, textiles, paper, and glass—sent between 60 and 90 percent of their products to Russia. At the beginning of the twentieth century, the domestic market absorbed only 26 percent of Latvian industrial production, and 67 percent of it was sold in Russia. The small nation of Latvia produced 28 percent of the empire's rubber, 13 percent of its wood, and 10 percent of its processed metal. The level of industrialization reached a much higher degree than in the empire as a whole, where only 17 percent of the gainfully occupied population was employed in industry; in Latvia, the figure was 31 percent. In the Livonian and Courland provinces, 53 percent of domestic products were industrial, a situation that illustrated the more mature stage of structural modernization in the Baltic countries.

Although the Polish and Baltic rim of the empire was more developed than Russia, it still suffered from Central and Eastern European backwardness. "In the Kingdom of Poland," as Jacek Kochanowicz states, "industry constituted islands of modernization in a sea of traditional peasants whose . . . level of civilization was almost untouched by industrial development" (Kochanowicz 1989, 122). These countries preserved their overwhelmingly agricultural character along with their relatively undeveloped domestic markets. The structural changes that occurred, judged according to per capita income and other structural parameters, reached a medium level, rather similar to developments in Hungary.

Hungary's Semisuccessful Modernization

Increased export possibilities led to an impressive trebling of Hungarian agricultural production during the nineteenth century. The construction of a railroad system, Europe's sixth most developed network in terms of "railroad density," and the massive influx of German-Austrian capital after 1867 (40 percent of all investments until 1900) combined to create a social environment in which the export-led development fostered industrialization. The wheat merchants of Budapest, who made their fortunes from exports, recognized the advantage of investing in a flour mill industry. As a result, this industry soon became the second largest in the world, surpassed only by the industry in Minneapolis. Unlike Russia and Romania, Hungary exported flour over unprocessed wheat at a ratio of 67 to 33 percent respectively. The success of Hungarian milling was also connected with a major technological invention—the rolling mill made from cast iron—credited to one of the oldest Hungarian engineering firms, the Ganz Co. This machinery revolutionized flour milling, giving a technological advantage to the Hungarian milling industry. Spin-offs from this revolution included huge investments that originated from the wheat export and flour milling industries. Jewish entrepreneurs, such as the Deutsch and Weiss families, built up new branches of sugar, iron, and engineering industries. Extensive railroad construction facilitated the development of coal, iron, and engineering industries, and Hungary's railroad industry became self-sufficient around the end of the nineteenth century.

Domestic capital accumulation diminished the role of foreign capital. The share of foreign capital in Hungarian investments declined from 70 percent between 1867 and 1873, and 40 percent between 1867 and 1900, to 25 percent during 1900 to 1913 (Berend and Ránki 1979).

In spite of its impressive structural modernization and growth, Hungary remained an agricultural country. Some 64 percent of her population was still occupied in agriculture, and nearly the same percentage of gross domestic product (GDP) was produced by agriculture. The country continued to supply farm products to the Austrian-Czech parts of the Austro-Hungarian Empire.

This was even more the case for the other eastern territories of the empire. Some 78 percent of the Croatian populace was engaged in agriculture. In Dalmatia the figure was 82 percent. Bosnia-Herzegovina still employed nearly 88 percent of her population in agriculture, in spite of the deliberate industrialization attempts of the Austrian government, utilizing the territory's rich lumber, coal and iron sources. Bukovina and Polish Galicia employed 73 percent. The economy in most of these territories resembled that of the Balkans more than that of Central Europe. Their industrial consumption needs were partly covered by a traditional cottage industry but mostly supplied by the well-developed industries of the Western parts of the empire (Good 1984).

Industrial Breakthrough in Austria and the Czech Lands

The only truly successful structural modernization in Central and Eastern Europe took place in the Austrian-Czech parts of the Habsburg Empire. The empire itself represented a peculiar self-sufficient unit in Europe, with its industrialized west and agricultural east, and it reproduced the European division of labor inside its borders. The mercantilist-protectionist economic policy of Maria Theresa, accompanied by other state interventionist measures, generated an early protoindustrialization in the eighteenth century, when a large textile industry emerged in Lower-Austria, Voralberg, and Bohemia-Moravia. This nonmechanized textile manufacture represented more than 40 percent of the industrial production of the Habsburg Empire and ensured the supply of the entire empire.

The Austrian-Czech protoindustrialization of the late eighteenth and early nineteenth centuries generated an important chain reaction by ensuring an ever-increasing market for Hungarian agriculture. This, in turn, inspired further advances in industrialization in the western part of the monarchy. A second wave of industrialization began during the 1830s and 1840s, when food processing for export played the leading role. The Bohemian-Moravian sugar industry ensured a third place to Austria-Hungary in European sugar production and became the leading export branch of that region's industry. Plzen became the center of the other star of Czech industry: beer production. Until 1880, Austrian-Czech food processing increased its production by three times, eventually representing one-third of its total industrial output. From the 1880s onward, during the third wave of Austrian-Czech industrialization, the modern textile industry played the leading role and became one of Europe's most developed textile industries, surpassing the French capacities and approaching those of Germany and Belgium. As a result of the division of labor inside the empire, two-thirds to three-quarters of its textile production was sold in the Hungarian market and the eastern parts of the empire. In addition, strong iron, coal, and engineering industries developed, making Austria-Hungary the fifth largest industrial power of Europe, as measured by volume of output. It ranked fourth in world trade, behind Britain, France, and Germany (Olšovský 1961).

In the Austrian-Czech parts of the empire in 1910, nearly half of the active population was employed in industry, and barely one-third was employed in agriculture. Before World War I, Austrian industry was located primarily in the Czech lands (56 percent of total), whereas 64 percent of coal mining and iron-steel capacities, 90 percent of sugar production, and 60 percent of textiles were concentrated in Bohemia and Moravia. The western parts of the Habsburg Empire, and especially the

Czech lands, approached the development levels of the West. According to David Good's thorough examination and balanced evaluation, "Though the western regions of the Empire more or less kept pace with western European contemporaries throughout the nineteenth century, the relative economic backwardness of the Empire as a whole probably intensified. . . . The Habsburg economy should still be classified as relatively backward on the eve of World War I." Good describes the region's moderate economic failure and medium position within Europe: while the empire "lost some ground with respect to Western Europe, it gained with respect to most areas in the European periphery" (Good 1984, 238–44).

The Semifailure of Central and Eastern European Modernization

"Alongside the advanced economies," notes David Landes in his *Unbound Prometheus*, "a number of what we could call today 'underdeveloped' nations embarked during these years of technological transition upon their own industrial revolution. . . . Hungary and Russia assimilated only pieces of modern technology, and these advances, achieved at discrete points of the economy, were slow to break down the tenacious backwardness" (Landes 1969, 236). Certain economic advances characterized the entire European continent, including each of the Central and Eastern European countries. The railroads and the belated agricultural revolution, the increased raw material extraction and export activity, were all definite signs of modernization according to nineteenth-century economic development. The least successful Balkan countries, those totally incapable of breaking out of their preindustrial state, also closed a chapter of their history and, as John Lampe and Marvin Jackson express it, moved "from imperial borderland" to become "developing countries"(Lampe and Jackson 1982).

Although Central and Eastern Europe witnessed a quickening of economic growth, it was not enough to narrow the gap between the two parts of the continent. According to Paul Bairoch's calculations, in the best period of their development, between 1860 and 1910, the countries of the region could not surpass Western growth rates. Austria-Hungary annually increased its per capita GDP by 0.98 percent (Bairoch 1976). The Russian Empire reached 0.96 percent, Romania reached 0.86 percent, and Bulgaria and Serbia reached only 0.50 percent.

During this half-century the European average growth rate was 0.96 percent, but core countries such as France, Germany, and Switzerland had 1.25, 1.39, and 1.25 percent respectively. The rapidly developing Scandinavian countries, which caught up and joined the European core on the eve of the war, reached a nearly 2 percent annual per capita rate of growth. According to the new calculations of Angus Maddison, twelve West European countries, including the Scandinavian ones, reached, as an average, 1.3 percent annual per capita real GDP growth between 1870 and 1913. The advanced overseas countries had a 1.5 percent annual growth. Central and Eastern Europe, including Russia, achieved a 1.2 percent growth rate; however, this impressive result still lagged behind the advanced world's accomplishment. The arithmetic average per capita GDP (in 1990 international dollars) reached $1,527 in the region, compared to the $1,788 South European, and $3,482 West European, let alone $5,051 overseas per capita average income (Maddison 1994).

In other words, Central and Eastern Europe, in spite of its attempts to modernize, achieved only partial results. The region could not change its position relative to the West and consequently remained on the backward periphery of Europe. Austria-Hungary, because of its more advanced western territories, was near to the European average: 93 percent of it in 1860, and 94 percent in 1910; but because of its eastern territories, the region could not climb above the average. Hungary represented only 74 to 75 percent of the European average. The Russian Empire and the Balkans together, in spite of their progress, remained in the same place: 58 percent both in 1860 and in 1910 (Berend and Ránki 1982). These figures, one should not forget, represent the relation to the European average and not to the most developed core. When compared to the core, the ratio remained 1:2, and, in the more backward cases, even 1:3.

Except for the Austrian-Czech Western provinces of the Habsburg Empire, which achieved a real economic success in industrialization, the region, though changed, was not able to catch up. Its industrialization had a minimal impact, creating little structural change. Therefore its economic structures remained ossified and radically different from those of the enlarged, advanced core.

2

The Peculiar Pattern of Central and Eastern European Societies

The Remnants of Noble and Incomplete Societies

The Deficiency of the Dual Revolution and Its Social Impact

Economic and industrial progress in Central and Eastern Europe during the second half of the nineteenth century was too little to generate radical social change yet too rapid to be socially digestible. Partial economic success underscored the obsolete character of the former noble societies and the traditional ruling elite. Incomplete patterns of modernization underlined the fact that the road followed in these regions toward modern society was paved by defeated revolutions, by reforms from above, and ineffective compromises. In all cases, the transformation was led and controlled by the ruling elite of the former ancien régimes. It is small wonder then that this road remained bumpy and full of potholes. The adoption of Western institutions and legal systems, the incorporation of values of the Enlightenment, and the legacy of the French Revolution and of British liberalism lay in the hands of Austrian and Austrian-Czech aristocrats of the Habsburg court, of Hungarian nobility, of Polish Szlachta, of Russian and Romanian boyars, of semienlightened monarchs, and of members of the military elite. These groups were motivated either by fear—of foreign challenge, incipient mass movements, and peasant revolts—or by a desire to preserve their rule in a modernized form. Their best members, however, genuinely desired progress, expressed a sense of the historical responsibility of their noble class, and participated in the awakening of national sentiment.

It is only natural that members of the established ruling elite did their best to salvage as much as possible from the past. Their actions derived neither from an understandable nostalgia for "the good old times" nor from the consequences of a coded behavior pattern and value system. They were vitally interested in safeguarding their positions and in preserving their leading role in the transformation of society and state.

The Large Estate and the Remnants of Noble Society

East of the River Elbe, in Prussia, Austria, the Czech lands, Romania, Hungary, Poland, the Baltic area, and Russia, the liberation of the serfs did not change the forms of land tenure. Because the noble elite had helped reform and transform the old feudal regimes into modern capitalist systems, the large estate survived in Central and Eastern Europe and provided a solid basis for conserving the economic powers and sociopolitical roles of landed aristocracy and gentry.

This situation existed even in the Austrian-Bohemian lands of the Habsburg monarchy and in the eastern territories of Germany, where economic modernization had progressed the most. In Posen and Pomerania, 50 percent of the land belonged to large estates over two hundred hectares (roughly five hundred acres), in Mecklenburg, 56 percent, and in Silesia, 40 percent. In Austria in the late nineteenth century, 47 percent of the land was owned by 97 percent of the landowners (peasant farmers) and another 47 percent was owned by a mere 1.2 percent of landowners (mostly a handful of aristocratic families and the former lower nobility). In the Czech lands, the contrast was even sharper: 63 percent of the land was occupied by 99 percent of the landowners, but 33 percent of the land was ruled by 0.5 percent of the landowners (the nobility). In Hungary in 1895, nearly 33 percent of the land belonged to 0.2 percent of the estates with holdings over six hundred hectares (roughly fifteen hundred acres). After the liberation of the serfs of the Polish Kingdom in 1864, roughly 50 percent of the land remained in the hands of the former Polish Szlachta; at the turn of the century, this proportion had only declined to 35 percent. In Romania, 42 percent of the land was owned by 95 percent of the landowners (peasant farmers), but 48 percent of the land was owned by 0.6 percent of the landowners (boyars). In Estonia and Latvia, roughly 40 percent of the land was occupied by the Baltic barons. In Russia, the tsarist reform left the bulk of landed estates in the hands of the noble estate (which legally existed until 1918), but during the following decades roughly 40 percent of the land was sold or became peasant holdings. At the beginning of the twentieth century, however, nearly 33 percent of the land was still occupied by 0.3 percent of the estates. In the fifty provinces of European Russia, including the Baltic and Polish territories, there were 887,000 hereditary and tsar-appointed nobles in the mid-nineteenth century. By 1897, paradoxically, their number increased to 1,373,000.

Altogether, between 30 and 50 percent of the land remained in the hands of the old ruling elite, which retained considerable power and political influence. "In the Dual Monarchy as a whole there were at least two dozen aristocratic families with over 250,000 acres apiece," states Arno Mayer. "In Southern Bohemia Prince Schwarzenberg lorded over a small kingdom of 360,000 acres. . . . In Transleithania . . . the Magyars were giant landowners, even by European standards. . . . The Esterházys alone held close to 1 million acres" (Mayer 1981, 27). The Schwarzenbergs, Lichtensteins, Stahrembergs, Windischgrätzes, Esterházys, and Somssiches not only kept their noble titles as princes and counts in modernized Austria-Hungary but also continued to exercise political power and, as in the case of the Hungarian aristocracy, to control about one-third of the country's gross national product. They kept their control over the army and continued to populate the inner circle of the imperial court and the core of the administration. Aristocratic birth was the main condition for assignment to top government positions in Vienna: two-thirds of the senior officials of the Ministry of the Interior and half of those of the Ministry of Agriculture were aristocrats. Compared to the Prussian imperial-Junker authority, the political and social power of the imperial landowning military bureaucracy in Austria-Bohemia was certainly milder and more bourgeois in character—or, perhaps, only more *gemütlich*: *Gemütlichkeit* and *Schlamperei* (untranslatable terms for frivolous, pell-mell Viennese joviality) belonged to the "national" virtue, or, more precisely, to the Viennese attitude, and tempered the rigors associated with the continued rule and pomp of the traditional, noble elite.

In Hungary, continued political power of the aristocracy after 1867 was evident by the fact that half of the prime ministers, one-third of the cabinet ministers, and one-sixth of the representatives in the parliament (though it was no longer a noble institution) were recruited from their rank and file. The exclusive "gentlemen's" upper-class casinos, those hotbeds of political intrigue, were genuine power centers, more important than the government bodies themselves.

The social hierarchy of the ancien régime, with its traditional emphasis on noble birth, left indelible marks on the face of the middle class as well. The middle and lower strata of the former nobility, having lost their privileges, exemption from taxes, and free serf labor, were unable to hold onto their estates in the competition of the market economy and, thus, rapidly lost their lands. In the second half of the nineteenth century, this was the fate of 20,000 out of 30,000 landowning families. Nevertheless, the déclassé Hungarian gentry and Polish Szlachta retained their social status. Noble birth, a family name with a historic ring adorned with a title of nobility, and the concomitant network of family and social connections opened the doors to government and county offices. Military careers, positions in the civil service and county administration, and legal posts connected with the state (often with only a meager salary in junior posts) enabled the gentry to remain part of the ruling elite. In Hungary, the gentry held one-third of the positions in the central government offices and two-thirds in the county administration nationwide. In other words, between 1875 and 1918, more than half of the executive class originated from the old ruling elite. These positions, closely associated with the state authority, ultimately conserved the traditional social prestige of the gentry. The well-born, elegant gentleman, perennially in debt but spending with an aristocratic lavishness despite his modest salary, stood higher on the social ladder than people who were much better off or even rich but who belonged to the entrepreneurial and business world (Hanák et al. 1993). In these noble societies, the tiers associated with capitalism, those of property and wealth, occupied lesser status because of the survival of feudal ranks and the principle of birth. This explains why the dueling, rollicking gentleman, breaking glass to the accompaniment of gypsy music and doing nothing useful, became a model for the attitudes and behavior of the bourgeois middle class. Although dueling was outlawed, the old elite in Austria-Hungary considered it "both a right and a duty denied to the lower classes." The privilege of dueling remained an important criterion of membership in the ruling elite (Mayer 1981, 110). The historically formed features of this elite—the *kultura szlachecka*, as the tradition and attitude was called in Poland—accrued the aura of an eternal national character and exercised a powerful fascination for the entire society. Not even those who hated its representatives could escape this influence. Their vision of social emancipation often consisted of the dream of one day being able to do all the things appropriate to the lifestyle of a "gentleman."

The conservation of the old could not inhibit the emergence of the new. Although partial and limited, a modern economy was developing, banks and industrial firms were being founded, market institutions were appearing, and trade was flourishing. As a consequence, a modern new elite—rich merchants, entrepreneurs, top-ranking managers, and the bourgeoisie—appeared. Men such as Karl Wittgenstein (the father of the philosopher) and Ernst Škoda established and owned vast iron, steel, engineering, munitions, and other industrial complexes and "measured themselves with Europe's largest captains of industry" (Mayer 1981, 59). Though such entrepreneurs remained in the shadow of the traditional ruling elite and avoided politics, their wealth often surpassed that of their noble counterparts. Moreover, they sought to assimilate themselves into traditional status patterns and rushed to buy noble ranks that were on sale in some countries. The Hungarian Jewish industrialist Manfred Weiss and his sons bought a noble title, thereby becoming Baron Csepeli-Weiss by incorporating into their family name the name of the Danube island in a southern suburb of Budapest where their factory was located. Jewish industrialists bought landed estates. Baron Hatvani-Deutsch, owner of a large sugar factory located in the northern Hungarian township of Hatvan, became one of the country's leading landlords. These nouveau riches had themselves portrayed in traditional noble dress, sword at side, on paintings hanging above the fireplaces of their countryside mansions—and considered their mansions a status symbol more important than the largest factory (Silber 1992).

In these traditional noble societies, the old social structure was not replaced by the new one but rather coexisted with it, in a relationship of close connections but strict separation. As a result, a social system emerged that Ferenc Erdei and István Bibó have called a "dual-society." The dual-society was characterized by the parallel existence of the aristocratic landowner and of the bourgeois ruling elite. It also manifested a dual structure of the middle class, which contained a traditional gentry and a bureaucratic military elite on the one hand, and a modern bourgeois middle-strata, a new intelligentsia, and a white-collar business bureaucracy on the other.

One of the most important features of this type of society was the survival until the twentieth century of a semitraditional peasant society. The peasantry remained the largest lower class, representing 60 to 70 percent of the populace. Legally emancipated but still virtually excluded from the society, differentiated by lifestyle, education, language, and even clothing, peasants could not elevate themselves into the middle class. Even well-to-do peasants remained subordinate and marginal in the society.

The Central and Eastern European peasants were entirely different from their Western counterparts. One of the most important differences lay in the large numbers and deep poverty of the landless peasantry. Though figures varied from country to country, in general 40 to 60 percent of the peasantry was landless. The landless peasants fell roughly into two main categories: servants, domestic and otherwise, who worked permanently on large estates, and temporary workers, who moved from place to place and job to job. The peasants on the large estates had permanent employment and a stable income, but their status remained nearest to that of pre-emancipated serfs. A late-nineteenth-century Farm Servants Act in Hungary forbade servants to leave the estates or to receive strangers in their houses and announced a penalty of sixty days imprisonment for inciting a strike. Working hours were unregulated, income was paid mostly in kind, and physical punishment was legal (Berend and Ránki 1979).

The larger part of landless peasantry enjoyed greater freedom from the old feudal forms of bondage but had an uncertain existence due to the lack of permanent work. Although they wandered throughout the country looking for work, found temporary employment at the large estates during harvest season, labored on huge construction works, railroad buildings, and water regulation sites, and were sometimes hired as seasonal workers in the food processing industry in the fall, these peasants worked on average only one hundred and fifty to two hundred days each year.

Peasants lived in deep poverty. "The Galician peasant employed on the estates," writes Oscar Jászi, "receives as his yearly income 900 pounds of bread less than would be necessary for the maintenance of his family. The people must permit their children to have rickets, or they must educate them to be thieves and scoundrels" (Jászi 1964, 236). Nor was there much difference between the landless peasantry and those who owned less than five acres of land (one million families in Hungary alone), who could hardly manage on their minuscule holdings without an additional occupation and income.

Of the thirteen million peasant holdings at the turn of the century in Russia, only 10 percent were able to produce a surplus for market. Despite this fact, the autocratic Russian state overtaxed the peasantry in seeking to increase its income. To pay the taxes, the peasants were forced to sell their produce and thus had less to feed their own families. In the Russian countryside at the end of the nineteenth century, famine was a regular visitor.

In Romania, the percentage of landless peasantry was much smaller than in other countries with large landed estates. Because of the special Romanian system of leaseholding, many peasants were not obliged to resort to wage labor. This system was dissimilar to any Western, Central, or Eastern European system; it was based on a bi-level leasing and subleasing method. The boyar landowners let their land to lessors, usually to Jewish tenants, who acted as intermediaries between the landlords and peasants, and who then sublet the land in small plots to the latter. Almost 40 percent of the landless peasantry was able to obtain land in this way. Around the turn of the century, 73 percent of the biggest estates (over seven thousand acres) lay in the hands of leaseholders, and 60 percent of farms with more than two hundred and fifty acres were farmed by tenants. Nonetheless, the terms of subletting were usurious, and peasant subtenants had to pay between one-third and one-half of their products as rent, a fact that kept the bulk of the peasant population near starvation. It is small wonder that the exploited peasantry expressed its despair in a spontaneous peasant revolt in 1907 (Stavrianos 1963).

The fact that the peasant class remained in Central and Eastern Europe did not preclude the development of a modern working class. Through several stages and over two generations, the landless semi-peasant and part-time wage earner who worked at construction and seasonal jobs gradually became the permanent worker. These transitory layers of society—people without land or with impoverished, minuscule holdings—represented one of the largest single groups of Central and Eastern Europe, nearly one-third of the population.

Additionally, a modern industrial working class was emerging. It was insignificant in size, since the peasantry represented at least 60 to 70 percent of these societies, whereas industrial workers numbered only 10 to 18 percent, but the new workers were densely concentrated in big cities. Austrian-Czech industrial workers, an exception to the general pattern, embodied roughly one-third of the population and resembled their working-class counterparts in the West.

Until the end of the nineteenth century, the majority of Central and

Eastern European industrial workers were employed in small-scale industry; only one-fifth to one-quarter of the industrial workers were occupied in modern factories. At the beginning of the twentieth century, however, in the more developed Polish, Baltic, and Hungarian areas, about half of industrial workers were employed in huge plants.

Central and Eastern European blue-collar workers were mostly unskilled, first generation workers. Many of them shuttled between their village home and the workplace. In contrast to this semipeasant, semiworker type, a highly skilled labor force was attracted to the East from Central-Western Europe, especially Germany and Austria-Bohemia. These skilled workers brought with them the experiences and attitudes of the German-Austrian social-democratic movements. Their ideas spread rapidly and took root among the emerging and enlarging native workforce, a process aided by the fact that the typical features of early capitalism—ten- and sometimes even twelve-hour working days and the lack of social legislation—became increasingly less common in turn-of-the-century Europe.

Unlike in the West, the historical trend toward the "disappearance" of peasantry had not yet begun in the East, and the working class did not become the largest stratum of the society. The dual social structure—near-traditional peasantry on the one side and a rising modern working class on the other—thus characterized the lower layers of the society as well as the upper layers.

The economic and social structures of the countries of Central and Eastern Europe at the end of the century of industrial revolution ensured that these nations remained primarily rural. In the West, industrialization led to a rapid development of the cities, and the urban population became the majority of the populace. But in Central and Eastern Europe, the special pattern of economic and social development produced few new industrial cities. Plzen, Brno in the Czech lands, Lodz in Poland, and Budapest in Hungary were among the exceptions. In the three parts of partitioned Poland before World War I, 16 percent of the population was concentrated in towns (settlements with more than ten thousand inhabitants). In the less developed Galician region, only 13 percent were town-dwellers. In Hungary, according to the 1910 census, 18 percent of the population lived in towns. Urban population in the other countries of the region, except in the industrialized and urbanized Austrian and Czech lands, varied between 10 to 13 percent.

Of existing cities, very few were large in 1910. Belgrade and Tallin each had 90,000 inhabitants, and Sofia had 100,000 inhabitants.

Bucharest with its 350,000, Riga with nearly 500,000, and Prague with 600,000 inhabitants did not compare to the West European metropolises. Vienna (population 2 million), Petrograd (2 million), Moscow (1.5 million) and Budapest (1.1 million) represented the pinnacle of Central and Eastern European urban development.

The stormy rise of Budapest, created from the three independent cities of Buda, Pest, and Óbuda in 1873, was almost unparalleled in the region. In 1850 the three cities had only 150,000 inhabitants, but in the year of unification the population had already reached 300,000. The population of the city increased by 40 percent during a single decade between 1890 and 1900. Even before the war, Budapest, with its industrial suburbs that contained more than half of all Hungarian industrial workers, was a cultural, administrative, and industrial capital, the seventh largest city of Europe. One-third of the urban population of Hungary lived within its boundaries (Enyedi and Szirmai 1992).

Large cities, however, not only remained islands in a sea of rural, peasant settlements but were isolated by their unusual economic structures and population. In turn-of-the-century Budapest, 56 percent of the population was bilingual, nearly every fourth inhabitant was Jewish, and, besides half of the industrial working population, the city also contained two-thirds of the nation's intellectuals and modern middle class.

The Weakness of the Middle Class: *Lücken-Positionen* and the Emergence of the "Jewish Question"

One of the most striking characteristics of Central and Eastern European noble society was its traditional rigidity, which offered only a narrow path for upward mobility within society. Déclassé elements and groups, because of their noble origin, could grab at various state positions and preserve their status in the lower layers of the ruling elite. Rising elements and groups of the peasantry were unable to enter the rank and file of the middle class. The relative weakness of the modern middle class constituted one of the most outstanding aspects of the structure of the society. In the Western societies, in contrast, the rapid rise of middle-class, white-collar workers, of intellectuals, and of a professional class became the most characteristic new trend of structural change from the 1870s onward. Few signs of such development existed in Central and Eastern Europe. Moreover, because of the lack of social mobility and castelike rigidity of social stratification, it was difficult to fill the gap in the middle of the society with indigenous elements. The gradual modernization of the economy, however, required these social functions and layers. This conflict between social reality and structural economic need led to a peculiar social phenomenon: the "nonindigenous" origin of the middle class.

It is as important to recognize this nonindigenous origin of the middle class as it is to recognize the special dual structure of Central and Eastern European noble societies. In identifying the ethnic and religious background of the nonindigenous people, we may understand a source of conflict between "old" traditional and "new" modern societies of the region. In particular, we may see how the fact that many of the nonindigenous people were Jewish, coupled with a growing disappointment with modernization, led to the emergence of the so-called Jewish question.

The *Lücken-positionen*, the gap-positions in the middle of society, as Karl Marx called this curiosity, were filled either by people who had lived in the given country for generations but were not integrated into the native society; or by immigrants who settled relatively easily into the new social niches. These people, considered nonindigenous, were already "over-represented" in modern trading, moneylending, and business positions in the countryside during the eighteenth century and had become the dominant inhabitants of isolated urban settlements even earlier. Greek merchants and early-modern bankers played a key role in the Romanian Principalities and contributed important functions in Hungary. Ethnic Germans represented the largest single minority group in several countries of the region. In the late nineteenth century, one-quarter of the population of the Czech lands and half that of Silesia consisted of ethnic Germans. In Hungary, one-tenth of the population was German, and that percentage was nearly the same in Transylvania. In addition to a massive emigration from the Russian Empire (Jews, Poles, and Lithuanians represented respectively 41, 29, and 9 percent of these emigrants), there was an even more numerous emigration from the Western part of the continent. In the nineteenth century, 4.2 million people immigrated to Russia, two-thirds of them from Europe, mostly from Germany. Germans also became predominant in urban development in the Czech lands, in Hungary, including its northern part inhabited mostly by Slovaks, in Transylvania, in Croatia, in the Baltic countries, and in parts of Poland. In these areas, the inhabitants of the townships spoke German, whereas the residents of the countryside spoke their native languages. Even some of the capitals of these countries were mostly German-speaking around the turn of the century. In Prague, for example, 40 percent of the population used a German mother-tongue, and in prewar Riga, 22 percent of the inhabitants were German. The German influence is clearly expressed by the fact that fifty-one of the eighty seats on the city council were occupied by German representatives.

A relatively great number of Westerners were included among the first and most successful entrepreneurs in the region. John Thornton from England set up the first mechanized cotton spinning mill in Pottendorf (Bohemia), and the Robert family, a father and son from France, became pioneers of the enormous sugar industry in the Czech lands. Another Frenchman, Phillipe de Girard, founded the first mechanical linen-weaving work in the vicinity of Vienna in the early nineteenth century. Among the pioneers of industrialization in Hungary, the Swiss Ganz and Haggenmacher families, the Bavarian Mechwarts, the Norwegian Gregersons, and the Austrian Drehers, Drasches, and Fellners played an outstanding role. The majority of the Polish bourgeoisie had a foreign origin: the Steinkellers, Kronenbergs, Szlenkers, and Epsteins illustrate the point.

An equal and in some cases even more important role was played by the Jewish communities of these countries. Present in Central and Eastern Europe since the Middle Ages, they were numerous in regions such as Ukraine, Poland, Lithuania, and Eastern Romania. Nineteenth-century emigration from this Eastern reservoir of Judaism played an important role in enlarging the Jewish population in countries such as Austria-Hungary. Polish Galicia, incorporated into the Habsburg Empire during the partition of Poland, became one of the main sources of an unrestricted Jewish immigration into the Hungarian and Austrian parts of the empire.

In relative terms (when compared to the entire population of the country), the largest Jewish populations in the world in the early twentieth century lived in this region: Poland (10 percent), Lithuania (nearly 8 percent), Romania (5 percent), Latvia (5 percent) and Hungary (5 percent). From the mid-nineteenth century on, these Jewish communities played an important role in filling social gaps to create a bourgeois, modern middle class in Central and Eastern Europe (Mendelsohn 1983).

The Jewish minority, occupying middle-class positions, had an inverse social pyramid in comparison with the rest of the populace. In Romania, where nearly 80 percent of the population was occupied in agriculture, only 2.5 percent of the Jews worked in this branch of the economy. In contrast, whereas roughly 10 percent of the gainfully employed in the general populace worked in trade and industry, 80 percent of the Jewish community worked in these sectors. In the rural society of Romania, only 20 percent of the populace lived in urban settlements, whereas 80 percent of the strongly urban Jewry did. The big cities of the country had large Jewish populations: though Jewish citizens represented 5 percent of the population of Romania, they were 33 percent of the urban population.

This pattern in Romania held throughout the countries of Central and Eastern Europe that had large Jewish populations. Although 5 percent of the population belonged to the Jewish minority in Hungary, every fourth inhabitant of Budapest was Jewish, a fact that inspired Karl Lüger, the anti-Semitic mayor of Vienna, to nickname the Hungarian capital "Judapest" (Janos 1982). Budapest, with its cosmopolitan culture and high level of commercialization, was indeed different from the countryside. A great many of the top industrialists and bankers, and even more visibly, roughly 66 percent of shopkeepers and 57 percent of service employees, clerks in banking, and entrepreneurial bureaucrats were Jewish. Half of the intellectual component of the lower middle class was recruited from this community. Around the turn of the century, 45 percent of journalists and advocates, 49 percent of medical doctors, and 24 percent of high school teachers were Jewish, as were roughly 33 percent of university students (Silber 1992).

Jewish entrepreneurs and intellectuals played a considerable part in Austrian life as well. Whereas in 1869 there had been only 33 Jewish lawyers in Vienna, at the turn of the century they represented more than half of the city's lawyers, and their ratio among journalists was no less than 75 percent. In 1914, nearly 28 percent of the student body of Vienna University and 35 percent of that of all elite gymnasiums (secondary schools) was Jewish. Certain trading professions, such as furniture, retailing, and advertising, were almost entirely controlled by Jewish entrepreneurs. It must be added, however, that Austria's Jewish population was concentrated almost exclusively in the capital: 8 to 9 percent of Vienna's population was Jewish, whereas the ratio nationwide was little more than 2 percent.

The special role played by newcomers or nonintegrated ethnic-religious groupings characterized not only the upper and middle class, but also the lower class of the Central and Eastern European societies. Western institutions and technology, economic modernization, and the requirements of the industrial revolution had no antecedents in the region. Protoindustrialization, the development that paved the road for mechanized, large-scale industry in the West, scarcely existed in the eastern half of the continent. Educational systems remained backward as well. As a consequence, the educated and specialized skilled labor that was needed when industrialization began could not be supplied from domestic sources. A great many of the German immigrants to Russia were attracted by the higher salaries they were offered in Russian industry. The lack of skilled labor also led to the employment of German, Austrian, and Bohemian workers in Hungarian industry. In the most sophisticated sectors, such as the Budapest engineering industry, roughly one-quarter of the workforce spoke a German mother-tongue in 1880. Moreover, the language and official newspaper (*Arbeiter Wochenkronik*) of the first workers' organization and labor movement in Hungary was German.

Jews also filled labor shortages. In Poland, a surprisingly high percentage — one-third of industrial workers — was Jewish. The *Bund*, a socialist workers' organization founded in Vilna in 1897, signaled the presence of a strong Jewish component in Polish and Lithuanian working classes and related labor movements. "In our city," Czeslaw Milosz, the Polish-born American writer, notes in his memoirs about his childhood in Vilna, "people called May 1st [the socialist holiday, initiated by the II. International] the 'Jewish holiday'" (Milosz 1981, 95).

Similarly, 35 percent of Hungarian Jews earned their living as workers. In addition, many unskilled laborers were recruited from other minority nationalities, such as Slovaks, Croats, and Romanians. In the early twentieth century, 44 percent of foremen and workers spoke non-Hungarian mother-tongues. Gyula Szekfü, the conservative historian, concludes in *Három nemzedék* (Three generations), his influential historical essay on the background of the working class in Hungary, that "nearly half of the organized masses of the workers, originating from non-Hungarian ethnicities, moved into the industrial centers. . . . [They] submitted to the international workers movement . . . [because] the working class was never entirely Hungarian" (Szekfü 1922, 32).

As this discussion has shown, the modern entrepreneurial, intellectual, and industrial occupations, and the modern urban settlements and social layers connected with them, were highly nonindigenous. Therefore it is not enough to recognize the special dual structure of Central and Eastern European noble societies. It is equally important that the ethnic-religious content of the "old" traditional and of the "new" modern societies receive recognition. In a simplified model, it might be suggested that, whereas the traditional structure of the aristocratic upper class, gentry middle class, and halfheartedly emancipated peasantry was primarily native (meaning that other ethnicities were assimilated and integrated centuries before and considered to be native), the modern social layers of the bourgeoisie, the modern middle class, and the industrial working class—the layers of the emerging modern society— were largely nonindigenous. The "otherness" and special role of the Jewish minority, their different social and occupational structure, their over-representation in decisive spheres of the economy and society, and their carefully preserved identity became, in an atmosphere of growing disappointment and disillusionment with modernization, the points of departure for the emergence of the so-called Jewish question.

In the Western societies this kind of social phenomenon was rarely present. First of all, the size of the Jewish population was negligible, usually not exceeding 0.4 percent of the populace. Second, in modern Western societies the social-occupational structure and urbanized character of the Jewish communities was not significantly different from that of the majority. The powerful integrating forces based on a gradual and permanent advance of capitalism within the stable framework of an absolute state that had characterized the early-modern centuries in the West reduced the significance of ethnic and religious differences. The small Jewish population of Western Europe was largely assimilated and, though preserving its religious differences, merged with the increasingly homogenized citizenship of the emerging nation-states.

This process of assimilation had begun in Central and Eastern Europe as well. It was, however, as slow, partial, and inhibited as general national development in the region. Ethnic and religious diversities and the lack of ethnic homogenization and the integration of the Jewish population in the multinational empires was an integral element of the delayed nation-building process. Major differences, however, existed inside the region, the result of diverse experiences with modernization. Consequently, one may distinguish three differing categories or types of Jewish assimilation.

The Western-type assimilated Jew had German, Hungarian, and Czech counterparts. These Jews often became leading representatives of their adopted culture and language. They totally identified with the ruling ethnic group of the host country or, as Péter Hanák so aptly notes in relation to Austria, if not with the nation, then with the state (Hanák 1984). These Jews described themselves as Czechs, Hungarians, or Poles "of Mosaic belief." They joined the Hungarian gentry's struggle against Austria and the struggle of the Polish nobility against Russia. By 1910, 92 percent of the Jews living in Galicia professed to be Poles. Furthermore, in 1910, 700,000 of the 900,000 Jews living in Hungary professed to be Hungarians. In 1908, Robert Seaton-Watson painted the Hungarian Jewry as one of the pillars of Hungarian chauvinism. When Chaim Weizmann, the leader of the Zionist Congress, went to Warsaw at the beginning of the twentieth century, he found two markedly distinct groups—the assimilated Jews and the staunchly traditionalist Hasidic communities.

Assimilated Jews looked like the other inhabitants of the countries where they lived. They wore similar clothing and had similar habits. Several of them were baptized and mixed marriages were common. Most of them, however, kept their parents' belief and even celebrated the religious holidays, but belonged to the "neolog" religious branch and were not at all strict in keeping "obsolete" religious rules.

In contrast, the Eastern-type of nonassimilated Jews lived in a closed ethnic-religious enclave under the leadership of a rabbi, spoke a unique language—the German-Hebrew mix called Yiddish—and wore traditional clothing and hair styles. Married women cut their hair, and men did not shave or cut their payee. They followed their own religious rules and scarcely shared anything in common with the non-Jewish population of the countries where they lived. The social environment of most of the Central and Eastern European countries was not receptive and contributed to the segregation of these Jewish communities. Huge nonassimilated Jewish enclaves existed in Ukraine, in Lithuania, in Galicia, in the famous Szatmár region of Transylvania and in the Sub-Carpatho-Ruthenia, both of which belonged to Hungary, and in certain parts of Poland.

Czeslaw Milosz paints a vivid picture of his Polish homeland in his previously cited memoirs: "There was no bridge between these two groups in our city. The Catholic and Jewish communities (some districts were almost entirely Jewish) lived within the same walls, yet as if on separate planets. Contact was limited to everyday business matters; at home different customs were observed, different newspapers were read, different words used to communicate. . . . Everyone in Wilno went to his 'own' school. Only at the university did we all gather in the same lecture halls, and even there student organizations were divided into

Polish, Jewish, Lithuanian, and Byelorussian. Thus the barriers were still kept up in accordance with an unwritten law" (Milosz 1981, 95).

Between these two extremes lay a wide range of degrees of assimilation marked by varying degrees of lingualism, by the easing of religious orthodoxy, by adjustment of clothing and customs, and by variations in the extent to which ordinary religious practices were observed. This type of partially assimilated Jew was present throughout the entire Central and Eastern European region.

The "otherness" and the special social role played by the Jews in the noble societies of Central and Eastern Europe made it possible to misinterpret the actual sources of the acute antagonisms within these societies. The markedly high concentration of Polish, Romanian, and Hungarian Jews in middle-class positions, in business, and in intellectual professions made it easy to explain most social ills as a consequence of this Jewish presence. "Jewish expansionism" was perceived as blocking the road of social advancement for the "native" masses by occupying the most profitable positions of the society.

In the same way, capitalism, with its destruction of certain traditional communal values, with its extreme individualism and "alien" Western philosophy, and with the inhuman features of its early stages, could also be blamed for the "Jewish problem," because the shopkeeper, the moneylender, the lawyer, and the entrepreneur were often Jewish. (In the Hungarian countryside the terms *Jew* and *shopkeeper* were often used as synonyms.)

In countries with large Jewish communities, the coincidence of these two "alien phenomena" suggested an easy and convenient link between the two. Consequently, the emerging capitalism was labeled as nonindigenous "Jewish capitalism." Furthermore, the revolutionary, anticapitalist socialist labor movement—also connected with "foreign" ideologies and international organizations and heavily supported by Jewish workers and intellectuals—was also accused of being alien, or Jewish. Only one step was needed to connect the two: that of assuming a worldwide Jewish conspiracy in which Jewish capitalism worked together with Jewish socialism against healthy national forces in an effort to undermine and to destroy them.

In this manner, political anti-Semitism, which drew on medieval traditions, religious prejudices, and superstitions, emerged around the turn of the century. It was by no means limited to the Eastern half of the continent. In France, the Dreyfus Affair produced a notorious example of anti-Jewish sentiment. In Germany, *The Victory of Judaism over Teu-*

tonism, a pamphlet by the journalist Wilhelm Marr, published in twelve editions in seven years, transposed anti-Semitism from religious to racial grounds. It maintained that in the nineteenth century the Jews had developed into a world power that was turning Germany into "New Palestine." Otto Glagan attacked Jewish profiteering and speculation, which he said was encouraged by liberalism and was destroying the German middle class. The ground was thus being prepared for the distinction between *schaffende*, creative capital generated by German industrialists, and the *raffende*, parasitic, usury capital that was commercial, foreign, and Jewish (Lukács 1974).

French political thinkers and German and Austrian politicians such as Stöcker and Lueger had transformed anti-Semitism into a political program after the stock exchange crash and the first Great Depression of the 1870s. These ideological seeds had fallen on well-prepared soil in Central and Eastern Europe. In Russia, popular discontent was deliberately channeled into bloody pogroms to relieve, if only for fleeting moments, the tensions of society. As a result, millions of Jews emigrated, especially from Ukraine. The Tiszaeszlár trial in Hungary, with its medieval charge of ritual murder, and the activity of Istóczy's Anti-Semitic Party at the end of the nineteenth century clearly reflected the existence of political anti-Semitism in the region.

This political ideology, however, was not yet influential enough to appeal to large numbers of people. This lack of influence was the result, to a considerable extent, of economic successes and liberal governmental policies that promoted assimilation rather than segregation. Nevertheless, the appearance of political anti-Semitism was already a clear sign of the gathering storm.

The Incomplete Societies and the Bureaucratic-Military Parvenu in the Balkans

The Balkan societies had a nature different than that of the rest of the region. Because they lived under the Ottoman yoke for nearly half a millennium, these people did not have a native feudal hierarchy, and the ruling elite was formed from the ranks of the Ottoman occupiers. In other words, these people had an incomplete society that lacked a ruling elite. After the liberation from Ottoman rule, no landed aristocracy or gentry could move into power. Land that had belonged to the Sultan became the property of the peasants and was more or less equally distributed. In Bulgaria at the end of the nineteenth century, 94 percent of the land was divided into plots of less than two hundred and fifty acres; only two hundred and fifty peasant families possessed a larger plot, altogether not more than 6 percent of the arable land. In Serbia, only eighty farms existed larger than two hundred and fifty acres each.

Landlessness, the main source of poverty in the countries of large estates in the region, did not exist in the Balkans. However, the Balkan peasant farm was not comparable to that of the West. First of all, its size was small: 87 percent of Bulgarian farms were smaller than twenty-five acres. Balkan villages were highly overpopulated because the population had more than doubled in the second half of the nineteenth century, and there were virtually no possibilities for employment outside the villages. Backwardness, isolation, lack of information, and lack of mobility blocked even the road of emigration, and few people moved from the area. Thus the Balkan peasants—who constituted almost the entire population—lived on small impoverished plots that were cultivated in traditional, primitive ways using wooden, animal-driven ploughs and that provided small yields. An industrial working force was practically nonexistent because the countryside was mostly self-sufficient. In the small townships, the artisan class represented only 7 to 9 percent of the active population, and large manufacturing industry counted for only a few factories, which employed altogether only 1 percent of the population.

In modern terms, most of the population was unemployed or underemployed, but this did not become manifest in the surviving village communities. The South Slav *zadruga* system, a form of extended family, preserved the features of primitive common-property holding. The *zadruga* members numbered between ten and one hundred people, and male members were related by blood. As Jozo Tomasevich, an expert on the Balkans, points out,

The headman of the zadruga was called the *domakin*; he was chosen . . . for his ability, and could be replaced. . . . Morally he was a kind of father to the whole family; economically, he was a kind of elected director of a company holding common, undivided property. . . . The rights and duties of the male members can be summarized in the communist principle: from each according to his strength and to each according to his needs. And, in truth, whether a member was sound of limb or unsound, ill or well, he was bound to hand in to the zadruga all he could earn according to his strength. In turn, whether he was married or unmarried, childless or with a dozen children, the zadruga had to provide him with house, food and clothing according to his family's needs. (Tomasevich 1955)

Although the *zadruga* made the disguised mass unemployment tolerable and assured at least a minimal level of subsistence for everybody, the *zadruga* system became an obstacle to modernization along Western market principles. It remained a self-sufficient unit that inhibited the development of social mobility and a market economy.

Around the turn of the century, however, village communities began disintegrating and a primitive capitalism emerged. Independent peasant farms, in need of manufactured goods, had to go to the market to buy and sell; consequently, they fell rapidly into debt. This was particularly so because of the absence of advanced forms of credit.

A small, rich peasant-merchant elite exploited this situation and lent money at usurious rates of interest (sometimes as outrageous as 100 percent). This peasant-merchant stratum was one of the elements forming a new, native bourgeois elite. Some urban merchant-artisan-speculator groups already existed under the Ottoman rule (*carshija*) and now became influential and closely connected to the newly established state power. The independent state authorities determined and controlled activities, and the powerful people rallying around them formed the core of a developing upper social stratum. Some of the new rulers, who were recruited from a leading bureaucratic-military group that had played an important role in the struggles for independence, belonged to the small, native elite—local *knazes*, or leaders, who had enjoyed self-government under Ottoman rule. They now rapidly enriched themselves, becoming a genuine *Ersatzklasse*, a substitute, bureaucratic-military ruling elite, which, in this case, became notorious for its extraordinary corruption and for the manner in which they held office in order to aggrandize themselves financially. This group had flourished under the autocratic and dictatorial Ottoman administration, and it continued to thrive after the demise of Ottoman control. The representatives of this robust, aggressive parvenu ruling elite obviously had learned the methods of the hated parasitic Ottoman tyranny. Their only excuse for their behavior lay in the fact that this was the sole model they knew.

Minorities and National Conflicts

The emergence of the "Jewish question" in Central and Eastern Europe indicates the importance of their unusual and extraordinarily mixed ethnic-religious character in creating national conflicts. As Hannah Arendt observes, in Austria-Hungary, tsarist Russia, and the countries of the Balkans conditions did not exist for the realization of the "Western national trinity of people — territory — state" (Arendt 1966, 232).

Indeed, the 224 million people living in the multinational empires of Austria-Hungary and Russia, and in the Balkans before World War I, showed a remarkable ethnic, linguistic, and religious diversity. Because it lacked a centuries-long history of nation building, of independent statehood, and of associated ethnic homogenization, and because the multinational states had survived, the area stretching from the Baltic to the Adriatic Sea remained a "belt of mixed population,"as it was often called. Whereas three-quarters of Latvia's population was Latvian, one-quarter belonged to the Russian, Byelorussian, Polish, and Jewish minorities. Nearly 20 percent of Lithuania's population belonged to Russian, Polish, German, and Jewish communities. The Western, so-called hereditary provinces of the Habsburg Empire had roughly 10 million Austrian Germans, 6.5 million Czechs, 1.3 million Slovenians, and more than a million people from smaller ethnic groups such as Croats, Serbs, and Italians. In the Czech lands, roughly one-quarter of the population was of German ethnicity. Some 10 million Hungarians, 3 million Romanians, 2 million Germans, 2 million Slovaks, 1.8 million Croats, 1 million Serbs, and roughly 1 million other nationalities lived under the Hungarian crown (Kann 1971). Within the post–World War I borders of Poland, less than 70 percent of the population was Polish; nearly 20 percent belonged to the Ukrainian and Beloruss, and 10 percent belonged to the Jewish and German minorities. Although the Balkan countries were ethnically more homogeneous, 30 percent of Bulgaria's population belonged to Turkish and other nationalities, whereas every tenth person in Romania and Serbia belonged to a great variety of different ethnic groups.

Some particularly mixed areas existed: Czech-Silesia, with its German, Polish, and Czech population; Transylvania, with its Romanian majority and large Hungarian, German (Saxon), and Jewish populations; and Macedonia with its ethnic Bulgarians, Serbs, and Greeks.

The religious mix of the region was similarly colorful and important. In an area of permanent foreign occupation that lacked independent statehood, religion played an important role in self-identification. In the modernized West, medieval religious self-identification had been replaced by national cultural affiliation and citizenship after the dual revolution, but in Central and Eastern Europe, what we now call national identity remained a sort of religious-national consciousness (Sugar 1980).

Furthermore, religion never consisted merely of a faith in God, affiliation with a special church, or the practices of certain rituals. Religion encompassed much more, functioning as a cultural package that offered a philosophy of and attitude toward work, life, and members of the opposite sex. The Muslim world of the Balkans, quite apart from its ethnic component, developed along different lines because of its religious-cultural heritage. The Orthodox legacy in Russia, Ukraine, Romania, and most of the Balkans displayed peculiar features and contributed to creating a dividing line within Central and Eastern Europe. In fact, according to several historians of the region, this religious dividing line distinguishes Central Europe from the truly Eastern regions of the continent.

A well-known theory about the crucial role played by Protestantism (versus Catholicism) in fostering a puritan attitude toward work, savings, and lifestyle assigns it an important role in the emergence of capitalism and modernization. In this light, it may be significant that the Protestant legacy was present only in a few areas of the region (in the Baltic, in the Eastern parts of Hungary, in Transylvania, and in certain Polish territories). Instead, Catholicism dominated most of Austria-Hungary, Poland, and Lithuania, although Greek-Orthodoxy was also present in some areas.

The special role of religion in Central and Eastern Europe was the most evident in the Balkans, where the South Slavic people expressed not a national identity, but rather a Greek-Orthodox identity that contrasted with the Muslim Ottoman overlords. This identity in religious terms had been strengthened by the Ottoman administration, which had differentiated among people according to their religion and had ensured autonomy to the Greek-Orthodox administrative unit called *Millet*. Religious self-consciousness gradually transformed into a national self-identification in the nineteenth century Balkans, but religion itself remained an important determining element of self-identification (Petrovich 1980).

Religion played the same role in Poland, Lithuania, Estonia, and Latvia. It functioned as the strongest element of self-identification against foreign invaders and oppressors of different faith. In Poland, the Catholic identity helped unite the nation against Protestant Germans and Orthodox Russians during the partition of the country, and Catholicism consequently became an essential and inseparable ingredient of Polish and Lithuanian national consciousness. Similarly, in Estonia and Latvia, Protestantism played a central role in maintaining a distinct self-identity in the face of overt Russification programs.

In certain cases, religious beliefs, which lacked genuine national or ethnic content, developed into a secularized national consciousness. Assimilated Jews, who had a secular national identity distinct from their Jewishness, developed in some instances a Jewish national self-identification and advocated Zionism. Muslims in Bosnia-Herzegovina, although mostly ethnic Slavs, gradually developed an independent sense of nationality.

Ethnicity and religion in Central and Eastern Europe were not only extremely intermingled but also highly interrelated with and amalgamated to social stratification and class status. Estonian and Latvian peasants worked on the estates of the Baltic German barons. Slovak and Transylvanian Romanian peasants were subordinated to Hungarian landlords. Turks constituted the majority of artisans in Bulgaria. Romanian peasants subletted their parcels from Jewish renters. Hungarian workers were employed by Jewish industrialists. The Ukrainian and Beloruss minority in Poland belonged almost entirely to the peasantry and worked on the estates of Polish landlords, and Polish industrial laborers worked for German and Jewish entrepreneurs.

The sharp class conflicts of the nineteenth century that were construed as a social problem in the West appeared partly as national and religious conflicts in Central and Eastern Europe. When Romanian peasants revolted against the exploitative subletting system in the early twentieth century, they did not rise against a "capitalist class," but burned and stabbed the Jews. Slovak and Transylvanian Romanian peasants, rebelling against the system of large estates, revolted against Hungarian rule.

The various national minorities and ethnic enclaves frequently displayed a social structure similar to that of the incomplete societies of the Balkans under Ottoman rule: because they were unable to develop a full social hierarchy, their ruling administrative, intellectual, landowning, and entrepreneurial classes were formed by members of the majority in the nation. Minorities remained peasants, woodcutters, miners, and unskilled laborers and could rarely rise above these positions. Therefore, infinite variations of classic class conflicts masqueraded as national-religious disdain and hatred, disguising the socioeconomic content of the conflicts.

Ethnic diversity also distorted economic disputes between agriculture and industry, or between lesser and more developed regions. Economic phenomena became politically charged because disparities did not appear merely as consequences of disadvantageous versus advantageous position, but seemed instead to involve discrimination against one or another ethnic minority. In reality, it was difficult to distinguish between the random effects of regional differences and the outcome of deliberate government policy.

In the "belt of mixed population," social, national, and religious differences and conflicts intermingled with important historical consequences. The idea of nationalism and, later, the progress of capitalist modernization furnished the grounds for the awakening of national sentiments and aspirations for self-determination. Each step forward, each success in this realm, fueled national consciousness and fed hope that eventually the region could catch up with the successful countries of the West. But the obstacles to modernization and failed expectations generated even stronger and more explosive emotions and political efforts. Painfully slow progress and petrified social-economic structures led to frustrations that fueled hatred and rebellion. These historical processes finally coalesced and turned Central and Eastern Europe into a crisis zone. People questioned whether the road they were trying to take was the right one. Their sense of backwardness was overwhelming, and even the progress that had been achieved was questioned. This was both a crisis of modernization and a predicament arising from the relative lack of modernization. The tensions created were similar in most of the countries and nations of the region, although various countries had experienced different degrees of success and failure. Whatever their experience, they could not escape the bitter sense of being dependent upon other nations. Relative successes did not lessen but rather served to increase the sense of frustration.

Social tensions in Hungary combined with frustration at the slow progress of modernization and fed a tendency to blame all failures and peripheral backwardness on Austrian rule. In the northern Slovak, eastern Transylvanian, and southern Croatian regions of the Hungarian Kingdom, socioeconomic ills were blamed on Hungarian oppression.

The Poles explained their disadvantaged position by blaming the partition and foreign occupation. Estonians and Latvians accused both the Baltic German barons and the Russian tsar of causing their plight. These patterns helped to produce an increasingly explosive situation in a region where national political allegiances were far from self-evident.

The Central and Eastern Europe of the early twentieth century might be characterized as ominously gathering clouds on the horizon. In the words of the prophetic Hungarian poet, Endre Ady, "We are running into revolution!" But the truth of this fact was not as evident at the time. The future champion of Czechoslovak independence, Eduard Benes, concluded his doctoral thesis on the Czech problem with the following words: "People have often spoken of the dissolution of Austria. I do not believe in it. The historic and economic ties which bind the Austrian nations to one another are too powerful to let such a thing happen" (May 1968, 437).

3

The Ideologies of Revolts and Revolutions

The Birth of Nationalist, Communist, and Fascist Ideas

Around the end of the nineteenth century, a euphoric Europe was celebrating new achievements. Railroads and bridges had been built, the first electric trams and subway lines had opened, and the first automobiles were threatening proud pedestrians on the modern ringroads and avenues of newly built European metropolises. The world admired the miraculous engineering products exhibited at the Paris world exhibition in 1900. At the same time, the long and triumphant reigns of Queen Victoria in Britain, of Kaiser Wilhelm II in Germany, and of Victor Emanuel in Italy symbolized the stability of power in the European order, which had been established at the Congress of Vienna in 1815.

Reasons enough existed for celebrations and pride, and not only in Britain and Germany. An entire nation welcomed Franz Joseph I with a resounding ovation when he arrived in Budapest in 1896 for the grandiose celebration of the millennium of Hungarian settlement in the Danube Valley. This hated emperor, the suppressor and hangman of the 1848 Hungarian Revolution, now was celebrated as a beloved friend and as a father figure to the nation. However, neither the official excitement and sparkle nor the real achievements of capitalist modernization could counterbalance the frustrations of the masses, who were still laboring in backward conditions in the countryside or suffering in the nascent capitalist urban-industrial economies of peripheral Central and Eastern Europe. Sensitive intellectuals saw through the moderate successes and facade of progress and recognized the numerous failures and crisis of modernization in this part of the world. They were humiliated by the backwardness of their countries and suffered from the feeling of belonging to "second rate nations" that were "shifting back to Asia." A large, desperate segment of the population living near or below the poverty level thus combined with a frustrated, rebellious group of intellectuals to create an explosive force, especially in those countries on the periphery where tensions and conflicts were the strongest. Precursors of the coming explosion revealed the danger: the Russian revolution in 1905 revealed the deep desperation and potential power of the relatively small but highly concentrated industrial population in the big cities. The medieval-type Romanian peasant revolt of 1907 uncovered the potential violence of the openly exploited East European peasantry. The noisy constitutional crisis in Hungary in 1905 and the bloody first and second Balkan wars in 1912 to 1913 illustrated the volatile nature of the national issue and of border questions.

At the turn of the century, the European balance of power and the multinational empires of Central and Eastern Europe still seemed strong enough to respond to the challenges, but the powder keg was filling. It needed only the ideology of rebellion to spark widespread conflagration.

Ideas and ideologies are international. Their birthplace is often only the point of departure, and a triumphant ideology may rapidly conquer entire continents. As the history of the second half of the nineteenth century demonstrates, British liberalism and the ideas of the French Enlightenment penetrated the entire European continent and inspired Central and Eastern Europe to adopt and follow Western ideologies. Similarly, the leading ideological trends—nationalism, communism, and fascism—emerged first in the more advanced western and central part of the continent and thereafter inspired twentieth-century Central and Eastern European rebellions against peripheral backwardness. Nationalism was a product of the newly born Western nations and nation-states in the United States of America, France, and other core countries. Communism, in its genuine form of Marxism, was worked out by German scholars and political thinkers as a response to early British capitalism and was implemented in organized movements first in Germany and France. Fascist and national socialist ideas were formulated by French, German, and Italian philosophers and ideologues and embodied in right-wing populist movements. These ideas transplanted easily to Central and Eastern Europe, since the seeds of revolt had fallen onto well-prepared and fertile soil. Yet none of the imported ideas and concepts remained unchanged. Adoption of the ideas was accompanied or followed by adaptation, and the original ideas were often transformed and deformed.

The ideas of nationalism, communism, and fascism reached Central and Eastern Europe in the last decades of the nineteenth century, just as the failure or semifailure of modernization was manifesting itself. Disappointed peoples and nations looked for new ways to modernize. As Barrington Moore suggests in his *Social Origins of Dictatorship and Democracy*, three alternative routes existed for agrarian societies moving toward modern industrialization: a bourgeois route ending in national revolution; a conservative route involving revolution from above and ending in fascism; and a route of peasant revolution ending in communism (Moore 1967). Before World War I, all of these routes were being taken in Central and Eastern Europe.

Nationalism

The most powerful political driving force in nineteenth- and twentieth-century Central and Eastern Europe was a highly emotional nationalism that mobilized tens of millions to act on its "eternal" principle. Millions were sacrificed in an almost permanent struggle of national interests. Entire ethnic groups and vast numbers of minorities were eliminated as enemies in host nations.

Yet nationalism was a surprisingly modern "import" in the region. Generations of preeminent historians and experts on the topic—from Arnold Toynbee, Hans Kohn, and Benedict Anderson, to Eric Hobsbawm—agree that nation and nationalism were born in the late eighteenth and early nineteenth centuries. Pluralism in state and nation emerged first in revolutionary France and in the United States of America after its successful fight for independence.

The birth of nations was a consequence of a centuries-long homogenization process in Western Europe, initiated and propelled by the appearance of capitalist market economies that integrated into one economic unit previously isolated self-sufficient feudal estates and scattered rural-local communities. The process of creating an integral domestic market (by abolition of internal tariffs, introduction of unified measurement systems, and so on), the abstract ideas of humanism and the Enlightenment, and the leading national slogans of the French Revolution contributed to the formation of nations.

The so-called melting pot was the absolute state that, building on the economic-social-political trends of the sixteenth through eighteenth centuries, gradually integrated and homogenized different ethnic groups, religious minorities, languages, and dialects and, by means of standardizing norms, nurtured a new form of self-identity: that of belonging to a nation and being a citizen of a state. From the late eighteenth century on, supreme loyalty was theoretically given by citizens to their nation-states.

The concepts of nation and "love for an abstraction of the nation" became the most powerful myths of the modern age. The "imagined community" — as Benedict Anderson called the nation — postulated the existence of a "unified community" and a nationwide "horizontal comradeship," although none of these in fact existed (B. Anderson 1983). Standardized national languages, education, military service, literacy, mass consumption, and public transportation systems helped to create a uniform national consciousness that suppressed and replaced older myths left from the feudal centuries. The earlier myths postulated the existence of a natural and divinely instituted hierarchical order. Subjects owed absolute loyalty to both the landlord and the monarch who ruled a multiethnic, multilingual dynastic state that bore no resemblance to a modern nation. National self-consciousness also replaced the "Christian myth," that set of beliefs in the existence of a universal religious collective, which had for centuries provided the ultimate sense of identity for most Europeans. National consciousness aroused extreme emotions because it created a new myth, one of common national characteristics and of a common national destiny, that emphasized collective history and culture and the existence of traditional linguistic community. The concept of the national, linked easily and often with racial perceptions, manifested itself in talk about "common blood."

In the emerging modern Western societies, the nation was equated with the bourgeois "Third Estate," or with the entire people. Nationalism was linked to political systems that stressed individual rights and popular sovereignty. The notion of the nation as that which deserves and demands supreme loyalty developed from interpretation of the concept of "liberty, equality, and fraternity." This notion, a product of Western development, rapidly conquered the entire European continent, arriving in Central and Eastern Europe before actual nations were born. Nationalism was not therefore a consequence of national awakening, but instead helped to cause this phenomenon.

The Eastern European Approach
to Nation Building

Nation building had a different history in Central and Eastern Europe than in the West. In the sixteenth and seventeenth centuries, the region became a peripheral food supplier of the rising Western core by preserving rigid feudal structures. The so-called second serfdom in those years reconstructed the manorial estate system and reinstituted mandatory labor service for serfs.

Paradoxically, as Immanuel Wallerstein notes, Central and Eastern Europe became a part of an emerging new capitalist world economic system by conserving its traditional precapitalist character, consolidating its agricultural structures, and expanding production, as much as possible, to satisfy West European demands (Wallerstein 1974). The consolidation of the power of the nobility worked against the rise of an absolute state, a fact that has been convincingly demonstrated by Pál Zsigmond Pach (Pach 1994). As the model country during the second serfdom, Poland provides the best illustration of the political consequences of the reinforcement of feudal institutions. Instead of an integrating power in a central government, the Polish-Lithuanian *Rzeczspospolita* granted all the power to the Szlachta, as the nobility was called, which established a special democracy of noblemen based upon direct representation. Each noble man was a member of the local *Sejm* (parliament), which in turn elected representatives to a central *Sejm*. In 1652, in an event unparalleled in history, a so-called *Liberum veto* was introduced that gave the veto right to each member of the noble *Sejm*. In other words, the vote of one person could decide anything. No elected king could challenge this power. For Poland, the consequence of this right to veto was disintegration, increased vulnerability, and, in the end, foreign occupation and the partition of Poland by the three neighboring great powers.

It was exactly the fear of external military challenge, coupled with the recognition that a state could be defended only by a strong central power, effective taxation, and a strong army—and not by the economic-social integration process of developing capitalism—that led to the foundation of Central and Eastern European absolute states. The birth of these states, as Perry Anderson stresses, was "militarized." For example, the emerging state apparatus in Prussia was "a side product of the military machinery." A tax system, public services, and local administration "came into being as a technical subsection of the Generalkriegskommissariat [General War Commission]" (P. Anderson 1974, 212–13). Vasilii Kluchevsky emphasizes the same fact regarding Russian centralization under Ivan IV and Peter I: "The chief characteristic is the military character of the state organization" (Kluchevsky 1912, 319).

Although absolutism was thus transplanted into Central and Eastern Europe as a response to military pressures, the militarized Eastern absolute states were unable to adopt the entire network of political and cultural institutions of Western absolute states because of the Eastern states' internal social and economic conditions. As they adjusted to their backward domestic economic and social environments, they became the guarantors of revitalized feudal institutions and of noble societies. In some cases, a special type of "service-nobility" closely linked to the state was created and integrated into the new state bureaucracies; this service-nobility became a pillar of support for the new system and supported the continued existence of the old order. As a result, the Central and Eastern European absolute states did not play integrating roles between the old and new, between noble and bourgeois, by gradually paving the road for the advance of the latter and the *Verbürgerlichung* (the embourgeoisement) of the former. Because neither the requisite economic changes nor the accompanying social transformations of the West prevailed in the absolute states of Central and Eastern Europe, these states could not become melting pots from which might emerge homogenized ethnic groups of equal citizens who spoke one standardized official language. In the absolute states of the region, the ethnic and linguistic pluralism of the medieval feudal states was preserved and states remained multinational, lacking a uniform national character.

When nations and nationalism arrived as a powerful ideology in the East, most of the ethnic groups of the region—Czechs, Poles, Hungarians, Croats, Slovaks, Estonians, Latvians, Serbs, Slovenes, Bulgarians, and millions of Romanians, as well as many others—lived in three multinational empires, ruled by the dominant dynasties and cultures that occupied the area.

The Peculiarities of National Ideology: Nation-State versus *Kulturnation*

Because nationalism arrived in Central and Eastern Europe before nations were born, it became the driving force behind the creation of modern nations. Mobilized by the national idea, the intellectual elite of the different ethnic groups in the region sought to substitute new political and cultural institutions as well as a sense of national consciousness for the economic, social, and institutional factors that had spurred nation building in the West but were lacking in Central and Eastern Europe.

Nationalism emerged in the early nineteenth century when the Western challenge was becoming frighteningly evident. The triumphant industrial revolution was dramatically broadening the gap between the rising Western core of nations and the stagnating and declining peripheral regions. Moreover, Napoleon had led the army created by the French Revolution on a campaign to destroy feudal systems and conquer the weak European peripheral nations from Spain and Italy to Croatia and Russia. In this atmosphere, the value of the strong nation-state as an effective defense was easily exaggerated. Status as an independent state appeared to provide the key needed to open all the gates that remained closed to the backward countries of Europe. It seemed to offer the chance of beginning once more the march down the admired Western road of modernization. And standing ready to supplement the concept of nation-state derived from successful Western capitalist development was the German concept of *Kulturnation* (cultural nation).

The concept of *Kulturnation* derived from the peculiar German experience. Johann Gottfried Herder, irritated by the absence of a strong, united German state during the eighteenth century, pioneered a German national ideology. He sought to create a spiritual Germany, united in its language and literature, which were, for him, the main expressions of a "national character." Herder rejected the concepts of "Mankind," of rationalism and universalism associated with the French Enlightenment. He said that the *Nationalgeist* (national spirit) demands self-realization by the national community, not through imitation of foreigners but through cultivation of the individual national character as embodied in language, poetry, and national costumes. No nation should follow another, but each should develop its own consciousness, because "every nation carries within itself the central point of its own happiness, just as every ball contains its centre of gravity" (Herder 1952, 465) The classical German philosophy painted a spiritual way of building nations.

Herder formulated the concept of "linguistic-nation," later called the

Kulturnation, in the last third of the eighteenth century, at the time of the birth of Western national ideas. Johann Gottlieb Fichte, shocked by the victorious advance of Britain and by the defeat from Napoleon, formulated the concept of national isolation and suggested the cultivation of the genuine German "national character" of the *Urvolk* (the ancient people), a character that he linked in turn to a special, pure *Ursprache*, an unspoiled genuine language. On that basis, the German people would unite into a nation (Fichte 1920).

The German ideology of nation building was born from the relative backwardness of the fragmented German states and from the absence of social-political integrating forces that might have established a united absolute German state, a true nation-state. This ideology was ready-made for other peoples of the even more backward and belated Central and Eastern Europe, who, at least in part, genuinely belonged to the sphere of German cultural influence. Large German minority groups existed in the region, and urban populations spoke German. Moreover, German was the official administrative language of the Habsburg Empire. But Herder and the German ideology strongly and directly influenced the Slavic peoples of the region as well.

In the early twentieth century, the outstanding German historian, Friedrich Meinecke, analyzed the role of the *Kulturnation* ideology. In his *Weltbürgertum und Nationalstaat*, Meinecke aptly compares two different types of nation-building. In the first — the Western case of the nation-state — a nation emerged from "a smooth functioning of the state, with various elements combining in it in slow, long-term evolution"; it was the product of the "unifying force of a common political history." The second type was characterized by the lack of "the driving force that would have turned [the absolute state] into a nation-state." Consequently, because the common history found in a smoothly functioning state was lacking in this second type, the nation was built from a "cultural property [which was] in some way commonly acquired and experienced" by a people. Cultural nations were born, after an initial spontaneous or semiconscious stage of national revival, from a conscious *Selbstbestimmung*, a strong will: "A nation is a community," Meinecke states, "that wishes to be a nation." After the French Revolution, the idea of "democratic individualism" gave rise to a national activity that led to the birth of new nation-states from "nations that for centuries had only a cultural existence" (Meinecke 1908, 7, 9).

From Cultural Movement
to Mass Organizations

Nation building in Central and Eastern Europe began with powerful cultural activity: language reform, the promotion of a national theater, opera, and arts, the historicization of the past, and the creation of national literatures and myths about a glorious legacy. Cultural nationalism in this region of peoples who lived under foreign domination in multinational empires was a defense against Germanization, Magyarization, or Russification. It compensated for the depressing feeling of national inferiority and humiliating subordination. In short, the cultural movement of national awakening was not only self-justifying but also self-creating.

Frustration caused by backwardness and lack of independence were often overcompensated by the concept of being in a "selected nation" or in a superior race with unique characteristics and a heroic past. Several historical myths maintained that one or another given people represented the only nation in the area that had defended the civilized world against barbaric attacks; this nation's people supposedly had lived the longest possible time in the region, predated the arrival of other groups, were descended from the greatest ancient people, were peaceful and creative in contrast to their aggressive, destructive neighbors, and exhibited cultural superiority as well as advanced state-formation skills. Nationalism in Central and Eastern Europe, as in most other backward areas from the second half to the last third of the nineteenth century, turned from the belief in the "brotherhood of free nations" toward, as Hans Kohn phrases it, aggressive exclusivism that announced "historical rights" and supremacy (Kohn 1929). In so doing, it laid the groundwork for many of the region's future conflicts.

According to the well-based analysis by Miroslav Hroch, there were three major stages in the rise of nationalism: folklore, propaganda, and mass movements (Hroch 1985). In the beginning, around the turn of the eighteenth and nineteenth centuries, the national idea initiated a romantic, apolitical folklorizing by a handful of intellectuals. At this time, the Slovak Jan Kollár dreamed about a unified Slav nation stretching "from the River Elbe to the Pacific Ocean," and his compatriot Bernolak created the first Slovak grammar and dictionary, selecting the West Slovak dialect, nearest to the Czech language, as the basis for standardization.

This folklore stage continued as Frantisek Palacký published the first volume of his huge ten-volume synthesis of Czech history in 1836, presenting that history as a constant struggle against bellicose, antidemocratic nations such as the Romans, Huns, Germans, and Magyars, who had constantly attacked the peace-loving, spiritual, democratic Czechs and Slavs. The national mission of safeguarding freedom and superior values against a permanent aggression and the special peerless national character, as revealed by romantic historiography, became basic elements of emerging national ideology.

In the Balkans, the "Great Illyrian" concept postulated the existence of a single South Slavic nation between the Black Sea and the Adriatic, supposedly descended from the ancient Illyrians. On the basis of this concept, Ludevit Gaj reformed the Croat language, elevating the vernacular derived from the *Shtokav* dialects into a literary language. This dialect was almost identical with the South-Slavic dialect of Herzegovina, the same that was chosen by Vuk Karadzić, the most influential Serb language reformer of the early nineteenth century. These activities constructed the basis for a unified Serbo-Croat language.

Meanwhile, the long static-theocratic orthodox world of the Balkan societies shifted gradually toward a national awakening. The first revolts against the Ottoman rule in the early nineteenth century were uncoordinated, bitter, spontaneous local uprisings against uncontrolled terror and exploitation and against the robber hoards of Ottoman Janissaries. Local uprisings of 1804 and 1815, with limited local goals, spread in the context of an advantageous international situation and evolved into the beginning of a series of national struggles for independence that led to the foundation of the small independent Balkan states of Serbia, Bulgaria, and Albania (Stavrianos 1963).

Also during this initial stage, the theory of the so-called Daco-Roman continuity emerged at the end of the eighteenth century and served as a foundation of the romantic Romanian national identity. Samuil Klain-Micu, working in Hungarian-ruled Transylvania, and Petru Maior, operating in the Ottoman-dominated Romanian Principalities around the turn of the eighteenth and nineteenth centuries, rediscovered early myths about the glorious origins of the Romanian people. According to this myth, the Dacs, the alleged genuine ancient population of Transylvania, had mixed with the conquering Romans, who had occupied the territory and founded the last province of the Roman Empire, named "Dacia." This Daco-Roman nation was the ancestor of the Romanians, who are, consequently, the native population of both Transylvania and the principalities. In his book on the *History of the Ro-*

manian's Dacian Origin (1812), Maior presented a powerful national ideology that established the "historical right" of all Romanians, including those of Transylvania, to be united.

That right was the basis of a turn-of-the-century language reform initiated by Văcărescu and Eliade Rădulescu, who claimed that Romanian and Italian are not two different languages but rather dialects of the same great language. A Romanian literary language, however, had not evolved because of the barbaric influences in the Romanian lands. As a result of the work of the enthusiastic reformers, Klain-Micu, Maior, and Gheorghe Şincai, Greek educational and Church Slavic languages, together with the Cyrillic alphabet and "alien [Slavic] words" used at that time, were eliminated and a "pure Romanian language" was created. The *Lexicon Budense* (1825) derived all Romanian words from Latin.

The second stage in national development arose when the linguistic, anthropological, and historical works of the folklorizing intellectuals were turned into propaganda and found their way to the literate public, thereby contributing to the formation of a national self-consciousness. That was the very stage when the *Kulturnation* was created and the concept of nation was established among people who lacked an independent nation-state. The national ideology became the driving force in the struggle for independent nationhood.

The third stage of national development emerged at the end of the nineteenth and early twentieth century, when the organization of mass national movements began. At that time, the advocates of the national idea deliberately and consistently urged and prepared for the establishment of independent states. Eric Hobsbawm characterizes the advocates as believing that nations must find their expression through independent sovereign states (Hobsbawm 1990), state building therefore had to complement and complete nation building.

During this third stage, the Czech national movement responded to the rejection of a proposal for a federalist reorganization of the monarchy by boycotting the 1870s' parliament of Austria-Hungary. Intense emotions led to bloody clashes between Czechs and Germans in Prague, where martial law was introduced in 1893. Slovak nationalists sought to "emancipate the life of Upper Hungary from Magyar influence," and in 1896, Slovak students in Prague founded the *Československá Jednota* (Czechoslovak society). At the head of the Realist Party, Thomás Masaryk led the Czech national movement toward new heights and, during World War I, organized a quasi-government in exile and the nucleus of an army, the Czech Legion.

In Transylvania, Romanians demanded the restoration of autonomy, established a National Committee and party, and also boycotted the Hungarian parliament. Their national struggle occupied the last third of the nineteenth century and concluded in the declaration of Alba Iulia in 1918, when Transylvanian Romanians expressed their will to join Romania.

During the same decades, a Hungarian national movement provoked a crisis in the Austro-Hungarian dual monarchy, and in 1905 a coalition of national opposition led by the Independence and 1848 Party won election for the first time in the half-century long history of Austria-Hungary. Leaders of the national movement demanded an independent Hungarian army (instead of the common, Austrian-led, German-speaking army) and the abolition of the common market of the empire. The latter reform was to be accomplished by introducing an independent Hungarian tariff system. Although the national coalition gave up its principles so that it could successfully form a government and then became compromised during its few years in power, a leading representative of the new generations of the Independence and 1848 Party, Count Mihály Károlyi, became the founder of independent Hungary. When a Hungarian army unit refused to go to the front, generating the peaceful October Revolution of 1918, Károlyi, the head of the newly founded National Committee, declared Hungarian independence.

In Poland, the former socialist and new leader of the Polish national movement, Jósef Piłsudski, was inspired by the Japanese defeat of Russia in the 1905 Japanese-Russian war and revitalized the concept of an armed struggle for Polish independence. Despite the fact that, from the mid 1860s onward, the nineteenth-century decades of "organic work" had expressed themselves in peaceful nation building, modernization, and the beginnings of industrialization in Poland, the tradition of three consecutive generations of uncompromising freedom-fighters who had lived between the 1790s and 1860s, along with memories of the heroic uprisings of 1794, 1830–1831, and 1863–1864, remained vitally active. After a half-century long intermission, Piłsudski drew upon this tradition and these memories. He took up the cause of independence, moving in 1910 to Galicia from Russian Poland and organizing his First Brigade, the nucleus of an independent Polish army. A window of opportunity was opened by the upheaval of World War I, when Piłsudski's army, under Austrian command, participated in a war against Russia that liberated Poland.

Zionism constitutes another special example of the emergence of organized Central and Eastern European national mass movements around the turn of the century. The idea of restoring the ancient independent Jewish state was born in the earlier decades of the nineteenth century in Germany and Russia. The real turning point, however, was brought about by the publication of *The Jewish State* by Theodor Herzl, a writer and journalist who was born in Budapest and who settled in Vienna with his family at the age of eighteen. Herzl's precursors were, to use David Vital's expression, proto-Zionists. Herzl himself created a complete movement and an organization with its own program. Its essence was simple, summarized in one sentence: "We are people without a country, we need a national home" (Herzl 1970). According to Herzl, the "Jewish question" was not a social or religious issue but a national one. Traditional Jewish Messianism and religious self-identification—the routinely expressed wish "Next year in Jerusalem!"—was translated into a secularized national ideology that became the driving force behind a large organization. In August 1897, the first Zionist Congress was held in Basel and resolved that "Zionism means the creation for the Jewish people of a home in Palestine, secured by public law. To this end the Congress wishes the following: 1. the systematic settlement of Jewish farmers, artisans and tradesmen in Palestine . . . ;3. the strengthening of the Jewish national feeling and consciousness" (Vital 1975, 4). In pursuit of these goals, Herzl initiated dialogues with the German, British, and Turkish governments.

Zionism was certainly the most peculiar national movement in the region. It sought to reestablish an independent state two thousand years after its collapse (instead of after one hundred and fifty years of Polish partition or after five hundred years of Ottoman occupation of the Balkans). It wanted to revitalize a language that had fallen into disuse except in religious rituals. Moreover, the newly founded state would be distant from the places where the Jewish diaspora actually lived. In spite of these peculiarities, the Jewish national movement was no more utopian than the greater Illirian movement or Czechoslovakism.

Organized mass movements, parties, and liberation armies prepared for the foundation of independent states that would realize national dreams. Most of these ideas, however, still seemed unattainable, even at the dawn of the twentieth century. What was the chance of Piłsudski's First Brigade against the tsar's army? What could a Slovak or Transylvanian Romanian organization do against the powerful bureaucracy, police force, and army of the fifth greatest power of Europe? It seemed a dream. But these movements and organizations gained momentum during the war that destroyed nineteenth-century Europe and promised a new arrangement.

The explosion of the war itself was connected with the passionate national conflicts of the region. Although great power conflicts, the formation of alliance systems, and a sharp arms race paved the road to major international confrontation, the first shot of the five-year-long war exploded in Sarajevo. The young Bosnian Gavrilo Princip, a member of the pan-Slav-oriented Black Hand Society, assassinated the Archduke Franz Ferdinand, who was visiting the city. The archduke died because he had attempted to safeguard the Austro-Hungarian Monarchy by replacing Austro-Hungarian dualism with a so-called "trialist" arrangement. This argument would have emancipated the Slavic nations of the Austro-Hungarian Monarchy, forming a new *Ausgleich* (compromise) and offering the same autonomy to the Slavs that had been granted earlier to the Hungarians.

Gavrilo Princip, like the Great Serbian, or "Yugoslav"-oriented Bosnian Serb nationalists in general, did not want to accept this solution. The nationalists sought to block the road of a trialist reorganization of the monarchy and to join Serbia and the other South Slavic nations in an effort to realize their dream of true national independence. The nationalist ideology had thus conquered Central and Eastern Europe and, from the early twentieth century onward, embarked on its triumphant march toward self-realization.

Communism

Communism, in its genuine Marxist form, was born in the most advanced countries of the West. Its utopian ideas were rooted in the beginnings of Western civilization and revitalized in eighteenth and nineteenth century France and Britain. Although Karl Marx preserved utopian characteristics in his work, he developed a scholarly analysis of British capitalism, anticipating its trends and maintaining that increasing social polarization and exploitation would lead to a proletarian revolution. The "grave digger" of capitalism, the ever-increasing and internationally organized proletariat of the most advanced West, would, in a common revolutionary action, eliminate the capitalist class society and introduce a just communist society without private ownership, money, and state power that was alienated from the masses.

Marxism became the secularized religion of the emerging workers' movement, mobilizing millions of workers and intellectuals into trade union organizations and creating huge social democratic parties in France, Germany, and Austria. In 1914, the German Social Democratic Party with its more than one million members and the two-million strong trade union movement formed the world's largest Marxist mass party and won nearly 35 percent of the votes in the 1912 elections, making it the single largest party in the German parliament, the Reichstag.

In *German Ideology* (1847), Marx and Engels had warned that "local communism" would fail in backward countries that could do little but redistribute poverty (Marx and Engels 1970). Marxist socialists around the turn of the century heeded this warning and maintained that proletarian revolution was not on the agenda for backward, agrarian, authoritarian countries. The small and weak proletariat first had to help the emerging bourgeoisie realize its revolution in order to destroy obsolete traditional societies, to establish democratic order, and to secure the free development of capitalism. This would prepare the ground for the rise of a modern proletariat and, later, for its revolution.

History, however, did not follow the advice of these socialists. Marxism became very popular in the peripheral areas of Central and Eastern Europe. Miserable living conditions, minority oppression in multinational states, the land-hunger of millions of landless peasants, and the lack of democracy in highly hierarchical societies with their autocratic governments all gave special endurance, audacity, and bitter determination to the region's small revolutionary socialist organizations. Backward capitalism thus did not mean a backward workers' movement, with weaker organization and fighting spirit. On the contrary, the frustration caused by the failures and partial successes of modernization generated a strong rebellion against early capitalism—a desire both to sweep away obsolete society and to create a new, more advanced and just social order.

Although backwardness provided a hotbed of revolutionary ideas and actions, it offered a different soil for Marxist seeds than that of the West. Russia, a peasant country with little industry operating in an environment of ruthless Asiatic oppression, naturally would not see a mass working-class political party on the German scale. Imprisonment and exile were the state's principal means of frustrating revolutionary organization. In Germany, the twelve years under Bismarck's antisocialist "emergency law" was the exception rather than the rule. In Russia, a similar state of affairs was "normal." In 1902, Lenin remarked that the Russian proletariat would have to undergo trials immeasurably more grave than those in Germany and would have to fight a monster compared to which the German Anti-Socialist Law would seem but a pygmy.

The tension and oppression in Russia soon led to the *Narodnaya Volya* (People's Will), a movement of individual terrorism. *Narodnaya Volya* conducted a series of terrorist actions by self-sacrificing revolutionaries such as Zasulich, Soloviev, and Khalturin. The assassination of Tsar Alexander II in 1881, of the minister of education in 1901, and of the minister of the interior in 1902 showed the potential danger represented by this movement. But revolutionary development went beyond these desperate actions by intellectuals. The laboring masses also began to stage reckless acts, that, especially in certain crisis situations, demonstrated the growth of a revolutionary tension. On January 22, 1905, during the Japanese-Russian war, tsarist troops opened fire on tens of thousands of demonstrators who were marching toward the Winter Palace in St. Petersburg. This January massacre triggered strikes and peasant revolts throughout the country. A general strike paralyzed transportation, and delegates of the strike committees formed workers' councils, or soviets. Although the tsar succeeded in restoring order and initiated a new wave of reforms, including an elected legislative assembly, his regime sought to keep centralized, authoritarian rule. The elected Duma—the principal legislative assembly in tsarist Russia—and the promise held out by the introduction of a parliamentary government failed to accomplish much, and when the majority of Constitutional Democrats (*Kadet*) advocated land reform and emancipation of Jews, the tsar dissolved the Duma. A second Duma, with a Social Revolutionary and Social Democrat majority, was also dissolved. The regime turned out to be unreformable, and the revolutionary events of fall 1905 became, as Lenin called it, the "dress rehearsal" for revolution.

Revolutionary organizations in Central and Eastern Europe often had a special relationship with proletarian landless peasants and agricultural workers. The well-organized harvest strikes and a strong Agrarian Socialist movement in late-nineteenth-century Hungary suggested the possibility of combining revolutionary peasant forces with the small but highly concentrated urban proletariat. Half of the industrial workers of Hungary were concentrated in Budapest, where they had their first bloody clash with police forces in 1912.

The illiterate, unorganized Romanian peasantry, indulging in a medieval jacquerie-type revolt in 1907, turned simultaneously against the rural Jewish leaseholders, shopkeepers, and moneylenders, the incarnation of a fragile early capitalism, and against the landowning boyars, who personified a preserved ancien régime.

The Rise of Western Socialist Reformism

At the turn of the century in the industrialized West, the distinct polarization of the early capitalist society was replaced by the rise of a modern middle class and of white-collar workers. Social legislation, a welfare system, and increased income improved the situation of the industrial workforce. In contrast to the statement of the *Communist Manifesto*, Western workers already had much more to lose than their "chains." Paradoxically, while the Marxist prediction for the West failed, the European periphery raised the banner of Marxism to become a potential center of revolution against backward, semifeudal capitalism. This was a turning point in Marxist theory, a crossroads where two kinds of Marxism—Western social democracy and Eastern revolutionary Leninism—separated and departed from each other.

In the highly developed Western and Central European countries, including Germany, revolutionary Marxism adjusted itself to transformed capitalism. In 1896, Eduard Bernstein, a leading theorist of the German Social Democratic Party who belonged to Engels's circle, launched his landmark article series, *Probleme des Sozialismus*, and urged the revision of Marx and of the Erfurt Program of the party. Bernstein argued that capitalism had developed in a different direction from the one indicated by Marx. Poverty had not grown but had diminished. Welfare reforms had been won peacefully by organized mass movements and had been instituted by parliamentary legislation. Capitalism had not collapsed but had changed and matured. Bernstein concluded that social democracy should not seek proletarian revolution but should advocate and carry out reforms. In that manner, it might obtain victory within the parliamentary system (Bernstein 1899).

The leading figure of post-Marxian Marxism, Karl Kautsky, provided the first analysis of the new phase of capitalism that emerged in the 1880s. Colonialism, the annexation of regions that contained valuable raw materials and agricultural resources, had prolonged the existence of capitalism. In his *Imperialism* (1914), Kautsky recognizes that capitalism does not reach its "final phase" but might be followed by "ultra-imperialism," a period when capitalist powers will replace the "imperialist policy" of colonialism and expansionist conflicts. From the economic trends of the concentration of capital and broader international integration, Kautsky predicts that "cartel policy will be applied in foreign policy" and that the great powers, instead of struggling against each other, will reach agreement and build cooperative alliances (Kautsky 1914).

Rudolf Hilferding went even further in analyzing the modern, twentieth-century phenomena of transforming capitalism. In his book, *Das Finanzkapital* (1909), Hilferding suggests that the modern economy had created a "consciously regulated social relation" and that the anarchy of capitalism had been eliminated. Thirteen years later, in spring 1923, at the refounding congress of the Socialist International at Hamburg, Hilferding stated that within the system of capitalism it is possible to "eliminate the faults of capitalism" (*Protokoll* 1923, 58). In 1927, at the Kiel conference of the German Social Democratic Party, he announced: "We arrive at a capitalist organization of the economy, where the road leads from an economy determined by the free play of forces to an organized economy. . . . In reality, organized capitalism means that the capitalist principle of laissez-faire is replaced by the socialist principle of planned production" (*Protokoll* 1927, 166–68).

Marxist social democracy thus deviated from the genuine revolutionary principle of Marxism when it adapted to the post-Marxian reality of the capitalist system. The social democratic parties developed an ideology of regulating, reforming, and renewing capitalism and turned it into an organized, state-controlled welfare system.

The Emergence of Eastern Revolutionary Leninism

In backward, authoritarian, and explosive Eastern Europe, a second type of Marxism emerged. Unlike social democracy, it preserved the revolutionary principle of genuine Marxism but diverged from its democratic foundations and became the communist ideology of revolt.

While Bernstein worked on revising Marx, Vladimir Ilyich Ulianov (Lenin), the son of a Russian schoolteacher and the brother of an executed revolutionary, was arrested and exiled to Siberia by the tsarist police for founding an illegal revolutionary organization "to emancipate the working class." Lenin did not believe in peaceful reforms or in parliamentary forms. He began to work on a book based on the analysis of extensive local statistics: *The Development of Capitalism in Russia*, published in 1899, which illustrated that the Russian economy had already been profoundly and decisively capitalized. In light of this illustration, he rejected the romantic anticapitalist view of the *narodniks*, the Russian populists, who sought to avoid capitalist forms by relying on traditional peasant village communities (*obshchina*). In Lenin's opinion, it was "gibberish" to say that "Russia . . . can bypass capitalist development, escape from capitalism, or skip it in some way other than that of the class struggle, on the basis and within the framework of this same capitalism" (Lenin 1971, 76).

Led by the attempt to prove the advancement of Russian capitalism, Lenin also analyzed the special characteristics of East European agricultural development. He distinguished between the American and Prussian paths of capitalist agrarian development, the latter being a capitalist transformation of former feudal latifundia, and concluded that the rise of capitalism in Eastern Europe did not have to occur along Western lines.

In the political conclusion to his analyses of economic history, Lenin maintained that it was neither possible nor necessary to wait for the emergence of Western forms and complete capitalist transformation in backward countries and that Russia was ripe for proletarian revolution. He rejected the widespread social democratic view that the process must first launch a bourgeois revolution and capitalist development in order to create the preconditions for proletarian revolution.

In rejecting this social democratic tactic in his *Two Tactics of Social Democracy* (1905), Lenin advocated a special form of combined bourgeois and proletarian revolution. In backward countries, he argued, this special revolution would manifest its bourgeois character by toppling authoritarian regimes and by establishing democratic republics and political liberty. The twentieth-century bourgeoisie lost its revolutionary character and could not be expected to fight. Consequently, the proletariat must fight "for the revolution to be carried to its conclusion . . . , [and since] the bourgeoisie is incapable of carrying the democratic revolution to its consummation, while the peasantry is capable of doing so . . . we must exert all our efforts to help it to do so." This special revolution would then establish "the revolutionary-democratic dictatorship of the proletariat and the peasantry" (Lenin 1971, 78, 106). This would eventually bring about a permanent revolution, that would in turn lead directly to the socialist revolution:

The proletariat must carry the democratic revolution to completion, allying to itself the mass of the peasantry in order to crush the autocracy's resistance by force and paralyze the bourgeoisie's instability. The proletariat must accomplish the socialist revolution, allying to itself the mass of the semi-proletarian elements of the population, so as to crush the bourgeoisie's resistance by force and paralyze the instability of the peasantry and the petty bourgeoisie. (Lenin 1971, 117)

Lenin's concept of the proletarian socialist revolution in a single backward peasant country abandoned Marx's theory of socialist revolution. This sharp divide with Marxist theory was bridged by the theory of permanent revolution. Lenin and Trotsky both maintained that the revolution in backward Russia would be permanent in a double sense, partly coupling the bourgeois and the proletarian revolutions in one process and partly serving as a generator of the socialist revolution in the advanced West. The victory of the Russian revolution would be used "for carrying the revolution into Europe" (Lenin 1971, 103). Lenin differentiated between the possibility of the socialist revolution and the possibility that socialism could be built in one single country. Whereas the first, according to Lenin, was possible, the second was not.

Despite the compromise represented by the theory of permanent revolution, Lenin's concept departed drastically from Marx. According to Marx, the attainment of the highest level of capitalistic development creates the necessary preconditions for proletarian revolution and socialism. Leninism reversed this formula by maintaining that revolution must be carried out in order to create the preconditions of socialism.

Another pillar of Leninism was its theory of imperialism, which differed noticeably from the social democratic concepts of Karl Kautsky and Rosa Luxemburg. The brilliant, Vienna-trained economist and Bolshevik theoretician, Nikolai Bukharin, in his *Imperialism and World Economy* (1915), described the internationalization of the world economy into a single integrated system. In this global framework, even the backward, "agrarian, or semi-agrarian peripheries" and noncapitalist countries became part of the capitalist world system. Unlike Kautsky and Hilferding, he did not anticipate an unlimited concentration of capital that would lead to an alliance of imperialist powers and to a single world cartel. He clearly recognized the contradictory character of the economic process: "Together with the internationalization of the economy and of capital, there is also an emerging 'national' or 'nationalizing' trend." As a consequence, reinforcing borders and protection of national markets will remain an imminent need that contributes to "the extraordinary growth of militarism" and the "mad hurricane of world wars" (Bukharin 1966, 80, 158).

Lenin, who also published a small popular booklet on imperialism, summarized most of the arguments of previous socialist theoreticians, emphasizing the inequality of development trends and noting that "capitalism is growing with the greatest rapidity in the colonies and in overseas countries. Among these latter, *new* imperialist powers are emerging (e.g. Japan). The struggle among world imperialism is becoming more acute" (Lenin 1971, 240). The struggle was all the more acute because "the colonial policy of the capitalist countries has completed the seizure of the unoccupied territories on our planet. For the first time the world is completely divided up, so that in the future *only* redivision is possible" (Lenin 1971, 223). Therefore, "we must define imperialism as moribund capitalism . . . [as] the eve of the social revolution of the proletariat," which made imperialism the final stage of capitalism. In these new conditions, in the united imperialist world system that is the stage of an ever-increasing rivalry and struggle among the countries of unequal economic development, the victory of a proletarian revolution even in backward or semideveloped countries became possible. A new powerful ideology was being born: Leninism was aiding the rebellion of backward countries against the entire capitalist world order.

In developing his theory on socialist revolution in backward countries, Lenin described what he considered to be the logical organization of the proletarian party. In dictatorial, oppressive monarchies where there are no opportunities for broad-based legal working-class movements, the European social democratic party organization is impossible. In his *What Is to Be Done? Burning Questions of Our Movement* (1902), Lenin distinguishes between a spontaneous interest-protecting mass labor movement and the narrow circle of the party, "an organization that will consist of professional revolutionaries." This party "must of necessity be not too extensive and as secret as possible" to prepare the revolution. Arguing that the broad democratic principle cannot be asserted amidst conditions in Russia, Lenin refuses the "infantile playing at 'democratic forms'" and urges the creation of a quasi-militarily disciplined party that will replace the "rearguard of opportunists" by the "new guard, a genuine vanguard" of "militant Marxists." The power of decision and control within the party must be given to

Populist *sezession* in Transylvania

Ödon Lechner's national *sezession* building in Budapest

Alfons Maria Mucha's *sezession* poster

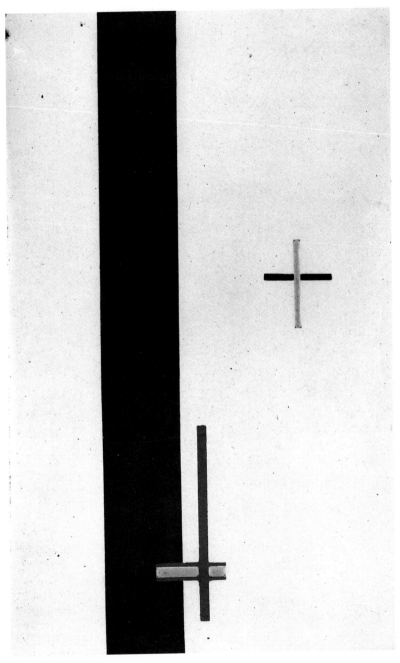

László Moholy-Nagy: *Telephone Picture*

Katarzina Kobro: space composition

Lajos Kassák: *Picture Architecture*

Constantin Brâncuşi: *Princess X*

Kazimir Malevich: *White on White*

Béla Uitz: *Red Soldiers, Ahead!*

Lajos Kassák
with flyers for his
periodical, *Munka*

Max H. Maxy:
Tristan Tzara

Long live the war! Demonstration in Budapest

Trenches, where soldiers of Austria-Hungary languished for years

The disabled came home

Aleksandr
F. Kerenski

Béla Kún (middle)

Hungarian poster:
"Join the Red Army!"

Aleksandur
Stamboliski

Declaration of the Hungarian Republic in 1918

Thomás Masaryk with the Czech Legion marching into Prague

Thomás Masaryk and Eduard Benes

Signing the Soviet-Estonian peace treaty in Tartu in 1920

Hungarian irredenta in kindergarten: "No, no, never!"

Nikola Pašić

Stjepan Radić

Father Hlinka

the elected leading bodies. This central importance of the party lies in being able to organize and to lead the masses, who are driven by spontaneous discontent. The party will be the Archimedean fulcrum with which the entire archaic Russian world can be overturned (Lenin 1947, 213, 222, 269). After the revolution, at the Tenth Party Congress, Lenin went even further and declared the mandatory "unity of the Party," the necessity of "iron discipline," and the need for "complete elimination of all factionalism"—a declaration that Stalin 'translated' as "The Party becomes strong by purging itself of opportunist elements" (Stalin 1972).

The Leninist concept of the party and its organizational principles were rooted deeply in Russian reality and its revolutionary legacy (in particular, the concept resembled the views of the so-called *Zemlovolets* of the 1870s). The Leninist ideas convinced the majority of the Russian social democrats, who clashed sharply with the minority *Menshevik* wing of the party—a wing led by Martov and loyal to European democratic socialist traditions. A confrontation at the second congress of the party in Brussels and London in 1903 split the party and led to the independent formation of the majority party, the Bolsheviks. The Bolsheviks held an independent congress in Prague in 1912 and formed a rigorously centralized revolutionary vanguard.

A split subsequently became unavoidable in the entire international social democratic movement. The Leninist concept of the party, with its centralist, military-type organization, was rejected by most Western socialists, who insisted with Rosa Luxemburg and Karl Liebknecht that democratic principles and spontaneous mass involvement must be preserved in any revolutionary action. In contrast, the peripheral countries of Europe found the Leninist concept appealing.

In the countries on the European periphery, several Bolshevik-type communist parties were founded, and the communist ideology became a prime mover in the region's most radical revolutions. "The first half of the twentieth century is richer than any previous period of human history in the activities of revolutionary movements," notes Hugh Seton-Watson. "But there is one important feature of the twentieth-century revolutionary movements which distinguishes them from those of the nineteenth century. The earlier movements arose in culturally and economically advanced countries, while those of the present century have for the most part affected backward regions and peoples" (H. Seton-Watson 1964, 36).

Fascism

Parallel with nationalism and communism, as a sort of deformed combination of both, a third robust ideology emerged. This ideology relied on an extreme national fundamentalism and subordinated both citizens and their individual human rights to the "eternal interests" of the nation. It was hostile to other nations, aggressively demanded the rights of the nation, and rejected the existing, Western-dominated world order and values. It advocated and attempted to create a strong, authoritarian state that was intensely antiliberal and antiparliamentary. It developed a cult of charismatic leadership that drew on irrational sources for its strength and power. Rejecting class differences in the national community, it sought to establish a homogenous, communal, collective society, which would realize a "national socialism" in its struggle against the West, against international finance, and against the society's alien elements (such as minorities and other races).

These ideas, which were coalescing in the 1880s into right-wing radicalism, grew in the political soil of France, Italy, and Germany. During the last third of the nineteenth century, after the defeat by Prussia, the maltreatment of the *gloire*, the loss of Alsace-Lorraine, and the world's first communist revolution in Paris, French conditions generated bitter and wild right-wing philosophies. Maurice Barrès revolted against a hypocritical, socially restrictive society and called for total individual liberty. The idealist hero of his *L'Ennemis des lois*, André Maltere, first turned toward socialism, but deserted the "utopian collectivism" and found his ideal in unrestricted individualism. Individualism, however, was linked to an authoritarian and antiliberal nationalism—the need of *l'homme national* to voice the hopes and needs of the people and to provide strong leadership. In opposition to Marxian "cosmopolitan socialism," Barrès called his program "national socialism" and attempted to combine "nationalism, protectionism, and socialism." With Barrès, Bergson, and Maurras, protofascism was born—and so, too, were born its cult of the French countryside and the war dead, its exalted anti-Semitism and Germano-phobia, and its covert and later overt racial views.

Another method for coupling national and social ideas was formulated in Italy. Lying on the South European periphery, Italy had enjoyed a glorious past but languished in the nineteenth century. The Italian peninsula consisted of two distinct regions: the undeveloped south (and the "south of the south," Sicily), and a Westernized north. In this environment, Enrico Corradini developed his "national socialism," a prefascist theory that contained two major elements: nationalism and syndicalism. Unlike Marxism, it denied the validity of class struggle inside a national community. Instead, it substituted an ideology of "class solidarity" that would be created and maintained by a strong state power. "Syndicalism and nationalism together," declared Corradini, "these are the two doctrines that represent solidarity." Accordingly, syndicalism "must stop at the national boundaries. . . . It must abandon its international role and function within the framework of the nation. . . . [Then] the differences between the two doctrines would disappear" (Eicholtz and Grossweiler 1980, 104). The "corporate state" must subordinate and coordinate different class interests so that a just national community could be created. Mussolini borrowed these ideas and translated them into actions and institutions. As the Fascist Confederation of Industrialists declared in 1939: The main purpose of the corporate state was "that of correcting and neutralizing a condition brought about by the industrial revolution of the nineteenth century which dissociated capital and labor in industry, giving rise on the one hand to a capitalist class of employers of labor and on the other to a great propertyless class, the industrial proletariat. The juxtaposition of these classes inevitably led to the clash of their opposing interests" (Arendt 1966, 258).

According to Corradini's theory, the unified national community must act together against rival and hostile nations. Marx's concept of class struggle was thus transformed into the concept of the struggle between "proletarian nations" and "bourgeois nations." In December 1910, when he addressed the First Congress of Nationalists in Florence, Corradini stressed the significance of international struggle. Italy, a proletarian nation, could only assert herself through fighting. Natural selection, the "sacred mission of imperialism," to use Corradini's words, would assure the victory of the strong. Following the pattern of aggressive expansionism of the rich Northern countries, Italy could secure colonies and raw material sources, thereby elevating itself into the ranks of industrialized nations.

The most powerful "national socialist" ideology and organization emerged in Germany. One school of thought has traced its origin to the early-nineteenth-century antiliberal, nationalist German political philosophy and political economy. In a book on the roots of national socialism, the British historian Rohan D'O. Butler notes the critiques of laissez-faire liberalism by Johann Gottlieb Fichte (*Der geschlossene Handelsstaat*) and Friedrich List (*Das nationale System der politischen Oeconomie*) and identifies these critiques as early forerunners of national socialist ideas. "This embryonic German socialism," states Butler on Fichte's ideas, "is national socialism" (Butler 1941, 44).

The Hungarian philosopher George Lukács believes that irrational German philosophy supplied the roots of Nazi ideology and claims that "Germany's path to Hitler in the sphere of philosophy . . . constitutes the road from Schelling to Kierkegaard, and also the road from a feudal reaction against the French revolution to bourgeois hostility to progress" (G. Lukács 1974, 6). He places among the forerunners of national socialism most of the leading nineteenth-century philosophers: Kant, Schopenhauer, Nietzsche, and Spengler.

Nazi ideologues sought to prove that their roots stretched far back into the intellectual and cultural history of Germany. In the thirties, several Nazi authors "proved" that the Third Reich was an embodiment of Georg Wilhelm Friedrich Hegel's ideas about the state. The chief Nazi ideologue, Alfred Rosenberg, listed in a 1933 article in *Völkischer Beobachter* "those personalities whom national socialism has an existing and direct linkage"; he mentioned Richard Wagner and Friedrich Nietzsche as particularly important (Eicholtz and Grossweiler 1980, 295). In truth, political thinkers and philosophers, the so-called individual forerunners of Nazism, did formulate statements that, removed from the context of their extremely complex rebel legacy, served as elements for Nazi ideology and "proved" the existence of historical antecedents. But these ideas played a much smaller role than did the turn-of-the-century *völkisch* (populist) and Pan-German ideologies and movements.

George Mosse called attention to the "*völkisch* German revolution," which appealed to millions and facilitated the organization of a vast youth movement based on strictly authoritarian leadership. The *völkisch* idea with its "idealized and transcendent concept of *Volk* (people) became a symbol of unity against the reality of the present" during the first two-thirds of the nineteenth century. It embodied a rejection of the values of the industrialized, urbanized Western rivals. The *völkisch* concept of an undivided, mythical community of "people and nation" was also linked to the ideal of a "Third Way," a rejection of both western capitalism and Marxist socialism. The "third way" offered a "true German socialism . . . , the community of the Volk" (Mosse 1966, 15).

It was the concept of a people's nation that linked the *völkisch* movement with pan-Germanism. First organized in 1886, the pan-German movement, as Emil Deckert phrased it, fostered an "enlarged tribal consciousness" by maintaining that people with German origin (based on racial distinction) belonged to the German nation, regardless of where they happened to live. According to Heinrich Class's terminology, Germans who lived in non-German countries were *Staatsfremde* (alien from the state) Germans. A *völkisch*, racial-national purification excluded all the non-Germans from the German nation even if they had lived for several generations in the German territories. In Class's categorization, these were *Volksfremde* (alien from the people) elements. At this point, anti-Semitism became a leitmotiv of national socialism, providing, in the Austrian Georg von Schoenerer's opinion, the "foundation" of *völkisch*-pan-German ideology.

In a manner similar to that in which Corradini transformed the Marxist class struggle into the concept of the struggle of the proletarian nations against the bourgeois nations, so the *völkisch* and later Nazi movement translated the antibourgeois struggle into an anti-Jewish revolution. Dietrich Eckart, a prominent representative of the *völkisch* movement, stated that "the central problem of mankind is the Jewish question." In a direct linkage between the *völkisch* and Nazi movements, Gottfried Feder, founder of the *Deutsche Arbeiter Partei* (Hitler joined the party after he attended one of Feder's lectures in the summer of 1919) differentiated between the Aryan-German *schaffende* (creative) capital and the Jewish *raffende* (usury) capital. Alfred Rosenberg reformulated this traditional *völkisch* concept in his *Der Mythos des XX. Jahrhunderts*, stating: "Marxism raises the question falsely and consequently works for international Jewry when it condemns capital in general. The real question is 'in whose hands this capital lies,' and by what principles it is regulated, guided or supervised. This last issue is the crucial one" (G. Lukács 1974, 570).

The Origins of Totalitarianism (1950), a seminal book by Hannah Arendt, points out the central role of racial, "tribal nationalism" in national socialism. "[T]ribalism appeared," Arendt explains, "as the nationalism of those peoples who had not participated in national emancipation and had not achieved the sovereignty of a nation-state." From the 1880s on, tribalism merged with the concept of "continental imperialism," which "frustrated ambitions of countries which did not get their share in the sudden expansion of the eighties" (Arendt 1966, 227). These were the years of the "triumphant imperialist expansion of the Western nations. . . . The Central and Eastern European nations, which had no colonial possessions and little hope for overseas expansion, now decided that they 'had the same right to expand as other great peoples and that if [they were] not granted this possibility overseas, [they would] be forced to do it in Europe'" (Arendt 1966, 222–23, quoting Ernest Hasse's *Die Zukunft des deutschen Volkstums* of 1907). This continental imperialism—the search for colonies within European boundaries and the desire to establish geographic continuity from a specified center of power—provided new impetus for the pan-movement.

In a synthesis of the German ideology, Oswald Spengler—a "despicable parodist of Nietzsche," to borrow Thomas Mann's description—expressed the following views at the end of the war: "The Prussians and Socialism *together* are opposing the English spirit, a penetrating *Weltanschauung* that destroys the entire spiritual life of our people." He called for a "final battle between Democracy and Caesarism" and prophesied that "the advent of Caesarism will break the dictatorship of money and its political weapon, democracy. . . . The sword shall triumph over money" (Spengler 1973, 464–65, 506–7). "The true International is possible only with the victory of one race over the others. . . . The true international is imperialism . . . not via agreements and concessions but through victory and annihilation" (Spengler 1920, 84–85).

Zeev Sternhell is correct when he states: "The author of *Mein Kampf* had nothing to say which had not already been said, and not by men on the lunatic fringe, but rather by the ranking intellectuals of the day" (Sternhell 1979, 337). Regarding the ideology of fascism, he adds:

Anti-liberalism, anti-parliamentarism . . . the cult of the elite, of youth, of force and violence; the revolt against the rationalism of the Enlightenment; the advocacy of political authoritarianism—every one of the elements which went to make up fascism was by now in existence, and not merely in the shape of raw materials for they already had been elaborated into a relatively coherent system. By the time the old world crumbled away in August 1914 fascist ideology had a past history going back to the 1880s." (Sternhell 1979, 352)

Thus fascism and Nazism entailed a right-wing revolution of nations that had experienced a troubled and delayed process of national emancipation and that were unable to create their nation-states at the same time as the major Western powers. Consequently, these countries lagged behind in the tense race between nations during the age of imperialism. They were latecomers in colonial empire building and could not join the club of the self-satisfied Western nations that dominated the world order.

In the heated debates about the social base and political content of fascism, various conflicting views exist. James Gregor links fascist ideology to countries that were "partially developed or backward and consequently statusless national communities in a period when sharp international contest was being waged for position and status. . . . Fascism characterized the partially industrialized nations of Europe," nations such as the countries of the Mediterranean and East-Central European regions. In the case of industrialized Germany, "the traumatic experience . . . after the First World War, its degradation into a second-class power at precisely that historical moment when it had every prospect of becoming a first-class world power . . . , the substantial loss of status can help to explain why she identified herself with the up-and-coming revolutionary countries" (Gregor 1969, xii–xiv). Eugen Weber says much the same regarding Romania, connecting fascist ideology with backwardness (Rogger 1966, 501–74).

The official statements of the Third International and the communist parties during the 1920s to 1930s, however, stressed the counterrevolutionary content of fascism, which, as the Executive Committee of the Third International stated in 1923, "reveals its true nature after its accession to power, when it serves the interests of the industrial capitalists" and becomes a dictatorship of the "most reactionary wing of imperialists" (Eichholtz and Grossweiler 1980, 26). Several analysts have concluded that fascism is a "preventive counterrevolution" that emerged in the political tensions after World War I and in the deep desperation of the Great Depression, historical situations that were (or were assumed to be) pregnant with the potential for communist revolution. In this analysis, the "revolutionary" slogans and rhetoric are mere demagoguery. John Weiss remarks that the Nazis did not really believe in their ideological statements and that, whereas they exploited the masses' dissatisfaction, in reality they served the interests of the ruling elite and defended the existing class system. Well-known documents and facts have proved the existence of a pact between Hitler and both the Junker-led army and circles of powerful industrialists (Thyssen 1941; Pool 1948; Turner 1985). Socialism was almost immediately dropped from the political package of both Italian fascism and German Nazism once their leaders attained power, and those who continued to support the link between nationalism and socialism were purged and massacred in the early stages of fascist power.

For Central and Eastern Europe, this debate has little relevance. Socialist class struggle, transformed into anti-Semitic struggles and antibourgeois aggressiveness, and the promise of attaining social modernization and rapid industrialization through antiliberal economic nationalism and protectionism, was very attractive in Central and Eastern Europe. The ideology of right-wing nationalism gained ground in the area, and the pioneering advocates of fascism of Western countries provided patterns and models. Moreover, in the strong populist movements, Central and Eastern Europe possessed natural "carriers" for national socialist ideas.

Populism and Rising Right-Wing Radicalism in Central and Eastern Europe

Populism emerged in late-nineteenth-century Central and Eastern Europe. The Russian term *narodnik*, the Romanian *poporanismul*, and the Hungarian *népies* had the same linguistic meaning as the German *völkisch* (populist), and populist movements displayed certain fundamental similarities. They usually emerged in backward peasant societies where large landed estates occupied a great part of the arable land. They reflected existing social tensions in the countryside, unequal land distribution, poverty, illiteracy, the absence of personal freedom, and lack of political rights. They intended to elevate the peasantry to a determinant social-political position and to provide solutions to backwardness and social-political marginalization.

Despite these similarities, populism was not a uniform movement, but rather contained several different sociopolitical contents. An occasional modernizing and Westernizing populist movement sought to follow the pattern of capitalist transformation of the West in an effort to solve problems having to do with peasants. For example, certain populist groupings in interwar Hungary followed the Danish cooperative movement and even introduced Sunday schools to promote the embourgeoisement of peasantry.

Populist revolutionaries more often founded militant movements and aligned themselves with socialists, communists, or fascists. The main stream of populism sought not to follow but rather to avoid capitalist transformation and rejected the idea of cooperation with workers' movements. Capitalism and socialism were equal evils that endangered the intact, idealized peasant society. These populist revolutionaries made a virtue of necessity by celebrating the survival of medieval village communes, which had long since disappeared in the West, as a unique and superior institution of democratic, just society. Consequently, they wanted to protect the communal village society with its traditional values and militantly opposed its destruction by international capitalism or socialism. Foreign and alien influences, both outside and inside the society, were a danger to the peasantry and therefore to the nation.

In this regard, populism met both nationalism and xenophobia: populists reacted defensively to a potential social transformation even before it happened. Eric Hobsbawm explains that, on behalf of a romanticized traditional national community, populists condemned selfish, individualistic, international capitalism (Hobsbawm 1990). Conservative anticapitalism in East European societies easily merged with harsh anti-Semitism. As a consequence, populism was vulnerable to the conservative and even extreme right in the twentieth century.

One of the strongest populist movements emerged in late-nineteenth-century Russia. Unlike the German *völkisch* movement, it arose as a utopian revolutionary socialist trend in the 1870s. This loose assemblage of small independent revolutionary groups embraced the goals of social justice and equality, locating their roots in the Russian village community (*obshchina*). According to Franco Venturi, the respected scholar of Russian populism, "the true founder of populism" was Herzen, who created the ideology, but "its politician" was Chernyshevsky, another great democratic revolutionary, who translated "populist Socialism into active politics" (Venturi 1983, 1, 129). The elitist groups formed secret, strictly centralized organizations, *Zemlya i Volya* (Land and Liberty) and later *Narodnaya Volya* (The People's Will), and sent representatives to the villages hoping to enlighten and mobilize the peasants. They acted in the name of the peasantry, whose members they believed embodied uncorrupted virtue and would provide the foundation for a free democratic Russia. The *narodniks* denied the need for industrialization and sought to avoid its destructive consequences. They maintained that the path of Western capitalism is degrading, inhuman, and destructive and that it destroys the natural egalitarian values of villages. These villages needed to be preserved because they could serve as units of self-production and self-governance. Populist economists such as Vorontsov rejected the "imitation" of alien conditions because prosperity and growth might be generated in independent, non-Western ways. Danielson suggested an economy based on small-scale ownership and the cooperation of small, independent units. Mikhaylovsky and other populists asserted the possibility of an autochthonous future Russian historical development that would bypass capitalism and avoid following the West.

The peasantry played a central role in their ideology, for if liberated and made owners of the means of production, the peasants might establish a free, efficient, genuinely Russian society. To achieve that end, oppressive tsarism should disappear. Populist groups were "dominated by a single myth," declares Isiah Berlin, "that once the monster [tsarism] was slain, the sleeping princess—the Russian peasantry—would awaken and without further ado live happily forever after" (Berlin 1983, xxviii). From the seventies onward, chased, arrested, and even killed by the tsarist authorities, uncompromising populist revolutionaries resorted to terrorist tactics in an effort to overthrow the tsarist system. In a single year, Russia was engulfed by a wave of revolutionary terror: Vera Zasulich attempted to kill General Trepov, governor of St. Petersburg; Osinsky attempted to kill prosecutor Kotlyarevsky; Popko killed Geykin, a secret police officer in Kiev; Kravchinsky fatally stabbed Mezentsov, head of the secret police; and Goldenberg assassinated Prince Kropotkin, governor of Kharkov. Morozov emphasized that terrorist actions were the best weapons to mobilize the masses in the given circumstances. Conspiracy and assassination attempts culminated in the assassination of Alexander II on the bank of the Yekaterinsky Canal in St. Petersburg in March 1881. Afterward, revolutionary movements and parties proliferated, creating not only the revolutionary socialist workers' movement and bolshevism, but several other movements as well.

It was easy to transform classical populists view into nationalist xenophobia and concepts of a mythic Russian mission. After the assassination of the tsar, the authorities helped to spur the outbreak of a series of anti-Jewish pogroms. More than two hundred were recorded in 1981 to 1982. In this context, several *narodniks* welcomed the pogroms as a clear expression of a "mass revolutionary movement" to which—as Romanenko, a new member of the executive committee of *Narodnaya Volya*, stated in the party's journal—local conditions had lent an "anti-Semitic complexion" (Offord 1986, 45). Together with tsarist officials, some *narodniks* maintained that the Jews themselves provoked the pogroms because they had "replaced the landowners" and had become the main local exploiters. This view echoed that of Ignatyev, the new minister of the interior, who stated that Jews "conspired to exploit the indigenous population" (Offord 1986, 44).

In spite of major differences, similarities existed between revolutionary populists and conservative, nationalist, religious Slavophiles and pan-Slavs. *Narodniks* and nationalist Slavophiles, and pan-Slav missionaries shared the view that Russian society, in contrast to Western capitalistic society, was based on a common ownership of peasant land and that this ownership institutionalized a "real and concrete equality." They linked this view to the unique character of the Russian and Slavic people. This mystical nationalism, as Nikolai Danilevsky states in his *Russia and Europe* (1869), differentiated between two distinct types of European peoples: the "Germano-Roman type" with their distorted despotic Catholic Church, who were power-loving and aggressive, and those who declined into the religious anarchy of Protestantism. These two types were in decay because they believed in materialism and embraced the philosophical and sociopolitical anarchy of democracy. Thus the Westernization process would be a disease in Russia. In contrast, the mission of Russia's "chosen people" was to liberate and unite the Slavic nation to which all Slavic peoples inseparably belonged. As a premise for their argument, Slavophiles appealed to the existence of a strong racial and linguistic similarity, asserting that this similarity generated a resemblance in Slavic civilization and political ideology and a natural desire for union. The Slav nation exhibited a different type of human being, possessing superior, peaceful, and creative national characteristics derived from the "religious truth" of orthodoxy and from the superiority of communal society.

Early revolutionary Polish populism emerged among exiled groups, such as *Gmina Londynska* (London Commune), *Lud Polski* (Polish People), and the *Grudziaz* section of the Portsmouth solders, after the defeat of the uprising of 1830–1831. Although they embraced a utopian, antiproperty collectivism and an idealized view of the peasantry, they were also nationalists par excellence. "Polish nationalism and French Utopian socialism were its parents," states Peter Brock, an expert on Polish populism. Peasantry was the real reservoir of pure, preserved Polish nationality and "kept it from Western influence" (Brock 1977, 4, 7). The Polish mission was to liberate Poland and become the "France of the Slavs" by completing the French Revolution in the Slavic world and creating a free and equal society. Thus populist views were translated easily into nationalist programs.

Nationalism was the focal point of Romanian populism as well. Constantin Stere, the Bessarabian leader of early-twentieth-century Romanian *poporanismul* (*popor* means "people") condemned the country's Westernization and asserted that a Golgotha lies at the end of the capitalist road. Stere dreamed about a country of smallholders with their own political representation. He opposed industrialization and denounced trade as nonproductive activity. In contrast to the Romanian peasantry, the repository of popular and national values, the Jews embodied the alien "plundering capital." The large Jewish population of the country was preoccupied by this activity and consequently embodied a "parasite group," a heavy burden on Romania. A sizable portion of the Romanian intelligentsia, including some of the finest intellectuals, supported this extremist nationalist and anti-Semitic ideology around the turn of the century: Alexander Cuza, the influential professor of economics at Iasi University, and Nicolea Iorga, the leading historian of Bucharest, together with the popular poet Goga, shaped the thinking of generations of Romanians (Ioanid 1992).

Lower-class populism led to the organization of a Romanian National Christian Socialist movement as early as 1919, with a strong Italian-type corporative concept. Pancu, the founder of the movement, declared in 1919:

I believe in the one, undivided Romanian State from the Dniester to the Tisa, the representative of all Romanians and only of Romanians . . . [the] State that furthers social harmony by minimizing class differences by nationalizing factories (the property of the workers) and distributing the land among the peasants. It would distribute benefits between the state and the workers. The former owner, in addition to his own salary should get a percentage calculated proportionally to the size of his original investment. . . . The state would provide storehouses for food and clothing for workers and civil servants who, organized in trade unions would have representatives on the administrative boards of the various industrial, agricultural and commercial institutions. (Codreanu 1976, 15–16).

Students of interwar Romanian fascist movements such as Henry Roberts and Stephan Fischer-Galati maintain that "the followers of the anticapitalist fascist movement of the interwar era were the agrarian, anti-Semitic populists . . . the followers of Constantin Stere" (Fischer-Galati 1991, 51). Armin Heinen denounces this view as "mistaken" because of Stere's "further political career in the twenties" in the left wing of the National Peasant Party (Heinen 1986, 83). If Stere himself did not become a fascist, his populist anticapitalist corporativism and anti-Semitism culminated in the next generation. Corneliu Zelea Codreanu, a student of professor Cuza at the University of Iasi and an early follower of Pancu, combined traditional populism with modern fascist ideas.

It is of psychological interest that, as in so many other cases, the Romanian xenophobic populist patriot's father, Ion Zelenski (his Slavic name probably suggests a Polish origin) immigrated to Romania at the end of the nineteenth century from Austrian Bukovina, with his wife, the daughter of the Bukovinian German Brunner family. The immigrant grammar school teacher joined Cuza and Iorga, becoming a leading figure in the nationalist anti-Semitic movement. He Romanized his Slavic name to "Zelea" and, with reference to his forester ancestors (*Codru* means "forest" in Romanian), added "Codreanu." His firstborn son was named after the Roman centurion Cornelius, who converted to Christianity. His other children were named after Dacian and Romanian national heroes, and his daughter was given the characteristic name of "Irredenta."

Codreanu's populist fascism rejected the "worn-out framework" of democracy. "Democracy breaks the unity of the Romanian people, dividing it into parties, stirring it up, and exposing it, disunited, to face the united forces of Judaism. . . . Democracy forms millions of Jews into Romanian citizens, by making them their equal. . . . Why should we be the same as people who have been here for barely 5, 10 or 100 years," asked Codreanu with neophyte zeal. "Democracy is incapable of continuity of effort. . . . One party negates the plans and the efforts of another. . . . Democracy is incapable of authority. It lacks sanctions . . . [and] is at the service of great finance." Instead of democracy, a "naturally" selected elite must rule on behalf of the people. Because "the people are unsuited to govern themselves . . . just as the bees elect their 'queen,'" so the people must elect their own elite from those who are made suitable "by virtue of their abilities, willingness to make sacrifices, love of justice, the homeland and the people" (Codreanu 1976, 304–9).

Romanian fascist populism advocated the subordination of individuals and their human rights to the mythic interests of an eternal nation. Codreanu differentiated among three distinct groups: the individual, the totality of the individuals in the same nation, and the historical entity of the nation, whose life extends over centuries. Individual human rights must be limited by the rights of populace and the latter made subordinate to the right of the historical nation. The right and interest of the eternal nation is, of course, defined by the charismatic, "naturally selected" elite and leader.

Romanian romantic *völkisch* anticapitalism rejected modernization, because "from its very beginning, the industrial age destroyed our spiritual culture but it did not [offer] anything better in its place. It rather established a false culture, which corrupts us," stated Codreanu's deputy, Mota, who later died in Spain in Franco's ranks. "Under the existing conditions," he added, "our ideal has to be an illiterate country" (Nagy-Talavera 1970, 268).

To defend the Romanian folk's interest and culture, its main enemy, Jewry, must be destroyed. Codreanu echoed the old German *völkisch* accusation about a Jewish conspiracy that was "effected against Romania according to a well-established plan. The great Judaic council probably intends to establish a new Palestine on a section of land extending from the Baltic Sea down through parts of Poland and Czechoslovakia, then covering half of Romania to the Black Sea" (Codreanu 1976, 106). The Jews must be persecuted because they represent a danger to the state, support corrupt politics, maintain capitalism and communism, and exploit the Romanian people. "Communism's triumph coincides with Judaism's dream of ruling and exploiting the Christian nations," warned Codreanu. He added that the destruction of the Romanian state "by the triumph of communism . . . [would] place [Romania] under the heel of complete Jewish domination" (Codreanu 1976, 271).

The Hungarian *népies* movement was born at the end of World War I. The pioneer of this trend and the main architect of Hungarian *völkisch* ideology was Dezsö Szabó, who presented a cohesive program in the form of a novel entitled *Az elsodort falu* (A village is swept away) published in 1919. The village, in this novel, is a symbol of national purity, all that is moral and good, and the "cradle of the race" in the face of the corrupt and corrupting town. Szabó's cult of the peasantry was linked to the new "rebirth of barbarism." Fed up with the world of intellectuals, János Böjthe, the hero of the novel, turns against the aristocratic and alien worlds that have joined forces to destroy the Hungarian people. He castigates Germans, Jews, capitalism, war, and communist revolution. The leading motif of the novel is János Böjthe's "submerging back into the people." Symbolic of this is his marriage to a peasant girl, Mária Barabás, an act that symbolizes the preservation of both racial purity and the traditional village.

Hungarian populism was a social rebellion on behalf of peasant emancipation against the old, noble ancien régime. It sought land reform and proper education, but it incorporated these reform programs into a program of nationalist hatred against the spirit of capitalism, Marxist socialism, and "aliens"—primarily Jews—who, in the populist view, embodied all these anti-Hungarian elements.

There were, at this time in the early twentieth century, still some points of agreement among various populist and conservative antiliberal trends. Gyula Szekfü, the conservative Hungarian historian, published his influential book, *Három nemzedék: Egy hanyatló kor története* (Three generations: The history of a declining age), in the same year that Dezsö Szabó's book appeared. Although its "hero" is the "historical middle class," the former gentry, Szekfü shared the view that nineteenth-century Hungarian history had been permeated by poisonous and subversive elements—capitalism and liberalism—that were alien to its national spirit. "There exist essentially non-capitalist peoples," declares Szekfü. "We Hungarians display anti-capitalist talents" (Szekfü 1922, 32). According to Szekfü, alien capitalism was the province of a non-Hungarian Jewry and urban proletariat, more than half of whom belonged to different nationalities and were immigrants. These alien trends generated a historical dead-end: liberalism—capitalism—Marxism—communism. As Szekfü expresses in his book's preface, he wanted to combat the forces "that had removed the nation from the mainstream of development." To "escape from our mistakes involves the establishment of genuine national traditions" (Szekfü 1922, 4–5).

Thus, Central and Eastern European populism, although expressing deep social disappointment and rebellion against the traditional political environment, contributed significantly to establishing the peasantry as an independent sociopolitical force. It also became a reservoir of nationalist and conservative anticapitalist concepts. Hence it provided a base for radical right-wing, xenophobic, and anti-Semitic views that equated all social ills with Jewry. Populism, then, provided the meeting point for the various ideologies that emerged around the turn of the century in Central and Eastern Europe.

4

Revolution in Art and the Art in Revolution

When Central and Eastern European nations began experimenting with Western values and institutions, they experienced varying degrees of success and failure. Over time, the relative lack of success led to frustration and disillusionment. The turn-of-the-century generation expressed doubts about the efficacy and desirability of Western institutions and sought alternative solutions to their societies' political, social, and economic problems. Their bitter disappointment was expressed clearly by sensitive artists. Endre Ady, the leading Hungarian poet of the turn-of-the-century generation, wrote in 1910: "Our ideals are outdated rubbish elsewhere!" The next year, in an article with the telling title, "People with a Schizophrenic Belief," he added: "We want proper democracy and are crying for universal suffrage and the secret ballot . . . yet the achievements of far more cultured societies that have been ahead of us for centuries have destroyed our appetite for such things" (Ady 1973, 137–38). The turn-of-the-century generation lost their fathers' and grandfathers' absolute confidence in Western institutions. After the Russian theater season in Paris in 1909, Alexander Benois declared proudly: "'We have shown the Parisians what theater should be. . . . This trip was clearly a historic necessity. We are in contemporary civilization the ingredient without which it would corrode entirely'" (Eksteins 1989, 47–48). The Russian artists, Mihail Larionov and Natalia Goncharova, went much further in 1913 and expressed not only doubts about but also revulsion toward Western values: "Long live the beautiful East! We are against the West, which is vulgarizing our forms, and which is bringing down the level of everything" (Larionov 1988, 90).

The longing for change and for new solutions manifested itself equally in political ideologies, party programs, concepts of economic modernization, and artistic trends. Sociopolitical rebellion, however, was often more possible in the arts than in politics in the nondemocratic, oppressive, and even despotic political regimes of Central and Eastern Europe. Rebellious artistic groups sought to play a direct political role in mobilizing people and destroying old values that they considered false and hypocritical.

The early-twentieth-century Central and Eastern European environment offered fertile soil for revolutionary avant-garde art. Modris Eksteins notes:

If an important impulse behind experimentation in the arts at the turn of the century was a quest for liberation, a break, in aesthetic and moral terms, from central authority . . . from bourgeois conformity, from, in short, a European tradition that had been dictated to a large extent from Paris, then it was no surprise that much of the psychological and spiritual momentum for this break came from the peripheries, geographical, social, generational, and sexual. The emphasis on youth, sensuality, homosexuality, the unconscious, the primitive, and the socially deprived originated in large part . . . on the borders of traditional hegemony. (Eksteins 1989, 48)

This does not mean, of course, that avant-garde art was a product of socioeconomic processes in the peripheral regions. The development of art is governed by its own internal logic, independent of social concerns and political boundaries. According to Benedetto Croce's diagnosis, the transformation of the public spirit, expressed partly by new art trends and scientific concepts, in Europe after 1870 was a sign of the end of an age. The last nineteenth-century European war between Prussia and France heralded the bloody mass world wars of the twentieth century. The Paris Commune, which ended with the "Bloody Week" of May 21–28, 1870, when twenty thousand communards were slaughtered, offered a harbinger of the twentieth century's mass uprisings, revolutions, and counterrevolutions. Cruel early-nineteenth-century capitalism with all its striking contrasts and poverty, so brilliantly described by Charles Dickens, began to die after 1870, the very year of that author's death. The stormy augmentation of the middle class halted the tendency toward polarization in the advanced societies and, after the death of Karl Marx in 1881, eliminated the social-political trends that, according to Marx's analysis, would lead to the proletarian revolution in the most developed countries of Europe.

It was an age of uncertainty, not only in politics but also in science, philosophy, and psychology. These uncertainties affected art, particularly in the countries of the European periphery, who were just jumping on the bandwagon of a disappearing social and economic order and were both attracted to and frightened by their experiment. In physics during these decades, the dominant eighteenth-century concept of the universe and of physical laws was transformed. The Copernican and Newtonian *Weltanschauung* was replaced by the new world of relativity, the achievements of Maxwell (1864), Hertz (1888), Bequerel (1896), Planck (1900) and, most of all, Einstein (1905). The basic concept of physical matter changed with the discovery of electromagnetic space and waves and pointed to a physical reality other than that of impenetrable bodies. Absolute space and absolute time disappeared; permanence and rigidity disintegrated into transience and relativity in the newly evolving image of the physical world.

The same may be said in regard to the long-lived rationalistic, positivist concept of the human being, history, and morals. Nietzsche and Rimbaud both revolted against traditional morals and values. From 1895 on, as a result of Roentgen's work, the human being became transparent. Weissman's new findings divulged the secrets of biological inheritance, and the science of genetics opened a new stratum of self-knowledge. In November 1899, Sigmund Freud published his *Dream Analysis*, and in 1901, his *Psychopathology of Everyday Life*. A scientific interpretation of the mystical, irrational, superstition-filled realm of dreams was born. Misspoken words and mistaken movements, the Freudian slip, the accidental short-circuits of consciousness, coalesced into a complex but resolvable system of signs that provided access to the deepest layer of the human psyche. All these developments opened new means for conquering the irrational and established an entirely new view of the human being. Nevertheless, with this increase in knowledge, "reality" became increasingly uncertain. Science had not yet offered a unified, coherent new image of the physical world to replace the old one; that would not occur until the period between the two world wars. Several generations would pass before a simplified version of the new concepts could become a natural element of general thought, just as happened with the Copernican and Newtonian views.

The state of uncertainty and the discovery of the mythopoeic subconscious challenged earlier artistic concepts of validity. The transformation of the public spirit was facilitated by rebellious, transforming art—from William Morris's Arts and Crafts movement to the "anarchy of art," the destruction of "real" colors by Van Gogh, and the destruction of "real" forms by impressionism and expressionism. The geometrization of Picasso and the abstraction of Kandinsky destroyed visual reality in the early twentieth century. The relativity of time and the internal psychological world composed of memory, emotion, and impression were explored by Proust, Joyce, and Musil. An aggressive attempt to change an obsolete world was expressed by various and rapidly transforming trends of the challenging avant-garde.

Prior to the turn of the century, most art trends were born in the advanced art capitals of Western Europe. As vanguard left-wing parties and right-wing movements emerged in Central and Eastern Europe, avant-garde art became an integral component of social revolt and a deliberate attempt to change an obsolete public spirit. For the first time in its history, Central and Eastern Europe became the center of a new art trend: the modern, turn-of-the-century avant-garde. Vienna, Prague, and Budapest formed a triangular center of modern art. "Fin de siècle Vienna" and "Budapest 1900"—brilliantly described by Carl Schorske and John Lukacs respectively—became legendary capitals of high culture and modernism. The major centers of Russia—Moscow and St. Petersburg—together with the "provincial" capital of Balkan backwardness, Bucharest, nurtured outstanding groups of rebellious writers, artists, and musicians. Attracted by the "world capitals of art," many of these individuals subsequently moved to Paris and Munich and played a pioneering role in creating the new literature and avant-garde art of the twentieth century.

Art Nouveau, *Jugendstil, Sezession*

Art nouveau was the first act in Central and Eastern Europe's leading role in modern art. The short-lived art trend, which had three different names in Europe within an area of less than one thousand miles, emerged simultaneously in Paris, Munich, Vienna, and Moscow. Samuel Bing opened his gallery, the "Art Nouveau," in Paris in 1896. The art journal *Jugend* was founded in Munich in the same year. In the following year, Gustav Klimt, Josef Hofmann, and Joseph Maria Olbrich established their *sezession* group in Vienna. In 1898, *Mir Iskustva* was founded in Russia, and Sergey Pavlovich Diaghilev's modern ballet was linked with the Russian opera and ballet during the short period of the directorship of Prince Volkonsky.

Central and Eastern European artists turned toward a passionate ornamental abstract naturalism that was at the same time mystical, symbolic, stylized, extravagant, and practical. Its roots related to William Morris's workshop, which produced posters, paintings, furniture, and wrought-iron gates. Known as *sezession*, this abstract naturalism featured embellishment with meandering lines, leaves, and flowers. Within the framework of wavy lines, plants, and flowers, we find women who move with snake-like grace, their hair flowing in rich curls. The application of these motifs as well as homogenous, strong patches of color and clean contours characterized art nouveau.

One of the uncrowned kings of *sezession* was the Austrian Gustav Klimt. The warm sensuality of his female figures was presented in an extraordinary richness of colors and Oriental decorativeness—as in his masterpiece paintings of *Judith* (1901) or the portrait of *Adele Bloch-Bauer* (1907), as well as *The Kiss* (1908). Another pioneer of *sezession*, the Czech Alfons Maria Mucha established a school of poster art. The Hungarian Ödon Lechner designed landmark buildings—the City Hall of Kecskemét and the Postal Savings Bank and Museum of Arts and Crafts in Budapest—in which he created a Magyarized version of *sezession* architecture characterized by profuse majolica ornamentation and stylized folk art elements. The most homogenous *sezession*-style city center of Europe was built in turn-of-the-century Kecskemét, a unique small township in the Great Hungarian Plain.

Central and Eastern European *sezession* was often linked to the search for a new national identity (Kelbeceva 1993). As populism turned toward the peasantry, the arts attempted to replace aristocratic traditions with a peasant style. Around the turn of the century, Endre Ady adopted György Dózsa, the leader of the sixteenth-century peasant revolt in Hungary, as part of the national heritage. Folk art became an inseparable source of high culture in architecture and music.

In Romanian painting, "Arta 1900," an art nouveau group that used stylized, sculpturesque figures and static equilibrium, represents "a narrative-allegoric interpretation of [Romanian] national history" (Dragut, Florea, Grigorescu, and Mihalaci 1977, 221). It was, in a way, a precursor of the monumental stylized national painting of the interwar years. The stained glass windows of Cecilia Cutescu-Storck, which decorated the building of the Academy of Economics in Bucharest, translated the romantic historical works of Nicolae Iorga into the language of image. The rich leaf-ornamentation of the frame of *Motherhood*, with the stylized figures of mother and child, although typically *sezession*, carried the influence of Romanian folk art.

Sezession's use of folk art elements, which served a predominantly decorative goal, became closely linked to the trend's functionalism. *Sezession* found its true course in interior design, industrial art, and the manufacture of various functional objects such as lamps, furniture, and dishes. Apartments wallpapered with bright, rich colors and stylized ornamentation, furnished in *sezession* style, became fashionable. Vases, lamps, and tableware designed in *sezession* style were supplied by factories, such as the Zsolnai ceramics firm in the South Hungarian town Pécs (the producer of lavishly colored majolica tiles for Lechner's *sezession*-style buildings). Chica-Budesti, a central figure of Romanian *sezession* and the architect of loggia-faced structures in downtown Bucharest, was also an interior decorator and furniture designer. The Czech Mucha, in addition to his posters, also designed textiles. The best works of the Polish *sezession* were collected in the *Polska Sztuka Stosowana* (Polish Applied Arts), an arts and crafts society in Kracow.

Although the ornamental motifs and baroque crowdedness of *sezession* soon came to seem artificial and contrived, its use of strong colors had a more lasting effect on art, as did its use in functional objects. *Sezessionist* use of color led to expressionism and stylized abstraction. *Sezessionist* functionalism led to the avant-garde idea that everyday objects have artistic worth. A direct road led from *sezessionist* functionalism to avant-garde. The Diaghilev ballet ensemble, the most important and complex Russian workshop of the *sezession*, created its own stage design and music and became one of the most influential propagators of *sezession* all over Europe. Diaghilev's Russian Ballet functioned as a bridge between art nouveau and the revolutionary avant-garde.

Serge Diaghilev, the son of a provincial aristocrat and owner of distilleries, studied law in St. Petersburg but soon turned to music and arts and entered the conservatory to study composition. He also began to paint. Yet he became neither a lawyer, nor a composer, nor a painter but remained an amateur; or as he himself said, a "great charlatan" in all of these fields. His unique talents bore fruit when he melded his varied interests and knowledge to create the world's most complex and genuine art-workshop. He was, however, too independent and extravagant, too rebellious, to be accepted in Russia, and in 1901 he was fired from his job as advisor to the imperial theater. Diaghilev's international career began with the organization of an extraordinary exhibition of four thousand Russian historical portraits in St. Petersburg's Tauride Palace in 1905, which attracted forty-five thousand visitors. "It must be emphasized that Diaghilev," notes Modris Eksteins, "the budding experimentalist who was to become manager-extraordinaire of the 'modern spirit,' launched himself from the foundations of the Russian past" (Eksteins 1989, 23).

In 1906, Diaghilev organized a Russian exhibition in the Petit Palais in Paris. His personal mission consisted of redeeming a declining old culture through confrontation with the elemental Russian arts. "Russian art will not only begin to play a role," he wrote before his first Paris exhibition, "it will also become, in actual fact and in the broader meaning of the word, one of the principal leaders of our imminent movement of enlightenment" (Eksteins 1989, 32). During the next year he presented five Russian concerts and, in 1908, Modest Mussorgsky's *Boris Godunov* at the Paris Opera. The real breakthrough occurred in May 1909, when Diaghilev opened the *Ballets russes* (Russian ballet) at the Théatre du Chatelet. The ensemble conquered Paris and subsequently performed in most major European cities. The stage designs for their operas and ballets, especially the *Schéhérazade* of 1911, offered vibrant art nouveau designs, which were the work of Bakst and several other leading Russian painters and artists. The characteristic colors and decor, enriched with exotic Oriental motifs, influenced both fashion and interior design in Europe. *Sezession* did more to transform the everyday bourgeois environment than any other preceding art trend. The *Ballets russes* itself became one of the strongholds of Russian futurism and avant-garde art. Diaghilev invited the best futurist artists, Larionov and Goncharova, to join his ensemble, as well as the revolutionary dancer and choreographer, Nijinsky. He inspired the young Russian composer, Stravinsky, to compose the works, which, together with the entire activity of the ensemble, ultimately revolutionized ballet, music, and visual arts.

These are the byways that led this short-lived art trend into an architectural functionalism that shed ornamentation and ultimately created expressionist painting and the avant-garde idea that everyday objects have artistic worth. *Sezession* itself disappeared in a few years: *Jugendstil* became "elderly," and art nouveau "archaic."

"Ornamentation Is Sin"

Early-twentieth-century Vienna, a city of beautiful baroque and Louis XVI-style palaces and buildings, turned against ornamentation in architecture and became a cradle of modernism. In the late nineties, Otto Wagner, an architect who was part of the Vienna *sezession*, had used mirrors and colorful flower-motif ceramics for decoration, but he soon abandoned them in favor of a purer functionalism, maintaining that "only the practical can be beautiful." With this shift Wagner abandoned not only ornamentation but also historical allusions and nostalgia. In 1909 to 1910, he built the corner-house at 40 Neustiftgasse with its smooth, unornamented facade, a building that became the prototype of modern, standardized city buildings. A handful of his public buildings also helped change the architectural face of Vienna. The *Steinhof Kirche* introduced thorough modernism into its spatial plan, abandoning the traditional elements of church architecture. Although the impressive *Postsparkasse* building preserved some church elements, it did so in a most unconventional setting; with its enormous tellerroom, built in the style of a classical basilica with main hall and two side naves, the building was constructed around iron pillars and frame, which were covered only by glass and thus remained visible. Wagner's "cathedral of money" heralded a new architecture (Haiko 1984, 104).

Wagner believed that it was necessary for architecture to meet the requirement of a new way of living and the need for cheap, hygienic dwellings and workplaces. Building construction must be standardized, and therefore individual buildings would lose their aesthetic-ornamental purpose. Aesthetic pleasure would reemerge in the "monumentality of standardization," when the monumentality—an impressive, "heroic scale"—of the streets as a whole was observed. Wagner proposed semi-independent city-sections of a hundred to a hundred fifty thousand inhabitants; the sections each had their own centers and workplaces, open spaces and greenery, long chains of identical buildings, and unbroken lines of glistening shops on the ground level. At the same time, Adolf Loos, a pupil of Wagner and an equally innovative architect, began his work in Vienna. The telling title of one of his articles, *Ornamentation and Sin*, passionately expresses his architectural philosophy. His *Steinerhouse* (1908) was the first cube-shaped villa with a flat roof, devoid of architectural decoration. The rooms received light through wide, undivided windows.

The new architecture that emerged in Vienna around 1910 and spread rapidly throughout the area broke radically with the past by placing functional, human concerns at its center (*Czech* 1987; Kojić 1979). We are faced here with the same phenomenon, the same passion to tear down the old and create the new, as existed in literature.

The Expression of "Irrational Reality" in Literature

At the end of the nineteenth century, Arthur Schnitzler and a group of Viennese writers who gathered in the Cafe Griendsteidl to form the *Jung-Wien* (Young Vienna) group, and Hugo von Hofmannstahl, the librettist of *Der Rosenkavalier*, turned against the euphoria of the *Gründerzeit*—the age of great constructions and investments—and realized that the old values were decaying. They expressed doubts about both the "eternal" ideals and the atmosphere in which they were eroding. A turning point was reached by the Viennese engineer-mathematician, Robert Musil, who in 1908 wrote his doctoral dissertation on Mach's epistemological theory. Musil was a successful writer, who published his first novel, *Die Verwirrungen des Zöglings Törless* (The confusions of young Törless), in 1906. The story of Törless, based on his very personal calvary in the military school of the Dual Monarchy and written in an apparently neutral style that nonetheless contains a hidden passion, became an early expression of human defenselessness, torture, and humiliation. In expressing the reality of turn-of-the-century Austria-Hungary, Musil became the literary-philosophical spokesman of the "depersonalization syndrome" and an intellectual rebel who unmasked, as Marie Louise Roth phrases it, the "fundamental crisis" and the "irrational reality" of a hypocritical society (Roth 1972, 47). Musil himself said one and half decades later that he wrote about a "fragmented period," when "homogenous culture and ideology disappeared and the members of the society had to face unanswerable questions. . . . [It is thus] understandable that they are reacting in a pathological way" (Gargani 1984, 246).

Prague's role in modernism was also decisive. A powerful artistic message of "disruptive revival" was sent from the city, which served as the capital of Bohemia. A hereditary province of the Austro-Hungarian Empire, which had lost its independence in the early sixteenth century, Bohemia had failed to achieve cultural-political autonomy during the permanent struggles from the 1870s onward but had nevertheless become the most advanced and industrialized part of the entire empire.

Nearly half of Prague's population was German-speaking, including Franz Kafka, who wrote in German and belonged to the city's Jewish community. The multilayered, hierarchical social structure of Prague and Kafka's minority status—belonging to the German-speaking Jewish minority among a larger Czech minority under the autocratic-bureaucratic "K. und K." (*Kaiserlich und Königlich*) regime—influenced Kafka's first and most expressive writings on alienation, a phenomenon characteristic of the coming age. Kafka masterfully presented the human being as both frightened and frightening and depicted the terror of a faceless power upon defenseless and hopelessly apathetic people. He revealed the dire absurdity of impersonal power and the rule of irrationality embodied by *The Castle* and the lonely man in the endless, horrifying labyrinth under the roof. "The secret king of German prose," as Hermann Hesse called Kafka, did not sound a revolutionary call, did not even revolt, but bitterly exposed the irrationality of an irrational world. Future decades have proven how deeply realistic his sense of absurdity was.

Along with Vienna and Prague, Budapest became a center of rebellion. The city was a Western center of modern industry in an Eastern country; more than half of the Hungarian industrial workers were concentrated in the capital, along with nearly two-thirds of the modern middle class and intelligentsia of Hungary. The highly Western culture and atmosphere of the capital was integrally interwoven with its strong and emancipated Jewish community, which comprised 20 to 25 percent of the city's population. A city with six hundred coffeehouses and three centuries of coffeehouse culture, where even revolutions were connected with coffeehouses—the March 15, 1848, revolution in Budapest started from the legendary Café Pilvax—Budapest was rife for rebellion.

That Budapest was the scene entered by the poet Endre Ady in 1906, the same year in which Musil's Törless appeared. Ady published his *Uj versek* (New poems), which he characterized as "new songs of a new time." His poems had an enlightening and revolutionary impact on an entire generation. John Lukacs notes, "I know of no instance in the history of world literature—or in the history of any country—where such a volume of poems . . . had a comparable impact. . . . In Hungary in 1906 this volume produced a veritable explosion" (J. Lukacs 1988, 164). "I am sending you a volume of poems by Ady," writes Béla Bartók in a letter to a Romanian friend in January 1912. "The first poem states that the Hungarians, Romanians and Slavs in this country, must unite, because they are all one in being oppressed. We have never had a poet who dared to write anything like this" (Bartók 1976, 186). Ady seemed to embody the feeling of crisis, and his work functioned as a harbinger of coming revolution. He attacked rural, "Oriental" backwardness, the autocratic regime of the dominant aristocracy, and the prime minister István Tisza with vitriolic passion. He also rejected Hungarian nationalism, calling for the reconciliation of the nationalities. "Ten thousand people had run ahead and were becoming European in mind, need, nerves," writes Ady in an article in 1905. Hungary, however, existed "in the middle of Europe as a living negation . . . in a struggle against Europe for a thousand years, . . . [like a] ferry-boat country sails from the East to the West, but more likely back to the East" (Ady 1990, 634–35). Ady's "Hungarian Europe," by which he meant a European Hungary, had to be created.

Hungarian activist avant-garde writers quickly and deliberately turned to sociopolitical action. In the introductory issue of their periodical *Tett* (Action) they declared: "Beauty dominates art but life is a broader beauty than beauty itself. The artist and writer will again be worker among workers and fighter among fighters" (Bojtár 1977, 74). Lajos Kassák, a former worker, who became a poet, writer, painter, and editor and the central figure of Hungarian avant-garde, organized a group of young writers and artists who advanced the radical stylistic endeavors of the 1910s. According to Kassák, the "Red Issue" of *Tett* in November 1918 "was a burning protest, not merely against the war, but against a society that tolerated such a war, and against an art that had its source in such a society and thrived on it, like the flower of perdition lives on marsh weed" (Kassák 1972, 243).

In 1907, the Spaniard Pablo Picasso began to paint his *Young Ladies of Avignon*. The geometrization of Cubism had begun. In the Netherlands in 1910, the "de Stijl" group of Piet Mondrian introduced geometric abstraction. Something new surfaced with these works. Italy, although relatively backward in economic terms, became one of the cradles of futurism, a movement that attempted to create a cult of "perpetual motion, aggressive struggle, and the art of speed." Italian futurism grew from a bitter and desperate revolt against the past. After a night of revelry, a group of inebriated young artists imposed the wild and incendiary program of futurism, declaring that "we want to destroy the museums and libraries" (Marinetti 1959, 349–54).

These themes, the tearing down and burning of the old with the accompanying demand for speedy change and aggressive dynamism, became a popular program in peripheral Central and Eastern Europe. Many people shared the view of Lajos Kassák, the leading Hungarian avant-garde artist and writer: "Art is not an aesthetic ideal standing outside the laws of society, but a manifestation of life . . . determined by the forces of the age . . . a will for and demand of change as a crisis, transformation, and new harmony of spiritual development" (Kassák 1972, 8).

Thus Central and Eastern European avant-garde erupted with a compelling talent, passion, and extremism, which powerfully articulated the general sense of crisis and the need for a radical transformation of the old order. This art was born and nurtured in the stuffy atmosphere of the Austro-Hungarian Monarchy, the Russian Empire, and Romania. But some artists did not want to go beyond demonstrating the absurdity of that world. To quote Kassák again: "Most of them were not the heirs of utopian builders but the victims of an oppressive past and a feverish sense of the future. . . . [It was not] a conscious purpose . . . [but] the unbearable cause" that was expressed (Kassák 1972, 47). Others sought more radical results. Diaghilev, himself, looking back to the early 1910s, stated in an interview in 1916, "We were all revolutionists . . . when we were fighting for the cause of Russian art, and . . . it was only a small chance that I escaped becoming a revolutionist with other things than color or music" (Eksteins 1989, 42).

In tsarist Russia, another birthplace of futurism, poems of Victor Khlebnykov were published in the almanac *Studio Impressionists 1910*. The "ego-futurist" and "cubo-futurist" groupings of Petrograd and Moscow attracted a new generation of writers, painters, and musicians. Their first manifesto—signed by Burlyuk, Khrutchenik, Khlebnykov, and Mayakovsky—bore the provocative title "We Gave Common Taste a Slap on the Face" and declared: "We alone are the face of our era. Through us does the bugle call of the era sound in the artistry of words. The past is narrow. The Academy and Pushkin are unintelligible hieroglyphics. Pushkin, Dostoyevsky, and Tolstoy should be thrown out of the steamboat of the Present Age" (*Futurizmus* 1967, 236).

As a provocative avant-garde *Gesamtkunstwerk* (total art), the opera *Triumph over the Sun* was presented by Russian futurists in Petrograd in 1913. The performers wore papier-mâché heads, moved like marionettes, and recited nonsense text by Khrutchenik to the music of Matyushin. The costumes and stage were designed by Kazimir Malevich. The next year they tried their creative potential in a new art form, the cinema. Kasyanov's film *Drama in Futurist Cabaret No. 13* turned to everyday life. Leading avant-garde artists—among others, Larionov and Goncharova —were featured in this film, which parodied symbolism and stressed the new futurist philosophy: back to reality! Into the streets! The new films presented the creators' daily lives, showing them out walking, eating, and shopping. The aggressive futurist *épater les bourgeois* was a leitmotif of Russian avant-garde: the men wore earrings and hung spoons in their buttonholes in public places. Yevreinov's provocatively illustrated book *Nudity on the Stage* (1912) was adapted to real life when topless women and men wearing nothing but a hat appeared in the streets of Petrograd and Moscow.

Emerging modern Russian theater had a more permanent and much more widespread impact than futurist theater and film. The new theatrical art was seeking its own independent path by freeing itself from the shackles of literature. In the years between the appearance of Yevreinov in 1908 and the opening of Tairov's Moscow Repertory Theater in 1914, a new theatrical movement was born. The director, a figure who had previously been relegated to the background as an intermediary between writer, actor, and audience, now moved into the foreground. He became both the composer and the conductor of the performance—the director who is playing himself. Modern Russian theater produced a long line of innovative directors such as Yevreinov, Meyerhold, Tairov, Vachtangov, and Granovsky—creators of a new language that increasingly diverged from Western theatrical traditions. In this "total" theater, the actors and actresses became the implementers and component parts of the central concept of the director, "tools," like the lighting and scenery and the script itself. The evolving new "theatrical theater," a complex and collective art form—herald of an emerging "age of collectivism"—often became a conduit for revolutionary political propaganda and for radical social and political ideas.

The Revolution in Music: Schönberg, Stravinsky, and Bartók

By the turn of the century, music had undergone a profound transformation. The origins of the transformation can be found in late romantic European music, in the last creative periods of Franz

List and Richard Wagner as well as in the postimpressionist early-twentieth-century Debussy. Yet the main sites for change were the Central and Eastern European cities of Vienna, Budapest, and Petrograd.

It is a strange paradox of history that new music first appeared in Vienna, the capital where operetta and waltz enjoyed their greatest successes. The Hungarian-Austrian Ferenc Lehár's *Merry Widow* (1905) and *Graf von Luxemburg* (1909), the Austrian Strauss's *Dreamwalzer* (1907), and the Hungarian Imre Kálmán's *Csárdásfürstin* (1915) conquered generations of audiences. Operetta helped the people of early-twentieth-century Austria-Hungary cope with difficulties and desperation (Bender and Schorske 1994). "Glücklich ist, der vergisst, / was doch nicht zu ändern ist" (Happy is he who forgets what he cannot change) — as the king of the operetta, Johann Strauss, summed it up in his *Die Fledermaus*.

Traditional harmony and melody suddenly disappeared in the music composed by Arnold Schönberg between 1906 and 1908.. His *Kammersymphonie Op. 9 für Soloinstrumenten* was first performed on February 5, 1907. Part of the audience demonstrated their displeasure by leaving the concert before the end. As contemporary critics stated, this work was a great step toward the emancipation of dissonance, because this music was "an unbroken chain of cacophony." The reception was similar in 1908, when Schönberg's *Second String Quartet (Op. 10)* was presented to an outraged, laughing, and mocking Viennese public. The harmonies of his songs and the subsequent six short piano pieces, as well as the melodramatic cycle of *Pierrot lunaire* (1912), became harsh. Tonality was unresolved and the melodies broken: this music was shouts and cries.

Schönberg's music, the theoretical foundation of which was laid down in his "Treatise on Harmony" in 1910–1911, broke with the traditional concept of harmony. In shattering the diatonic structure of music, which had dominated during the centuries of baroque and romantic music, Schönberg revolutionized musical structure and language. An end was put to the world of major and minor modes and to the hierarchy that assigned major sevenths and minor fifths to marginal positions in harmonic progressions. Schönberg's atonal music used all twelve notes of the scale and gave them equal value, an act that resulted in new, "barbaric," offensive chords. As Carl Schorske aptly characterizes it, this was the musical "language of flux, of dissolution" (Schorske 1980, 347). In the words of the Czech composer, Ernst Křenek, "The imminent catastrophe was clearly predicted in this music" (Křenek 1961, 99).

The outline of a mighty symphony on which Schönberg was working between 1912 and 1914 expresses clearly his artistic consciousness and the message of his musical idea. This unfinished opus would have sung the death of the "bourgeois God." The introduction begins with the "transformation of life." The idea of the fourth movement, that "the bourgeois God is inadequate," turns into a "dance of death of principles" in the second part of the symphony. Schönberg speaks of the agony of a bourgeois world where "everything is simultaneously order and disorder." In the fifth part of the outline, the "faith of disillusionment," a skeptical consciousness mingles with the fatalism, "the mystical is hidden within the simple." The worldview so clearly expressed in the outline was, in the end, not translated into music, but it nevertheless illustrates the goals and philosophy of the composer.

It is, perhaps, the philosopher and the innovative theoretician whom one should appreciate most of all in Schönberg. A contemporary Hungarian music critic noted in 1912:

Thus the music of subconsciousness is characterized by great awareness, exaggerated contemplation, and little invention. . . . Let us be grateful for the new, because it reminds us that there can be no end to ecstasy. Schönberg brings to us, in a masterly fashion, not so much the beautiful, but rather the new. The error either lies in us, or his work is only preparatory. . . . In this instance, the theory seems viable, but the creation . . . is not. . . . Schönberg is a striving, thoughtful talent . . . and shall, perhaps, inspire the composer who will do less theorizing and sing more and more beautifully to the world. (Molnár 1912)

Igor Stravinsky, a young law student from Petrograd, first attracted attention with his musical experiments in the same years as Schönberg's debut. The son of an opera singer, Stravinsky was quickly invited by Diaghilev to compose a work for his world-famous ballet company. The resulting work, *L'oiseau de feu* (Firebird), still bears the mark of the young composer's master, Rimsky-Korsakov, and was first performed in 1910. Stravinsky's real creative breakthrough and lasting world fame were achieved in the following year with the presentation of his second ballet, *Petrushka*. It was followed in 1913 by the third ballet, *Le Sacre du Printemps* (Rite of spring). The elemental, raw, brutal music of these works created the greatest of scandals and lasting impressions, perhaps because its deliberately primitive subject-matter was expressed through the medium of the traditional, overrefined genre of the ballet.

By his own admission, Stravinsky traveled the long road that leads from the fantastic to the universally human in the extraordinarily short time between *Firebird* and *Petrushka*. As the French critic Gachot observed, *Petrushka* "is no longer the sort of work that can be considered apart from the real world. . . . Russian melancholy already cries out from its first notes in an unparalleled mix of deep secrets and carnival atmosphere. There is drama in these notes" (Gachot 1926).

The barbaric, elemental strength of Stravinsky's music acquired symbolic meaning in the *Rite of Spring*, which presents an ancient rite that celebrates the emergence of humanity and the purification of the soil. The virgin who is the intended sacrifice for renewal is herself a symbol of purity. As Gachot states, this music represents "order, willpower, and rigor in an effervescent, turbid and disintegrated era."

Béla Bartók, the third member of the Central and Eastern European triumvirate of revolutionary geniuses of music, was performing as a pianist by the age of ten. His first symphony, the *Kossuth-Symphony*, was composed in 1903 and influenced by both the Hungarian romantic-national idea and Richard Strauss. By 1905, however, Bartók found a new direction. With Zoltán Kodály, he set out to collect folk music in a conscious and methodical manner. In 1920, he noted in a letter that "the peasant music of our country had the greatest influence on me. Perhaps you will be interested to know that for fifteen years I have collected the music of Hungarian, Slovak, and Romanian peasants" (Bartók 1976, 262).

Folk music had already been absorbed into romantic music, which itself had often been associated with national awakening. Hungarian dances and songs, such as the Hungarian rondo, had been integrated by Haydn into his piano trio and by Beethoven into the Eroica Symphony. Liszt and Brahms both enriched their music with Hungarian dances and *verbunks*.

Bartók, however, did not continue this line but introduced something entirely new. Turning toward authentic, Asian-born, pentatonic Hungarian folk music and using its rhythms and harmonies, he created a new type of music. Folk music no longer merely enriched melodies but subversively transformed music, creating new rhythms and chords. With its painful, broken tones and dissonances and nervous, gloomy chords, this music eloquently expressed a depressing personal and social malaise. As one of its first eulogists, the contemporary Hungarian painter Robert Berény noted in the summer of 1911 that this music "causes the most excruciating ecstasy" (Berény 1911). One can consider it almost symbolic that in Bartók's balladic, depressingly tense one-act opera, *A kékszakálu herceg vára* (Bluebeard's castle; 1911), the key that

Judith demands so insistently from Bluebeard finally opens the door to bloody horrors.

The pioneering Austrian-Russian-Hungarian trio of composers was accompanied by others in Central and Eastern Europe. The Czech Leos Janácek was already fifty years old in 1903 when he composed his opera *Janufa*, which was based on a Moravian folk song. After the belated success of its Prague performance twelve years later, further successful works followed: a second opera, *Vylety Pane Brouckovy* (The excursion of Mr. Broucek; 1917), and an orchestral rhapsody, *Taras Bulba* (1918). Although Janácek collected folk songs and published essays on them, his special interest was the melody of speech. In the region of Hukvaldy, Janácek's birthplace, word endings were cut off by the peasants as if by a knife. The rhythm of speech was broken, with abbreviated articulation, and this was varied in the folk songs of the region by the repetition of the broken parts of speech. Janácek's music transformed this practice, giving it dramatic force. Melodic recitatives based on folk speech and folk songs together with declamatory semimelodies played a particular role in Janácek's opera. The broken rhythms and kaleidoscopic short themes and motifs of his music and the frequent, rapid, increasing and barely-changing repetition of particular words, sentences, and musical phrases was hypnotic and had an elemental power.

Other contributions were made to the new Central and Eastern European music by two young composers, the Polish Karol Szymanowski and the Russian Sergei Prokofiev, both of whom embarked on successful careers just before the war. But the musical revolution of the region had only entered its first stage.

Revolt against Traditional Beauty and Harmony in Visual Art: Kandinsky, Kupka, Brâncuşi, and Archipenko

Painters and sculptors who came from Moscow, Vityebsk, Prague, and Bucharest wanted to negate traditional "harmony," "beauty," and self-evident "reality." This was the mightiest revolution in the art of the times.

The most effectual pioneer in the resultant destruction of form and negation of object was the Russian painter, Vassily Kandinsky. Leaving behind an aristocratic family and a Moscow law degree, he moved to

Munich, where, in 1909, in the incomparably freer atmosphere of Germany, he founded the New Society of Munich Artists with his fellow countryman, Alexej Jawlinsky. Three years later, this time with Franz Marc, Kandinsky established a new group, *Der Blaue Reiter* (The Blue Rider), which gathered rebellious artists from Germany, Austria, and Russia. In their first exhibition, the Russians Kandinsky and Burlyuk, the Germans Marc and Macke, and the Austrian composer-painter Schönberg together attacked old artistic values and, as Schönberg's maxim expressed, explored the harmony of the age "by direct antigeometrical and illogical means" (Weissenberger 1984, 287).

Kandinsky's revolution occurred between 1905 and 1910. A 1905 portrait of his friend and colleague, Gabriele Münster, was painted in a traditional style, with "real" colors and forms. The fine female face and the white blouse contrast sharply with the dark lilac background. Five years later, the same model was presented in a typical expressionistic way, in exciting yellows, greens, and blues: all the "real" forms and colors had disintegrated and been replaced. In 1909, in two landscapes of Murnau, forms started to disappear and the decorative use of strong yellows, reds, and blues took their place. In 1910, several *Improvisations* and two paintings titled *All Saint's Day* offer a special harmony of strong colors that sometimes suggest human and animal figures or objects, but more as colors than as figures. All such traits gradually disappeared from Kandinsky's paintings. On the large-scale *Four Seasons*, only imagined memories and moods are expressed by burnished colors. Much of the prevalent expressionism was present in this decorative abstraction, but decorative abstraction was only the transition toward a strict abstraction that overtook fine arts around the 1910s.

Kandinsky played an epoch-making role in this artistic revolution. As the contemporary young German professor Wilhelm Worringer explained, Kandinsky's searching for pure abstraction was "the only possibility of peace within the turmoil and darkness of the world." Arnold Hauser gives another interpretation: the artist sought to force "the laws, the ideal existential stamps of a higher structural order upon the realities he refused to accept" (Hauser 1968, 91).

Sculpture experienced a similar change of direction. One of the most powerful pioneers in abandoning form was the Romanian Constantin Brâncuşi, who "simplified" objects down to their "essentials" and created sculpted pieces of barbaric primal power. The desire to simplify is already present in the charming oval-shaped, white marble head of *Mademoiselle Pogany* carved in 1912 and repeated several times. Similarly, the stylized half-figures of *The Kiss*, embracing and forming an integral limestone block, and the *Three Penguins* with their heads bent toward each other, both executed in the same year, mark the boundary between figurative sculpture and spatial construction. The *Sculpture for the Blind* (1916), an oval, head-shaped piece of white marble, playfully but still aggressively exemplifies that philosophy. The same should be said of the ambiguous *Duchess X* (1920), which may be perceived simultaneously as a peculiarly shaped female bust or as an enormous gilded male genital. *Hony soit qui mal y pense* (Evil be to him who thinks evil)? (Florea 1984).

The Russian Alexander Archipenko, another pioneer of modern art, opposed traditional ideals and reality by contrasting convex and concave forms in his collagelike sculptures. The son of a university professor in Kiev, who was expelled from art school in 1905 because of differences with his professors, Archipenko arrived in Paris in 1908, bringing his innovative ideas with him. What influenced him besides Russian icons and Byzantine art? To what extent was he affected by the archeological excavations in the Ukraine in which he had participated as a student and which exposed him to the influences of Neolithic art? Although it is difficult to answer these questions, the simplicity and power of primitive art and ancestral images can be seen in the massive block-shapes of the half-torso *Susanna* (1909) and in the *Woman with Cat* (1910). This stability, however, soon vanished. The arched composition of the *Kiss*, and the two seminal works, *Woman Striding* and the novelty *Medrano I* (both in 1912), are examples of a new sculptural idiom. This new language, like the new musical language of Schönberg and Bartók, bears a new message. The "arrangement figures" in the entwined forms of the *Boxing Match*, which can be interpreted as closed space or spatial form, express the conflicting duality of the single entity and a new concept of harmony as a confrontation between forces. Naum Gabo, Archipenko's countryman, went even further, rejecting traditional materials and creating statues made of glass and metal in Oslo in 1916. He also broke with the traditional subject matter and created spatial constructs instead of "meaningful" figures.

The question here arises: on what basis can we categorize Russian and Romanian artists who lived and worked in Munich, Paris, or Oslo as artists of Central and Eastern Europe? One certainly cannot doubt that Paris and Munich, the capitals of arts and artistic freedom, provided inspiration without which the work of many Central and Eastern European artists would not have developed. And yet, the culture of modern avant-garde art in Paris was determined by exiles from Spain, Russia, and the peripheral countries of Europe. "[In] the second decade of this century, Paris seemed to be far more entranced by foreign culture than by its own. . . . All the . . . excitement seems to have been generated by foreign composers and artists . . . the Russians in particular" (Eksteins 1989, 47).

Artists such as Stravinsky, Kandinsky, Brâncuşi, and Archipenko brought their previous experiences with them. Their education, their first impressions of society and the arts, their family traditions, inherited history, culture, and language all had an enduring impact on them. Decades after he came to France, where he spent most of his long life, Marc Chagall painted the experience of his Russian-Jewish herring-merchant father and his Russian-Jewish environment in Vityebsk. Artists in their twenties and thirties carried with them the imprints of the world they came from, no matter where they were ultimately tossed by fate.

An interesting and convincing, though at first glance not self-evident, example is the case of the Czech Frantisek Kupka, who arrived in Paris in 1896 at the age of twenty-five. Fourteen years passed before the new, truly "Kupkaesque," nonfigurative art emerged. For this reason, many regard Kupka's art as having evolved under French influence. This view is convincingly debated by Meda Mladek. On the basis of thorough research, she proves that the young Kupka's years in Prague were decisive and that his art studies in Bohemia influenced his future career. The young man encountered spiritualism in Prague and even acted as a medium, experiences that shaped his unusual view of the world. While Kupka was studying art in Jaromer, his teacher, Studnicka, an expert on folk art and abstract decoration, influenced him to an extraordinary degree. Studnicka made his students draw simple and complex geometrical figures, spirals, curves, and above all, circles with a single line, and he taught the decorative function of colors. Admiration for Czech Nazarene painting, particularly for Mánes whom Kupka regarded as his ideal, had its roots in this school. It is easy to see a relation between Mánes's figure of a woman, painted in 1865–1866, dancing gracefully with scales in her hands and surrounded by ornamental lines and circles, and Kupka's *Girl with a Hoop*, painted in 1903–1905, where the hoop held by the gracefully moving female figure forms a natural frame. His painting in 1908 of a little girl with a ball was still in the style of the turn of the century. But his studies for the same painting made in the following year already point to defiguration. Kupka's *Piano Keys* (1909) are a rare example of the direct path from realism to abstraction.

From 1910 onward, he painted circles of blue, red, and white—an example of decorative geometric abstraction. The geometric forms from Czech folk art and his early school years in Prague had thus matured, becoming elements of a conscious artistic expression. "A musician who has heard a peasant tune or popular song in childhood," argues Mladek, "finds it cropping up as the theme in a symphonic movement that he composes in adult life. An idea or an image has moved from the subconscious into the conscious mind" (Mladek 1975, 23).

"Destruction, Too, Is Creation"

Writers who destroyed "reality" and chronology and who expressed the irrational or presented the past in a moment of the present; composers who destroyed harmony and made music with broken melodies, dissonance, and nervous cries; and painters and sculptors who replaced real forms and colors with abstract geometrical designs and spatial constructs were instinctively or deliberately reflecting the crisis of old values and ideals. Their new aesthetic forms attempted to demolish the old. Although these artists, composers, writers, and architects were committed to creating new art and designing comfortable buildings that would serve people, they sought also to assist in constructing a new society on the ruins of hypocrisy and lies; thus, the most spectacular and widespread characteristic of the early-twentieth-century avant-garde was the destruction of the old world. Most of these artists shared the Russian revolutionary anarchist Mikhail Bakunin's view that "destruction, too, is creation." This bitter artistic crusade to annihilate the old world culminated during World War I, and rebellious artists from Central and Eastern Europe played an authentic and outstanding role in the process.

The most extreme attempt at destruction was made by the so-called Dada movement, which was created in February 1916 at the Cabaret Voltaire in Zurich. Its founders—the Romanians Tristan Tzara and Marcel Janko and others committed grotesque, absurdly boastful, aggressive, shocking outrages against the bourgeois taste that had been developed by artist-intellectuals during the decade of the 1910s. As Europe entered the period of World War I, the Dadaists thus self-consciously declared their own war against what they believed was an irrational reality. As Tzara himself characterized the movement, it was "the most horrifying protest, a private guerrilla war, a denial, and," he added to avoid pathetic seriousness, "the chocolate of despair." Dadaist art was conceived as *action gratuite* and a negation of bourgeois culture and society; it even included a self-destructive attack on art itself. Its followers never transcended these nihilistic goals, even in practice. They consciously strove to confuse the distinction between the artistic and the vulgar, the tasteful and the tasteless. "As far as Dada goes," their manifesto proclaimed, "it is odorless, it means nothing, absolutely nothing. Dada is like your hopes: it is nothing. It is like your Paradise: it is nothing. It is like your idol: it is nothing. It is like your political leader: it is nothing. It is like your heroes: it is nothing. It is like your artists: it is nothing. It is like your religion: it is nothing" (Tzara 1959, 277–85).

The Dada performances at Cabaret Voltaire expressed the same spirit. In one of the programs, Tzara appeared on the stage and shaved himself; then the program was over. In Dada paintings, the well-known method of collage, already used by cubists and futurists, took on a new sense, or rather senselessness: ridiculously arranged rubbish, newspaper scraps, and pictures were arbitrarily pasted-on to prove that reality is also unreal and that even material objects are meaningless in a disintegrated world. The total effect expressed a senseless chaos.

The same held true for Dada poetry. Tristan Tzara's poetry cookbook in his "Pamphlet on Feeble and Bitter Love" gives detailed advice on how to write poems: "To write a Dadaist poem, take a newspaper. Take a pair of scissors. Select an article about the length of your intended poem. Cut out the article. Carefully cut apart the words of the article, then put them all in a bag. Shake it gently. Take the words out, one by one, and put them together in the order you have found them." Indeed, Dada poetry sought to reflect a world where, as Tzara stated, "words should not be believed," because "they express the opposite" of what they should mean in a world where "lies circulate" (Tzara 1959, 286–95).

Poems comprised of jumbled words, paintings made of litter, a real chamber pot offered as a sculpture, or a copied Mona Lisa adorned with a jaunty mustache all belonged to their deliberately degraded, empty and artistically meaningless art. Dadaists sought to shock and wake up society. The same goals were shared by the Russian Dada movement, although it was born independently during the war years. In Rostov in April 1917, Rurik Rok delivered a famous, intentionally provocative lecture on *The Shattering of Art*, which launched the nihilist "Nichevoky" movement.

The sense of crisis in society and the desire for change found an extreme yet transient expression in Dada nihilism. Revolutionary art, however, did not seek to negate and destroy all values and society but to transform them in a revolutionary manner. The sense that this was a period of flux was captured in the words of the manifesto of the Hungarian avant-garde group *Ma* (Today): "We are witnessing the last phase of the disintegration of a passé, hierarchical society, and in part the agony of trying to give birth to a new belief. Thus we are in a totally undefinable, transitory state" (Bajkay 1979, 234–35).

"Wipe Out the Past Once and for All": Constructivism and Suprematism

Negation was a point of departure for several new paths. The Italian futurist avant-garde arrived at the cult of irrationality and the glorification of aggression and war, "the destructiveness of the liberated" and "the sole purifier of the world" (Marinetti 1959, 349–54). At the same time, the majority of the avant-garde artists in Central and Eastern Europe around World War I joined leftist movements. The total negation of the past became a common idea of the revolutionary avant-garde and of the extreme communist left. Although the marriage was rather short-lived, and the communist political movement later excommunicated "bourgeois nihilism" and "empty formalism," for a short while in the critical period of the 1910s and early 1920s, the union was undisturbed and clearly expressed in both Hungarian constructivism and Russian suprematism (Vlcek 1990).

The Hungarian László Moholy-Nagy, who occupies a notable place in the vanguard of constructivism, gives an interesting account of positions in 1922:

The man of today (and most interestingly, if creative, he is intuitively revolutionary without taking a conscious political stand) is fed up with the "formal and social" meaning of the heretofore existing culture. At first he destroyed the inherited bounds . . . and attempted to build a new whole from the disintegrated parts (cubism, futurism, expressionism). After realizing that the new cannot be created from the remnants of the old, he scattered the pieces again with a despairing laugh (Dadaism). New work had to begin to create the new life of the new order. The simplest elements of expression, color, form, material, and space had to be regained. In a manner similar to our striving for a new life, which cannot be satisfied with the dogmas of the old society but only by searching for the laws of our humanity, so the work to ascertain the relationships among colors, shapes, and tensions had to start from scratch (suprematism, constructivism). (L. Moholy-Nagy 1979, 203–4)

This particularly interesting constructivist current of the avant-garde was closely connected with the emergence of an independent Russian school. Although many prominent Russian avant-garde artists streamed to Paris and Munich after the turn of the century, an avant-garde school evolved in Russia as well. The central figures of this powerful Russian avant-garde movement were Mikhail Larionov and Natalia Goncharova. The latter developed her "primitivist" style between 1903 and 1905. It had a great impact on Kazimir Malevich, who arrived in Moscow in 1905. His first experiments had been influenced by Matisse and the fauvists, but now he developed his own "decorative and primitive" style. Two influential brothers, David and Vladimir Burljuk, and the theoretically oriented Vladimir Tatlin joined the movement as well, and their first joint exhibition opened in 1910. By March 1912, their "Donkey's Tail" exhibition became, as Camilla Gray notes, a milestone in their "conscious breakaway from Europe" and in their assertion that they were founding an "independent Russian school" (Gray 1962, 121).

By the outbreak of World War I, Kazimir Malevich, the son of a foreman of a Kiev sugar refinery, had become the leader of the Russian School. The most original phase of his painting began in 1913 and was first presented to the public in 1915, the same year in which Larionov and Goncharova left Russia to join the artistic staff of Diaghilev's Russian ballet in the West. Malevich's role as leader was, henceforth, unchallenged.

The new suprematist (*supra materiam*; beyond the material) movement, as Malevich named it, was launched with his *Black Square on a White Background*, painted in 1913. It was followed by a series of haphazardly placed black squares, rhombi, and triangles on a white background (*Malevich* 1990). The development of the trend—with the participation of Xenia Bogoslavskaya, Ivan Klyun, and Nadieshda Udaltsova—was divided, as Malevich characterized it, into three stages: black, red, and white squares, or black, red, and white eras. At the end, white shapes appeared on white backgrounds. All three periods of development lasted from 1913 to 1918.

The artists interpreted white space as the sole adequate reflection of infinity and offered arranged and rearranged geometric shapes as an expression of planning for future society. Lajos Kassák, Malevich's Hungarian contemporary, passionately argued that Malevich's geometric forms were the "embodiment of a collective *Weltanschauung*." He attacked the hostile critique that mocked "the squared *Weltanschauung*," and he added: "As people's longing for God gained artistic expression in the pointed arches and stone-laces of Gothic architecture, so the collective view of the world found its artistic expression in the square that suggests stability and equality in pure colors and unornamented surfaces. Instead of coming to pointed arches, instead of decoration, there is economy in all areas" (Kassák 1972, 26).

A contemporary and fellow-sympathizer Ernö Kállai argued in 1921 about Kassák's constructivist art in a similar way: "'Nonobjective' in this art does not mean an attempt to escape from the world; it is not romantic and even less a mystic effort to go beyond the body. This is an uncompromising revolutionary will to reshape law and life. . . . This is an active art. . . . It is creation that establishes borderlines and auguries of the future community in the infinite and shapeless space" (Bajkay 1979, 188).

The constructivist and suprematist experiments went to extremes. Malevich's landmark painting during his "white period," *White Square on White Background*, was a genuine tabula rasa in the strictest meaning of the term. Another Russian, Alexander Rodchenko, echoed the idea with his *Black on Black*. When wartime Russian artists were first introduced to the European public in Berlin in 1922, the German art critic Westheim noticed that "these Russian artists—like people in Russia at large—are driven by the compulsion to create something new. . . . There is a suggestion hanging over Russia, that only now can everything come into being and that now everything will have to be created anew. This could lend courage and daring creativity, the like of which Europe has not seen for centuries." Westheim also recognized the "unbridled fanaticism" of this art. He quotes from Dostoyevsky: "When we Russians reach the shore, and we truly believe that this is the shore, we go immediately to the other end. Why is this so? If one of us converts to Catholicism, he immediately becomes a Jesuit. . . . if he becomes an atheist, he will immediately demand that belief in God should be exterminated, even by force if needed." Following the words of Dostoyevsky, Westheim adds:

Here is Malevich. He espoused the thesis of the need for simplification. Thus Malevich simplifies. More and more is left out of the painting. Everything that is objective, of course. Then color. The contrast of black and white still remains: an abstract shape, a black square or a black circular surface on white background. But this is not quite the final simplification. Malevich removes the black as well, and paints his "famous" picture, *White on White*. Now there is only white on a white background. Simplification progresses until there is nothing left in the white frame except an empty white canvas. This intellectual experiment can, of course, not be carried any further. . . . This painting of "white on white" means nothing less than total resignation from painting. (Westheim 1979, 267–68).

Constructivists and suprematists believed in art as a form of social action that could exert power over nature and an archaic society. A group of the Russian suprematist artists led by Tatlin and El Lissitzky united engineering and the arts. A new approach to reality appeared in Tatlin's sculpture-painting reliefs, which used wood, metal, and cardboard—real material in real space. In a later description of this movement, El Lissitzky remarked that they did not want to create the illusion of color on the canvas but to work with iron, wood, and glass. They perceived the world through the prism of technology and maintained that a difference between the work of art and the product of technology does not exist. El Lissitzky rejected even the world of abstraction by using a technological parallel: "Are radio waves abstract or naturalistic?" This new art of construction, however, had to serve the society: "We are unable to imagine any creation of new forms in art," wrote the artist in 1922, "that is not linked to transformation of social forms"(Lissitzky and Ehremburg 1974, 56). The same concept was expressed by one of Kassák's poems: "The word is dead, there now ensues the demonstration of facts and objects" (Bojtár 1977, 23).

In industrially backward Eastern Europe, modern technology symbolized a better future. Russian and Hungarian avant-garde artists envisioned a new rational human society where the social ills of Western capitalism would be cured and both arts and society renewed through industry and technology. This dream of a future society founded on modern technology provided a spiritual and intellectual meeting point for left-wing avant-garde artists and Bolsheviks (Passuth 1985). Thus, Central and Eastern European avant-garde became closely connected with the aim of revolutionary transformation and modernization. In 1922, David Sterenberg stated in the foreword of the catalogue of the first Russian exhibition in Berlin that the Russian Revolution "created the opportunity for the artist to bring their works into the squares and streets. . . . The greatest part of their artistic works, during the first years of the Revolution, was intended to decorate public places" (Sterenberg 1922, 3–4).

Russian constructivists collaborated in planning mass demonstrations and making street decorations. So did Mark Chagall after he returned to Russia. Malevich and Rodchenko made posters to help mobilize the Russian masses, and Hungarian avant-garde painters such as Sándor Bortnyik designed posters to propagate the Hungarian Councils' Republic.

Avant-garde artists eagerly awaited the revolution because they thought that a new society would allow them to realize their goal of bettering the human environment. Their artistic program sought to create a new relationship between art and reality that would liquidate art if necessary (*Devitsil* 1990). As the Polish avant-garde artist Mieczyslaw Szczuka stated in the twenties, the proletariat does not need the "stucco-art of Sunday," but, as he announced in 1924 in an editorial of *Blok*, the Polish avant-garde journal, constructivism is a "search for the practical application of creative impulse" (Bann 1974, 104). Tadeusz Peiper, the avant-garde artist of Krakow, added: "Design is not an internal affair of industry. . . . We need art with which life will be enriched and made more beautiful" (Peiper 1986, 148). The Russian Sterenberg enthusiastically proclaimed in 1922 that ornamentation and decoration destroy the meaning of objects and that it is more important and difficult to make a new chair or a new cup than to paint a picture. Lyubov Popova, one of the most important Russian avant-garde artist of the war years, painted and created stage sets for the Mayerhold theater, but she also designed textiles for a factory. "No artistic success has given me such satisfaction," she declared, "as the sight of a peasant or a worker buying a length of material designed by me" (Gray 1962, 192). In this sense, the new art consciously ceased to be art. And yet, the purpose of art was located not only in producing more useful and functional objects but also in collaborating with the process of changing society emotionally, intellectually, and sociopolitically. As Lajos Kassák put it in 1921: "The problems of contemporary life cannot be solved by relying on organized force alone, or concentrating exclusively on the economic revolution. The militarism and bureaucracy of the capitalist social system is useful not only for patricide, it has terrible moral forces as well. . . . Art transforms us, and enables us to transform our environment" (Bajkay 1979, 183).

László Moholy-Nagy, who was born into a Hungarian landowning family, also sought to join the revolution. He explained his motivations in his diary on May 15, 1919:

At the time of the War, I developed a feeling of social responsibility, and today I feel it to an even greater extent. My conscience spoke to me: is it fitting to be a painter in an era of social change? In the past century, art and reality were separate. The personal joy of artistic creation contributed nothing to the happiness of the masses. . . . Today I already know: . . . as a painter I can serve the meaning of life. (S. Moholy-Nagy 1977, I/92).

When he painted his *Bridges* in 1919, a disorderly jumble of geometrical shapes, iron triangles, elements of bridges, and flying numbers on a cheerful background, Moholy-Nagy sought to serve the revolution. "When Béla Kún destroyed the hated structures and declared the Hungarian Councils' Republic," Sybil Moholy-Nagy, his wife, observes, "Moholy, together with many of his generation looked upon him as the Messiah of a new world. With the flare enthusiasm of youth he offered himself, his art, and his desire to teach, to the communist regime" (S. Moholy-Nagy 1977, 13).

The artists who felt socially responsible for transforming art and society—the constructivist and suprematist artists—saw their own artistic revolution realized in social, political, and economic realms with the triumph of the October Revolution in Russia in 1917 and the establishment of the Hungarian Councils' Republic in 1919. As Tatlin said: "What happened in 1917 in a social sense had been carried out in our fine craft in 1914" (*Tatlin* 1988, 239). Malevich referred back to the cubist and futurist period of the prewar Russian avant-garde when he stated that "cubism and futurism were the revolutionary forms in art foreshadowing the revolution in political and economic life in 1917" (Bojtár 1977, 35–36).

Nathan Altman, a member of the Russian avant-garde school, explaining the reason why futurism went "hand in hand with the October Revolution," added: "Futurism is a revolutionary art that has broken with old ideals and was thus near to the proletariat. . . . The connection, however, is deeper. . . . As was the old capitalist world itself, old art was individualistic. Only futurist art was based on collectivism. Today only futurist art is the art of the proletariat" (Altman 1984, 149–50). The revolution in the arts thus became the art of the revolution.

PART II

Class Revolutions and Counterrevolutions

National Revolutions and Their Right-Wing Deformation, 1918–1929

Introduction

Despite the partial successes of modernization, revolt was brewing at the turn of the century and during the first decades thereafter. Consistent ideologies were being formulated, and social and ethnic groups organized with almost military discipline; vanguard parties emerged, and avant-garde art began to flourish in Central and Eastern Europe. All these movements presaged the forthcoming upheavals in society.

The World War I years, and the ensuing misery, poverty, and humiliation, created a social and political environment in which these ideas could be translated into political reality. The war generation could not escape the shocking effects of the war, and social discontent was increasingly linked to disappointment and disillusionment. Privations never before experienced and the huge loss of life drove the masses to take up arms. Many people who had thought of the war as a means of "purification" changed their minds. They viewed war as neither a purgatory nor a vehicle of renewal. But they recognized that it had destroyed the old, stable framework of society and created an opportunity to pursue the social and national aspirations that had been fermenting for decades. In 1905, the French revolutionary Jean Jaures had prophesied this outcome of a possible war:

"From a European war a revolution may spring up and the ruling classes would do well to think of this. But it may also result, over a long period, in crises of counter-revolution, of furious reaction, of exasperated nationalism, of stifling dictatorships, of monstrous militarism, a long chain of retrograde violence" (Joll 1973, 195).

Each word of Jaures's prophecy came true after the war. New European political maps were created at the peace conference and new borders were drawn. But it was not an easy and peaceful rearrangement. The internal situation in each nation was in flux. On the one hand, opportunities existed for revolution through the mobilization of the masses. On the other hand, the old regimes might be restored and shored up with minor reforms. People were rebelling everywhere, sometimes against the old empire, sometimes against the capitalist structure of their societies. Right-wing radical revolt was as common as left-wing action and offered an alternative to both Western capitalism and parliamentarism and to Marxist class revolution and socialism.

Although peculiar to Central and Eastern Europe, these phenomena were part of a broad postwar pattern. The new despair that was affecting all classes was part of a general rejection of old values that was occurring throughout Europe. The economic and social progress that had characterized the long nineteenth century came to a halt, and international trade, the locomotive of nineteenth-century modernization, derailed.

In 1928, at the height of a gradual increase in European prosperity, the outstanding liberal Western economist, Joseph Schumpeter, published "The Instability of Capitalism" in *The Economic Journal*. Schumpeter noted that politics, society, and economics in capitalist countries are frequently unstable. But he rejected the view that made this instability integral to the structure of the capitalist economic system. In fact, he saw the existing system as inherently stable and able to recover even from great crises. Although economically stable, capitalism nevertheless generated sociointellectual effects discordant with its spirit and institutions. According to Schumpeter's analysis, these dissonances will bring about the transformation of the system.

Our diagnosis [on the economic stability of capitalism] is, therefore, no more sufficient as a basis for prediction than a doctor's diagnosis to the effect that a man has no cancer is a sufficient basis for the prediction that he will go on living indefinitely. Capitalism is, on the contrary, in so obvious process of transformation into something else, that it is not the fact, but only the interpretation of this fact, about which it is possible to disagree . . . although not by economic necessity and probably even at some sacrifice of economic welfare, [it transforms] into an order of things which it will be merely matter of taste and terminology to call Socialism or not. (Schumpeter 1971, 41–42)

Karl Polanyi goes further than this when he states that for the origins of the cataclysm we must turn to the rise and fall of market economy:

The root cause of the crisis, we submit, was the threatening collapse of the international economic system. It had only haltingly functioned since the turn of the century, and the Great War and the Treaties had wrecked it finally. This became apparent in the twenties when there was hardly an internal crisis in Europe that did not reach its climax on an issue of external economy. . . . Market society was born in England—yet it was on the Continent that its weaknesses engendered the most tragic complications. . . . Market economy, free trade, and the gold standard were English inventions. These institutions broke down in the twenties everywhere—in Germany, Italy, or Austria the event was merely more political and more dramatic. (Polanyi 1964, 23, 30)

Polanyi continues by asserting that the leading capitalist powers, grown prosperous on Atlantic trade, were naturally reluctant to acknowledge the collapse of a world economy and of national economies that had been based on the notion of the self-regulating market system. After World War I, they stubbornly strove to revive that system. In contrast, the vanquished countries, where civil conflicts were more dramatic and which, in any case, were "opposed to the *status quo*, would be quick to discover the weaknesses of the existing institutional order. . . . Thus Germany, once defeated, was in the position to recognize the hidden shortcomings of the nineteenth century order, and to employ this knowledge to speed the destruction of the order" (Polanyi 1964, 28–29).

Polanyi is partly right when he identifies the crisis of capitalism circa World War I as the social and economic background for "right-wing" or fascist revolution. One should add that the same situation catalyzed "left-wing" or communist revolution, and the national-nationalist revolutions. Polanyi is likewise correct in saying that right-wing revolution was a factor to be reckoned with everywhere, especially since conditions particularly favored it in the defeated countries. As he argues:

The appearance of such a movement . . . should never have been ascribed to local causes, national mentalities, or historical backgrounds as was so constantly done by contemporaries. Fascism had as little to do with the Great War as with the Versailles Treaty, with Junker militarism as with the Italian temperament. The movement appeared in defeated countries . . . and in victorious ones . . . , in countries of Aryan race . . . and non-Aryan race . . . , in countries of Catholic traditions . . . and in Protestant ones . . . , in soldierly communities . . . and civilian ones. (Polanyi 1964, 237–38)

It is true that particular causes should not be overrated. Still, in the final analysis, the only universal factor emphasized by Polanyi, the "collapsed market society," did not, after all, give rise to fascism—or any other kind of serious revolutionary challenges, including bolshevism—in the Western world. These upheavals occurred only in the relatively backward, historically disappointed and humiliated, peripheral regions of Europe, or in countries where modernization had either failed or only partly succeeded, or where achieved successes were endangered. Meantime, the capitalist system in the advanced, prosperous countries was consolidated by important Keynesian reforms and changes, by the replacement of self-regulated markets with regulated market economies, and by the substitution of state interventionism for the laissez-faire regime. Western capitalism adjusted flexibly to a changed environment.

5

Class Revolutions— Counterrevolutions

Russia's Two Revolutions in 1917

The sensitive Hungarian poet Endre Ady felt before the war that he was "living in revolution." If the specter was already in the air in some countries of the region, the war turned these premonitions into reality.

The appalling wartime misery, the loss of several million lives, and the years of deprivation in Russia, led that country—one where modernization had largely failed—to the first and greatest of the European revolutionary explosions. On February 23, 1917, a series of spontaneous demonstrations began in Petrograd. Workers engulfed the streets, demanding food and chanting "Down with war! Down with the tsar!" They did not heed the warning by General Khabalov, the commander of the capital's garrison, that he would keep order. After three days of growing and apparently unstoppable demonstrations, the tsar issued orders to shoot. The police opened fire on the crowd in Znamenskaia Square, but the soldiers who had been summoned to deal with the disturbances—who had themselves been through three years of war misery—refused to shoot and joined the demonstrators' cause. The Pavlovski Guard Regiment was the first to revolt against their officers. When other regiments declared themselves revolutionaries, several officers were killed. The workers and soldiers revitalized the revolutionary soviets of the 1905 revolution and elected delegates who established the Provisional Executive Committee of the Petrograd Workers'

Soviet on February 27. In response to the crisis, the president of the state Duma, Nicholas Rodzianko, immediately called a special session to create a temporary Duma Committee. On March 1, Tsar Nicholas abdicated in favor of his brother Mikhail, who refused to accept the crown. The Duma Committee appointed a cabinet of ten ministers as a provisional government headed by Prince Georgii Lvov.

The revolution could no longer be halted. Was it a mere consequence of the war, or was it a genuine revolution? Although there are several who argue the first view, the obsolescence and rigidity of the autocratic tsarist regime and its resistance to adequate reforms strengthen the position of those who speak of a genuine revolution. "In these circumstances it was only a matter of time before the rebelliousness of alienated workers and poor peasants outran the government's capacity to respond, and Russia erupted again" (Rosenberg 1982, 39). The events are well-known and there is no reason to describe them here in detail.

The February revolution was not the end but the prelude to revolutionary breakthrough. The liberal democratic provisional government sought to introduce major social and political reforms, including desired land reforms, but wanted to legitimize its actions by setting up national elections to form a constitutional assembly with full legal competence. Moreover, the liberal Russian elite and its government sought first to conclude the war with Germany in a manner that would keep the empire intact and establish Russian control over both the Bosporus Strait and the Balkans.

It was a severe miscalculation. The revolutionary masses of Russia wanted to stop the war and demanded instant social reforms. The genuine revolutionary character of the events was demonstrated by the exceptional strength of mass movements, expressed in the establishment of *dvoevlastie* (dual power system) from the beginning of the February revolution. The provisional government agreed to share power with the Petrograd Workers' Soviet on March 2 and henceforth could not take any important steps without the agreement of the soviet. Moreover, in certain provincial cities such as Saratov, several Latvian cities, Tbilisi, Baku, and Tsaritsin, local power was controlled by the soviets (Releigh 1992). The strength of the labor movement was expressed by the fact that between March 3 and October 25, 1917, 2.4 million workers participated in strikes. The climax of the labor unrest occurred in September. Spontaneously formed workers' militia and fighting *druzhina*, the so-called Red Guard, represented the strongest armed force in industrial areas and towns. "The workers' armed bands arose out of . . .

the tremendous drive of self-assertion, the spontaneity, that character-ized the Russian population after the February revolution. . . . The orig-inal urge seems to have come from below and to have been resisted at first by higher-level leaders" (Wade 1992, 55). Detailed research has re-vealed that between February and October 1917, more than sixteen thou-sand peasant disturbances rocked the countryside, 20 percent of them involving seizure of land. In other words, a spontaneous revolutionary land reform began without any governmental action.

The soviet leadership, expressing the view of the masses, aggressively opposed the continuation of "war to complete victory" and demanded "peace without annexations." Mass demonstrations condemned the war and the "bourgeois ministers" on April 20 and 21. Miliukov, the for-eign minister of the provisional government of Prince Lvov, did not understand the popular slogan "Either the revolution will kill the war, or the war will kill the revolution" and "waged an active struggle . . . against Zimmerwaldism [the antiwar stand of the Socialist Interna-tional] in favor of maintaining our general foreign policy with our al-lies" (Miliukov 1967, 416, 429). He and the provisional government of the prince were forced to resign. A socialist-liberal coalition took over, but the cabinet headed by Alexander Kerensky began to prepare a new offensive in May. The new provisional government continued the for-eign policy of the previous provisional government.

On April 3, Lenin arrived at Petrograd's Finland station, having been secretly transported from Switzerland. In 1914, he had called for "the transformation of the present imperialist war into a civil war." In Oc-tober 1915, he had predicted the possibility that proletarian revolution might break out in peasant Russia. Now, on April 16, Lenin delivered his famous April Theses, announcing that the Russian revolution was passing from its first, bourgeois stage to a radicalized second, proletar-ian stage. The first of his ten theses was devoted to the issue of the un-changed character of the "robber imperialist war" and to rejection of any concession to "revolutionary defensism." The popularity of Lenin and the Bolsheviks increased because they embraced the demands of the masses, which were being expressed in spontaneous demonstrations for peace and in seizure of land and factories. Unlike the liberals and the moderate socialists, the Bolsheviks did not want to avoid conflicts but to intensify them. They rejected the dual government, demanding in-stead that all power reside in the soviets.

Open confrontation broke out in July when the Kerensky govern-ment offensive began and the Bolshevik Petrograd garrison revolted.

After three days battle, the uprising was suppressed, Trotsky and other Bolshevik leaders were arrested, and Lenin went into hiding in Finland. The Russian war offensive was successful for the next two weeks, but a powerful German counteroffensive destroyed the hopes of the provisional government. In August, General Kornilov, the commander-in-chief, initiated an abortive "preventive" right-wing military coup against the "imminent Bolshevik uprising." Even his own troops refused to follow his orders. The authority of the provisional government was totally undermined. Lenin and the Bolsheviks were validated in the eyes of the masses. The Bolshevik Left gained ground. In July, only an eighth of the delegates to the All Russian Congress of Soviets at Petrograd had been Bolshevik, but the September elections brought a Bolshevik majority in the key Petrograd and Moscow soviets. Trotsky was released from prison and became the president of the Petrograd Workers' Soviet. Lenin made a motion urging the preparation of an armed insurrection; the motion was accepted—ten to two—by the Central Committee. The Trotsky-led Military Revolutionary Committee began preparations for the uprising. On October 25, Bolshevik armed units met practically no resistance as they occupied key strategic points of the capital. Kerensky escaped, but the other cabinet ministers were arrested. The Second All Russian Soviet Congress proclaimed the victory of the proletarian revolution.

The Bolshevik Russian October revolution was a reflection of popular desire and enjoyed the support of the masses. The provisional government had lost its legitimacy in the eyes of the population because it could not and did not seek to enforce its will. The revolution, although prepared and executed in a conspiratorial manner, was thus definitely not a coup d'etat but a genuine revolutionary expression of the Rousseauian "General Will."

The revolution was a response not only to the inhuman war, humiliating collapse, and misery but also to the unfinished, halfhearted reforms of the preceding fifty years. It challenged the landlessness and ruthless exploitation of the overtaxed peasantry, providing a "wakening call" to the "sleeping giant." In this interpretation, the Russian revolution was an early-twentieth-century answer to "semifailed" modernization and economic backwardness, to unsolved social conflicts, to unfinished nation building, and to nondemocratic political systems.

In a paradox of history, the revolution began to deform into a dictatorship by a new elite almost immediately after its victory. Although the Bolsheviks demanded "All power to the soviets!" they did not oppose the creation of a constitutional assembly but sought to gain, at least together with the Social Revolutionaries (SRs), a majority of votes that would allow them to establish a broadly based socialist government. In the November elections, however, the peasantry cast the majority of its votes for the SRs, and the Bolsheviks were excluded from control. The assembly met only once, in January, before it was forcibly disbanded. Even the soviets, the agents of democratization and the embodiment of "General Will" between February and October, became the local organs of an increasingly centralized one-party state after the October revolution. The All-Russian Central Executive Committee of Soviets, or the "soviet parliament," which was authorized to control the government, became an institution that set up uncontrolled, centralized power.

Until the summer of 1918, there was a Menshevik and SR opposition in the soviet parliament, but on June 14, 1918, the Bolshevik majority passed a decree that excluded the opposition. The action was crowned by the expulsion of the left-wing SRs on July 9. A radical purge "cleansed" the soviets of "hostile" elements and accomplished the *Gleichschaltung* (forcing into line) of the soviets. In addition, a secret extraordinary commission to combat counterrevolution, the infamous *Cheka*, was established. Sergei Dukhovski, secretary of the Collegium of *Cheka*, warned in October 1918 that "All power to the soviets" was turning into "All power to the *Chekas*" (Getzler 1992, 30). Meanwhile, the inevitable outbreak of civil war and of open class confrontation accomplished the deformation of revolutionary power.

The immediate impact of the Russian revolution was immense in Central and Eastern Europe. As J. C. Smuts noted: "There is no doubt that Mankind is once more on the move. The very foundations have been shaken and loosened, and things are again fluid. . . . The great caravan of Humanity is once more on the march" (Toynbee 1955, 196). Smuts was right, although only a few peoples joined the "great caravan": the Bolshevik revolution reverberated in other humiliated and desperate countries. Even Thomas Mann, a great intellect and moralist, roared hopelessly in March 1918, "Rejection of the peace by Germany! Rise up against the demagogical bourgeois! A national uprising . . . even in the form of communism. . . . I am perfectly willing to take to the streets and yell 'Down with the lie of western democracy! Long live Germany and Russia! Long live communism!" He wrote in his diary, "I feel a growing sympathy with that which is healthy, human, national, anti-Entente . . . in spartacism, communism, bolshevism" (Mann 1994, 2–3). Even in May

1918, after a few weeks had passed and he had calmed down and rejected communism "as the most appalling cultural catastrophe" that ever threatened the world, Mann still predicted an unavoidable communist revolution: "What is going to happen? Will the phase of bolshevism not spare any part of Western Europe? It does not look as though we can evade it" (Mann 1970, 151).

Another peaceful German intellectual, Stefan Zweig, protested the humiliating peace and noted in a letter to Romain Rolland on January 2, 1919, "The only hope left is the world revolution, and there are signs of it everywhere" (Klein 1994, 4). But both Mann and Zweig were mistaken: the world revolution or a Bolshevik revolution in Western Europe was not on the agenda. The flames of revolution, however, soon reached the crisis-ridden Central and Eastern European nations.

Hungary's Two Revolutions

Revolution arrived in Hungary one year after the events in Russia. On October 31, 1918, a battalion refused to obey orders to go to the front, and this was enough, in the explosive atmosphere of desperation, to spark revolution. Political prisoners were liberated from prisons, and a revolutionary crowd occupied public buildings. The workers of the capital declared a general strike. Power passed almost without resistance into the hands of the democratic opposition. Some violence occurred, including the shooting of former prime minister Count István Tisza, but the shift of power was largely peaceful. The National Council was established on October 25 by the liberal and radical democratic parties, and the social democrats formed a new government. Count Mihály Károlyi, a member of one of Hungary's most powerful aristocratic landowning families but a liberal democrat and a pro-Entente Westernizer, was appointed prime minister and formed a coalition government of the parties in the National Council.

This revolutionary government swore its allegiance to the Habsburg king but rescinded that allegiance the very next day and declared that its central goal was to establish the independence of democratic Hungary. Radical electorial reform, the guarantee of human rights and freedoms, and the institution of fundamental social reforms would support the new democracy. The first decree of the revolutionary regime, issued November 16, 1918, abolished the kingdom of Hungary and established the Hungarian Republic. The government managed to stabilize its power, earning approval in early November from the spontaneously founded Soldiers' Council and Budapest Workers' Council.

Although the rapidly accumulating economic and social problems seemed overwhelming, the new revolutionary democratic government first had to address the border question, its central problem. The declaration of Hungarian independence had initiated the disintegration of the multinational, historical, Hungarian kingdom and the loss of two-thirds of its former territory. This loss was formalized by an armistice agreement signed in Belgrade on November 13 by Károlyi, the head of the Hungarian delegation. The agreement demanded that the new Hungarian government withdraw from large areas of the old Hungarian Kingdom. Serbian, Czech, and Romanian armies had already partly occupied these areas. In November and December, the Transylvanian Romanian council declared the joining of the new Romania, and the Sub-Carpatho-Ruthenian council declared the joining of the newly created Czechoslovakia. The Austrian government demanded transfer of the West-Hungarian Burgenland to its control. Thus Hungary's neighbors, with the help of their Entente allies, made large territorial demands that ignored ethnic borders.

The democratic government of Hungary was in a deadly trap: it desired to follow a pro-Entente policy but could not assist in dismembering its own territory, especially when ethnically Hungarian territories were to be given to new neighboring multinational states. Three million Hungarians became minorities in Romania, Czechoslovakia, and Yugoslavia, about half of them living in almost intact Hungarian communities next to the Hungarian border.

In addition to losing much of its territory, the Hungarian government was paralyzed and unable to solve difficult domestic economic and social problems. In February 1919, a law on land reform was enacted, which declared the parceling out of landed estates larger than approximately 750 acres and of church estates larger than approximately 300 acres. Count Károlyi himself split up his own estates in Kápolna on February 23. In a peasant country where 40 percent of the land belonged to big estates, this symbolic beginning of land reform promised the realization of the peasants' dreams. The liberal-democratic government, however, was unable to satisfy the expectation of the masses. The land reform was still incomplete six months later, and spontaneous seizures of land and factories began. Rampant inflation, a 50 percent decline in agricultural output, and scarcity of food, coal, and most consumer goods fueled mass dissatisfaction and intensified the revolutionary atmosphere.

Unsolved social problems and the collapse of supply systems, together with the national tragedy and humiliation of the war settlement, paved the road for the Left. The Russian revolution pointed the way. Hundreds of thousands of Hungarian peasants and workers had been incarcerated in Russian prisoner of war camps when the Russian revolution broke out. Many of these prisoners sympathized with the revolutionary cause, and about one hundred thousand Hungarians joined the Red Army to fight against the White Russians. A Hungarian communist party was established in revolutionary Russia: first, on March 24, 1918, as the "Hungarian Group of the Russian Communist Party," then as an independent party, still in Moscow, on November 4, 1918 (Völgyes 1971). Its leader, Béla Kún, returned to Hungary two weeks later, and at the end of the month the party began revolutionary activity following Bolshevik party lines. The party daily, *Vörös Ujság* (Red newspaper), declared its goals of abolishing capitalism and of introducing the dictatorship of the proletariat through the medium of socialist revolution. The party assured its popularity by embracing the goals of the poorer classes, but also by militantly advocating the national issue. "There is only one thing that may smash the robber plans of the Entente," declared the *Vörös Ujság*, "the victory of bolshevism!" (*Vörös Ujság* 1918).

After a deadly armed conflict, several communist leaders were arrested in February 1919. The party, however, continued to prepare the proletarian revolution and to fulfill the resolution of the Communist International, which had been founded in early March 1919 in Moscow. To follow "the Bolshevik road," the Hungarian party mobilized the unemployed for a mass demonstration on March 19 and organized a strike to paralyze the publication of newspapers.

In this explosive situation, Lieutenant-Colonel Fernand Vix, the head of the Entente military delegation in Budapest, presented an ultimatum to President Károlyi that demanded an immediate Hungarian withdrawal from additional territories in the heartland of the kingdom. Major cities such as Szeged and Debrecen lay in the new zone of demilitarization. On March 20, 1919, Károlyi and his government refused the Entente demand and resigned. Károlyi described the events in his memoirs: "The ministers had tendered their resignation, not having the courage to accept or refuse the ultimatum. I . . . proposed that the Cabinet should resign, after which I would charge the Social Democrats, in conjunction with the Communists, to form a new Government. . . . Only a homogeneous, strong and united Government backed by organized labour . . . would have the authority to refuse" (Károlyi 1956, 154).

In this crisis situation, the social democrats and councils of soldiers and workers decided to unite forces and merge with the communists. The agreement with the communist leaders, who were still under arrest, was signed in a Budapest prison. Károlyi had not been informed and refused to sign a proclamation "that I was resigning and handing over power to the Hungarian working class. . . . [The proclamation, however,] had been published before being presented to me, and my signature forged. . . . For the torpedoing of democratic Hungary," added Károlyi, "and for Communist *coup d'état*, the Entente was responsible" (Károlyi 1956, 155–57).

The Socialist Party of Hungary, as the united party was named, declared its intent to introduce the dictatorship of the proletariat and to defend the national interest by rejecting the Entente ultimatum. The Budapest garrison immediately offered its assistance. Bourgeois and nationalist sympathizers and a significant proportion of the officer corps also offered their services. Oscar Jászi, Károlyi's cabinet minister who emigrated after his resignation, characterized the situation as follows:

[I]n the first days of the dictatorship everyone was jubilant. . . . Acceptance of the dictatorship . . . was thoroughly popular, strange to say, among the middle-class and the petty bourgeoisie. . . . The majority of the . . . intellectuals not only associated themselves with the dictatorship but tried to out-howl the wildest of the wolves. [Beside a triumphant socialist feeling,] the second reason for the popular acceptance . . . lay in the demagogic . . . way [the dictatorship] played upon popular chauvinism . . . after their national humiliation. . . . This enthusiastic readiness for *revanche* . . . [was] attributed at least as much to nationalist as to socialist feeling." (Jászi 1924, 110, 115–17)

A bloodless revolution introduced the dictatorship of the proletariat and established the Hungarian Councils' Republic on March 21, 1919. A revolutionary governing council and a council of people's commissars modeled on the Russian pattern were founded. The cabinet was headed by the social democrat Sándor Garbai, but its most influential member was the communist leader, Béla Kún, who served as people's commissar for foreign affairs.

The Councils' Republic followed the Bolshevik example by banning all other parties and associations. Local power was exercised by directly elected councils. All the so-called class alien bourgeoisie and even well-to-do peasants were excluded from the franchise. Altogether 4.5 million people, only half of the population, gained the right to participate in the early April council elections. Police and gendarmes were replaced by a newly organized Red Guard. Revolutionary courts and militia (the so-called Lenin-boys) exercised "revolutionary terror" against the class enemy. The government copied soviet "war communism" by national-izing most of the economy, including small-scale industry and retail shops. The "Decree on Land" nationalized all estates larger than ap-proximately one hundred acres. The land was not parceled out but rather assigned to newly created cooperatives. A compulsory agriculture de-livery system was also immediately introduced. These measures alien-ated not only the landed peasants but even their landless counterparts.

The council government introduced comprehensive social legislation and guaranteed the right to obtain work. The disabled and the unem-ployed were supported by the state. Work days were regulated and the forty-eight-hour workweek was introduced. Poor families were moved into large bourgeois houses, and proletarian children were sent for sum-mer vacation to elegant resorts.

The central question, however, remained the national and border is-sue. General Franchet d'Espérey, commander of the French Balkan army, reported to Clemenceau on the preparation of military interven-tion in Hungary on April 6, 1919: "It is indispensable that the Entente shows its sternness," wrote the general, "against the first nation that re-sists its decisions" (Balogh 1985, 101). The Entente could rely on the armies of the newly established or enlarged neighboring countries: on April 16, a successful Romanian offensive began from the east, and on April 23, the Czechoslovak army started its attack from the north. The two armies soon met and occupied vast portions of Hungary while the French army occupied important cities in the south. The Hungarian Councils' Republic was surrounded. In an almost hopeless situation, the government began to recruit and mobilize soldiers: the sixty-thousand-strong army in March doubled in one month, reaching two hundred thousand by early June. This new Hungarian Red Army began its suc-cessful counteroffensive in the north in May. After a large part of Slo-vakia had been reoccupied, a Slovak Councils' Republic was declared.

This transitory success was halted by a harsh French ultimatum, and at the end of June, the Hungarian Red Army withdrew. A desperate new offensive, launched against the Romanian army in the east, collapsed at the end of July, and the road to Budapest lay open to the Romanians. On August 1, 1919, after 133 days of rule, the Hungarian Councils' Republic collapsed. Most of its communist leaders escaped to Vienna, relinquishing power to an entirely social democratic government.

Was the Hungarian revolution of 1919 a genuine Bolshevik-type revolution, or was it a nationalist upheaval against the dictates of the victorious Entente and its allies around Hungary? The peace dictate, no doubt, crippled the country, causing one of the most moving postwar national tragedies. Undoubtedly, the Hungarian Councils' Republic was a strange hybrid of both bolshevism and nationalism. On the one hand, it was a child of the Russian revolution, and as such, deliberately international. "The destiny of the Hungarian Councils' Republic," Béla Kún stated at the very first session of the Revolutionary Governing Council on March 22, 1919, "is based on the advance of the international proletarian revolution" (Balogh 1985, 92). Kún and the other revolutionaries assumed that their revolution was a part of an emerging general European proletarian revolution and eagerly waited both the victory of the Russian revolution and the beginning of upheavals in Austria and Germany. On the other hand, without the national tragedy in Hungary, the communist revolution could not have happened. National self-defense became the most important legitimizing factor for the revolution and helped, at least transitorily, to establish national unity. The merger of the social democrats with the communists, and the collaboration of a great part of the officer corps and other populist-nationalist elements, all became possible because of the national question.

Yet the mix of the seemingly antagonist communist and national factors did not undermine the concept that the revolution had social-class causes. National questions, after all, could and would generate fascist-type nationalist revolutions as a response to national tragedy. History, especially that of post–World War I, demonstrated this fact in events such as the victorious fascist takeover in Italy and the aborted Nazi putsch in Germany. Backwardness and a modernization crisis, as in the case of Russia, created a firm sociopolitical basis for left-wing revolutions. Additionally, the unsolved social and national questions were, at last, also consequences of the unfinished modern transformation of the country along the Western lines. The modernization crisis, deepened by the lost war and the collapse of the empire, led thus to the desperate revolutionary endeavor.

Bulgaria's One and a Half Revolutions

Bulgaria was one of the least industrialized countries of Europe. If Hungarian modernization was a semisuccess and Russian modernization a semifailure, the Bulgarian attempt was a humiliating failure. The country had only a short time—hardly more than a third of a century—to transform from a robbed borderland of the Ottoman empire into a modern European state. The process simply could not occur in such pressured conditions. In addition, the short history of independent Bulgaria had been characterized by permanent conflicts and three major wars. One-fifth of the male population between the ages of twenty and fifty died on military fronts during this period. Strikes and bread riots rocked the country. An exhausted and frustrated population finally revolted against the regime. In September 1918, a peasant army rebelled in Vladaya, and Daskalov's "republican" troops began marching toward Sofia before being defeated with German assistance. Tsar Ferdinand's dream of "Great Bulgaria" produced not only total defeat but also the collapse of his authoritarian regime. Ferdinand abdicated in favor of his son, Boris. World War I ended for Bulgaria when its government signed the armistice at the end of September 1918.

Three coalition governments were constituted between October 1918 and September 1919, each expressing a further political shift toward the Left. During these months, certain democratic rights and freedoms were guaranteed, censorship was abolished, and political prisoners and revolutionaries were freed by general amnesty. The ruins of the autocratic tsarist regime were gradually swept away and the first democratic election was held on August 17, 1919. The election transformed into a peaceful revolution when three left-wing parties gained nearly two-thirds of the votes. The Agrarian Union, led by Aleksandur Stamboliski—who, together with Daskalov and other peasant leaders, regained his freedom after more than three years in prison—garnered 31 percent of the vote, followed by the communists (18.2 percent), and social democrats (12.8 percent). Various liberal and conservative parties were eliminated.

Stamboliski, an ardent antiwar advocate and peasant revolutionary, formed a coalition government. But he had higher ambitions and soon introduced his peculiar left-wing populist dictatorship of the peasantry. Stamboliski did not hesitate to use the "Orange Guard," the paramilitary organization of the Agrarian Union, against rivals; with the guard's help, he crushed a communist-organized general strike. By introducing compulsory suffrage, Stamboliski mobilized "his" peasantry, dissolved the freshly elected parliament, and set up a new election in March 1920. As a result of the new compulsory electoral rule, more than 77 percent of the voters participated, and the Agrarian Union gained more than 38 percent of the seats. With some manipulation, including the invalidation of thirteen mandates of opposition parties, the Agrarians assured themselves an absolute majority in the parliament and formed their own government.

In the fall of 1922 and early 1923, the populist peasant dictatorship was strengthened. The Orange Guard physically attacked leading liberal and conservative politicians, who were jailed in "protective custody." The guard clashed with other opposition groups and invaded the Sofia offices and meetings of other parties. Several communists were arrested. After these atrocities, a new election was held in April 1923. Stamboliski this time gained the absolute majority and a quasi one-party system was introduced.

A charismatic populist revolutionary, Stamboliski sought to use the dictatorship on behalf of the interests of the peasantry. In May 1921, his parliament enacted a land-reform law that redistributed landed property. Although large estates did not exist in Bulgaria, the maximum size of a landholding was set at thirty hectares (about 75 acres). The territory of estates larger than this—roughly 6 percent of the arable land—was expropriated and distributed among more than a hundred thousand landless and small-landholding peasants. As another measure of social equalization, Stamboliski introduced compulsory labor service for the state in June 1920. The younger generations of the male and female population had to serve eight and four months respectively. The new labor units built roads, railroads, canals, and dams.

The populist dictatorship sought to liquidate the "parasitic" merchant class and bureaucracy. The political activity of lawyers was restricted and, to eliminate private traders, a state monopoly on grain trade was introduced in December 1919. Intellectuals were excluded from the Agrarian Union, progressive taxation was introduced according to class principles, and those who made profit from the war or played any role in its preparation, including twenty-two wartime cabinet ministers and leading businessmen, were tried and punished (Bell 1977).

Stamboliski strongly opposed war and territorial revisionism and dreamed of establishing a confederation of the agrarian countries of the region that would include closer ties with Yugoslavia, the archenemy of Bulgarian nationalists. His "third road," the anti-Western and anticommunist populist regime, adopted a populist version of the Marxist slogan: "Peasants of the world unite!"

The unique postwar Bulgarian left-wing populist revolution boldly challenged the traditional ruling class, and the coalition of the army, state, and local bureaucracies, intelligentsia, and rich urban merchant classes. The endangered former elite formed its own organization, the *Naroden Sgovor* (National Concord) in 1922 and, under the leadership of Professor Tsankov and Colonel Velchev, prepared a coup d'etat. On June 9, 1923, Velchev's troops, in cooperation with the Macedonian terrorist organization, IMRO, occupied the Bulgarian capital. The poorly armed peasant troops were defeated and several thousand peasants were slain. The rebels captured Stamboliski and handed him over to the Macedonian terrorists, who brutally tortured and killed him. His body was mutilated, dismembered, and beheaded.

The Communist Party of Bulgaria, which was strongly rooted in the poor peasantry, called a meeting of its Central Committee on the very day of the putsch and adopted a platform of neutrality. From the doctrinaire platform of a direct proletarian revolution, they assessed the clash as merely a conflict between the various groups of the bourgeoisie. As the party newspaper put it: "The government formed after the *coup* replaces one type of military and police dictatorship, that of the peasant bourgeoisie, with another type, that of the urban bourgeoisie" (*Rabotnicheski* 1923).

Soon, however, the Bulgarian communists relinquished their neutral stance. The Communist International in Moscow and Vasil Kolarov, the Bulgarian secretary general of the organization, rejected neutrality in a telegram of June 14 and called for a joint struggle with the peasantry. Kolarov returned speedily to Bulgaria, where he convinced the obedient party to prepare for a proletarian uprising. The government, informed by an intercepted communication from Moscow to Sofia, launched a preemptive attack and arrested more than two thousand communist functionaries on September 12. Nevertheless, uprisings erupted on September 23, 1923, in the districts of Nova Zagora, Stara Zagora, Pleven, and Trnovo. Villages and towns were occupied and revolutionary committees were set up.

The belated and soon isolated communist uprising suffered a fate similar to Stamboliski's earlier experience. In reprisal for the revolt, Macedonian terrorist groups again played a leading role. The number of their victims is estimated, according to various sources, at between ten and thirty thousand. After the attempted rebellion of 1923, the Bulgarian communist movement turned to desperate individual revolutionary acts of terror that resembled the acts of the nineteenth-century Russian *Narodnaya Volya*. Two bomb explosions took place at the central Sveta Nedelia Church on April 16, 1924, killing 128 people gathered for the funeral service of a murdered general; the explosions failed to kill Tsar Boris, who arrived late. The terrorist act prompted the government to settle accounts with the communists. According to highly uncertain estimates, another thirty thousand people fell victim to the government's bloody revenge.

Revolutionary Attempts in the Baltic Countries and Austria

In contrast to the enduring revolutionary movement in Russia, the communist and left-wing populist revolutions of Hungary and Bulgaria could not survive longer than a few months or years. The revolutionary tide reached other countries of frustrated Central and Eastern Europe, but the class revolution of the poor workers and peasants could not occur. Failed revolutionary attempts characterized the immediate postwar years in the Baltic area and Austria.

The historical opportunity to regain independence arrived in the Baltic countries, which had been part of the Russian empire for more than a century, as a consequence of the turmoil of the war. Repeated German attacks and German occupation of the area were followed by the defeat of Germany and a weakening of revolution-ridden Russia. In March and August 1917, first Estonia and then Latvia demanded autonomy. The march toward independence began. However, radicalization of Baltic politics and the rise of strong left-wing revolutionary groups also accompanied the Russian revolution. The Latvian social democratic party turned toward the Bolsheviks, and the Estonian Bolsheviks gained ground from the summer of 1917, earning 35 percent of the popular votes at the local soviet elections. For Narva, the figure was 47 percent. The Latvian municipal elections resulted in an even more spectacular breakthrough of the radical Left: the Left obtained 41, 64, and 70 percent in Riga, Valmiera, and Limbazi respectively. The provincial assembly elected a Bolshevik president in September. "Between March and September 1917, the single power-center of Latvia was the Workers' Council" (Kalnis 1974, 195). After the Bolshevik revolution in

Russia, Latvia became a stronghold of bolshevism. In the November election for the Constitutional Assembly, in contrast to the 24 percent of votes cast for Bolsheviks in Russia, or to the 45 percent in Petrograd, Latvian Bolsheviks in the Latvian part of Livonia captured 72 percent. Though less enthusiastic, Estonia also elected a Bolshevik-led military committee in Tallin.

The German withdrawal and collapse in November 1918 strengthened the national forces in their struggle for independence, but the Russian Red Army rapidly advanced and occupied the Baltic area. The soviet leadership considered Lithuania, Latvia, and Estonia the keys of world revolution because they provided a link between Soviet Russia and rapidly revolutionizing Germany. Leon Trotsky, the war commissar, stated in December that the Red Army would advance into Western Europe. Consequently, the occupying Bolshevik authorities created a new Lithuanian Communist Party, Bolshevik-led councils, and Bolshevik government. Baltic revolutionaries assisted the Russian military endeavor: the Latvian light-infantry regiment was the nucleus of the invading Red Army in Latvia, and four Estonian light-infantry and other regiments fought in the soviet army, which advanced on the Narva front. On November 29, 1918, the Estonian Workers' Soviet proclaimed the Soviet Government of Estonia. "But the Communist rule proved to be a fiasco. The Estonian army, helped by units of the British Navy, 2,000 Finnish volunteers[,] and . . . German Balts . . . [freed] the whole country . . . about the middle of January 1919" (*Report* 1972, 33).

Yet subsequent military events, a new German invasion, an arriving British naval unit, British and French political and diplomatic assistance, and most of all the strengthened national forces that could exploit military success changed the fate of the area. Baltic nationalists grew stronger in response to the extensive "red terror" that accompanied the Bolshevik occupation and that concluded with mass killings of Baltic Germans, priests, and bourgeois elements, especially in Tartu and Riga. The communist class revolution could not compete with the rising forces of national revolution. The inspiring goal of restoring independence and building a nation proved much stronger and more popular than internationalist and pro-Russian communism. Mobilized by nationalist politicians and parties, the Baltic countries joined with Polish, Finnish, and White Russian troops to struggle successfully against both Russian and local Bolshevik forces. The Estonian national troops, the Latvian Balodis Brigade, the Baltic German's *Baltische Landeswehr*, and the Lithuanian national army defeated the Russian Bolsheviks, who were preoccupied by a deadly civil war and sought to consolidate their power by territorial sacrifices and compromise. At the turn of 1919 and 1920, successive peace negotiations and agreements between Soviet Russia and each of the Baltic countries ended confrontations and led to the triumph of the Baltic national revolutions.

Communist revolutionary forces were eliminated and communist parties proscribed in the independent Baltic states. The last act of the revolutionary era was symbolic: the ill-prepared attempt at an adventurous coup d'etat in Tallin, organized by Jaan Anvelt, the former head of the Estonian Soviet Government, with the participation of a few hundred armed communists in December 1924, had nothing in common with a mass revolution. It was easily and immediately suppressed and harshly punished. Communist revolutionary forces were totally defeated.

If the failed communist revolutionary attempts in the Baltic countries were closely connected to the Russian revolution, the Austrian events were greatly influenced by the revolutions of other nations that surrounded the country. A desperate, defeated, and mutilated Austria, which had been one of Europe's great powers but now was a small and miserable country, witnessed the bitter rebellions not only in Russia but next door in Hungary and Bavaria as well. The failed German revolutionary attempts in 1918–1920 had a strong impact on German Austria; not even hoping for independent survival, the country toyed with the idea of *Anschluss* (joining Germany). Small wonder that powerful revolutionary mass movements emerged at the end of the war.

The strike of January 1918 and the uprising of the sailors of Cattaro on February 1, when the red flag was hoisted on forty warships, indicated the discontent unequivocally. Spontaneous nationwide organization of workers' and soldiers' councils followed the military collapse. In Graz, the Styrian capital, a welfare committee was set up in October. A few days later a *Volksrat* (People's Council) was elected in Salzburg, and the Carinthian provisional executive committee and the *Tiroler Nationalrat* (National Council of Tirol) were founded. In Vienna, a mass demonstration demanded the release of Friedreich Adler, the celebrated antiwar hero. The Viennese Soldiers' Council systematically removed and crushed the imperial eagles that adorned public buildings. A provisional national assembly vested its elected state council with executive power. Karl Renner's draft of a republican constitution was adopted, and the social democratic leader became the first chancellor of the Austrian Republic, proclaimed on November 12, 1918.

Whereas administrative power was organized on a strict coalition basis at both local and national levels, elections held in the soldiers' councils mostly produced left-wing social democratic majorities. As Julius Deutsch, the party's military expert stated: "Not always old and tried comrades [gained ground] . . . but often more radical youngsters who had joined us but very recently" (Carsten 1972, 80). Left-wing socialists took over several soldiers' councils, including the Viennese council. While the imperial army collapsed, the revolutionary socialist paramilitary organization, the Viennese *Volkswehr*, became a strong and disciplined army of seventeen thousand soldiers with armored units and cannons. One of its units in the center of the city—under the command of the revolutionary journalist, Egon Erwin Kisch—was called the Red Guard. When the republic was proclaimed, revolutionary masses demonstrated in front of the parliament, cutting out the white strip from the red-white-red Austrian flag and clashing with the police. Two people died and several were wounded.

The revolutionary crisis, however, did not intensify in Austria. Austrian social democrats, even their left-wing leaders, remained sober and regarded a revolution in Austria as impossible. In a reply to an appeal from the Hungarian Councils' Republic in March 1919, Victor Adler, the celebrated socialist leader, announced in the *Arbeiter Zeitung* on March 23, 1919: "You have issued the call to us to follow your example. We would joyfully do so but unfortunately cannot at the moment. In our country there is no food. Even our meager bread ration depends upon the food trains sent to us by the Entente. Thus we are entirely the slaves of the Entente" (Carsten 1972, 113). In the same month, a brochure of Julius Braunthal with the characteristic title *Rätedictatur oder Demokratie* (Council-dictatorship or democracy) refused the possibility of socialist revolution because of the hostile attitude of the Austrian peasantry and concluded "that only the road of democracy was open" for Austrian socialists (Goldinger and Binder 1992, 32). In October 1918, Otto Bauer accurately pointed out the radical difference between the Russian and Austrian situations:

Many people are captivated by the idea that the methods of our Russian comrades, the Bolsheviks, could without much ado be transferred to Austria; that workers', peasants' and soldiers' councils could be formed and take over the government. But to this end not only the cooperation of workers and soldiers is needed but also that of the peasants. The great difference between our situation and that in Russia is, above all, that the Russian peasant— socially, culturally, economically and legally—is quite different from our peasant here. While the Russian peasant . . . felt like a proletarian . . . our peasant feels like a bourgeois and a determined enemy for the working class. (Carsten 1972, 31)

In Austria, concluded Bauer, only the power of a minority would be possible, which would soon collapse in the wake of hunger, for the peasantry would not give up food, and if forced to do so, would revolt in bloody civil war.

Thus, Austrian socialists rejected the possibility of revolution. "In the case of Austrian Social Democracy," maintains Peter Loewenberg, "the words were of . . . revolution, and a new world, but reality was of accommodation and use of the parliamentary system and integration into bourgeois social values. . . . Otto Bauer was the personification of the ambivalence of Social Democracy in the 1920s and 1930s" (Loewenberg 1985, 161). Relying on their urban strength and parliamentary weight, they even feared that a Bolshevik adventure would impair the chances of establishing democracy. Accordingly, whenever necessary, they emerged in the role of "pacifier": they purged the *Volkswehr* from communist influence, and on June 15, 1919, they led armed socialist units to arrest 115 communist functionaries in order to prevent any kind of revolutionary adventure. *Volkswehr* units occupied the inner city of Vienna. Detachments lined up in Hörlgasse and opened fire on the masses who were demanding the release of communist leaders. The twenty dead and eighty injured constituted alarming evidence of the steadfast stand of the Austrian social democrats.

A conservative Austrian majority, however, rejected even the rule of moderate social democrats. Powerful extreme right-wing organizations commenced in the provinces. Officers in Styria and Carinthia, led by Dr. Pfrimer and Dr. Steidle, an anti-Semitic Christian Socialist in Tyrol, organized private armies. The extreme right-wing paramilitary *Heimwehr* was established, and open armed confrontation seemed inevitable between the socialist factions and right-wing conservatives, who hated the "red" and "parasite" Vienna and who had broad and indisputable support in the countryside. In the fall of 1920, the social democratic party was forced out of government. The revolutionary attempts of weak left-wing groups ended and "a general cry for a strong government," as a Vienna police report characterized the atmosphere in November 1919, paved the road for right-wing conservativism. Even the socialists' seemingly sober strategy to avoid revolutionary adventure and defend democracy had failed.

For the time being, the revolutionary historical circle had closed.

With the single exception of Russia, which remained a strong bridge-head of communism, attempts to bring about social revolution in Central and Eastern Europe failed. The crisis-torn area was engulfed by a wave of harsh counterrevolutions to restore "law and order" and reestablish or introduce conservative, autocratic, right-wing regimes.

The Wave of Counterrevolutions

The "Red Dawn" in several Central and Eastern European countries was a desperate rebellion of frustrated groups, led by utopian-revolutionary intellectuals. Their mass support at certain moments was quite significant. One should not forget, however, that this was a bold attempt by a well-organized minority. In revolutionary Russia, the Bolsheviks were able to preserve their power by introducing harsh revolutionary terror and by mobilizing a huge part of the poor rebellious peasantry. They thus defeated a powerful counterrevolution that was assisted by the great powers.

For external and internal reasons, other countries could not repeat the Bolshevik success. In the Hungarian case, a French-orchestrated military alliance and offensive by neighboring Romania and Czechoslovakia brought defeat. In the Bulgarian case, an alliance of the traditional army elite, with the bureaucracy, the urban intellectual and merchant classes, and extreme nationalist-terrorist forces worked to undermine left-wing revolutionary power. Left-wing populist and communist forces and the masses under their influence grew isolated from the rest of society, and during their short period in power, the left-wing leadership made crucial mistakes, alienating many potential allies. The withholding of land reform in Hungary and the populist crusade against the sins of the urban "Sodom" in Bulgaria tragically contributed to the Left's defeat. In countries where revolutionary attempts could not lead the revolutionary minority to power, the left-wing "centers" or spontaneous forces were isolated, easily surrounded, defeated, and destroyed. The island of "Red Vienna" could not prevail against the ocean of a conservative-Catholic countryside. The Bolshevik forces of the Baltic countries could not compete successfully with nationalists who mobilized the bulk of the population under the banner of national independence, a century-long dream and goal of the region's occupied and oppressed people.

The revolutionary attempts and the parties that represented them were adventurist and refused to analyze the balance of forces objectively. They believed with almost religious fervor in the world revolution or in the alliance of the peasant countries that would solve all internal problems. This attitude and the dictatorial methods of red terror that they used against broadly defined "class enemies" generated a savage reaction in which ruthless, similarly dictatorial counterrevolutionary regimes were established. The historical alternative to Bolshevik and populist dictatorships in postwar Central and Eastern Europe was not Western-type democracy but "white" terror and conservative autocracy.

The most "classic" counterrevolution emerged in Hungary. Although the Hungarian Councils' Republic was suppressed by foreign military intervention, organized Hungarian counterrevolutionary forces consolidated a new government. The old gentry-military-bureaucratic elite had established antirevolutionary organizations in the spring of 1919 in Vienna, where a Hungarian Anti-Bolshevik Committee was founded in April, and in the foreign-occupied southern city of Szeged, where a counterrevolutionary government was established in May under the premiership of Count Gyula Károlyi. The minister of defense of this government, Admiral Miklós Horthy, the last commander of the Austro-Hungarian navy, began to organize his "national army," recruiting a few thousand former officers and noncommissioned officers from the demobilized former royal army.

In the second week of August, Horthy announced his departure from the Szeged government and the independence of his military headquarters. His national army began to occupy the Western part of the country that was not held by the Romanians. (The transitory governments in Budapest had no military power, and the capital as well as the central and eastern parts of the country were under Romanian control.) Horthy's military units and the Prónay- and Héjjas-detachments launched an anticommunist crusade, torturing and executing members of local communist councils, hanging revolutionary peasants and members of the Red Army, and promoting bloody pogroms against Jewish burghers. Because the Romanian army—following the command of the Paris Peace Conference—was gradually withdrawing from Hungary, Horthy's army took over and, on November 16, 1919, arrived at Budapest. At Horthy's headquarters in the Hotel Britannia, the purging and punishment of "guilty Budapest" began, and courageous journalists who reported the actions were murdered. The "white terror" killed two to four times as many people—various sources estimate the number of victims between 626 and over 2,000 — as had the red terror, whose victims are estimated as numbering between 342 and 578 (Janos 1982, 202). "Disciplinary" procedures were initiated against those who had served in the Hungarian Councils' Republic, including famous writers and musicians such as Béla Bartók and Zoltán Kodály. Tens of thousands of left-wing people, including social democrats and liberal intellectuals, were imprisoned or interned. The decree of internment made it possible to arrest without legal procedure anybody who was "dangerous for the state, society, and security." Thousands, including leading liberal intellectuals, emigrated. "The brain of the unhappy country has been destroyed," stated Oscar Jászi in the early 1920s.

The four or five thousand men who represented European ideals and culture among us are either languishing in the prisons, or interned, or starving in exile, or . . . never know when they will be insulted in the street . . . by some gang of "Awakening Magyars." . . . The White party [attempts] to rouse the fanaticism of large sections of the population . . . [by advocating] the restoration of the territorial integrity of the country . . . [and by] the "ending of Jewish domination." (Jászi 1924, 199, 202–3)

The Entente powers initiated procedures to consolidate power in Hungary by sending the British diplomat George Russel Clerk to Budapest. Clerk's successful mission led to the formation of a transitory coalition government and to preparations for parliamentary elections to be held in January 1920. Democratized electorial rules extended voting rights to nearly 30 percent of the population (up from 7 percent before the war). The new parliament restored the kingdom with its first decree in February 1920 but did not reinstate the Habsburg dynasty. Horthy's army surrounded the parliament, which elected Horthy governor of Hungary on March 1, 1920. The consolidation of counterrevolutionary power had begun. Horthy's national army and detachments provided the nucleus of a new military. Anticommunist terror was legalized by an enacted law (1921.III) that banned and harshly punished all communist activities. Under the provisions of this act, as Andrew C. Janos notes, the prosecutor general was authorized to ban the distribution of newspapers and books without legal proceedings; this happened roughly fifty times in the twenties (Janos 1982, 215–16). Another law (1920.XXV) introduced the *numerus clausus*, the law restricting admission of Jews to universities, the first anti-Semitic legislation in Europe. It limited the number of Jewish students at the universities according to their percentage in the entire population. In consequence, as Jörg Hoensch describes, "the proportion of Jewish students fell from 34 percent in 1917–18 to only 8 percent in 1935–36. Deliberate measures were also introduced to eliminate the Jews completely from the state bureaucracy. . . . Jews . . . were eventually no longer allowed to conduct business in which the state had a monopoly" (Hoensch 1984, 106). As a symbol of the newly introduced and "consolidated" power, the decree XVI.1920 introduced medieval forms of corporal punishment. The institutionalized parliamentary system was counterbalanced by the creation of a united, monolithic governing party, accompanied by the elimination—in a peasant country—of genuine peasant parties. Further stability was created by broadening the authority of the governor and by strictly limiting the voting right, excluding both the younger generations and the less-educated strata. This act excluded three quarters of a million people from the franchise, most from the lower classes. In rural areas, the open ballot was reintroduced because a secret ballot was "irreconcilable with the open character of the Hungarian people," according to Prime Minister Count Bethlen. Miklós Horthy's "Christian-national course" restored the ancien régime but eliminated its liberal characteristics and institutionalized a conservative, anti-Semitic, oppressive authoritarianism. In spite of its conservativism, this regime preserved the limited constitutional and legal parliamentary framework that guaranteed legality both for the trade unions and for the social democratic party. Faked "parliamentarism," however, was based on a "system of armed terrorism," as Jászi called the system and practice of open ballot. Indeed, whereas in the few districts in which secret ballot was obtained the government party gained only 18 percent of the votes, in the open ballot districts it gained 67 percent. "In four general elections between 1922 and 1935, the government party won 628 out of 980 available seats (64.1 percent), 578 of them in constituencies voting under the system of open franchise" (Janos 1982, 213). The government signed the Trianon Treaty and sought to adjust to the European order, but its leading principle remained territorial revisionism. Consequently, the regime became a natural ally of those countries that wanted to destroy the Versailles system. This fundamental foreign policy orientation strengthened right-wing, fascist political trends and their representatives in interwar Hungary.

The old aristocratic class regained its power in Hungary, and Horthy's prime ministers in the 1920s were chosen from the "old guard" (Count Teleki and Count Bethlen). The promised land reform, a powerful slogan against the communist regime, was a fraud. Only 6 percent of the land was parceled out in a country where 40 percent of the land belonged to large estates. The Catholic Church gained a leading position, stronger than before the war. According to Andrew Janos, it had a "virtually free hand in matters of the primary and secondary education . . . [and] a virtual power of veto over a whole range of public appointments—judgeships, notaryships, and candidacies to the House of Representatives from overwhelmingly Catholic districts. . . . In exchange, [the Church] became one of the pillars of the neo-corporalist order" (Janos 1982, 231–32).

Some of Horthy's intimate friends who demanded an uncompromising "change of guard" and sought to preserve both an open dictatorship and a harsh anti-Jewish policy were politically defeated and marginalized. Two leading figures of the group, Gyula Gömbös and Endre Bajcsy-Zsilinszky, formed the right-wing opposition party, the *Fajvédő Párt* (Race Protecting Party), in the parliament. However, Horthy's comrades in arms—companions from the days of the counterrevolutionary Szeged government and Horthy's national army, who were mostly descendants of landless gentry families with military-bureaucratic backgrounds and endorsed antiliberal, antidemocratic, and anti-Semite views—merged to form a new elite that became the most powerful group in interwar Hungary.

The coup d'etat against Stamboliski in Bulgaria also concluded with the formation of a combined constitutional-dictatorial counterrevolutionary regime. The Tsankov-Velchev government launched the most ruthless white terror against communists and populists. Both the communist and agrarian parties were banned, and "the next several years," notes Joseph Rothschild, "witnessed an ongoing vendetta. The government . . . tolerated, or even arranged, the frequent assassinations of radical Peasantist leaders at the hands of IMRO and police agents" (Rothschild 1977, 344). Because other opposition parties could compete in a parliamentary race and both communists and peasant politicians formed various "front organizations" to participate at elections, quite a few of them were elected from time to time as members of the parliament. But the guaranteed parliamentary framework was undermined by institutionalized terror. One of the most telling episodes was the infamous Petkov incident. Stamboliski's former associate, the imprisoned Petkov, was elected to the parliament and released from prison after the election in order to take his seat. He was assassinated in the street on his way to parliament. The government observed parliamentary rules, but General Velchev, the éminence grise of the 1920s, preserved close contacts with the IMRO, the violent Macedonian terror-ists who did all the dirty work for the Bulgarian regime. However, when leaders of the terrorist organization plotted to establish an independent Macedonia, Velchev arranged the assassinations of IMRO commander Alexandrov and of General Protogerov. Terror was thus an integral com-ponent of the regime.

Furthermore, though a multiparty system was allowed, a strong, un-beatable government party was created. Premier Tsankov's *Naroden Sgovor* (National Concord) was a coalition of right-wing nationalist par-ties that easily won 172 parliamentary seats out of 247 in the Novem-ber 1923 elections. As in Hungary, the communist and agrarians were banned, but the social democratic party was legalized as part of the Tsankov coalition. Its additional twenty-nine seats guaranteed a majority of more than 58 percent for the ruling party. Parliament was little more than a decoration in a regime that relied on terrorism to enforce its rule.

Alternative class revolutions in Central and Eastern Europe did not produce genuine parliamentary democracies. Counterrevolutions mo-bilized the seemingly defeated traditional ruling elite and other extreme dictatorial forces. Austria and Germany, where much weaker revolu-tionary forces could not even break through and were instantly sup-pressed, had similar experiences. Because further sansculotte-type rad-icalization did not occur, the old ruling elite and institutions—the nobility, army, bureaucracy, and the Church—prevailed. No doubt, ob-solete monarchies were replaced by constitutional parliamentarian re-publics and, in these cases, democratic legislation gained momentum. But as Francis Carsten, an authority on the Austrian and German rev-olutions, notes, Austria and Germany experienced "defeated revolu-tion." Because "the revolution of 1918 failed to destroy the strength of the forces opposed to it, they quickly revived. As the left-wing did not succeed in propelling the revolution on to a more radical course, the old social forces were able to stage a comeback." Despite great political-constitutional changes, Carsten continues, the societies and social sys-tems remained unchanged:

The task of the revolution was to overcome this discrepancy [between the advanced economy and the obsolete political and social structures], to re-form radically the political and social structure. This was done only in the political and constitutional sphere, and even there only partly. . . . Many may disagree with the thesis that the revolution of 1918–19 was defeated. It resulted, after all, in the disappearance of the dynasties and in the estab-lishment of parliamentary democracy in Germany and Austria. But this democracy was never secure; it was time and again shaken by severe crises, and it only lasted just over one decade. The "democratization" of the political structure failed. The workers' and soldiers' councils which would have contributed much to this "democratization" were dissolved or simply vanished from the scene. The old social ruling groups retained their positions. . . . There was not much reason to speak of a "victory" of the revolution. . . . The storm had passed, and the society settled down in its traditional grooves. (Carsten 1972, 330–31, 334–35)

"When the counter-revolutionary smoke dissolved," Karl Polanyi writes, "the political systems in Budapest, Vienna, and Berlin were found to be not very far different from what they had been before the War" (Polanyi 1964, 23).

The challenged but unchanged continuity is certainly highly exaggerated in these analyses. In the 1920s, a strong representation of social democracy characterized Austrian politics. Their forces, however, had to contend with the continuingly growing conservatism and the presence of putschist political groups. Social democrats were pushed out of coalition governments, and conservative Christian and right-wing *Heimwehr* forces gained ground. The author of a book on the history of the Austrian Republic rightly devotes a lengthy chapter to the "Crisis of the Parliamentary Democracy" beginning in October 1926, with the formation of the second Seipel cabinet (Goldinger 1992). Democracy was short-lived, but its true successor was not the old, reconstructed political structures and forces; these forces were not so much reconstructed as they were replaced, as Thomas Mann aptly noted in December 1922, by a new "reactionary obscurantism." "I protest against this reactionary wave that now sweeps over Europe. . . . Any form of obscurantism is highly attractive, but highly dangerous, to a humanity exhausted by relativism and yearning for absolute values" (Mann 1970, 201). Reactionary obscurantism became triumphant in the early 1930s.

6

Belated National Revolutions

At the end of World War I, when the most desperate social layers of the most despondent nations turned toward the most reckless revolutionary endeavors, and revolutions and counterrevolutions engulfed a great part of Central and Eastern Europe, the majority of the region's people placed hope in another solution: national revolution. This form of revolution seemed an attractive and effective response to the challenges of backwardness and peripheral social ills, particularly because the failure to create nation-states was one of the most striking characteristics of unsuccessful modernization. The process of nation building in the area had not yet been completed.

Over the course of the nineteenth century, the various peoples of Central and Eastern Europe who lived in the region's large multinational empires emerged as separately identified nations. Miroslav Hroch carefully describes the three-stage process (Hroch 1985). In the first stage, toward the end of the eighteenth century, national movements began in culture and linguistics. These movements were initially antipolitical, associated with romanticism and the study of folklore. In the second stage, an enthusiastic intellectual class became the prime mover and propagandist in building a *Kulturnation*, a substitute for nationstates where they did not yet exist. In the third stage, the movement extended beyond the boundaries of the literate public and became an organized mass movement, the carrier of national propaganda and agitation. Political parties dedicated to creating independent nation-states were established under the banner of national unification or national separation. People were ready to die for the idea of the nation and were convinced that the achievement of their goals would cure all the ills of backwardness and would bring them into the family of advanced countries in the West.

The Great War prepared the soil: it mobilized and armed the peoples and provided an opportunity for the entire adult male population to organize, train itself, and launch armed attacks against its enemies in the name of national aspirations. Goals that before the war had seemed impossible to achieve suddenly became reality at the end of the war. The oppressive and obsolete multinational great powers in the East were defeated: the triumph of the Entente combined with pressures created by internal unrest and revolutions to undermine their power. Nations without nation-states, nations that had never enjoyed independence, nations, in this sense, "without history," were liberated. Turkey, once a hegemonic power in the Balkans, became an impoverished small country in search of its own development, and the Balkans were liberated once and for all. The Czechs, Slovaks, Hungarians, Croats, Slovenes, Poles, and Romanians were now free of centuries of Habsburg-Austrian, or, in some cases, Hungarian domination. Russia lost Poland and the Baltic states. The three empires that had controlled Central and Eastern Europe either lost considerable territory or disappeared altogether.

Plans to Create Democratic Confederations

Several plans emerged to replace the autocratic, centralized, and oppressive multinational states with free, voluntary, and democratic associations of various nations organized in federative or confederative states. The forerunner of these plans was Friedrich Neumann's *Mitteleuropa* concept, which was inspired by the early German victories in 1915. Neumann drew the conclusion from modern economic development and the war that "no small or medium-sized power will henceforth be able to carry out high policy. . . . Only large states still have any significance." He was convinced that politics was "under the influence of big industrial and supra-state organizations" (Neumann 1915). Small countries had no other choice but to join together or become isolated. Germany would only be able to compete with the superstates of Russia, Britain, and the United States if she were to become a pivotal part of a new "Central European world power," the nucleus of which would be a union between Germany and Austria-Hungary. Neumann opposed the creation of a Great Germany—that is, a German-ruled and oppressed *Mitteleuropa*—and suggested as an alternative a democratic and voluntary confederation of nations located between the Baltic Sea and the Adriatic. The German-Austrian center would be enlarged by Romania, Serbia, and Bulgaria in the East and by the Netherlands and Switzerland in the West. The adjoining states would retain their sovereignty and independent governments. The confederation would be led by delegates from the member states, but Germany would be ensured military and industrial leadership. Although Neumann urged its realization during the war, the *Mitteleuropa* confederation plan vanished with the German military defeat.

Two other plans emerged as a result of the defeat and disintegration of the Austro-Hungarian Empire. The first was championed by Karl Renner, the social democratic president of the Austrian republic. Renner envisioned a voluntary, democratic unification of the empire's former German and Slavic nations—a union that excluded Hungary. The plan addressed the concerns of the new political elite of postwar Austria, whose members could not imagine the existence of the rump, mutilated country. Whether affiliated with the Left or the Right, these people believed that the mutilated Austria, which lost the larger parts of its former imperial territory, was unviable and that the only hope of survival lay in unification, either with Germany or with the former Slavic nations of the empire. According to the Renner plan, the confederation would have four equal and autonomous member states, a federal parliament, and centralized government.

The second proposal for a democratic confederation was born in Hungary, which, after the Austro-Hungarian Compromise of 1867, had become a ruling partner with Austria in the Dual Monarchy. Hungarians were shocked by the postwar dissolution of the former Hungarian kingdom, which resulted in the loss of two-thirds of its former territories when the Hungarian Councils' Republic failed in its attempt to resist the dictates of the victorious powers and their allies. Oscar Jászi, a liberal democrat and member of the Károlyi government, was an honest believer in the equal right of all nationalities; he suggested the transformation of the old Austro-Hungarian Monarchy into a democratic confederation. Moreover, he advocated the foundation of a Danubian United States composed of the free and equal nations of the Danube valley; in other words, he included the Balkan countries in his vision of the integrated union. Before the collapse of the Dual Monarchy, Jászi published his concept and called for the participation of five member states—Austria, the Czech lands, Poland, Hungary, and "Illiria." In 1918, he suggested that the Danube confederation would not even have a permanent capital but rather that the capitals of the member countries would play this role in rotation. According to Jászi's plan, Hungary would have remained intact without federalization because, he thought, the nationalities of Hungary lacked the will to build independent states (Jászi 1918, 52). As a minister of nationalities, however, he soon learned that this will was not lacking. When, for example, he offered independence to the Transylvanian Romanians in the suggested confederation, the Romanians refused flatly to join.

The Renner plan sought to preserve—in a transformed and democratic way—a great part of the former Austrian empire. The Jászi plan suggested an even larger confederation of Central and Eastern European countries. Other ambitious confederation plans advocated smaller, regional unification. In particular, plans for the Baltic and Polish area sought to avoid the "balkanization" of the newly liberated Baltic and Polish territories. During the war, German political-military interests in creating "a ring of 'barrier' states" against Russia caused the German government and high command to play the "nationality card" by sponsoring the League of Non-Russian Peoples. According to the plan of Chancellor Bethmann-Hollweg in 1916, the proposed Baltic alliance would consist of Poland, Lithuania, Courland, Livonia, and Estonia; in July 1917, the Bingen conference declared autonomy for this entire area. This German plan was complemented by the ideas of Jaan Tönisson, a charismatic Estonian politician, who in 1917 advanced the idea of creating of a Scandinavian-Baltic Bloc of "thirty million people." These were by no means the only plans for the area. The Helsinki conference in January 1920 and the Warsaw Accord of March 1922 both sought to establish large-scale Baltic cooperation between Finland, Estonia, Latvia, and Poland. Aleksandur Stamboliski, the Bulgarian peasant revolutionary, nurtured an anti-balkanization plan for a confederation of the Balkan peasant countries, suggesting in the early 1920s that Bulgaria and Yugoslavia unite in a federation. Jósef Piłsudski planned to "turn back the wheel of history" by establishing a new, democratic and federative version of the great medieval Polish state; he envisioned a federation consisting of Poland, Lithuania, Ukraine, and Byelorussia. President Paderewski, the popular Polish pianist-politician, even sent a memorandum to President Wilson, arguing for the acceptance of a "United States of Poland" constructed along the lines of Piłsudski's plan.

Despite their varying outlines, all of these plans failed. The peoples of Central and Eastern Europe—especially the political elite—sought to exploit the unique historical opportunity created by the collapse of the multinational empires and wanted to establish independent states. Having just gained their independence, these people were suspicious of confederation and federation plans; such plans seemed disguised attempts to preserve the domination of former ruling nations. For a Czech or a Slovak, a Croat or a Romanian, both Renner's and Jászi's plans embodied attempts by Austria and Hungary to reassert their hegemony, though in changed form. The Baltic people worried about a resurgent Polish power and did not trust each other. The same was true for the Balkan nations. Mutual suspicion, the desire to accomplish the unfinished nation building, and a rise of rival small-nation nationalism precluded the possibility of unity or cooperation and undermined all confederative attempts in Central and Eastern Europe.

The sole exception was Bolshevik Russia. In the oppressive climate of the multinational tsarist empire, the Russian Social Democratic Party had declared the "right of national self-determination" in the first manifesto produced at its founding congress in 1898. This principle became an inseparable part of the Bolshevik program. In his "April Theses" on *The Socialist Revolution and the Right of Nations to Self-Determination*, Lenin maintained that socialist revolution would create proper democracy, and, therefore, it would also have to recognize "the right of oppressed nations to self-determination, i.e. the right to free political secession" (Carr 1950–1953, 1:433). In Lenin's interpretation, the right of self-determination was no longer a "bourgeois democratic" principle. In the age of twentieth-century imperialism, the struggle for national independence had assumed prominence in backward Central and Eastern Europe, in Russia, and in the colonial and semicolonial world; therefore, according to Lenin, national movement had become a reservoir and an ally of socialist revolution. In April 1917, in a debate within the party that occurred after the February revolution and in preparation for the Bolshevik revolution, Lenin again underlined the right of "all nations forming part of Russia . . . [to] free separation and the creation of an independent state." In November 1917, shortly after the victory of the Bolshevik revolution, the *Declaration of Rights of the Peoples of Russia* proclaimed without any qualification the right of self-determination for all peoples. The party program of 1919 reformulated this concept and stressed the right of "nonsovereign nations to secession." The program, however, also proposed to create "a federal union of states organized on the Soviet model" (Carr 1950–1953, 1:268–69, 275). In opposition to Lenin's view, Stalin, the commissar for nationalities affairs, declared in an article in *Pravda* "that the demand for separation of the border regions, at the present stage of revolution, is a completely counterrevolutionary demand" (*Report* 1972, 23).

The first actions of Bolshevik Russia followed Lenin's principles. The right of self-determination was applied in the cases of Poland, Finland, and the Baltic countries. E. H. Carr, an expert on the Russian Revolution, comments: "[T]he initial recognition of the right of self-determination and secession was accorded after 1917 willingly, sincerely and, on the whole, unreservedly. . . . Lenin in his utterances of 1917 frequently coupled the Ukraine with Poland and Finland as a nation whose claim to independence was unreservedly accepted by the Bolsheviks" (Carr 1950–1953, 1:277, 295). The former Russian Empire was reorganized according to the Bolshevik principle: a decree of the *Vsesoyuznyi Tsentralnyi Ispolnitelnyi Komitet* (All-Union Central Executive Committee) on June 1, 1919, announced recognition of "the independence, liberty, and self-determination of the toiling masses of the Ukraine, Latvia, Lithuania, White Russia, and Crimea" (Carr 1950–1953, 1:385). The Russian Soviet Republic had nearly twenty autonomous units inhabited by non-Russian peoples, and the rest of the country was divided into eight separate and independent states: Ukraine, Byelorussia, Azerbaijan, Armenia, Georgia, the Far Eastern Republic, and two Central Asian Republics of Khorezm and Bokhara. The Ukraine treaty was signed on December 28, 1920, and a series of treaties between the independent states followed. In November 1922, each independent republic signed a separate treaty with Germany to extend the provisions of the Treaty of Rapallo.

This was, however, the last action of the independent republics. A process of reunion began immediately, first as a military alliance, which later became also an economic alliance strengthened by ideological links. Reflecting the new situation, Lenin stressed that the right of self-determination can be expressed in the voluntary union of free and equal nations. In December 1922, the soviet congresses of the independent republics announced the goal of establishing a federal Soviet Union. In July 1923, a draft constitution of the Soviet Union was adopted, which gained formal confirmation by the All-Union Congress of Soviets on January 31, 1924. Although the new constitution recognized the right of secession and created both a bicameral assembly system and the Council of Nationalities to safeguard the rights of the nations, it nevertheless represented a major step toward the creation of a single, united and centralized state.

In the soviet case, the realization of a federative state paradoxically brought about the total destruction of genuine federalism. A federation of the various nations of the former multinational Russian Empire—a unique exception in Central and Eastern Europe—was achieved, only to be immediately deformed into a dictatorial centralized power.

Versailles and the Great Powers' Policy of Balkanization

In postwar Europe, the ambitions of small nations and competing nationalisms coincided with great power political goals. Paradoxically, two entirely different types of leader, Lenin and Wilson, had quite similar views on postwar peace settlement. Lenin argued for "peace without annexation" and declared the right for national autonomy, including secession—that is, the right of self-determination. Bolshevik Russia, however, was not a determinant factor in the postwar peace arrangement. In contrast, President Wilson and the newly emerged American great power had a tremendous impact on the peace process, albeit in a different way than had been intended. Wilson entered world politics with a new doctrine of American political interest. Opposing traditional isolationism, he recognized that, in the modern world, international peace was of preeminent American interest, because war in Europe or other continents would endanger American well being. To safeguard international peace, Wilson became an advocate of American leadership. On January 22, 1917, the American president delivered his famous "peace without victory" speech before the Senate. He introduced a concept of a new world order and harshly criticized European imperialism, militarism, and balance-of-power politics that, in his interpretation, had caused the war. The new order would be based on a just and democratic principle, the "right of self-determination," which would guarantee freedom and equal status for all nations, without great power interference, and which would, consequently, create collective security for the free community and "league" of nations. In January 8, 1918, Wilson articulated this concept in a more detailed form in his Fourteen Points address.

Although somewhat utopian and naive, Wilson's principles were nonetheless practical. He maintained, for example, that a total defeat of militarist-expansionist autocratic Germany was one of the main prerequisites for a new world order. Wilson did not seek the destruction of the Austrian and Russian empires, but did grant autonomy for the various nations according to the right of self-determination—a right that he did not believe led necessarily to a deconstruction and balkanization of Central and Eastern Europe.

After its strong initial involvement, the United States withdrew from European politics and peacemaking, thus leaving postwar issues to its European allies, who continued to pursue their traditional imperialistic, balance-of-power politics. Versailles became a peace *with* victory, or as John Maynard Keynes called it, "outrageous and impossible," a "Carthaginian" peace treaty. Lenin expressed the same view: "The imperialist war was followed by an imperialist peace," "a robber peace dictate." The Wilsonian principles were cynically manipulated and applied in a selective way to advance the perceived interests of Britain and France.

French war policy sought to weaken and shrink Germany by any means and to replace the centralized Bismarckian empire by a loose confederation of several German states. These goals were compromised in order to ensure a permanent alliance with Britain and the United States as the main guarantee of French security. As a result, France accepted the existence of a weakened but united Germany. By the spring of 1918, however, Clemenceau developed the idea of dissolving Austria-Hungary, the second major power of the German coalition. In this matter, he was strictly following the French political and military doctrine that sought to construct an alliance surrounding Germany. Because Russia had dropped from the alliance system and the Habsburg Empire had not been split up with Germany, Clemenceau envisioned an alternative eastern barrier in a chain of newly established independent allied countries, especially Poland, Czechoslovakia, and Romania. The right of self-determination therefore served as the leading ideology and slogan of the peace settlement and was used successfully to dissolve Austria-Hungary. The principle was subordinated, however, to strategic and economic considerations in order to strengthen the member states of this new "corridor." As a consequence, Sudetenland with its homogeneous German population was granted to Czechoslovakia, and France supported Polish claims to the entire Upper-Silesia with its rich coal fields. Similarly, vast regions of Hungary with 3 million Hungarians in Transylvania and lower Slovakia and Vojvodina were amputated and given to the newly formed Czechoslovak, Romanian, and Yugoslav states in clear violation of the right to self-determination.

British policy, which followed the traditional balance-of-power doctrine, sought to secure British political interests not only against former enemies but also against former allies. In order to halt overly ambitious French expansionism, Britain joined the United States in defending a united Germany but agreed to the dissolution of Austria-Hungary and the formation of new independent states. The rhetoric was Wilsonian, but the practice remained that of British imperialism: having sought a new balance of power and sphere of influence, Britain manipulated the formation of small nations in Central and Eastern Europe. "Self-determination is quite *démodé*," noted a leading British peacemaker in a letter from the conference. He added: "Leeper and Nicolson [members of the Political Intelligence Department of the British Foreign Office and the British delegation to Versailles] determine for them what they ought to wish, but they do it very well" (Goldstein 1994, 4).

By following their presumed self-interests, victorious great powers of Europe allowed the realization of heretofore elusive national dreams about establishing or reestablishing independent statehood and achieving "small-nation imperialism." Central Europe was seen as a region ripe for political reconstruction. The journal *The New Europe*, edited by Robert Seton-Watson's influential group, spoke of the "*tabula rasa* in Central Europe," and Thomás Masaryk, a member of this group, stated that Europe was "a laboratory sitting atop a vast graveyard" (Goldstein 1994, 4). The experiments began as new countries with new borders were planned and new maps were drafted on the tabula rasa. The door for belated national revolutions was thus opened in postwar Central and Eastern Europe. The small nations, which had attempted fruitlessly to regain their independence during the previous centuries and had revolted after their national awakenings during the nineteenth century—even those nations "without history" who never had enjoyed independent statehood and whose right to self-determination had not been previously recognized—now, easily, could feel that they were the masters of their own destinies and that history was working for them. This misleading mirage reflected a world order in which the center of Europe lacked a direct great power presence. The former ruling nations, now defeated, lost their leading positions, and the new victors did not have the strength or the geographical proximity to dominate. Even the strongest continental nation, France, had nothing but indirect political-diplomatic control over the area. The peoples of the region experienced a unique and temporary power-vacuum that encouraged national aspirations. Thomás Masaryk, the father of Czechoslovak independence, voiced the general belief of the age when he wrote with considerable overconfidence, "Recent political evolution has been favorable to the small peoples. . . . In a new Europe of this kind, the independence of even the smallest national individuality can be safeguarded" (Masaryk 1927, 371). Latvia's representative in Geneva, referring to the Covenant of the League of Nations, similarly stated: "The debate regarding great and small powers is over—the League of Nations has made the equality of states an international dogma" (Peters 1979, 107).

The cause of national revolution thus enjoyed much greater opportunity and more international assistance than the contemporary, adventurous proletarian revolution, which collided head on with the interests of the victorious great powers. Besides, as Zeev Sternhell notes, the war taught that "the concept of class carried less weight, as a factor of solidarity, than the concept of nation. Confronted by the fervor which the idea of nation aroused, the idea of class was shown up in all its artificiality: the nation was a reality, which the International could never aspire to be" (Sternhell 1979, 352). The idea of nation also offered more to those people who conceived all their historic ills, whether social and economic backwardness or autocratic restrictions on liberty, as the product of their frustrated national aspirations. Hence, as a consequence of nineteenth-century national movements and aspirations, an exaggerated expectation developed that the long-awaited resolution of national questions would automatically solve all problems. The national concept also carried in its train the dreams and programs of modernization and the promise of joining the family of advanced and democratic countries of Europe. In most countries of Central and Eastern Europe, belated national revolutions took place in the context of postwar shock and exhaustion. They occurred, in most cases, without uprisings, ushered in through the terms of peace treaties.

The Polish Case

After the partitions of Poland in the late eighteenth century, a heroic and on-going struggle for independence began. Between the 1790s and early 1860s, regardless of previous defeats and bloody repressions, each generation of Poles renewed the struggle. After the crushing of the major uprising in January 1863, however, the chain of uprisings was broken and a half century of subsequent "organic work" partially modernized the still-partitioned country. By the 1890s, during the period of developing European conflict and preparation for war, the Polish national issue reemerged and gained international importance.

Two major centers of Polish independence arose. From the Polish League, which was rooted in the romantic traditions of the uprisings and which had been established in Switzerland in 1887, a new national camp was formed under the leadership of Roman Dmowski. His *Narodowa Demokracja* (National Democratic Party) was established in all three parts of Poland between 1897 and 1905. During the war years, intensive work began to prepare for independence. Dmowski, who left Congress Poland after it was occupied by the Central Powers in 1915, established the Polish National Council (a "government in exile") in August 1917. Located first in Switzerland, the council moved to Paris and was soon recognized by the Entente powers as the representative of Poland. Dmowski built his plans on the assumption that the Entente would defeat Germany and Austria, and the council established a Polish army under the command of General Józef Haller. The original plan for Polish unification under Russian control was gradually replaced by demands for genuine independence and for the reestablishment of a centralized historic Poland that would "Polonize" Germans, Ukrainians, and expatriate "unassimilable" Jews.

A second center was formed around Jósef Piłsudski, who began his political career in the labor movement and, at the age of twenty, was sentenced to five years of exile in Siberia. After his return in 1892, he played an important role in the Polish Social Democratic Party. At the Paris Congress in November of that year, the national question divided the party. The minority, led by Rosa Luxemburg, stressed the international goal of revolution and maintained that the proletarian revolution would automatically solve the national question. The majority of delegates, however, adopted the program of national independence as their first goal (to establish "an independent democratic republic"); only after achieving this first goal would they join the struggle for a proletarian revolution. A split in the party became unavoidable.

Piłsudski, editor of the underground journal *Robotnik* (Worker), emerged as the leader of the national wing. The Russian defeat in the Japanese-Russian war convinced Piłsudski that a Polish insurrection in the framework of international confrontation might lead to victory. He assumed that a confrontation between the Central Powers and Russia would occur, with victory going to the former. In 1910 as international crisis was building and war preparations were beginning, Piłsudski left Russian Poland for Galicia and, although he lacked formal military training, established a paramilitary unit. He began the methodical training of a general staff, officer, and noncommissioned officer corps for a future Polish army. In August 6, 1914, the hour arrived: in the march to Kielce, Piłsudski's "First Brigade," a unit of twenty to twenty-five hundred men, attacked Russian Poland, hoping to generate a Polish uprising in Congress Poland. The uprising did not occur, and the brigade was incorporated as an independent unit into the Austrian First Army, where, under General Dankl, it fought against Russia.

Piłsudski linked German-Austrian war goals and his program for liberating and uniting Poland. This link rested on historical tradition, because the Galician Poles favored the Austro-Polish concept of a trial resurrection of the Austro-Hungarian Empire. During the war, the Central Powers developed a plan for Polish autonomy in order to weaken Russia: the November 5, 1916, Two Emperors' Manifesto declared the creation of a self-governing Kingdom of Poland and called for the establishment of a Polish army. "While the Manifesto was a statement of intentions rather than a political arrangement," notes Piotr Wandycz, "it internationalized the Polish Question to a point of no return. What is more it placed the Poles in a position of being courted by both belligerent camps" (Wandycz 1994, 4).

Piłsudski sought to exploit the situation while remaining free to create a fully independent Poland. The opportunity to realize his plan was suddenly granted after the February revolution in Russia, when the provisional government in Petrograd declared the reestablishment of an autonomous Poland. At this point, Piłsudski turned against Germany and Austria but was arrested and imprisoned in Magdeburg in July 1917.

The Polish national question at this stage of the war, and at the beginning of the preparation of peace, urgently required a solution. In his Fourteen Points, President Wilson made the creation of an independent Polish state one of the requirements for lasting peace in Europe. On September 12, 1917, the emperors of Germany and Austria established a Polish State Council and a Regency Council in Warsaw, which, in turn, appointed Piłsudski *Naczelnik Panstwa* (head of state) in November. The new Polish power soon gained the recognition of the Entente. Its acceptance was closely connected with the French policy that sought the dissolution of Austria-Hungary and the creation of an eastern barrier of relatively small but strong, independent allied countries—a barrier that was to include Poland. The Bolshevik revolution in Russia made the implementation of the French plan much more important. The chain of independent Central and Eastern European countries that was proposed in the French peace settlement would isolate both Germany and Russia. As Lloyd George remarked, "A greater Poland suited French policy—and the greater the better." General Carton de Wiart openly declared that Poland "had been earmarked as a French sphere," and the French did not allow this to be forgotten "for one single instant" (Wandycz 1962, 39, 25). President Wilson commented that France sought to dominate Central and Eastern Europe and that "the only, real interest of France in Poland is in weakening Germany by giving Poland territory to which she has no right" (Wandycz 1994, 14).

Though great power rivalry created a climate in which the reestablishment of a united Poland could occur, the activities of the masses, led by an enthusiastic, nationalist elite, also played a decisive role. In Poland, powerful mass movements opened a new chapter in the struggle for independence and accomplished the national revolution. The first significant action was the armed uprising in Poznan that engulfed all of Prussian Poland. The various irregular revolutionary groups were soon united into a regular army of seventy thousand soldiers that liberated the province. About 350,000 ethnic Germans left the region for Germany, which caused their percentage in Prussian Poland to drop from over 38 percent to 16 percent. In Upper Silesia, three consecutive uprisings in 1919, 1920, and 1921 decided the fate of the region. At the eastern frontier, the Polish national army invaded Vilno and Suwalki in the spring of 1919, and the armed struggle continued through 1920 and 1921. During the Polish national uprisings and war for liberation, 250,000 Poles lost their life.

The new Polish political elite, which was divided into two main political camps headed by Dmowski and Piłsudski, reached a temporary agreement in the critical year of 1919. Piłsudski remained the head of state, Ignacy Paderewski, the outstanding pianist and diplomat, became prime minister and held the portfolio of foreign affairs, and Dmowski represented Poland at the peace conference. This agreement meant the defeat of Dmowsi's right-wing, aggressive nationalism and the victory of Piłsudski's democratic line. The former socialist became the virtual dictator of the newly born country—but, as he told friends and followers later as he was withdrawing from public life, "I was a dictator only for a few months" (Piłsudski 1936, 138). The uncrowned dictator wanted the new Polish state to be a democracy. He was deeply convinced that "in Poland of the twentieth century a democratically elected *Sejm* [parliament] can be the only source of law" (Piłsudski 1936, 45). Accordingly, on January 26, 1919, he held elections for a constitutional assembly and, on February 20, handed over power to the newly-elected *Sejm*. Despite handing over that power, Piłsudski continued to steer his country's course: he was confirmed in his office as head of state, and on March 19, his name-day, he was made first marshal of Poland. Until the spring of 1923, he was commander-in-chief of the Polish army, and he crowned his mission as founding father of his country by personally leading his troops against Soviet Russia in the spring of 1920. The peace treaty, signed in Riga on March 18, 1921, enlarged Poland by the occupation of Vilno (Wilna, Vilnius) and shifted the eastern border of Poland to the River Zbrucz, roughly 120 miles east from the Curson-line, which had been accepted by the Allied Powers in the summer of 1920 as the western border of Russia.

The new Polish constitution of March 1921 was inspired by the examples of Western democratic constitutions: it established the constitutional framework of a parliamentary democracy with a bicameral system and declared certain democratic and human rights, including equal rights for the more than 30 percent minority population. Presidential power was strictly limited, and a document became official only if, in addition to the president, the prime minister and the minister of the given portfolio signed it. Article 46 of the constitution made the president commander of the army, but it also stopped him from actually exercising the command in wartime. The legislature became supreme, and presidential power was transformed into a mere formality

The right-wing opposition to Piłsudski attempted to block his power. When the first presidential elections were held in December 1922, Piłsudski refused even to be nominated. His close ally and friend, Gabriel Narutowicz, was elected but assassinated by a right-wing fanatic at the opening of an exhibition in Warsaw a week later. A new government was formed by an ally and rival of Piłsudski, General Wladislaw Sikorski, but on May 28, 1923, after only a few months, a centrum and right-wing coalition took over. That was too much for Piłsudski,who resigned all his military posts in protest and retired from public life to his country home in Sulejowek.

Between 1918 and 1921, victorious national revolution helped a united Poland to reappear, created from lands formerly under Russian, German, and Austrian rule. New territories were gained and the new nation-state, with an area of 388,000 square kilometers and 27 million inhabitants, became one of the largest countries of Europe. The ethnic and religious composition of the country, however, was far from homogenous. Only 69 percent of the population was Polish; more than 14 percent was Ukrainian, roughly 8 percent was Jewish, almost 4 percent was Byelorussian, and nearly another 4 percent was German. The legal foundation for a parliamentary democracy had been laid, but a difficult economic situation, social conflicts, and a sharp power struggle among the new elite led to further turmoil.

The Independent Baltic States

The Baltic people, like their counterparts in Central and Eastern Europe, achieved independent nationhood. The success of their struggles for independence was guaranteed not only by the war and its conclusion, which brought the collapse of German expansionism and the crisis in the tsarist empire, but also by the policy of the victorious great powers, which wished to establish a chain of independent, allied countries as a *cordon sanitaire*, an eastern barrier between Germany and Russia.

The road toward independence was opened during the German occupation of the region from the spring of 1915 onward. The German high command flirted with the Baltic national issue in the spring of 1916, when it founded the League of Non-Russian Peoples and Bethmann-Holweg suggested creating autonomous countries under German patronage. An agreement was reached about this policy in July 1917 at Bingen. National committees, such as the Lithuanian *Taryba* (Council) were founded under German auspices, and Lithuania declared independence and its alliance with Germany on December 11, 1917. Germany recognized Lithuanian independence by the terms of the Treaty of Brest-Litovsk on March 23, 1918. Similar events occurred in Baltic territories under Russian control, where the provisional government in Petrograd granted autonomy to Estonia and part of Latvia. A provincial assembly, the *Maapäev*, was elected in Estonia in May 1917.

Although these steps were taken to secure Russian and German rule in the "autonomous" countries, they launched Baltic independence. The national movement became unstoppable. Estonia declared full independence on February 24, 1918, and Latvia followed in November. Both nations were officially recognized in a few weeks by the Allied governments. Although German and Bolshevik Russian occupation followed, Allied assistance was firm: the British sent the Royal Navy in support, and the presence of warships at Tallin coupled with the Allied military missions that were set up in the spring of 1919 clearly expressed Western interests in defending the autonomy of the region. Lord Curzon, the British foreign secretary, charged General Hubert Gough, the head of the military mission, with trying "to establish our influence in the countries between Germany and Russia" (Gough 1954, 191). "British politicians," notes John Hiden, "were talking of 'an old fashioned quarantine guaranteeing against infection.' In reality, this was directed as much against Germany as it was [against Bolshevik Russia]" (Hiden 1988, 373). The Baltic forces were equipped and reorganized by the Allies and played the leading role in the last stage of their war of independence in 1919. Estonian troops under Major-General Podder forced the Germans to withdraw, and the Estonian victory was recognized in the armistice of Strazdumuiza in early July 1919. Similarly, the Estonian army under General Tönisson successfully defended Estonian lines against a Bolshevik offensive, and an armistice agreement was signed in December 1919, then followed by the peace treaty of February 1920. Latvian armed forces under national leadership fought against both the Bolshevik and White Russian armies. In alliance with Poland, Latvia attacked Russia in January 1920 and liberated Latgale. An armistice of February 1920 was followed by the peace treaty of Riga in August, which guaranteed Latvian independence. Meanwhile Lithuania, after heavy fights in late summer and early fall of 1919, began peace negotiations with Bolshevik Russia in May 1920 and signed a treaty in July of that year. The "*de jure* recognition of the Baltic states was delayed," notes a study of the Royal Institute of International Affairs, "owing to the persistent hope entertained by the Allied Powers . . . that the Bolshevik regime might yet be destroyed. The Powers would have liked . . . to preserve a territorially indivisible Russia" (*Survey* 1938, 27).

In the end, however, the small independent Baltic nation-states were established: Estonia with 1.1 million, Lithuania with just under 2 million, and Latvia with just over 2 million inhabitants in the early 1920s. Together these three republics possessed territories roughly three times larger than Holland—Latvia alone was slightly larger than Holland—but they possessed a Baltic population only two-thirds that of Holland. The reestablished Baltic states hurried to reintroduce traditional national symbols. The Estonians borrowed a coat of arms from late-thirteenth-century knighthood. The Lithuanians adopted a thirteenth-century emblem consisting of a white knight bearing a sword and a cross on his shield. The Latvians used the traditional Livonian griffin and the lion of Courland.

In general, the new states were not ethnically homogeneous. Only Estonia possessed a relatively homogeneous population (nearly 88 percent Estonian). Both Latvia and Lithuania had significant minorities— more than 24 percent and 16 percent respectively. The Baltic Germans in both Estonia and Latvia, though not numerous, were still influential, especially in large cities such as Riga, Tallin, and Tartu. The Russian minorities (more than 8 percent in Estonia and nearly 8 percent in Latvia), the Jewish communities in Latvia (5 percent) and Lithuania (nearly 8 percent), and the Polish minorities in Latvia and Lithuania (roughly 3 percent each) created an ethnic mix of explosive character.

The new Baltic republics attempted to follow the pattern of Western nation-states by adopting their value system, writing Western-style constitutions, and establishing parliamentary democracies. All three countries introduced unicameral parliaments with elections based on a universal, equal franchise and direct and secret ballots. The Estonian Declaration of Independence declared the introduction of "general, direct, secret, and proportional elections, . . . equal protection under law and courts of justice [to all citizens], . . . cultural autonomy [to minorities, and] . . . civic freedoms" (*Declaration* 1974, 170–72). In April 1919, the first free elections in Estonia installed a constituent assembly, which ratified a new constitution in the summer of 1920 and thereby established parliamentary power. The parliament (*Riigikogu*) held all the power, and the government was a kind of parliamentary commission. The senior statesman (*Riigivanem*) served both as premier and as ceremonial head-of-state. Laws were enacted by the parliament, which also had the right to appoint a commander-in-chief. Dissolution of the parliament could occur only by referendum. In Latvia, a constituent assembly was elected in May 1920. The new constitution, which was enacted in November 1922, combined elements from the Swiss, French, and Weimar constitutions. The ultimate power went to the parliament (*Saeima*), which enjoyed the right to elect a president who also served as commander-in-chief. The Lithuanian Constituent Assembly was democratically elected in April 1920 and passed a new constitution in August 1922. Here, too, the parliament (*Seimas*) became the supreme authority, and the president was a figurehead. Indeed, the desire for democracy was in the air: "Everyone saw salvation only in democracy.

It was the alpha and omega of political wisdom. Like a sort of holy spirit, democracy was expected to enlighten the masses with political wisdom" (Vardys 1979, 320). All three countries guaranteed freedom of speech and of the press, religion, and conscience. Minorities gained far-reaching rights; in Estonia, they gained free choice of national identification, education in the minority's mother tongue, and a cultural autonomy that, according to the Royal Institute of International Affairs, "had no equal in Europe." The institute qualifies this assessment, however, by noting the fact "that democratic institutions, as operated during the period of parliamentary government . . . never functioned properly" and caused the "state of parliamentary atrophy" (*Baltic States* 1938, 43–44).

The political structure and party formation were similar in all the Baltic countries, but the parallels were especially notable in Estonia and Latvia. The Farmers' Union in Estonia, headed by Konstantin Päts and Johan Laidoner, and the Peasant League in Latvia, led by Karlis Ulmanis and General Balodis, were conservative nationalist parties, whereas the Left was represented by strong social-democratic parties. Communist parties were banned in Estonia after the 1924 coup but participated in national elections under various pseudonyms. In the center, nationalist liberal parties led by intellectuals played a leading role: the Estonian Peoples' Party under Jaan Tönisson or the Democratic Center in Latvia are examples. In Lithuania, the Christian Democrats represented agrarian interests with the National Party, whose ranks included the most important politicians in Lithuania—individuals such as Antanas Smetona and Augustinas Voldemaras.

Land reforms were the first and most important legislative actions enacted by the new Baltic legislatures. An Estonian land expropriation law of October 1919 destroyed the great estates and expropriated 98 percent of them to create more than fifty-six thousand new small holdings (more than doubling their number). The Lithuanian land reform of March 1922 fixed the size of private farms at 150 hectares (roughly 380 acres). The Latvian land reform in September 1920 expropriated more than one thousand large estates and created new farms from 22 percent of those lands while leaving 35 percent of the land, mostly forests, in state ownership.

Although radical land reforms resulted, in some cases, from the new democratic representation that, in the early years of independence, ensured a majority rule by coalitions of socialist, social democratic, and radical democratic parties, various peasant agrarian parties also played an important role. In fact the vast majority of the new political elite in the Baltic nations stemmed from peasant communities and represented their interests. But if these democratic and agrarian interests tended to support land reform in nations such as Estonia, so too did nationalist sentiments. Most large estates in the Baltic region had belonged to economically powerful, ethnic minority groups of Baltic Germans, Russians, and Poles. Nationalist goals could thus also favor the transfer of land from minority ethnic groups to the majority group, as happened in Lithuania. In all these countries, land reform proved an easy goal when independent states were emerging. But the merger between agrarian reform and nationalism eventually proved lethal to multiparty parliamentary democracy and social reform legislation, because they were quickly subordinated to more purely nationalist goals, which proved to be short-lived in the Baltic region. "Each started with an ultra-democratic Constitution, and each . . . passed through a phase of dictatorship" (*Baltic States* 1938, 41).

The Making of Czechoslovakia

Although the Polish and Baltic national revolutions aimed at reconstituting formerly independent states, national movements in other parts of Central and Eastern Europe led to the formation of entirely new states with no tradition of unity or independence. This occurred in the case of the northwestern and southeastern "brotherly" Slavic peoples, who formed the relatively small, new multinational states of Czechoslovakia and Yugoslavia.

By the end of the nineteenth century, the Czech national movement had reached the mature stage of an organized political mass movement, but it preserved the cautiousness and moderation that had characterized it from its incipience. Before World War I, motivated by fear of German designs on Bohemia, Czech nationalists attempted to gain extensive autonomy within the Austro-Hungarian Monarchy and to effect the Dual Monarchy's "trialistic" (Austrian-Hungarian-Slav) reorganization. Despite the inherent cautiousness of the movement, there had been signs of a trend toward radicalization even at the end of the nineteenth century—signs such as the popularity of the Young Czech movement.

The Slovaks in Northern Hungary originally had even more limited goals than the Czechs, because Slovakia had never existed as an independent country. The national movement did not reach its higher, separatist stage until the war. In spite of intellectual forerunners such as Bernolák, Havlíček, Srobar and his *Hlas* group, Milan Stefanik, and a few others, "Czechoslovakism" had an even less vigorous history, and a Czechoslovak movement barely existed. The masses were not mobilized by the concept of "a Czechoslovak nation in two branches," in which, as Stefanik stated, "the Czechs are Slovaks who speak Czech, and . . . the Slovaks are Czechs who speak Slovak" (Zacek 1969, 191). The few Slovak students who studied in Prague and established their *Československá Jednota* (Czechoslovak Association) at the turn of the century could not initiate a mass movement.

Yet a merged Czech and Slovak national movement gained momentum during World War I. Its history is inseparable from the role of its charismatic leader, Thomás Masaryk, the influential professor of sociology and liberal-democratic Czech nationalist member of the Austrian *Reichsrat* (Parliament), who was head of the Realists Party. Masaryk was convinced that the Entente would win the war, and he recognized the political opportunity to be gained through alliance with the presumed victors. In the fall of 1914, while walking in the old streets of Prague with his close ally, Eduard Benes, Masaryk broached the issue of gaining Czech independence and the tactics needed to achieve it. In a few weeks, he left Austria-Hungary for the West. In a few months, Benes followed him, and the two men began energetic organizational and propaganda activity. In April 1915, in a memorandum to the British and French governments, Masaryk argued for the establishment of an independent Czechoslovakia. In September, Masaryk and Benes founded the Czech Foreign Committee, which gained broad recognition from various Czech immigrant groups in the West. In February 1916, the committee was reorganized as the Czechoslovak National Council with the participation of Milan Stefanik, a Slovak émigré.

Masaryk recognized that a Czech army that could join the Entente to defeat the Central Powers would strengthen the bargaining position of the council. The opportunity to create a military organization was provided when Czech soldiers, including two entire regiments, deserted during the massive Russian offensive. In early 1915, Masaryk set up a Czech division, the *Druzhina*, which was placed under the operational command of the Russian army. In May 1917, Masaryk went to Russia, where, in discussions with the provisional government, he agreed to organize a Czech legion to be recruited from Czech and Slovak prisoners of war. The new Czech forces were to fight with the Entente army. In August 1917, Benes gained French authorization for this plan and the legion began expanding: in October, it numbered thirty thousand men and grew to roughly ninety thousand by the end of the war. A second Czech legion was organized in Italy. After the Bolshevik revolution, the Czech legion in Siberia fought against the Red Army, occupying Penza and Kazan, and assuming control of the strategically important Trans-Siberian railway. The unit's considerable service against the revolution—besides symbolizing the conflict between the class and national revolutions—significantly helped the Czechoslovak cause of independence. In the summer and early fall of 1918, the Entente powers recognized the Czechoslovak National Council as a government in exile. President Poincaré declared at the Versailles Peace Conference that "in Siberia, France and Italy, the Czechoslovaks have conquered their right to independence" (Masaryk 1927, 265).

Masaryk, Benes, and Stefanik also worked successfully together for a general recognition of the various Czech and Slovak emigrant organizations in the West. American Czech and Slovak organizations met in Cleveland as early as October 25, 1915, and approved the demand for "independence of the Czech lands and Slovakia" and for "the union in a confederation of the Czech and Slovak nations." Masaryk arrived in Pittsburgh, met with the leaders of these organizations on May 30, 1918, and signed an agreement that declared: "We approve of the political program which aims at the union of the Czechs and Slovaks in an independent state composed of the Czech Lands and Slovakia. Slovakia shall have her own administrative system, her own diet and her own courts. The Slovak language shall be the official language in the schools, in public offices and in public affairs generally" (Lettrich 1955, 289–90).

Beside the agreement with the Slovak emigrant leaders, Masaryk achieved another major diplomatic success with the Ruthenian emigrant organization. A Ruthenian National Council was formed by Ruthenian immigrants in the United States and declared its separation from Hungary at a July 1918 meeting in Homestead, Pennsylvania. Gregory Zhatkovich, the president of the council, turned to President Wilson for support and was advised by the latter to join the Czechoslovak state. Although the Ruthenians were not related either ethnically or linguistically to the Czechs and Slovaks and no national movement to join them existed, nevertheless, on October 26, 1918, Zhatkovich and Masaryk signed an agreement in Philadelphia to join the autonomous unit of Transcarpathia to the Czechoslovak state. Thus, the outlines of a new state were determined. But still missing was a spectacular endorsement, a revolutionary declaration at home of Czech independence. This soon followed.

The overly cautious, moderate national leadership in Prague was replaced by a militant group in the spring of 1918. Karel Kramař, the renowned leader of the Young Czech movement who had just been released from an Austrian prison, became the leader of the *Národny Vybor* (National Committee). Public discontent had become visible in January, when a series of strikes were organized. In July, all the parties joined a national council, and on October 14, a general strike took place. After the announcement of the unconditional surrender of Austria-Hungary, the Czech National Council declared independence: "We have thrown off the chains of slavery. We have risen to independence. With our unbreakable will and with the sanction of the whole democratic world, we declare that we are standing here today as executors of a new state sovereignty, as citizens of a free Czechoslovak Republic" (Lettrich 1955, 288–89). Two days later, in the famous Martin Declaration, the Slovak National Council announced that "the Slovak nation is a part of the Czecho-Slovak nation, united in language and in the history of its culture" and declared that the Slovaks would join the new independent Czechoslovakia (*Declaration* 1955, 289–90). In Stara Lubovna, a Ruthenian national council was formed, and on November 8, 1918, it declared the separation of Ruthenia from Hungary. "The work abroad was decisive," stated Masaryk on the foundation of the Czechoslovak state, but, he added with an evident exaggeration, "this work was rendered possible by the general resistance of the people at home to Austria-Hungary, and by the revolution after Vienna had capitulated to President Wilson" (Masaryk 1927, 367).

A map of Czechoslovakia was ultimately designed in the back rooms at the Paris Peace Conference. Masaryk and Benes attained all their goals in a masterful fashion. Using an argument from history, they restored old medieval frontiers in the northwest, incorporating more than three million ethnic Germans and nearly one hundred thousand ethnic Poles in the Sudetenland and Silesia. In the southeast, they were no such historical precedents, and thus they defended ethnic-national arguments against Hungarian rule, thereby incorporating more than seven hundred thousand Hungarians into the new nation. With nearly 140,400 square kilometers and 13.6 million inhabitants, Czechoslovakia proudly embodied the Wilsonian principle of self-determination for the region, breaking a nearly four-hundred-year-old tradition of Habsburg rule in Czech lands and a millennium of Hungarian domination in Slovakia. In the meantime, the structure of the new nation denied the same principle for the German, Hungarian, and Polish minorities, which represented nearly 30 percent of the population.

The roughly 6.5 million Czechs, more than 2.2 million Slovaks, and about 0.5 million Ruthenians in this common state had rather different images of their "marriage." Some believed firmly in "Czechoslovakism" and that the process of nation building in the twentieth century could create a united nation just as it had in the West a few centuries before. Most Czechs, however, thought that national homogenization should occur under their leadership within a centralized state. Even Masaryk, although a genuine democrat, held steadfastly to the vision that "Slovaks are Czechs despite the fact that they use their dialect as a literary language" (Kann and Zdenek 1984, 391). The majority of both the Slovak and Ruthenian political elite, however, desired autonomous status in a federal republic. Moreover, other national groups that were incorporated into the Czechoslovak state did not give up aspiring to rejoin their neighboring *Vaterland*. Multinational Czechoslovakia thus was extremely vulnerable to the burning national and minority issues.

Yet the founding fathers strongly believed that a prosperous, democratic, Western-type Czechoslovakia would cope with these initial difficulties. Although they rejected cantonization and federalization as alien to the envisioned Czechoslovak nation, they nevertheless established a democratic parliamentary system. The new constitution of February 1920 created a bicameral system consisting of a three-hundred-member parliament and a one-hundred-and-fifty-member senate elected according to a modified system of proportional representation which reserved a strong role for party leaders in deciding how seats were to be filled. Although the constitution was based on the British model, certain elements of the French and American systems were also incorporated. For example, the president was elected by a joint session of the two legislative houses (as in France) but enjoyed significant executive power (as in the United States). The post was designed for Thomás Masaryk, who was unanimously elected president by the first Constituent National Assembly in November 1918 and then reelected by the first National Assembly in May 1920. The democratic political system guaranteed extensive liberties and human rights. The republic was a *Rechtsstaat*, a constitutional state that guaranteed freedom of press, speech, and assembly. Czechoslovakia was the only country in the region where even the Communist Party acquired full legality and parliamentary representation.

The national revolution attempted to satisfy democratically not only political and ethnic needs but also basic social demands. Between 1919 and 1923, a powerful labor movement developed that caused strikes in over fifteen thousand companies and resulted in a loss of almost thirteen million working days. The general strike of December 10, 1920, developed into a bloody battle in three places and claimed the lives of thirteen people. The Czechoslovak government not only suppressed the violence that endangered the young republic, but also tried to satisfy the masses. Masaryk himself admitted that the capitalist social system was one-sided and, therefore, had to be eliminated. On the first anniversary of the founding of the republic, he warned that, in the process of socialization, "one must keep carefully in mind the special qualities of the individual and the nation," but he also recognized the need for nationalization. Karel Englis, a distinguished economist and cabinet minister, stated in the fall of 1920, "We will socialize the country together with the socialists, and we do it gladly. The Russian bourgeoisie failed to understand this and was, therefore, swept away." Even the right-of-center nationalist Karel Kramař said, "Mankind is, indeed, moving toward socialization" (Korbel 1977, 52, 60).

Although "socialization" did not take place, the government introduced important welfare measures. During the first five years of its existence, the parliament enacted 157 bills, introducing the eight-hour workday, retirement pensions, paid holidays, and social security. First in mines and then in industrial firms, over thirty workers' councils were legalized; these councils were authorized to supervise the social welfare system, to hire and fire, to supervise company books, and to mediate in disputes between workers and management. At the end of 1922, an unemployment benefit scheme was introduced that paid 20 percent of the daily wage, an amount higher, at that time, than in England, Germany, or France. In 1925, this percentage was raised to two-thirds of the daily wage, half of which was contributed by the government. Under an extensive housing program, more new homes were built during the 1920s than in the course of the preceding forty years. The Czechoslovak national revolution thus established a social welfare democracy, the only one of its type in Central and Eastern Europe.

The Making of Yugoslavia

In its earliest stage, the South Slavic national revolution created a common Serbo-Croat literary language and also nurtured the

"Yugo-slav" (South Slavic) or "Illirian" idea of unifying the various Slavic peoples of the Balkans. Although King Michael's plan for a co-ordinated Balkan revolt and the establishment of a Yugoslav Kingdom in 1867, a year before his assassination, was closely linked with emerging Serbian nationalism and independence, *Jugoslavenstvo*, the Yugoslav idea, appeared more militantly among the Slavs of Austria-Hungary. In its first stage, this movement sought cooperation among Serbs, Croats, Slovenes, and other South Slavic people within Austria-Hungary. Anton Tomšič and Josip Jurčič's *Slovenski Narod* (Slovene nation) announced this goal in 1868 and a "Yugoslav Congress" was held in Ljubljana in 1870. The Yugoslav movement, however, developed primarily in the early twentieth century. As Ivo Lederer notes, after the Bosnian crisis, *Slovenski Jug* (Slovene Youth), *Mlada Bosna* (Young Bosnia), *Ujedinjenje ili Smrt* (Unification or Death), and several other south Slavic societies,

shared two points in common: hatred of Austria-Hungary and the vision of an eventually united Yugoslav state. . . . By 1911, spurred by pro-Yugoslav currents in Croatia, Slovenia, Montenegro, and particularly in Dalmatia, Beograd, with the blessing of St. Petersburg, set out to realize earlier Serbian dreams of a Balkan concert. The new alliance produced dramatic results, and the triumph of Serbian arms in 1912–13 lent credence to Serbia's mission as the Piedmont of the South Slavs. (Lederer 1969, 428)

Ironically, the push for Serbian leadership and the establishment of a Yugoslav state emerged in Croatia, Slovenia, and Bosnia. Nikola Pašić, the charismatic Serbian nationalist leader and prime minister, was an advocate of Greater Serbia and supported the cause of liberating Serbs who lived outside the kingdom in places such as Bosnia. The Bosnian Serb national movement strove toward the same goal, a fact that motivated their extremists to assassinate Archduke Franz Ferdinand, who was advocating a "trialistic" reorganization of the Dual Monarchy. When Gavrilo Prinzip shot the archduke in Sarajevo, his act blocked those South Slavic national goals that demanded autonomy inside the Habsburg Empire.

The Yugoslav movement gained momentum in Austria-Hungary, where the traditional Croatian national movement, which had sought to gain autonomy in cooperation with Hungary, was challenged by the energetic work of Franjo Supilo, a Dalmatian Croat. Supilo initiated the Fiume Congress in 1905 and fostered the collaboration between Croats and Serbs within Austria-Hungary. When World War I broke out, the Croatian "Yugoslavists" recognized the opportunity and left the Dual Monarchy for Allied territory. Supilo, together with Ante Trumbić and Ivan Meštrović, established a Yugoslav Committee in London in 1915. It had three Slovene delegates as well. The committee called for the dissolution of Austria-Hungary and the foundation of an independent Yugoslav state. The Yugoslav movement was particularly strong in Slovenia, where whole military units deserted on the Russian front and the Austrian authorities sought to halt mass resistance by executing several hundred Slovenes for "political crimes." In contrast, in Croatia the demand was for autonomy rather than for an independent Yugoslavia. When the *Reichsrat* gathered in the spring of 1917, the South Slav delegates issued their May Declaration, which demanded the creation of an autonomous body of all South Slavs living in the Dual Monarchy.

The turning point was reached in the summer of 1917, when the Yugoslav Committee organized its Korfu meeting. Because Pašić and his government had been exiled to Korfu after the Bulgarian invasion and lost his powerful patron, tsarist Russia, Pašić yielded in his opposition to the creation of a Yugoslav state. An agreement was forged, and the Korfu Declaration, which demanded a united, unified, and independent Yugoslavia, was drawn up and ratified on July 20, 1917. Pašić's dream of a Great Serbia was replaced by a Serbian-led Yugoslavia, structured as a constitutional monarchy under the Serbian Karadjordjevič dynasty.

By 1918, the initial demand for autonomy was changed to one of full independence at home as well as abroad. In the summer, a Yugoslav Democratic Party was founded in Slovenia and large mass demonstrations in Ljubljana demanded an independent Yugoslav state. In Zagreb, a national council of Slovenes, Croats, and Serbs was established, and on October 29, 1918, the *Sabor*, the Croatian parliament, declared the dissolution of the union with Hungary and the foundation of a "State of the Slovenes, Croats, and Serbs." The provisional government of the South Slav peoples of Austria-Hungary announced the creation of the new state to the Entente on October 31. Negotiations began with Serbia on the formation of a federal state, but, in the difficult military situation, the council voted for a unitary state and invited Prince Alexander to become its regent. The Serbian army entered Zagreb on December 1, 1918. Meanwhile, Montenegro's assembly deposed King Nicholas and proclaimed a union with Serbia, which was ratified by both the Serbian *Skuptšina* (Parliament), and the Zagreb council. On December 1, 1918, Prince-Regent Alexander proclaimed the union of Serbia with the independent "State of the Slovenes, Croats, and Serbs," and thus the "Kingdom of Serbs, Croats, and Slovenes" (later renamed as Yugoslavia) was created.

Unlike the Czechoslovak state, Yugoslavia was established six weeks before peace talks began in Paris. It was not created as a result of extensive diplomatic activity in the Allied countries, but was created as a fait accompli at home, based on the leadership of the independent, strong Serbian "Big Brother." The talks at Versailles, however, produced the finishing touches to the new arrangement and settled the debates and previous violence over border questions with Italy, Romania, Austria, and Hungary. The Yugoslav demands were harshly opposed by Italy, whose government sought to actualize the provisions of the secret London Treaty, in which Dalmatia and Istria, along with the port city of Trieste, were promised to Italy in return for its support of the Allies. At last, Italy gained large areas in Istria and Dalmatia. Romania, in turn, expected to received the entire Banat, an area that it had been promised by the 1916 secret Treaty of Bucharest. Instead, the region was divided between Romania and Hungary along ethnic lines. In the end, an ethnically, culturally, and religiously pluralistic Yugoslavia of nearly 249,000 square kilometers and almost 12 million inhabitants was established. The nearly 9 million Yugoslavs consisted of Serbs and Montenegrins (43 percent), Croats (23 percent), Slovenes (less than 9 percent), Bosnians (6 percent), and Macedonians (5 percent). In addition, roughly one-half million Germans, Hungarians, Albanians, and "others" lived in the country. Ethnicity and religion did not necessarily correlate, although the Serbs were mostly Greek Orthodox (5.6 million), the Croats and Slovenes were primarily Catholic (4.7 million), and the Bosnians and Albanians were Muslim (1.3 million).The presence of a minority Protestant group (0.3 million) made the ethnic-religious diversity even more complex and subject to stress. Although the majority's mother tongue was Serbo-Croat, the eastern regions used the Cyrillic alphabet, whereas the western regions used the Latin alphabet. No other country in Europe—except the Soviet Union, which had preserved the old multinational empire—possessed such a diverse population.

Whether the new state would be constituted as a federal republic or as a unitary nation was not decided in 1918. Two major concepts were considered. A federalist structure was advocated by the Croats, especially by the Croatian Peasant Party of Stjepan Radić, and a centralized, unitary, extended Serbian-led Yugoslavia was envisioned by the Serbs, in alignment with Pašić's Radical Party and the prime minister. The elections in November 1920 for a constitutional assembly extended the franchise to all males over the age of twenty-one, except Germans and Hungarians. Although twenty-two parties competed, election results reflected a strict ethnic-religious division: the three leading Serbian parties gained nearly 44 percent, the Croatian parties nearly 20 percent, and the Bosnian Muslim Party 7 percent of the votes. Harsh political struggles occurred, and Radić's Croatian Peasant Party sought to block the road to centralism; in spring 1919, the Croatian nationalist leader had collected enough signatures for an appeal to the Allied powers to reestablish Croatian independence, and he pursued this anti-centralist course after the election. In response, Pašić prepared a draft for a centralist constitution and submitted it to the Constitutional Assembly on January 1, 1921. The draft proposed the destruction of the historical-national-minority framework by subordinating it to the framework of a centralized state. On this basis, an April 1922 administrative law introduced thirty-three *oblast* (administrative territorial units), each with a maximum population of eight hundred thousand people. The tiny units were intended to prevent grouping along national lines. The Serbs thus sought to destroy the historic-ethnic framework that had promoted separatism and to foster the emergence of a Yugoslav nation. Another significant guarantee of centralism was provided by the strong position of the Serbian king, who gained the rights to control the army and to choose the prime minister of the new constitutional monarchy. Pašić and the Karadjordjević king—like Thomás Masaryk and Eduard Benes in Czechoslovakia—believed firmly in the possibility of creating a Yugoslav nation from the various ethnic-religious groups. They thought that success was only a question of time and of the thorough suppression of the opposition.

Despite this attitude, the constitutional monarchy was built on democratic principles. The unicameral parliament (*Skuptšina*) was based on proportional representation. All religions and human rights were recognized, and the two alphabets gained equal official status. Local autonomy was granted. Nonetheless, the Act of August 1921 provided a legal basis for harsh repressions against persons, parties, and movements that were considered by state authorities to endanger "security and order." This law quickly became an instrument that was used against the opposition.

The Serb proposal to create a unified Yugoslav nation provoked a sharp Croatian response: Radić and 161 Croatian deputies walked out of the Constitutional Assembly, which, in their absence, easily passed the centrist "Vidovdan Constitution" on June 28, 1921. Its Article 126 created an effective legal guarantee against any changes by requiring a 60 percent majority for constitutional amendments. In response, Croat nationalists, who did not accept the concept of a Yugoslav nation and refused to amalgamate to it, began their crusade to build a Croatian nation. A permanent and dramatic Serbo-Croat conflict emerged, which undermined the peaceful and democratic development of Yugoslavia.

Making a Great Romania

After the unification of the so-called Romanian Principalities in 1861 and the foundation of the Romanian Kingdom in 1866, millions of Romanians still lived outside the country in Habsburg-ruled Bukovina, in Russian-dominated Bessarabia, and, most of all, in Hungarian-owned Transylvania. Transylvanian Romanians, who emerged in the late eighteenth century as the main carriers of Romanian national consciousness, initiated the first cultural-linguistic stage of the Romanian national movement, and developed the romantic Daco-Roman historical concept and supporting political arguments, becoming the prime movers of the late-nineteenth-century national mass movement. But they did not seek, at this stage, to join the Romanian Kingdom. The tradition of the famous *Supplex libellus Valachorum* of 1791—the petition that demanded that the Transylvanian diet recognize Romanians as a fourth nation of Transylvania, equal to the Hungarians, Saxons, and Seklers, with proportional representation in the administration— remained alive throughout the nineteenth century. During the on-going struggle for recognition, Romanians focused on establishing within Transylvania an equal status for Romanian ethnic groups (55 percent of the population of Transylvania in 1910), the Romanian language, and the Orthodox Church. When the first Romanian political party, the National Party, was founded in 1881, it called only for the restoration of Transylvanian autonomy, which had been abandoned in 1865 when the Transylvanian Diet approved the union with Hungary. The Romanian government in Bucharest also did not seek unification with the Transylvanian Romanians. In Bukovina, both the Romanian National Party— which controlled the province's diet—and the Romanian society at large remained loyal to the Habsburg Monarchy and demanded neither independence nor union with the Romanian Kingdom.

In fact, the Romanian national movements outside Romania did not develop goals beyond the traditional demand for autonomy within Austria-Hungary until World War I. Alexander Vaida-Voevod, one of the most prominent Transylvanian Romanian leaders, supported the traditional view when he stated in January 1913 that the idea of a Daco-Roman Empire that would unite all Romanians was nothing more than a "beer-table fantasy." He called for a strong Habsburg Monarchy but challenged its dualistic Austro-Hungarian arrangement, urging "a strong hand and a powerful will" to reorganize it. In the early twentieth century, the Romanians in Austria-Hungary preferred a "trial" reorganization of the monarchy as a guarantor of equal rights and protection against Hungarian oppression. But grotesque plans for unifying all Romanians also emerged along this line. Nicholas Filipescu, the Romanian minister of war, developed the idea of linking Romania and Transylvania by joining Romania to the Habsburg Empire. Under this plan, the Romanian king would have occupied the same position under Habsburg rule as the King of Bavaria in united Germany. Aurel Popovici, a Transylvanian nationalist, sought to transmit this plan to Archduke Francis Ferdinand in 1911. Aurel Onciul, the Romanian leader in Bukovina, also supported this plan when he declared as late as June 1917 that all Romanians should unite and that Romanian territories inside and outside the Habsburg Empire should be subsumed within it. Similar plans were advocated by Constantin Stere, the influential Bessarabian-Romanian politician who was often called the éminence grise of the Liberal Party, and who, after the death of Emperor Francis Joseph, issued a newspaper to propagate a personal union with Austria under Emperor Charles or his infant son.

But all these plans soon evaporated. As Robert Seton-Watson, the most influential foreign advocate of the Romanian case, observes, "The murder of the archduke at Sarajevo on 28 June 1914 was at once realized as a deadly blow to hopes of peaceful evolution. Nowhere did it cause greater consternation than among the Roumanians, on both sides of the Carpathians" (R. Seton-Watson 1963, 471).

Nonetheless, the assassination in Sarajevo turned out to be a most fortunate event for Romania. Hugh Seton-Watson, the renowned historian and son of Robert Seton-Watson, notes that "of all the Eastern European States Roumania was the most fortunate at the Peace Settlement. Although defeated in 1918, she acquired from her late Ally, Russia, the partly Roumanian province of Bessarabia, and, having signed a separate peace with Germany, declared war a second time just before the Armistice and presented herself at the Peace Conference as an Allied State" (H. Seton-Watson 1967, 198). This "most fortunate" postwar situation was not accidental but masterfully prepared. In Hugh Seton-Watson's interpretation, it happened because, at Versailles, the victorious great powers wanted to create a relatively strong chain of allied small powers between Germany and Bolshevik Russia. "Roumania's success at the Peace," he continues, "is almost solely due to the panic about Bolshevism, and . . . Roumanian statesmen cleverly exploited the Bolshevik bogey" (H. Seton-Watson 1967, 198). Great power competition for control over Romania had actually begun earlier when the Central Powers, seeking to attract Romania to join them, offered them Bessarabia. On August 14, Sergei Sazanov, the Russian minister of foreign affairs, pledged Russian help in acquiring Transylvania should Romania enter the war on the Entente side. When the Russian army entered Bukovina, Sazanov announced to the Romanian government that this was the first step toward liberating the Romanian provinces from the Austro-Hungarian yoke. In a secret treaty of 1916, the Allied powers promised Romania a large part of the Hungarian plain stretching almost to the line of Szeged and Debrecen in addition to Transylvania.

Although military misfortunes during the war had dramatic effects on Romania, the events of this period invigorated the national movement. Once deemed unrealistic, nationalist hopes now seemed quite realistic. Recognizing this great shift, Romanian leaders were flexible enough to change their stance and to ensure leadership of the struggle for independence and Romanian unification toward the end of the war. On October 12, 1918, the Transylvanian Romanian National Party met in Nagyvárad (Oradea Mare) and declared the right of self-determination for Romanians in Hungary. Vaida-Voevod presented this message in the Hungarian parliament, and a National Council of Transylvanian Romanians, headed by Iuliu Maniu, was established. The Bukovinian Romanians established their National Council in Chernivtsi on October 27, 1918, and appealed to the Romanian government to send troops to "liberate" the province. On November 28, a Bukovinian Congress voted for union with Romania; the union was formalized by a decree of the Romanian government on December 19. On December 1, 1918, 1,228 delegates of the Transylvanian Romanian organizations gathered in

Gyulafehérvár (Alba Iulia) where they declared the union of Transylvania with Romania. A directing council and cabinet were established under the leadership of Iuliu Maniu, and a delegation was sent to Bucharest.

Meanwhile, in Romania, the pro-German Romanian government of Alexander Marghiloman was replaced in November by the pro-Allied nationalist Bratianu government. The Romanian army entered Transylvania, and Bratianu traveled to Paris to urge the implementation of the secret treaty of 1916. "The union was effected without opposition and almost without bloodshed," concludes Robert Seton-Watson. "The secular dream of the Roumanian race, when at last it came, came 'as a thief in the night,' when preparation had ceased and hope had almost vanished" (H. Seton-Watson 1963, 534).

Final borders were established after long and detailed debates at Versailles. The Romanians argued for a safe "natural border" at the River Tisza, which, however, extended their state well into Hungary. Although the Tisza border was not accepted, a vast portion of the Hungarian plain inhabited by ethnic Hungarians was given to Romania because drawing the borders on purely ethnic lines would have created "an unworkable frontier" that cut communications between northern and southern Transylvanian territories. Consequently, frontier cities such as Nagyvárad (Oradea Mare), Arad, and Szatmárnémeti (Satu Mare), which had overwhelming Hungarian majorities of 91, 73, and 95 percent respectively, were assigned to Romania. The Romanian delegation proffered the same argument with respect to the Banat, demanding the entire province to the River Tisza. Here, however, the great powers decided not to follow the same principle of "workable frontiers" and divided the Banat according to ethnic lines, thereby cutting communication lines between major cities.

Just decisions based on the right of self-determination were totally impossible in these areas of dramatically mixed population. In Temes (Timis) county, of 500,000 inhabitants 70,000 were Serbs, 169,000 Romanians, 150,000 Germans, and 78,000 Hungarians. In Torontal county, 199,000 Serbs, 86,000 Romanians, 125,000 Hungarians, and 158,000 Germans lived together. In the center of Transylvania, surrounded by Romanian regions, there was a homogenous Hungarian-Sekler territory composed of three Sekler counties with more than 900,000 inhabitants. Marosvásárhely and Kolozsvár (Cluj) each had populations that were more than 83 percent Hungarian. Prior to the war, the former Hungarian counties assigned to Romania at Versailles contained 2.9 million Romanians (46.1 percent), 2.1 million Hungarians, more than 0.7 million Germans, and nearly 0.3 million Ruthens. In Bessarabia, there was an Ukrainian (Ruthen) and Russian population of nearly 1 million, and in Bukovina, a majority of Ruthens were mixed with Romanians.

Newly created *Romania Mare* (Great Romania) more than doubled its former territory and population from approximately 137,000 square kilometers and 7.5 million inhabitants to 304,000 square kilometers and nearly 18 million inhabitants. Roughly 30 percent of the population belonged to non-Romanian ethnic minorities. By far the most numerous were the roughly 2-million-strong Hungarian minority. In addition, 0.75 million Germans, 0.5 million Ruthens, and 0.5 million Russians, and nearly 0.4 million Bulgarians were included. The cultural diversity of the country was clearly demonstrated by its religious mix: the Greek Orthodox population (72 percent) was supplemented by Greek Catholics (8 percent), Roman Catholics (7 percent), Jews (5 percent), and various Protestant groups.

The victorious and belated Romanian national revolution thus produced a country larger than the one envisioned in the bold "beer-table" dreams of a united Daco-Roman Empire. As in the case of other small multinational states, Romanian leaders sought to "nationalize" or assimilate the various ethnicities and construct a Romanian nation-state. But, as in Czechoslovakia and Yugoslavia, these goals conflicted with those of ethnic autonomy and self-governance. Consequently, the minority goals, which had been promised in order to solicit support, were not realized. Instead, strict centralization was institutionalized and enforced by politicians and officials of the *Regat*, the old Romanian Kingdom. The democratic constitution and legal system of the constitutional monarchy were undermined by overambitious, conservative, authoritarian nationalism. When the postwar coalition prepared a radical and "comprehensive program of land expropriation and social reform . . . [and] professed national reconciliation . . . [taking seriously the Minority Treaty and] acting in consort with conservatives and nationalists, King Ferdinand dismissed the Vaida government in March 1920. . . . The royal 'coup d'état' was crucial in determining the course of Rumanian history in the interwar years" (Fischer-Galati 1991, 35). In Fischer-Galati's analysis, Wallachian supremacy, authoritarian government, rejection of social reform, anticommunism, anti-Semitism, and anti-Magyarism, together with an antidemocratic electoral law, "dealt a fatal blow" to democratic forces and reforms. And, thus, seeds of social unrest and ethnic conflict were sown.

The Unstoppable New Waves:
National Revolutions without Nations

The wave of national revolutions that engulfed Central and Eastern Europe seemed to offer solutions to certain unsolved questions. The reestablishment of independent Polish and Baltic nation-states, the unification of Slavic "brother" nations into Czechoslovakia and Yugoslavia, and the unification of Romanians into a Great Romania clearly illustrate the power of this wave. A successful national revolutionary movement became the political leitmotif in the region at the end of World War I. The pull toward national revolution proved to be irresistible—in some cases, it dragged people toward revolution before their national movements had reached the appropriate stage in the nation-state building process. Two cases in point were the Albanian and the Jewish national movements.

For centuries, Albania was an integral part of the Ottoman Empire. After the Ottoman occupation, its population converted to Islam and assumed important roles in the Ottoman hierarchy, becoming part of the military-bureaucratic elite of the empire. Thirty Ottoman grand viziers were Albanians. Mohammed Ali of Egypt and Ali Pasha of Janina, both powerful "local" rulers in the disintegrating empire, were also Albanians.

Unlike other European societies, Albania preserved a tribal social structure. In the mountainous north, the majority Geg tribe lived an isolated, nomadic tribal life. The southern, primarily peasant Tosk tribe had more contact with the world. The country remained at a non-European level of backwardness, lacking an educational system and railroads and possessing altogether only about two hundred kilometers of paved roads. In sum, Albania had not reached even the first, cultural-folkloristic stage in the development of national movements, let alone the stage of mass nationalist movements that dominated most of the nineteenth-century Central and Eastern European political milieus.

Albania was, in this sense, pushed into struggling for a nation-state before the concept of an Albanian nation had been born. The conscious sense of Albanian identity emerged initially as a response to territorial changes sanctioned by the Treaty of San Stefano in 1878, in which Albanian-Muslim regions in the east and north were assigned to Greek Orthodox Bulgaria and Montenegro. The Albanian elite established the League of Prizren to defend its territory. The first signs of a cultural-national movement—language reform and the introduction of the Latin alphabet—appeared after the league was established. The Balkan Wars in the early 1910s increased the danger of partition by neighboring Slavic and Greek states, a situation that generated a modest demand for Albanian autonomy within the Ottoman Empire. By November 1912, after the possibility of eliminating Ottoman rule in the Balkans became apparent, a national assembly of eighty-three delegates in Vlore declared Albanian independence. The new nation was recognized almost immediately by the great powers, who saw its value as a support for their international strategic goals. An independent Albania, however, proved unviable and was occupied by Greek, Serbian, and Italian troops during World War I. Again endangered by ambitious neighbors, the Albanian elite mobilized to defend itself. In January 1920, the national congress gathered in Lushnje, and by March, the National Legislative Assembly opened deliberations in Tirana. These events were made possible by a temporary suspension of tribal vendetta obligations on the part of participants. As a result, an independent constitutional monarchy was established and recognized by the great powers.

Within the framework of the independent nation-state of Albania, a small country of twenty-seven square kilometers and one million inhabitants, the task of creating an Albanian nation was difficult. The ethnically and linguistically homogenous country, the only Muslim country in Europe, was divided by religious differences: 70 percent of the population was Muslim (belonging either to the Sunni or Bektashi sects), 20 percent was Greek Orthodox, and 10 percent was Catholic. Boys were often baptized and then, at the age of thirteen, circumcised, so that they were both Muslims and Christian. An even greater obstacle to nation building lay in the strong tribal structure of the Albanian society. Leaders of rival tribes competed for political power; during the first half of the 1920s, every year saw at least one major rebellion or regional uprising. Occasionally, coup and countercoup followed each other in a matter of days.

Before a central power was established, these rivalries between tribes led to a series of stormy political events. On December 11, 1921, an armed group of Agif Pasha forced their way into the bedroom of Prime Minister Evangjeli, who escaped on horseback; two days later, Hassan Prishtina, who had replaced Evangjeli, had to face Ahmet Zogolli, the leader of several thousand armed men belonging to a Muslim Mati tribe, who marched toward Tirana and set up another government. Zogolli, who changed his Turkish name to the more Albanian "Zogu," attempted to disarm the rival tribes and succeeded in collecting thirty-five thousand weapons, but he soon had to build barricades to defend his power against the forces of hostile tribes who began advancing against Tirana. Having suppressed this threat, Ahmet Zogu became prime minister in December 1922. His regime was the first government to control the entire country, but two more years passed before he could consolidate his power. In 1923, Zogu had to cope with several revolts and an assassination attempt: Shevhet Korca, commander of the gendarmerie, and Colonel Hakki occupied the capital. Assisted by the great powers as mediators, Zogu retained his premiership but had to make severe compromises. To avoid coups, the key position of minister of the interior rotated weekly among the members of the cabinet. In February 1923, Zogu was wounded by three shots fired at him as he stood on the steps of the parliament. A few weeks later, in retaliation, the murder of two American tourists was used as a pretext to launch a campaign in which the leader of an opposition terror-organization was killed. In June, the opposition rallied and forced Zogu to flee with six hundred supporters. The new prime minister, Harvard graduate Bishop Fan Noli, stayed in power only for six months. Meanwhile Zogu, having returned from Yugoslavia to recapture Tirana and Noli, was forced into exile. By December 1924, Zogu once again became prime minister and, a year later, acquired the post of president as well. From then on, he proved to be charismatic and strong enough to halt tribal dissension and to consolidate centralized power. In these events, seminomadic, semitribal Albania embarked upon a bumpy, semi-European process of modern nation building.

In this era of flux, the most illusory and boldest national movement in the region, the Jewish national movement, also gained momentum. The shock of World War I and the new European arrangements made at Versailles strengthened Jewish nationalism and national demands. "This was particularly the case . . . where the change of regimes also produced a vacuum which . . . Jewish national politics was able to fill. As in most regions of East Central Europe (with the exception of Hungary), Jewish national councils were established under the control of nationalist Jewish elements" (Mendelsohn 1983, 194). In several countries, Jewish movements partly followed the general pattern. As in other cases, these movements developed strategies for acquiring autonomy. First came the demand for traditional minority rights—recognition as an autonomous nationality with the rights to use native languages, to operate schools, and to enjoy other collective rights. In some cases, however, territorial autonomy or even independent statehood within Europe was demanded. To distinguish these groups from Zionism, which sought the establishment of a Jewish homeland in Palestine, they were called "territorialists."

A Jewish National Council was set up in Prague in October 1918. Similar institutions were founded in Warsaw, Cracow, and Cernauti in the fall of the same year. Jewish representatives to the Paris Peace Conference sought to convince the great powers and the Polish delegates that a constitutional guarantee of Jewish national autonomy in Poland would serve the common interest. Jewish delegates wanted a general guarantee of human and collective national rights, proportional representation in parliament, recognition of the elected national councils, and the appointment of a government official responsible for Jewish affairs. Among nonassimilated Jewry in Poland and certain parts of Czechoslovakia (Sub-Carpatho-Ruthenia), the demand for recognition as a separate national minority was especially strong. In postwar censuses, 57 percent of Ruthenian Jews described themselves as a national minority, 80 percent of Polish Jews declared Yiddish their native tongue, and 8 percent named Hebrew. It pays to note, however, that religious Hassidic fundamentalism also had a strong base among these groups. The *Agudes Yisrael* (League of Israel), founded in Germany in 1912, was strong in certain parts of Poland and also in Sub-Carpatho-Ruthenia, especially around Rabbi Haim Eliezer Shapira of Mukachevo (Munkács) and among the so-called Satmar Jews in Transylvania.

In the more assimilated Jewish communities of Poland, Jewish political parties were formed and participated in the 1919 elections; they elected eleven representatives to the *Sejm*. In that same year in Czechoslovakia, a Czechoslovak Jewish Party was formed. In Romania, Jewish leaders allied with various parties, and the four Jewish representatives in the parliament formed the Jewish National Club to protect collective interests. In Lithuania in January 1920, an all-Lithuanian Jewish conference established a national council and drew up a list of Jewish candidates in the elections; the elected Jewish representatives fought for Jewish national autonomy, and in November 1923, an independent Jewish National Assembly was elected. It was in the postrevolutionary Soviet Union, however, that Jewish ambitions were most closely realized. Jews were recognized as an autonomous nationality (not religion), and the so-called Birobidzhan Jewish autonomous area was created.

In the Western part of Central and Eastern Europe, highly assimilated Jews in Austria, Czechoslovakia, Hungary, and Poland did not demand autonomy; rather, they rallied to democratic and socialist move-ments that advocated universal human rights and equality, hoping that such political approaches would automatically solve the problems caused by minority status. In fact, the majority of the Jewish national movements of the postwar period focused on the protection of Jewish minority interests in particular countries (*Gegenwartarbeit*, as it was called) and so remained distanced from the call for creation of an in-dependent Jewish region or nation.

Although regionally circumscribed, the most important and dynamic trend in the Jewish national movement of the period was Zionism. Theodor Herzl's dream of restoring the Jewish homeland in its historic location slowly began to achieve reality. As in all the national move-ments, the outbreak of war opened up new possibilities. In November 1917, Arthur Balfour, the foreign secretary of Britain, accepted a Zion-ist initiative from Chaim Weizmann to create a new Jewish state at Turkey's expense. The program fit well into British imperial plans. Zion-ism gained further impetus and mass support in response to the anti-Semitism that flared up amid the process of creating new nation-states in 1918–1920. The rebirth of Poland was accompanied by pogroms in Lvov in November 1918 and in Pinsk, Lida, and Vlno in April 1919. Everyday atrocities included the cutting off of Jews' beards and the im-prisonment as "potential traitors" of volunteer Jewish officers during the war against Soviet Russia. In Hungary, a strong and institutional-ized anti-Semitic course was established after the defeat of the com-munist revolution. Traditional Romanian anti-Semitism resurged in the postwar years. "Political freedom, extreme nationalism, and anti-Semitism combined with a huge unacculturated Jewish community rooted in traditional Judaism but undergoing a process of seculariza-tion, [and] produced a mass Zionist movement without precedent in modern Jewish history" (Mendelsohn 1983, 56–57).

The Jewish movement was by no means united. During the 1920s, six different working-class socialist and five different general Zionist or-ganizations existed in Poland. The political spectrum was rather broad, ranging from the left-wing, communist-oriented *Poale Zion* (Workers of Israel) to the religious *Mizrachi* (Spiritual Center) founded at the beginning of the twentieth century, and included Zeev Zhabotinski's "Revisionist" group, which broke away from the general Zionist move-ment in the mid-twenties, rejected compromise and negotiations with the British and Arabs, and advocated tactics of armed struggle and ter-ror to achieve the establishment of an independent Jewish state on both banks of the Jordan. Political fragmentation also characterized the Zionist youth movements: from the independent Marxist-socialist *Hashomer-hatzair* (Young Guard) to the militaristic *Betar* (The Covenant of Trumpeldore), they represented every shade of the political spectrum. Both the Revisionists and the *Betar* introduced military training to prepare their cadres.

The *Halutz* (pioneer) organization was set up to prepare for *aliyah* (emigration to Palestine) and to build a healthy society based on farming and industrial labor. Not much emigration occurred, however: even in 1924 to 1926, the years when Jewish emigration from Poland to Palestine first surpassed that to the United States, only thirty-two thousand Jews left Poland to settle in Palestine. Zionism was the strongest in Lithuania. In the first postwar national census, 98 percent of all "Jews by religion" declared themselves "Jews by nationality." The number of emigrants to Israel as a percentage of the Jewish population was the highest in the entire region. The Latvian movement was also strong: just 3 percent of Jewish elementary school children were enrolled in Latvian-speaking schools and emigration to Israel, again as a percentage of population, was also higher than in Poland. In 1926, the British authorities in Palestine stopped large-scale immigration, and the next wave did not arrive until the turbulent thirties.

Thus, the Zionist movement was relatively strong in Lithuania, Latvia, and Poland, the Ruthenian part of Czechoslovakia, and the Bessarabian province of Romania. Most Jews in the region, in spite of the increasing anti-Semitism, believed that their governments would defend them, if necessary. Those who were entrepreneurial and lucky enough fled to the West. But emigration to the West was limited because of the extremely stringent restrictions in the United States and Western Europe. Many Jews tried to assimilate, converting to Christianity or Magyarizing or Polonizing their "Jewish names." Local Jewish leaders tried to collaborate with moderate anti-Semitic regimes and with political parties in Austria, Hungary, and Romania. It was only in the second half of the 1930s that the Zionist movement gathered momentum, most of all in Poland and Romania. By this time, Jewish national movements were well-established in Central and Eastern Europe.

"Constrained" nation building began in Austria, the small and humiliated state that was left after the dismemberment of the Habsburg Empire. Both its people and political elite were convinced that Austria was incapable of independent existence, and they hoped to escape a bleak future by joining Germany. The idea of *Anschluss* — joining Germany —

was the most popular political view, equally shared, though for different reasons, by the Austrian Right and Left. The Austro-German *Volksbund*, an association of extreme nationalists, announced the slogan "One people, one state!" and, ironically, Otto Bauer, the leading socialist theoretician and politician, resigned in 1920 from the Renner government because it was dilatory on the issue of *Anschluss*. Plebiscites in the early twenties proved that 98 and 93 percent of the population of Salzburg and Tirol respectively voted for *Anschluss*. The majority of the delegates of the *Nationalrat* (National Council) signed an *Anschluss* appeal. But regional separatism also appeared: Voralberg, for example, sought to join Switzerland.

In this desperate situation, Austrian nationalism gradually emerged. Hugo Hantsch advocated national independence for Catholic Austria. A legitimist-Catholic radical youth organization, "Austrian Action," attempted to build an aggressive Austrian national consciousness. "The Alpine Austria of today," declared a leading representative of this group, "is culturally and racially different. The Austrian is racially a synthesis of German and Slav, culturally a synthesis of Roman and Byzantine. . . . Austria cannot return to the Reich since it never belonged to the German Reich of today" (Suval 1974, 200).

The wave of nationalism and the will to be an independent nation in a separate state engulfed Central and Eastern Europe. The Versailles Treaty system accelerated but did not accomplish this process of building nation-states. Continued national conflicts and a marked shift from democracy toward authoritarian regimes signaled the future of the newly created independent states by the second half of the 1920s.

7

From National
Revolution to Nationalist
Authoritarianism

Extreme Ethnic-Religious Diversity

The independent nation-states created in Central and Eastern Europe when the Treaty of Versailles gave formal recognition to the demands of national revolutionary movements not only failed to resolve inherited minority problems but also helped to create new ones. The Soviet Union remained a multinational empire even though it lost its former western rim. In Czechoslovakia, the dominant Czechs and Slovaks shared the land with minorities—Germans, Hungarians, and other ethnic groups—that constituted nearly one-third of the population. In Yugoslavia, a state composed primarily of Serbs, Croats, and Slovenes, nearly one-quarter of the population was Albanian, Hungarian, German, or some other minority. Only roughly 70 percent of the population of Poland and Romania was Polish or Romanian, respectively; the remaining percentage in Poland was Ukrainian, Ruthen, Byelorussian, German, or Jewish, and the remaining percentage in Romania was Hungarian, German, Ukrainian, Russian, Jewish, or Bulgarian. Even in the small independent Baltic countries, a significant percentage of the population—in Latvia, nearly 25 percent, in Lithuania, roughly 16 percent, and in Estonia, about 10 percent—was Russian, Polish, German, Jewish, or another nationality. Hungary, Albania, and Bulgaria were nearly homogenous in ethnic terms, but they wrestled with a "reversed" minority question: large numbers of Hungarians and Albanians (more than one-third and two-thirds respectively, of each group) and one-tenth of all Bulgarians became national minorities in neighboring countries.

Not counting the multinational Soviet Union, one in five persons in this region of 110 million inhabitants lived as national minorities in their new states. From this fact, as Hugh Seton-Watson describes, three distinct types of minority problems emerged (H. Seton-Watson 1967).

The first and most explosive problem occurred where national minorities lived in border regions next to their "motherland." Examples include the Sudeten Germans, Silezian Poles, and southern Slovak Hungarians in Czechoslovakia; Germans and Ukrainians in western and eastern Poland respectively; the Kosovo Albanians and Vojvodina Hungarians in southern and northern Serbia respectively; Hungarians in Transylvania; and Bulgarians in Romania's southern Dobrudja region.

The second, also highly explosive problem, was created by the existence of markedly mixed areas where just ethnic separation was entirely impossible. In Macedonia, for example, Serbs, Greeks, Bulgarians, and Albanians were not only hopelessly mixed but each group also regarded the region as its unique homeland. Transylvania possessed a mixture of inseparable Romanian, Hungarian, and German peoples. Bessarabia's population consisted of Romanians, Ukrainians, Russians, and Jews. The Banat was inhabited by Romanians, Serbs, Hungarians, and Germans, and Dobrudja had a population of Romanians, Bulgarians, Greeks, and Turks. The Macedonian, Transylvanian, and Bessarabian questions and the ethnic-national conflicts of the Banat and Dobrudja could not be solved by partitions or by granting these territories to one or the other rival nation.

The third minority problem arose in areas where members of a specific nationality lived well within the boundaries of their home countries, separated by great distances from their motherland. Thus, urban Germans in most of the countries, Hungarian-Seklers in the heart of Transylvania, Slovaks in southern Hungary, Romanians in Macedonia, and many other groups lived geographically separated and isolated from their ethnic roots. Jews in the region, meanwhile, lived in a special position: they lacked a "motherland" and identified in some cases with a specific country (German Jews considered themselves German, and Hungarian and Transylvanian Jews considered themselves Hungarian), yet they were denied membership in the nation-state majorities because of their ethnic and religious differences.

The successful drive to establish independent states and the triumphant principle of the right of self-determination increased the minority communities' appetite for independence, especially because most of the newly independent countries sought to create homogeneous nation-states by absorbing and assimilating their various ethnic minorities. As Hugh Seton-Watson declares:

In Czechoslovakia the Czechs, and in Yugoslavia the Serbs, each formed less than half—a smaller proportion, in fact, than the Russians in the old Russian Empire or the Hungarians in the old Kingdom of Hungary. All four [Poland, Romania, Czechoslovakia, and Yugoslavia] were multinational states, and all four insisted on pretending to be states of one nation, in which persons of other national origin could only be tolerated guests for a time, and the longer-term aim was the assimilation of all into the nationality of the dominant nation. (H. Seton-Watson 1964, 23–24)

The victorious great powers and peacemakers did not overlook the minority question and attempted to guarantee the peaceful existence of affected groups. To this end, the successor states were required to sign minority treaties and the League of Nations was authorized to ensure their execution. The minority problem, however, could not be so easily resolved. These agreements did not cover all minorities, and, in most cases, their terms were easily circumvented. Often the minority groups in question had not even requested this kind of "protection." Furthermore, though the League of Nations offered protection against discrimination, it also desired a "just and gradual" assimilation. Austin Chamberlain noted, "The object of the Minorities Treaties . . . was . . . to secure for the minorities that measure of protection and justice which would gradually prepare them to be merged in the national community to which [they] belonged." Briand's stance was no more reassuring to minorities: "The process at which we should aim is not the disappearance of the minorities, but a kind of assimilation" (Macartney 1934, 272–73).

Thus oppression and injustice continued, but with a reversed hierarchy. Members of former dominating nations became minorities, and the new dominating nations sought retribution for past grievances. The new minorities were satisfied with citizen rights but rejected assimilation. Waves of small-scale migration began. Roughly one hundred thousand Hungarians, mainly former civil servants and intellectuals, moved from Transylvania to Hungary. Turkish and Bulgarian populations were exchanged in the two nations, and about one-and-a-half million Greek refugees left Asia Minor for Greece. Several hundred thousand Bulgarians were expelled from Greek Western Thracian areas under a

Bulgarian-Greek population exchange program. Some two hundred thousand Bulgarians left Yugoslavian Macedonia and fled to their motherland. Similarly, hundreds of thousands of Turks fled Bulgaria. Yet the majority of minority populations could not flee.

The region was religiously as well as ethnically diverse. The population of Central and Eastern Europe was divided among five major religious groups: Roman Catholics, Greek Orthodoxs, Protestants, Jews, and Muslims. Divisions applied not only to the region as a whole but also to many individual countries. Catholic Poland also served as home to Greek Orthodox and Jewish communities (nearly one-fifth of the population), and predominantly Greek Orthodox Romania contained sizable Catholic, Protestant, and Jewish communities. In Muslim Albania, nearly one-third of the people belonged to the Catholic and Greek Orthodox churches. Hungary, too, was religiously diverse, containing Catholics (60 percent), Calvinist Protestants (approximately 34 percent), and Jews (5 percent).

Religious diversity was even more complex than these simple figures suggest. Nearly every religion contained significant inner divisions. For example, the Greek Orthodox Church was not centralized but instead was organized along lines of nationality. In contrast, during the sixteenth and seventeenth centuries, the Greek Catholic religion submitted to papal authority in Rome. The various divisions of Protestant Christianity included the Lutheranism of Slovakia and the German settlements in the area, Calvinism in Hungary, and Unitarianism in Transylvania. Judaism was likewise multifarious, with assimilationist neologists and isolationist Hasidic groups, Yiddish-speaking Askhenazi, and Ladino-speaking Sephardic Jewish communities (the latter mostly in Bulgaria). Muslims in the region were mostly Sunni, but the Bektash sect was of Shiite origin.

Religion played a determinant role in the nineteenth- and twentieth-century nation building efforts in Central and Eastern Europe—a role distinctly different from that in Western Europe. In the West, national identity emerged as a replacement for the older "religious myth" of identity, but in Central and Eastern Europe religious affiliation helped create ethnic identity (Petrovich 1980).

Allegiance to Greek Orthodoxy symbolized the unity of the Russian people during the Tatar conquest, and the Serbian and Montenegrin Orthodox Church provided one pillar of self-identification during the years of Ottoman rule. But Bulgaria offered the most telling example of the role of religion in national development. The Sultan refused to grant the Bulgarians an independent church, placing them instead under a Greek bishopric. Consequently, the Bulgarian national movement of the nineteenth century began with a demand for ecclesiastical autonomy. Similarly, the Greek Orthodox Church and the Greek Catholic Church, which were not among the officially recognized four religions, preserved and developed the language and "national" consciousness of Romanians in Transylvania.

Militant churches struggled for national survival during the centuries of foreign domination and sometimes even played an important military role. Catholicism and Protestantism served as weapons in the confrontation between the Habsburgs and Hungarians. Catholicism also provided a basis for Polish resistance against both Russian Orthodoxy and German Protestantism. Where oppressed peoples managed to win concessions from their conquerors, their success could often be attributed to actions of the churches: for instance, the Habsburg Serbs were allowed to elect their own leaders and even to organize a militia as a result of interventions by their church. Most commonly, however, church-state relations were only superficially theocratic and churches functioned as secular and temporal entities. Often the church was the sole institution in a civic community and, in this capacity, served as an organ of self-government and defense under foreign rule.

Seman Dubnow has demonstrated this process in the history of Central and Eastern European Jewry. By cultivating traditions, language, and "national" history, Jewish religious communities helped to preserve differences between them and the dominant peoples. In partitioned Poland and in territories under Ottoman domination, these communities were responsible for the local self-government out of which a national consciousness developed. The traditional religious wish "Next year in Jerusalem!" required secularization before it provided the foundation for a Zionist national movement. The religious community "provided the stateless nation with a substitute for national and political self-expression" (Dubnow 1961, 113).

The role of religions in national development was not over in 1918. Catholicism in Slovakia and Croatia and Islam in Bosnia provided building blocks for new minority movements that emerged within the new states. As the case of the Muslims in Yugoslavia illustrates, religious identity could spawn nationalist movements even when the participants belonged to the same ethnic group as the majority population. The diversity and the proliferation of minority groups—they made up almost half of the region's population—contributed significantly to the failure to develop Western, national, liberal values in Central and Eastern European nations. In fact, the values and institutions of parliamentary democracy were often violently rejected, and dictatorships were set up to enforce national unity in the name of national rebirth. Czeslaw Milosz notes in his memoirs on the interwar decades: "People shouted about a 'national revolution,' and the political scene swarmed with petty tyrants. . . . Demagoguery turned its sharp edge against foreign capital and 'Judeo-plutocrats'"(Milosz 1981, 103)—and, it should be added, against Czechs, Serbs, Hungarians, Jews, and "others" in general.

Nationalism Multiplies by Bipartition

In the new, small multinational states, concepts such as "Czechoslovakism" and "Yugoslavism," which were designed to create a homogenized nation, clearly violated notions of minority rights and the principle of self-determination. The political elite in Czechoslovakia, which included not only Czechs but also "Czechoslovakist" Slovaks such as the Social Democrat Ivan Derer and Vavro Srobar, minister of Slovak affairs, looked to the Czech "elder brother" as the carrier of social, economic, and cultural progress. The Czechs were well educated and trained in the skills needed in a highly industrial and urbanized country. In contrast, their Slovak counterparts still lived in a world dominated by agriculture, and one-third of the population was illiterate. As a consequence, the majority of central administrative offices went to Czechs. Of the 417 employees in the Ministry of Education in Prague, only four were Slovak, whereas in Bratislava's branch of the ministry, sixty-eight Slovaks worked with ninety-four Czechs. The staff of the Ministry of Defense numbered 1,300, but only sixty-six were Slovaks. Of the army's 139 generals and 436 colonels, only one was Slovak. Even in Slovakia itself, half of the judges and secondary-school teachers were Czechs.

Czech centralism linked easily with the "modernization mission," and the promises made to minority groups by the central government upon independence—minority rights, autonomy, and linguistic guarantees designed to create a "Central European Switzerland"—were either not kept or were manipulated. Bertram de Colonna offers a telling example of these manipulations in the treatment of Hungarian minorities:

The 1912 census showed that 20% of the population in the Pressburg area was Hungarian. In order to lessen this proportion the authorities resorted [to] arbitrary separation adding sixteen Hungarian communities to the neighbouring Galánta area and replacing them by non-Hungarian communities from the Bazin area. By virtue of the fact that a minimum proportion of 20% was necessary in order that a minority should enjoy the right to use their own tongue for all purposes these two areas were deprived of this right. The same treatment was meted out to Hungarian minorities in Kassa, Nyitra and Rimaszombat. (Colonna 1938, 20–21)

Similarly, the autonomy promised to Ruthenia was not realized on the grounds that this backward area was not mature enough for self-government and that at least another two decades would be needed before it reached the requisite level of development. In 1926, as a result, Czech became the official language in the province.

The most explosive conflict between the Czechs and Slovaks emerged as a consequence of broken promises of autonomy. The more moderate wing of the Slovak national movement, the National Party, challenged the notion of a "united Czechoslovakia and Czechoslovak nation" but urged more decentralization rather than separation. The Slovak Peoples' Party under Father Andrej Hlinka, the veteran Slovak national leader who, for a brief euphoric moment, had endorsed the Czechoslovak nation and who, in the 1920 elections, prepared a list of candidates in conjunction with the Czech Catholic Party that had won only 21 percent of the votes, changed his political stance. This outstanding orator emerged as a prophet of Slovak nationalism who rejected "Czechoslovakization." "We have never been one nation with the Czechs," he declared, and Czech "atheism could destroy us" (Korbel 1977, 100). The right wing of Hlinka's party was not satisfied by harsh rhetoric alone and began seeking action. It established the *Rodobrana* (Fatherland Defense), a paramilitary force with fascist goals. *Slovak*, the party's newspaper, enthusiastically proclaimed: "The brilliant example of Italy lights up the road for us. It calls us to action. We Slovaks shall stand guard. Our outstanding 'Rodobrana,' the Slovak 'Fascist' is fueled by enthusiasm, its muscles are straining with strength. . . . We are firmly convinced that by defending ourselves we are saving our fatherland, and giving service to all mankind" (Lettrich 1955, 75).

On January 1, 1928, *Slovak* gained considerable but dubious fame. Vojtech Tuka, professor of law, editor of the paper, and a leader of the party's right wing, published an article entitled "In the Tenth Anniversary of the Martinská Declaration," which stated that the Slovak National Council's declaration to join a united Czechoslovak state contained a secret clause according to which the union of the Czechs and Slovaks was intended to last for only ten years. If the promised Slovak autonomy had not materialized by the rapidly approaching end of those ten years, the Slovaks would be free to make new decisions. "On October 31, 1928, extraordinary conditions, a *vacuum juris*, will exist in one-half of the Czecho-Slovak Republic," declared Tuka. "On that critical day the ethical foundation of certain constitutional clauses will cease to exist, legal continuity will be interrupted" (Lettrich 1955, 76).

The central government decided to use force: Tuka was accused of conspiring with alien powers (meaning Hungary) to undermine the republic, placed on trial, and sentenced to fifteen years imprisonment. Defending Tuka at the trial, Hlinka said that "Czech despotism is not in the slightest degree different from the old Hungarian despotism. It is indeed worse. To impose . . . a prison sentence . . . based on an unproven charge is indeed a mockery of justice." On October 9, 1929, in *Jednota*, Hlinka spoke of "another chapter that has been added to the criminal melodramatic activities of Czech despotism within the so-called Czechoslovak republic" (Palickar 1948, 64–65). The existence of Czechoslovakia was challenged, and the Slovak national revolution embarked upon its separate path.

A strikingly similar fate characterized the decline of united Yugoslavia. The Serb and Croat conflict became deadly after the centralist constitution was enacted. The Croat political elite, a partner in the foundation of Yugoslavia, turned to anti-Serbian nationalism. At the second anniversary of the Vidovdan Constitution, the conflict was intensified by an assassination attempt against Pašić and an open appeal for assistance from fascist Italy in the Croatian struggle against Belgrade. The Serbian government did not hesitate: at the end of 1924, Stjepan Radić's Croatian Peasant Party was banned. The "legal" basis for the action was provided by the Law of 1921, which had been enacted as a safeguard against communism. Using a false passport, Radić fled to Prague and then to Moscow in the summer of 1923. His action dramatically "proved" the accusation that the Croat nationalist party intended, via the Peasant International, to establish contact with the Communist International and with anti-Yugoslav forces operating in Bulgaria and Hungary. After heavy political skirmishes, Pašić resigned and Radić returned to Yugoslavia in the summer of 1924. Instead of reconciliation between the parties, the conflict continued and a vicious press campaign was launched. *Smoprava* published an article in its December 7, 1924, issue, which accused Radić of aiding anti-Yugoslav Bolshevik subversion. In its December 18 edition, *Rec* revealed that contact had been established between Radić and Zinoviev, the leader of the Communist International. Before the February elections in 1925, Radić and other leaders of the Peasant Party were arrested for activities against the state, but the party nevertheless emerged in the elections as the largest opposition party in the country.

After this sharp confrontation, King Alexander stepped in to mediate. An agreement was reached in which Radić recognized the constitution in an open letter. A formal agreement was signed on July 18, 1925, and the "R-R Coalition" (the Radicals of Pašić and the Radićists) was formed. Radić became minister of education, and Croatia gained some control over appointments and endorsement of legislation in the Croatian, northern half of the country. The new compromise, however, turned out to be brief; after the death of Pašić in December 1926, chaos reigned in the political arena. Although he was a member of the cabinet, Radić continued to criticize and attack the institution and his colleagues. On February 1927, the coalition was dissolved and replaced by a Serb-Slovene coalition. By then, however, even the Serbian party system began to disintegrate. The government was rearranged several times. New elections in September 1927 were greeted with political apathy by a country that had lost confidence in government and parliament. Various corruption cases, which were highly publicized and used as weapons in political struggles, had a negative impact. The *Skuptšina* (Parliament) was virtually paralyzed by permanent obstruction. During the 1920s, twenty-four cabinets were formed and none of the elected parliaments served their four-year terms. Changing coalitions, new alliances between former enemies, a thorough "ethnicization" of political life, and party formation pushed the Yugoslav political system to the brink of collapse.

The blow that finally provoked a violent political crisis occurred on June 20, 1928, when, after a rude exchange between Radić and Puniša Račić on June 19, a highly emotional debate in the *Skuptšina* exploded in violence: the Montenegrin Račić, a member of the Radical Party, shot four Croatian representatives, including Stjepan Radić. A Serbian journalist, who less than a week before the assassination had openly demanded the liquidation of Radić, was killed a few weeks later. Political life was totally paralyzed, and the Croatian Party and its allies withdrew their representatives from the parliament. The king offered a surprising solution—a peaceful split of Serbia and Croatia—which was not accepted by the Croats, who were worried about an Italian and Hungarian intervention and, therefore, sought true federalism. But federation was not acceptable for the Serbian parties. In response to the crisis, the king appointed General Hadžić to lead a suprapartisan government. But when the *Skuptšina* reopened in Belgrade in early August, the Croats opened a counterparliament in Zagreb that declared the Vidovdan Constitution and the union with Serbia invalid. Demonstrations and clashes with the police led to the deaths of a dozen demonstrators in Zagreb in December. Ethnic-national conflicts brought Yugoslavia close to collapse.

The collapse, however, did not occur. On January 6, 1929, King Alexander, whose reputation gradually improved during the chaotic second half of the twenties and who enjoyed the absolute loyalty of the army, introduced a royal dictatorship. The constitution, the parliament, the political parties, the trade unions, and all civil liberties were suspended. In a symbolic gesture, King Alexander appointed the commander of the royal guard, General Zivković as prime minister. The king himself became the ultimate source of legislative and administrative authority. Order and law were reestablished, although one-third of the newspapers were banned and dozens of diplomats and generals were forced to retire. The administrative structure of the country was altered to eliminate official status for historic territories; nine provinces (*banovina*) were created and named mostly after rivers to avoid emotion-laden traditional signification. In October 3, 1929, the country itself was renamed, becoming the Kingdom of Yugoslavia. The democratic parliamentary system that had been introduced when the nation was created died.

Despite these sweeping changes, the Yugoslav crisis did not end. In 1928, a new political force appeared in Croatia when Ante Pavelić founded his extreme nationalist-separatist movement and allied it with Mussolini, replacing political struggle with terrorist action. The pattern was set: extreme nationalism and extreme right-wing politics merged.

Nationalism Breaks Loose: The Link to Right-Wing Authoritarianism

The dubious Balkan institution of royal dictatorship was not the invention of King Alexander. It was introduced first in Albania by Ahmet Zogu, who after gaining and consolidating power during the mid-1920s, continued to face frequent attacks by rival tribes. Zogu was seriously challenged in 1926. Although he suppressed the uprising in the north, he decided to replace parliamentary formalities with absolute central power. Such power was more suitable for his modernization program, which was linked closely to Mussolini's fascist modernization dictatorship of the twenties. The first step to concentrate power in Zogu's hands occurred in January 1925, when he was "elected" president of Albania and yet retained the posts of prime minister and commander of the armed forces. After becoming president, Zogu successfully pursued a far-reaching military and economic alliance with Mussolini's Italy, formalized by the Tirana Treaty of 1926. An Italian military mission arrived in Albania to build up and train the army. An Albanian National Bank was founded by Italian investments, and an Italian loan of fifty million gold francs assisted Albanian modernization programs. For this goal, the Italian *Società per lo Sviluppo Economico d'Albania* (Association for Albanian Economic Development) was established.

On September 1, 1928, Zogu elected himself "King of the Albanians" (generating an emotional Yugoslav claim of irredentism) and strengthened his personal power. Tayar Zavalani characterized Zogu's reign as "undemocratic and dictatorial" and pointed out that "[Zogu] swept aside all attempts at a parliamentary democracy and imposed his personal rule. . . . A constitutional monarchy on paper, Albania was ruled in actuality by a clique of court favorites. . . . The ruthless repression of any organization suspected of opposition and the harsh punishments imposed on its members were particularly resented" (Zavalani 1969, 84–86). Strong dictatorial power was put in the service of major efforts at modernizing the country. The practice of vendetta was restricted and modern civil, penal, and commercial laws were introduced. Moderate land reform, reductions in rates of illiteracy, and the secularization of the country all were, indeed, in Zogu's program. Tribal "nationalism" and extreme backwardness blocked the road of building a parliamentary democracy in Albania.

Western-style constitutions and parliamentary democracies collapsed in other newly independent countries of the region as well. The euphoria that followed postwar national revolutions and the resultant attempts to adopt Western patterns soon was confronted with the harsh realities of national conflict and severe internal socioeconomic turmoil. National conflicts and socioeconomic turmoil appeared in the Baltic republics in the mid-1920s and the first move toward nationalist dictatorship occurred in Lithuania. When the Sleževičius government signed a nonaggression treaty with the Soviet Union in September 1926, right-wing extreme nationalists, already highly agitated by previous border skirmishes with Poland and by the debate about Vlno (Vilnius), now decided to take action. In conjunction with the *Tautinikai* (Nationalist) party, right-wing officers led by General Ladyga occupied the parliament building on December 17, 1926, and dismissed the cabinet. A state of emergency was introduced, and Augustinas Voldemaras and Antanas Smetona assumed power as prime minister and president respectively. Voldemaras imprisoned political opponents and established a paramilitary organization, the *Gelezinis Vilkas* (Iron Wolf). In 1928, the sitting parliament was dissolved and a new constitution introduced a presidential dictatorship. Although a quasi-parliament was restored, parties became mere decorations embellishing the power of the president, who was assisted in ruling by the right-wing nationalist, eventually fascist *Tautinikai* party and by the armed forces. After the arrest of Premier Voldemaras, the dictatorship of President Smetona was consolidated and Lithuania was governed mostly by decree. Only a few years passed before Estonia and Latvia followed Lithuania's steps, each setting up a presidential dictatorship, the Baltic version of Balkans' royal dictatorship.

The shift in Lithuania from parliamentary democracy to nationalist-authoritarian rule was largely inspired by events in Poland. The triumphant Polish national revolution had embarked on the promising road laid down by the victorious Western powers. However, during the early 1920s, and especially after the resignation of Marshal Jósef Piłsudski violent confrontations halted this development. In 1923, strikes engulfed the country and the workers in Krakow revolted, clashing with the police. Eighteen people died and two hundred were wounded. Similar events occurred in Boryslaw. Roman Dmowski's ultra-nationalist, right-wing, highly anti-Semitic National Democratic Party also gained ground. In 1926, its leaders set up the Great Polish Camp, organized along the *Führer-Prinzip* (Führer principle), and began urging dictatorial actions. A secret organization, the *Pogotowie Patriotów Polskich* (Polish Patriots' Readiness), was formed to plot a coup that would introduce a dictatorial regime, and an antiparliamentarian putsch to be staged by Dmowski and Sikorski was prepared. Meanwhile, several rival officer groups made their own preparations to replace the "rotten" parliamentary system with strong government. In November 1925, President Wojciechowski even summoned General Sikorski, one of the most powerful military leaders of the country, and warned him not to instigate a

Hungarian aristocrats in 1916

Jewish shopkeeper
with Ruthenian
peasant women
in the 1930s

Washing the laundry in a Central European village in the 1930s

Lower-middle-class
fashion in 1930

Aristocrat wedding party in Hungary in the 1930s

Peasant wedding
party in Slovakia
in the 1930s

Jewish lower-middle-class wedding party in Budapest in 1938

Slum in the suburb of Budapest

Free soup for the un-
employed in Central
Europe in 1932

Peasant home in Verhovina

Ploughing in Central Europe in the 1930s

Harvesting in Central Europe in the 1930s

Export tobacco industry in Bulgaria

The *Škoda Work* in Czechoslovakia

Miklós Horthy with his soldiers

Jósef Piłsudski with his soldiers

King Alexander with his soldiers

Tsar Boris with his soldiers

Józef Piłsudski under the umbrella of the Church

King Carol, kissing
the hand of the Greek
Orthodox bishop

Tsar Boris, kissing
the hand of the
Greek Orthodox
bishop

The Romanian Iron Guard

The Austrian *Heimwehr*

Founding the Hungarian Arrowcross Party in 1935

Fascist-style student demonstration in Bucharest: "Heil King Carol!"

Fascist-style student demonstration in Sofia: "Heil Tsar Boris!"

Austrian Nazi poster

Mussolini and two of his admirers: Gyula Gömbös and
Engelbert Dollfuss

Corneliu Zelea
Codreanu (right)
in folk dress

Maniu and Ion
Mihalache

Ahmet Zogu and his family

Slovak fascist leaders (Father Tiso in middle)

Hungarian fascist leaders (the presidium of the Hungarian National Grand Council)

Ante Pavelić with Croatian peasant women

Ferenc Szálasi
in prison (an
Arrowcross poster)

Heinlein in the Sudetenland

coup. In the spring of 1926, three books were published by authors with vastly different political convictions, but all urged constitutional reform and the strengthening of central power. Coincidentally, during these months the first attempt at monetary stabilization collapsed and a new wave of inflation emerged. In the major industrial centers of the country—Warsaw, Łodz, Lublin, and Lvov—one-third of the work force was unemployed. Mass demonstrations and violence engulfed the urban areas, and "calls for dictatorship became ever more general and open" (Rothschild 1966, 21).

In May 1926, Marshal Piłsudski moved first. He had been preparing his action since November 1925, when he asked Professor Kazimierz Bartel to draft a political program and act as prime minister after the anticipated coup. As per the marshal's order, General Orlicz-Dreszer began military preparations in late 1925. On November 15, twenty generals and thousands of officers loyal to Piłsudski staged a demonstration outside his Sulejowek home, and on May 12, 1926, the marshal and his troops set off for Warsaw. The self-confident Piłsudski thought that his *Marcia su Varsovia* (March on Warsaw) would be a parade march and told his wife that he would be back for lunch by half past two.* His troops easily occupied the *Praga*-district of the capital, but then met resistance. The inner city was occupied only after a two-day battle and the death of three hundred people.

People imbued Piłsudski's move with manifold meanings. Because of his early socialist background, workers supported him and announced a general strike on May 19, calling for the removal of the president and government. The Warsaw workers even sought to join and assist Piłsudski in the fighting by organizing separate units. Warski, the communist leader, saw the *coup* as a road to the "revolutionary democratic dictatorship" and called upon the workers to support it.

But events soon dispelled peoples' illusions. "Despite the help that he received from the Left during his takeover in May 1926, Piłsudski turned to the Right in October" (Kozlowski 1978, 5–6). His closest aid, Colonel Walery Sławek, held a secret meeting on September 15 with leading aristocrats, and, at a three-day meeting at Dzikow, on the estate of Count Tarnowski, he tried to create a conservative power base for Piłsudski, who

---

*The parallel between Piłsudski and Mussolini was made as early as July 2, 1926, by Trotsky, who, at a session of the Communist International, maintained that "the movement he [Piłsudski] headed was . . . a populist solution to the pressing problems of capitalist society. . . . Here there is a direct parallel with Italian Fascism" (Trotsky 1971, 282).

himself visited Prince Radziwill in Niéswiez Palace in October. Piłsudski intended to weaken both the right-wing opposition led by Dmowski and his left-wing "allies" and wanted to create an autocracy with a strong executive power. He did not abolish the parliamentary system but greatly reduced its power, transforming it into little more than a formality. Real power lay in the army, which was strictly controlled by the marshal, who sometimes acted as prime minister, sometimes as minister of defense, but always as inspector of the army. The "colonels," his loyal comrades-in-arms from the First Brigade, supervised the state apparatus, which was filled by technocrats.

Piłsudski sought to overcome multiparty "corruption and chaos" by organizing a *Bezpartyjny Blok* (Nonpartisan Bloc) to cooperate with the government in regenerating the country. His so-called *sanacja* (economic rehabilitation) regime in the second half of the 1920s sought to impose a central state power that would reach "beyond" antagonistic partisan, social class, and ideological interests. Piłsudski believed in an "enlightened" modernization dictatorship but wished to preserve a quasi-parliamentary regime. In March 1928, he sought to legitimize his coup by a "multiparty election," because he had confidence in his Nonpartisan Bloc. However, the bloc won an ambiguous victory, gaining 24 percent and 31 percent of the seats in the *Sejm* and Senate respectively. Socialists, right-wing groups, and national minorities all preserved strong parliamentary positions. Opposition to Piłsudski's program gutted attempts to pass authoritarian constitutional reform, and a joint declaration by the opposition condemned the "illegal dictatorial" drive. A disappointed Piłsudski struck back. On the night of September 9, 1930, nineteen opposition representatives and senators were arrested, and another sixty soon followed them to the notorious Bržešć prison. Several thousand people were arrested and fourteen rallies were broken up, with much blood shed. Piłsudski, however, still insisted on observing democratic formalities and ordered new elections with the intent of securing an absolute majority in the *Sejm*. But these elections only parodied parliamentarism. The 1926 coup d'etat and the 1930 Bržešć incident effectively ended parliamentary endeavors in Poland and established a strong authoritarian-military regime instead.

After World War I, right-wing extreme nationalism became more vigorous and widespread, appearing not only in nations that had experienced Bolshevik and left-wing populist revolutions but also in the parliamentary democracies. In the Czech lands, a national-socialist German movement existed in the minority area of the Sudetenland. Hitler's party had a strong branch in the region, and after the war, the swastika on flags was a far more common sight there than in Germany. In 1923, the *Ustřední Vybor Československych Fašictú*, the first Czech fascist organization, was founded. Two years later, General Rodola Gajda, the legendary hero of the Czechoslovak Legion, then chief-of-staff of the new national army, established his National Fascist Community. In the spring of 1926, he planned a putsch to seize power, but he failed, was sent into retirement, and was stripped of his rank. Right-wing nationalists garnered less than 1 percent of the vote in the 1929 elections.

Extremist trends were more successful in Austria. Hitler's Nazi Party had a strong branch in Austria, and the Austrian German Labor Party changed its name to *Deutsche National-Socialistische Arbeiterpartei* (German National-Socialist Workers' Party) in 1918. At the May Day celebration of 1920, party members marched under their own red flag, which displayed a swastika at its center set against a white background. Departing from the genuine Austrian "left-wing" Nazism of the founding fathers—Rudolf Jung had advocated the nationalization of large industries, mines, and transportation and had suggested the introduction of a profit-sharing system and the inclusion of workers on companies' boards in 1921—Walter Riehl and other new leading figures put themselves forward as representatives of "the entire German people," designating *Judenherrschaft* (Jewish rule) as their chief enemy. At an Austrian Nazis' "rally in September 1920 Dr. Riehl asserted that Vienna's housing problem could be solved by the expulsion of 200,000 *Ostjuden* [Eastern Jews]" (Pauley 1990, 27). The Austrian Nazis established a paramilitary organization called the *Vaterländischer Schutzbund* (National Defense Alliance) in 1923. The membership of the Austrian Nazi organization, however, reached only thirty-four thousand by 1923. Between 1926 and 1929, two Nazi parties actually worked in Austria, a *Hitlerverein* (Hitler's Union) and the previously established Austrian Nazis. The Austrian right-wing extreme nationalists also developed several other organizations in the 1920s. Right-wing Christian Socialism led by Ignaz Seipel became more influential, as did the racist, anti-Semitic, antiparliamentarian Catholic movement directed by Lugmayer, Messner, and Othmar Spann. A paramilitary organization known as the *Heimwehr* (Home Guard) emerged by 1927 as a determinant factor in Austrian politics and cautiously plotted a putsch. Young Prince Ernst Rüdiger von Stahremberg, who had served as a lieutenant during the war, set up a small private army of seven hundred men. The various *Heimwehr* organizations in Tyrol were united by Richard Steidle, and in a few years, the *Heimwehr* grew into a national organization, a movement with a paramilitary structure and a distinctive anti-Semitic program.

In postwar Romania, Iasi University became the cradle of a right-wing, anticommunist, antiliberal, and anti-Semitic nationalist terrorism. As early as the fall of 1919, Constantin Pancu, a former trade unionist, convened a statutory meeting that was attended by some twenty students, shopkeepers, workers, and priests of the "Guard of National Consciousness." Early in 1920, this group attacked strikers, and in the summer of 1922, they broke up the Yiddish theatrical performances of the Kanapoff Ensemble in Husi, Barlad, Botosan, and Pascari. The right-wing terrorist trend gained impetus in March 1923 when the veteran Professor Cuza founded the *Liga Apărării Naționale Creștină* (Christian National Defense League). The *Fascia Nationala Romană* (Romanian National Fascio) and the *Actiunea Romaneasca* (Romanian Action) in Cluj were incorporated into the Defense League in 1925. When the prefect of Iasi attempted to restore order and restrict the violent organization, a student named Corneliu Zelea Codreanu, who was the leader of the league's youth section, simply shot him dead in the law court. In a summer day of 1927, Codreanu set up his own Legion of the Archangel Michael operating from his apartment. "Today, Friday, June 24, 1927 . . . 10 o'clock P.M.," Codreanu announced in his Order No. 1, "the Legion of 'Archangel Michael' was founded under my leadership." Codreanu firmly believed that he had been chosen by God "to guide the Romanian people in a healthier direction." The organization was shortly to become one of Central and Eastern Europe's most important populist-fascist mass movements, organized in small units or "nests" of three to thirteen members according to the *Führer-Prinzip*. As Ion Mota, Codreanu's lieutenant, stated: "An organization cannot be built and developed without order and hierarchy, but most of all without a Leader. Our organization has a Leader . . . the great leading personality . . . who with his secret strength established the first disciplined net of our organization. Our Leader is Corneliu Zelea-Codreanu" (Heinen 1986, 131,135, 142). All these movements were characterized by unconditional, aggressively nationalist ideologies, which equally opposed liberalism, democracy, Marxist socialism, and communism. They advocated authoritarian government and envisioned a mass party built around paramilitary organizations. Mussolini's fascist Italy was an explicit ideal and model. As Codreanu announced his political strategy in 1928: "Romania needs broad reforms that are fascist in character"

(Heinen 1986, 146–47). Terrorism was particularly suitable as a vehicle for expressing the right-wing movements' social frustration. As Hannah Arendt said: "What proved so attractive was that terrorism had become a kind of philosophy through which to express frustration, resentment, and blind hatred, a kind of political expressionism which used bombs to express oneself" (Arendt 1966, 332).

In postwar Central and Eastern European national revolutions, various shades of nationalist, counterrevolutionary ideology and fascism appeared in a peculiar mix. However, Karl Polanyi warns against treating them as a single interrelated movement. "By accident only . . . was European fascism in the twenties connected with national and counterrevolutionary tendencies. It was a case of symbiosis between movements of independent origin, which reinforced one another and created the impression of essential similarities, while being actually unrelated" (Polanyi 1964, 242). According to his analysis, the immediate starting point of "counterrevolution and nationalist revisionism . . . was the Treaties and the postwar revolutions." In contrast, fascism "was a revolutionary tendency," rooted in far broader causes of social origin and in the crisis of the entire market system. Counterrevolution and extreme nationalism "were easily confounded with fascism" because "the nascent fascist movement put itself almost everywhere into the service of the national issue; it could hardly have survived without this 'pick-up' job" (Polanyi 1964, 240–41).

Despite the usefulness of Polanyi's theoretical separation of three highly intermingled trends, which certainly helps us to understand the history of the twenties, he is wrong to suggest that nationalist-dictatorial regimes and fascist-type mass movements in Central and Eastern Europe merely "picked up" the nationalist agenda and the counterrevolutionary program. In fact, the various trends of this "nationalist-right-wing—sometimes fascist—authoritarian mix" actually derived from a common origin. All were rooted in the peripheral backwardness of the region: its economic backwardness, somewhat archaic social structure, and unfinished process of nation building. The nationalist dictatorial regimes and fascist-type mass movements were genuinely intermixed with the nationalist agenda and counterrevolutionary programs. The confusion of "national" and "social" was a special characteristic of the region.

In the West, where bourgeois liberal development proceeded unimpeded, the social question was posed far more openly on its own terms, without intermingling with the national one, and even where fascist

movements and ideologies appeared, fascism and right-wing dictatorships failed. Contrary to what Polanyi argues, the crisis of the market
economy in the interwar decades did not lead to the collapse of liberal
parliamentary democracies in the West. Instead, peripheral backwardness (or a post-Versailles shock and fear in Germany of being forced back
to the periphery) collapsed all these economic, social, and national
problems into one dramatic central question about national survival and
revival. This led to the goal of catching up by revolting against the values and institutions of the rival and triumphant advanced West, including its human rights, democracies, parliaments, and free trade. The social and economic goals all were expressed in a national program against
"race-aliens," nonnationals, Jews, foreigners, hostile neighbors, and foreign investors, which allowed social programs and national goals to mix
in calls for "social justice." Largely for this reason, postwar democratic
national revolutions could not follow the Western path of previous centuries and began to deform into nationalist authoritarian regimes. Nationalism provided an accessible freeway to nationalist dictatorship.

8

From Bolshevik Revolution to a National-Imperial Modernization Dictatorship

The Hope of a World Revolution

Although victorious, the Bolshevik revolution did not spread throughout Central and Eastern Europe. But what could be the destiny of an international revolution limited to one country? Following Marxist theory, Bolshevik leaders believed that the achievement of socialist goals was impossible if confined to a single, backward peasant country like Russia. Revising Marxist theory, Lenin maintained that the mission of the Russian revolution lay in inducing a European "world" revolution, but he denied that true socialism could be introduced in Russia. What history had prepared in Russia, Lenin argued in his famous April Theses of 1917, was only the beginning of the process toward socialism. At the Tenth Party Congress in 1921, Lenin reiterated his view that socialism is possible only in advanced countries and that the revolution in Russia would achieve its goal only with the assistance of revolutions in advanced countries. Until that time, the Russian proletariat would need to compromise with the peasantry, the majority of the country. This concept was firmly based on the views formulated by Lev Trotsky in *Itogi i Perspektivy* (Results and perspectives) (1906). Writing in the Peter-Paul Fortress where he was awaiting trial, Trotsky theorized that Bolshevik Russia would go through "a permanent revolution" in a dual sense. First, within the country, an antifeudal revolution would become anticapitalist, and second, that anticapitalist revolution would expand beyond the boundaries of Russia. Thus the national stage of revolution would eventually acquire international dimensions, and in the end, a united socialist world system would emerge.*

The crucial question for Russian radicals in the mid-1920s—what would happen if the revolution failed to spread and conquer Europe—was first posed by Trotsky in 1906. He suggested two possible routes to failure: the revolution either would be destroyed by a conservative Europe, or would be eroded by the primitive economic and cultural environment of Russia. Trotsky actually reformulated the warning of Marx and Engels, although at the time he could not know it, since the unfinished manuscript of their *German Ideology* (1847) was still unpublished. Like Marx and Engels, Trotsky asserted that socialism might be achieved "as the common action of the leading nations," but without high levels of development "only poverty would be distributed and the struggle for the necessities would start again . . . communism would be a local phenomenon." The development of communism in such nations and connections with the world system "would destroy local communism" (Marx and Engels 1970).

This warning was unchallenged and often repeated by Russian Marxists and Bolsheviks. In early 1924, Stalin himself recapitulated this view in his *Foundations of Leninism*. He questioned whether the final victory of socialism could be achieved "with the forces of only one country" and concluded that, no, it could not: "For this the victory of the revolution in at least several countries is needed." Peasant Russia could not be a "self-sufficient entity [of socialism], but . . . an aid . . . for hastening the victory of the proletariat in other countries" (Stalin 1972, 120). Yet Stalin also stressed the importance of "accomplishing the maximum that is achievable in one country."

The Road of Transition: The Introduction of War Communism

What was this "maximum" in Russia; what kind of "transition" was possible? In the beginning, Lenin advocated a cautious, grad-

---

* Trotsky based his thesis on Marx and Engels's "Address of the Central Committee to the Communist League" in 1850, where Marx suggested that "it is our interest and our task to make the revolution permanent . . . until the proletariat has conquered state power, and . . . not only in one country but all dominant countries of the world" (Marx and Engels 1962, 110).

ual path that monopolized the "commanding heights" of the economy but allowed many private enterprises to exist, even though they were controlled by the state and by workers' factory committees. The Bolshevik program accepted by the Seventh Party Congress in 1918 declared that the population would be concentrated into consumer communes, the monopolists of any kind of trading. All other trading activity would be banned. Wages and salaries would gradually be equalized and labor would become compulsory. Money, banking, and bourgeois expertise, however, would continue to be recognized and legitimized.

This Bolshevik program was harshly criticized by Nikolai Bukharin and Evgeny Preobrazhensky as a "savior of capitalism." As the leaders of the left-wing opposition of the Bolsheviks, they urged Lenin to instigate drastic nationalization policies and to collectivize agriculture. They also advocated replacing money and banking with a central system of distribution and accounting. The left-wing opposition was harshly criticized by Lenin and the majority of the party elite, but the program proposed by Bukharin and Preobrazhensky soon became triumphant. The short peaceful interval after the treaty of Brest-Litovsk was broken by the attacks of the Czech Legion and by the White Russian army of Kolchak and Denykin. From the early summer of 1918, the life-or-death struggle of the civil war began. In this new context, radical nationalization abolished private ownership. Before June 1918, chaotic, spontaneous actions by the masses nationalized 487 firms. Within a year, nearly 90 percent of large industry belonged to the state. By November 1920, all firms with more than five workers and those having any kind of machinery were nationalized. In practice, small-scale industry and village windmills were also nationalized. The number of state-owned companies reached thirty-seven thousand. (More than five thousand firms employed only one single worker.) The extreme "nationalization fever" is illustrated by the fact that all private libraries larger than three thousand volumes were nationalized.

The fatal food shortage and resultant famine of the winter of 1917–1918, when the daily bread ration of Petrograd workers was only five dekagrams (175 ounces), generated desperate state intervention. All private trade was banned and treated as crime. "Racketeers" were shot dead on the spot. Lenin ordered the "crusade for bread" and the *Narkomprod*, the people's commissioner of supply, was established in May 1918. Armed workers' units searched homes and confiscated food reserves. All the "superfluous" foodstuff held by peasants were requisitioned by the state. Because the state "paid" for the requisitions with valueless paper money, the compulsory delivery of farm produce actually meant confiscation of produce when supplies exceeded the minimal need of the families. In 1918–1919, nearly 108 million poods (one pood is roughly thirty-six pounds) of grain were confiscated, twice as much as in 1917–1918. In response, peasants dramatically diminished cultivation, and, consequently, a compulsory sowing plan was introduced in 1919.

The labor market was closed and labor was militarized. A "Labor Army" was recruited: 280,000 people were sent to construction and mining projects, and women between the ages of sixteen and forty-five were required to work for the Red Army. Compulsory labor service became a general practice.

A highly centralized, planned, bureaucratized economy was created. In addition to the Supreme Council of the National Economy (*Vesenkha*), which was established in December 1917 as the central ministerial organ for directing the economy, regional councils (*Sovnarkhoz*) were founded. Soon, a network of offices (*Glavki*), each of them responsible for a single industrial branch, was created but strictly subordinated to the Supreme Council. Production and distribution were planned; both market and money relations were consequently abandoned. This centralized, dictatorial war communism reintroduced an economy in kind. Most services, including housing, postal service, transportation, and food products rationed by the state were free of charge. The Bolsheviks made virtue out of necessity: it was not so much ideological commitment but rather an intolerable hyper-inflation that led to the introduction of a moneyless economy. In the years of revolution and civil war, prices increased eight thousand times. The value of money in circulation—based on the cost of living index—declined from 2.2 billion rubles in November 1917, to 29 million rubles in July 1921. As Zinovyev stated in a lecture during his 1920 trip to Germany: "The burden of inflation is almost unbearable in Russia. . . . However, there is hope of escape from the situation. We are totally eliminating money. Wages are paid in kind. Transportation, schooling, and electricity is free of charge, and rents have been abolished" (Zinovyev 1921, 47). The nationalized economy did not use the market or money as an exchange medium. As Larin declared at the second congress of the regional councils in December 1918, state-owned companies received raw materials and energy by central distribution. Their products were also distributed by central authorities, and the railroads delivered them free of charge. Money did not play any role in the economy.

Nikolai Bukharin, the leading theoretician of war communism, argues in his *Economy of the Transition Period* (1920) that market and money were not needed in the soviet economy. The reorganized national economy could be seen as a single gigantic combined company. Value, price, and profit therefore no longer existed. The "blind forces of the market" were replaced by conscious planning in an economy of kind. Direction came through state intervention and pressure (Bukharin 1971).

Hyper-inflation and severe shortages, combined with a doctrinaire revolutionary "enthusiasm" for accomplishing long-range goals and ideals, contributed to the premature introduction of communism in Russia. But the change was also urged by the plight of the impoverished masses. "The difficulty was not in the logic of civil war, as comrade Preobrazhensky thinks," argued B. Gorev in 1923 at a debate of the Socialist Academy, "but in the fact that the rebellious proletariat demanded equality, that is, consumer communism" (Nove 1992, 74).

A New Approach toward Transition: The New Economic Policy

War communism was a failure. With its utopian-dictatorial measures, across-the-board equalization, and return to an economy in kind, it killed economic incentives and increased rather than solved the problems of a collapsing nation. Industrial output in 1921 reached only one-fifth of the 1913 level. The harvest of the same year produced 37.6 million tons of grain, 43 percent of the average of agricultural output between 1909 and 1913. Railroads delivered 39.4 million tons of goods, compared to the prewar figure of 132.4 million. The starving urban populace fled the cities: the populations of Petrograd and Moscow decreased by 58 and 45 percent respectively during the three postrevolution years. The number of industrial workers dropped from 3 million to 1.24 million between 1917 and 1922. Lacking adequate fuel supplies, people burned their floors and entire wooden houses to get heat during the harsh winters. Famine decimated the population; millions starved to death. Bukharin complained about the "disintegration" of the proletariat at the Seventh Party Congress. Peasants revolted in the countryside, and gangs ruled in some regions. On February 28, 1921, even the sailors of Kronstadt, once a hard core of Bolshevik supporters, revolted against the regime. Further delays in bringing change would have been deadly.

Shocked by the sailors' uprising, a February 28 plenary session of the Moscow Soviet openly denounced the infamous *Prodrazverstka*, that brutal confiscation of the entire "surplus" product of the peasantry. In its place, a fixed taxation in kind was suggested. A year earlier at a session of the Politburo, Trotsky had made precisely the same suggestion, but his motion had been defeated as members, following Lenin, maintained that marketing the surplus product in the given circumstances would be a "crime." The 1921 reversal in policy was announced by Lenin at the Tenth Party Congress in March. The tone of Lenin's address captured the sense of danger and urgency:

We must try to satisfy the demands of the peasants who are dissatisfied, discontented. . . . We must admit that the masses are weary and exhausted. . . . We must say to the small farmer: "Farmer, produce food and the state will take a minimum tax." We now have an opportunity of coming to an agreement with the peasants. . . . We know that only agreement with the peasantry can save the socialist revolution in Russia until the revolution in other countries takes place. . . . We must this very evening announce over the radio . . . that the congress of the governing party has . . . substituted a tax for the food quotas. (Lenin 1937, 108, 110, 117, 120–22)

This was a genuine compromise with the peasantry. The quantity of tax in kind—240 million poods of grain in 1921—was significantly less than the quantity of confiscated grain—423 million poods—in 1920. In 1922, the tax in kind was only 10 percent of production, and peasants were allowed to employ labor, even to rent land and to market their products. Taxes in kind were replaced by taxes in money in 1924. Agriculture began to develop: grain production increased from 37.6 million tons in 1921 to 50.3 million tons in 1922, and to 76.8 million tons in 1926, thus approaching the prewar level of 80 million tons.

The *Novaya Ekonomicheskaya Polityka* (New Economic Policy) (NEP) went much further than replacing grain confiscation by moderate taxation. Although official positions stressed that war communism was only a set of emergency measures demanded by the war and not a consistent economic policy, NEP destroyed the consistent system of a nonmarket economy by reintroducing the market and private incentives. Milyutin, the deputy president of the Supreme Council, noted at the Tenth Party Congress that NEP is "not only a compromise with the peasantry, but a radical change of the entire economic policy that we consistently followed during the last two years" (Szamuely 1971, 131). Indeed, in May 1921, a decree legalized small-scale private industry and canceled the extreme nationalization measures. More than seven thousand state-owned industrial firms were offered for private leasing in the leather and food processing industries alone. Within a year, nearly four thousand firms were rented by private persons, who were sometimes the former owners. The management of state-owned industry also changed. The concept of the national economy as a huge, single, centrally-directed, nationwide company was replaced by *Hozrashchot*, the concept of efficient, market-oriented, independent firms. Larger units, the so-called "trusts," which merged on average about ten companies, appeared before the end of 1921. The largest trusts—such as the Ivanovo-Vozhnesensk Textile Trust—employed fifty-four thousand workers. The majority of state-owned firms produced for the free market, whereas firms of strategic importance—namely, investment good industries, engineering and steel firms, and so on—marketed half of their products. State distribution of energy was halted in March 1922 and replaced by a market system. In April 1923, state-owned firms became legally independent from the state administration and were allowed to operate on a profit basis in the market.

All the restrictions of war communism were curbed. In April 1921, a decree dissolved the "labor army" and ended the militarization of labor. A free labor market was reintroduced in which wages were to be fixed by agreement between firms and workers. The decree denounced "all kinds of equalization." All free supplies and services, including transportation, were abolished. State distribution, free of charge, was replaced by the market system. Before the introduction of NEP, 34 million people had been supplied with food by free state-rationing, even though it had covered less than one-third of the food consumption in cities. The illegal "black market" thus had played a role of central importance. At the beginning of NEP, soviet authorities sought to limit market activity to local framework; peasants and small-scale producers were allowed to sell their products in the village or township in which they operated. But it was impossible to realize this goal. After restrictions on traveling and transportation were lifted, the market became triumphant; it was officially recognized and legalized in May 1921. Trade became overwhelmingly private: 95 percent of Moscow's trade was in private hands by 1922, and the famous fairs of Nizhniy-Novgorod and Irbit were reopened.

Industrial output gradually increased. From the nadir of 1921, when it was only one-fifth of the 1913 level, output doubled by 1923 and doubled again by 1925. By 1926, industrial output surpassed prewar levels by 10 percent. The bold adventure to create a moneyless society had failed spectacularly. Symbolically, on the fourth anniversary of the October revolution, Lenin published an article on the importance of gold. The realization of the dream of a moneyless economy was postponed to the far-distant future of "world socialism." "When we are victorious on a world scale," stated Lenin, "we shall use gold for the purpose of building public lavatories in the streets" (Lenin 1971, 656). In the present, however, *Gosbank* (National Bank) was reopened in November 1921, and a new currency with a 25 percent gold reserve was issued in July 1922. The new currency, the *chervonyet*, equaled ten prewar gold rubles. The state budget was reestablished; in the 1923–1924 fiscal year, it was already balanced.

In this context, a new concept of transformation emerged. In his fourth anniversary article, Lenin stated: "We presumed . . . to be able to organize the state production and . . . distribution . . . directly as ordered by the proletarian state. Experience has proved that we were wrong. . . . Not directly relying on enthusiasm, but . . . on the basis of personal interest, personal incentive and business principles, we must first . . . build solid gangways . . . of state capitalism" (Lenin 1971, 651).

Debates on the Destiny of the Revolution: "Socialism in One Country"

The NEP was evidently successful but could not annul the fundamental questions about the destiny of the revolution. Most Bolsheviks assumed that the NEP merely represented a period of retreat from proper transformation policy; it might be, according to Lenin, a serious change that would last a "long period of time that one measures in years" and characterize an entire historical period—possibly even several decades long—but it was, nonetheless, only a temporary measure. Without specifying a definite time frame, Lenin declared in November 1921, half a year after the introduction of the NEP, that "we retreated to state capitalism, but we did not retreat too far. We are now retreating to the state regulation of trade, but shall not retreat too far. There are visible signs that the retreat is coming to an end . . . in the not too distant future" (Lenin 1971, 659).

In 1923, opponents of NEP began to criticize the policy for fostering the rebirth of capitalism and for "sacrificing workers' interests for the sake of the peasantry." Trotsky, who became the head of the left-wing opposition, protested against the application of the NEP in industry. In a memorandum to the Central Committee dated August 7, 1921, he deplored the zigzags in Bolshevik policy and demanded a powerful central authority, a planning office, and a reorganization of the economy with the central role assigned to heavy industry. Preobrazhensky, the talented economist of the left-wing opposition, criticized the NEP for creating a new bourgeoisie and urged collectivization. In April 1923, at the Twelfth Party Congress, Trotsky launched an open attack against the NEP. In sharp terms, he cited Lenin's own claims to support his own position: NEP was "established seriously and for a long time, but not forever . . . [and] had been adopted in order on its own foundation and to a large extent by using its own methods to overcome [NEP]. . . . Our success on the basis of the new economic policy automatically brings us nearer to its liquidation." The coming post-NEP period, stated Trotsky, would be the period of "primitive socialist accumulation" (Carr 1950–1953, 2: 379).

In October, the so-called "Group of '46," led by Trotsky, issued a declaration and an article in *Pravda*, which thoroughly condemned NEP policies and advocated a "dictatorship of industry" accompanied by central planning.

The fierce debate of that era was closely connected to Lenin's serious illness and his death in January 1924. Next to Lenin, Trotsky was the most outstanding Bolshevik theoretician and leader of the revolution and civil war, and with customary vigor he mounted an indirect campaign to assume Lenin's post. For the very same reason, Joseph Visarionovich Stalin, a member of the Politburo and hence one of the top Bolshevik leaders, stepped out as the chief defender of Lenin's party line against the left-wing opposition. Compared to the four other members of the Politburo during the civil war—Lenin, Trotsky, Kamanyev, and Bukharin, who were all highly educated men, scholars, theoreticians and outstanding speakers—Stalin was much less sparkling. The short reticent Georgian, whose studies began and ended in a religious seminar, rose to prominence because of his unlimited capacity for hard work and excellent organizational skills. It was, therefore, not accidental that he eventually became responsible for the ordinary administrative tasks of the party and was elevated to the newly created post of secretary general after Lenin's first serious illness. Stalin was not a theoretician and once, when he spoke on theoretical issues at a party meeting, Ryazanov, an old Bolshevik, interrupted saying: "Do not continue

Koba," (Stalin's nickname was Koba), "do not make a fool of yourself. Everybody knows that theory is not your field."

Ironically, in 1924, the year of Lenin's death, Stalin offered the most effective "theory," one that revised the basic principles of Marxism and Bolshevism. At the end of 1924, he published the study *Problems of Leninism*, in which he rejects the traditional internationalist concept of socialism and declares that Russia, although lacking the support of victorious revolutions in advanced European countries, would be able to establish a socialist economy and society. Since true socialism is possible only with a high level of economic development, socialism would be accomplished if Russia could become a highly industrialized, advanced country with a high standard of living. Enormous Russia with its unlimited natural sources could, with hard work, achieve this goal: "We can build socialism . . . [because] we possess . . . all that is needed to build a complete socialist society, overcoming all internal difficulties, for we can and must overcome them by our own efforts . . . without the preliminary victory of the proletarian revolution in other countries. . . . It is no use engaging in building socialism without being sure that we can build it completely, without being sure that the technical backwardness of our country is not an *insuperable* obstacle to the building of a complete socialist society" (Stalin 1976, 211–12). Stalin's thesis was simple and powerful: Russia is strong and can realize its goals even alone. She does not need the assistance of other nations; the destiny of the revolution and the fate of the country is not dependent on outside support. The future of revolutionary Russia became a "national" issue rather than one of international scope. Isaac Deutscher describes these events as follows:

Hitherto Bolshevism looked upon Russia as upon a periphery of modern civilization. On the periphery the revolution started; there socialism had found its practical pioneers. . . . Russia's role in the world-wide transformation of society was seen as that of the powerful initiator of the whole movement. But Western Europe still remained the real center of modern civilization; and, in the old Bolshevik view, it was there in the center and not on the periphery that the forms of a new social life were eventually to be forged. . . . In Stalin's doctrine Russia no longer figures as a mere periphery of the civilized world. It is within her own boundaries that the forms of a new society are to be found and worked out. It is her destiny to become the center of a new civilization, in all respects superior to that capitalist civilization. (Deutscher 1967, 293)

Stalin's "discovery" of the possibility of "socialism in one country" had far-reaching importance. It reinforced faith in the communist dream, and it strengthened Bolshevik self-confidence in their revolution by freeing it from dependence on a successful world revolution and making it a specifically national, Soviet Russian case. Russia's new proud goal consisted of establishing itself as a new center of a new civilization. Russian nationalism and communism were not contradictory movements any longer. As Edward H. Carr expresses it:

Socialism in one country might look like the nationalization of the revolution. . . . [It] was a synthesis between socialist and national loyalties. It was the point at which Russian destiny and Marxism joined hands. . . . Hitherto the economic development of Russia and the westernization of Russia had been integral parts of the same process. After 1925 they were separated. Industrialization would be pursued independently of the west and, if necessary, against the west. (Carr 1959, 50)

Stalin's motives for revising the basic principle of Marx and the Bolsheviks were manifold. The struggle for power, evidently extremely attractive to him, necessarily led him into open confrontation with Trotsky, the most likely heir to Russian leadership. Stalin also recognized the natural hopes and needs of the majority of his party, which sought stability and a clear vision on the future. In the eighth year of the revolution, the party needed to believe that it still held Russian fate in its hand. The concept of a backward Russia dependent on the West was humiliating, particularly after the hope for a world revolution evaporated. The mirage of a future advanced socialist society, the new center of an emerging new world civilization, served traditional Russian feelings of messianism and missionary zeal. Because a strong need for confidence in the future existed, Stalin had to be sure in his success. Although the influential Zinovyev maintained that the concept of "socialism in one country" was "national narrow-mindedness," and Trotsky called it "national messianism," the Eleventh Party Conference in March 1925 enthusiastically adopted the thesis. Nikolai Bukharin, who published his study "The Road to Socialism" in that year and who triumphantly announced that "the economy of our enormous country is beginning to stand on its own feet. . . . We are lifting ourselves out of poverty," accepted Stalin's thesis and added that "socialism . . . in the first stage of its development, before all the countries of the world merge into a single entity, will . . . be differentiated . . . by its own peculiarities . . . There is no cause for us to be ashamed of the fact that the socialism we are building is inevitably a backward type." Ignorant of Marx's warning that local backward communism would, of necessity, fail, Bukharin optimistically concluded: "We have the potential for endless progress, for perfecting these forms, for overcoming our backwardness" (Bukharin 1982, 209–10, 294).

Stalin's thesis was little more than a powerful slogan; it lacked specific strategic content. But it was effective enough in the struggle against the Left Opposition and Trotsky, who continued to propagate the idea that the final success of socialism depended on world revolution. Paradoxically, Trotsky and the Left Opposition actually worked out the economic strategies, institutional mechanisms, and political requirements needed to bolster "socialism in one country." But they and Stalin did not realize that their opposing concepts met on common ground. In 1926, Trotsky sharply criticized Stalin's view of socialism in Russia; Stalin, meanwhile, harshly rejected the economic strategy suggested by Trotsky and maintained that it would lead toward an economic and political disaster. The program of the internationalist Left Opposition, ironically, developed as an isolationist strategy for modernization in a backward peasant country. The initiator of the idea of the "dictatorship of industry," or, as it would be called in modern terminology, "modernization dictatorship," was Trotsky, but the main architect of its model was Evgeny Preobrazhensky. His concept was brilliantly summarized in his *Novaia Ekonomika* (The new economics), which was published first as a lecture series in 1924, and then as a book in 1926. Stalin rejected the ideas of the work and later (in 1937) deported and murdered its author, but he also "borrowed" and eventually put the ideas into practice.

The Concept of Forced Industrialization and Central Planning

Preobrazhensky worked out a new model of the transformation from capitalism to socialism in a backward country, embracing the concept of a fast road to industrialization and sustained economic growth. Preobrazhensky's point of departure was the thesis that, in a transitory period after the revolution:

the socialist system is not yet in a condition to develop all its organic advantages, but it inevitably abolishes at the same time a number of the economic advantages characteristic of a developed capitalist system. . . . [Therefore, the transition] is the most critical period in the life of the socialist state. . . . How to pass as quickly as possible through this period . . . [and reach] the moment when the socialist system will develop all its natural advantages over capitalism, is a question of life and death for the socialist state. (Preobrazhensky 1965, 89)

Preobrazhensky suggested that the nonindustrialized "backward economy must pass through a period of primitive accumulation in which the resources provided by pre-socialist forms of economy are drawn upon very freely." The central problem was the rate of capital accumulation, specifically, how to achieve accumulation in a poor country unable to save a high portion of its income. Nationalized, weak industry could not supply the resources that were required. In a peasant-agricultural country, only "petty-bourgeois producers" and peasants could be exploited. Preobrazhensky asserted that the idea that a socialist economy in its first phase of existence could manage "without touching the resources of the petty-bourgeois (including peasant) economy is . . . a reactionary . . . utopia." His concept of "primitive [or preliminary] socialist accumulation, as a period of the creation of the material prerequisites for socialist production"—a forced "accumulation in the hands of the state of material resources mainly . . . from sources lying outside the complex of state economy"—was based on Marx's interpretation of the birth of capitalism, when a period of "primitive accumulation" (the expropriation of the peasantry by a rising bourgeoisie) introduced capitalism.* As early modern capitalism required "a period of prolonged exploitation of petty production" in order to "be able to demonstrate its advantages over craft production . . . , in the same way . . . the previously accumulated means . . . of production is needed" for the socialist economy in the making. Moreover, "the task of the socialist state consists . . . not in taking from the petty-bourgeois producers less than capitalism took, but in taking more" (Preobrazhensky 1965, 81–82, 84, 89). Consequently, the policy of forced accumulation focused on extortion from the kulaks, the well-to-do peasantry. The state had to siphon off the resources of the private peasant

---

* The term *primitive socialist accumulation* was introduced by another soviet economist, V. M. Smirnov, but it is Preobrazhensky who gives a strong theoretical interpretation of it in the second chapter of his book, where he speaks of the "law of primitive socialist accumulation" (Preobrazhensky 1965, 81). Marx introduces the term *primitive accumulation* and analyzes its process in the British historical example in *Das Kapital*, vol. 1, chapter 24 (Marx 1919).

economy, transferring those resources to the state's accumulation fund, where they would eventually be invested in industry. This accumulation of funds would provide the basis for a forced industrialization that would renew the entire technological and structural basis of the soviet economy, lifting it to the level of the economies in advanced capitalist countries.

Preobrazhensky offered an arsenal of methods to achieve the requisite high rate of accumulation in a poor country. The central operator was the price system. By destroying the market economy and market prices and by introducing fixed prices, regulated by the state, it became possible to support high industrial prices and low agricultural ones. With this "price scissor," state-owned industry exploited the privately-owned agricultural economy and siphoned off its income. In addition, the "system of socialist protectionism"—a term that was introduced by Trotsky—based on the state monopoly of foreign trade, assisted forced accumulation by keeping domestic prices paid to the peasants at a much lower level than export prices, thereby ensuring a surplus profit for the state. High tariffs represented an extra taxation of private economy and the population. The "monopoly of price policy," Preobrazhensky said, is "only another form of taxation of private economy." With striking frankness, he suggested the "issue of paper money" and inflationary policy as "a channel for socialist accumulation . . . carried out at the expense . . . of the petty-bourgeois [peasant] . . . elements or of reduced wages of the state's workers and . . . employees" (Preobrazhensky 1965, III, 91).

In other words, the state-owned, nonmarket economy possessed all the instruments needed to guarantee an unprecedented high rate of accumulation at the expense of the non-state-owned sectors, the peasant economy and the entire population. In Preobrazhensky's theory, primitive socialist accumulation is a general rule and an unavoidable transitory period after the proletarian revolution, "not only for backward peasant countries like the USSR but to some extent . . . also for the socialist economy of Europe . . . , [because it] is economically and technically weaker than the economy of . . . North America" (Preobrazhensky 1965, 120–21).

The program of forced industrialization was a consistent, long-term economic strategy that contained the basic institutional requirements for its own application. Because the central goal consisted of reaching the highest possible capital accumulation by halting the "exchange of equal labor values" at the expense of private peasant agriculture, the market and market prices had to be abolished in a system of planned and state-directed economy.* The "law of the market" was replaced by central planning. The "law of primitive socialist accumulation" thus eliminated the automatic play of market relations and demanded a state-regulated economy in its place.

Preobrazhensky's thesis of socialist accumulation on the road to catching up to the industrialized West would eventually be realized later by Stalin as the basis for a modernization dictatorship. In the early and mid-1920s, however, only Trotsky and his followers called for the realization of the "dictatorship of industry" in order to siphon funds from the villages and peasantry to benefit industrialization. This demand, formulated first in 1923, became a focal point in the policy debates by 1926. In November 1927, Trotsky, Kamenev, and Zinovyev published articles in *Pravda* and presented a joint "counterthesis" to the Fifteenth Party Congress underlining the dangers inherent in the advance of the kulaks. They demanded an increase in the prices of industrial products and a two-million-pood compulsory grain tax to be levied on the richest 10 percent of the peasantry. Grain paid as taxes would be exported and therefore raise money for importing industrial investment goods.

In an agitated theoretical debate, a group of renowned economic experts including Shanin and Kondratiev suggested a diametrically opposed, agriculture-oriented strategy. The increase of agricultural productivity and exports, according to the advocates of the notion, would lead to an increase in export incomes, which would be reinvested in agriculture. Over time, agriculture would reach high levels of development, and, on this base, industrialization would later occur.

The Stalin-led majority in the Bolshevik leadership rejected both strategies. Stalin was able to place himself in the advantageous center position on the Central Committee. At the Moscow Party Conference in January 1925, Stalin rejected Trotsky's and Preobrazhensky's "ultra industrialization," stressing that the destiny of socialism and the soviet economy is dependent on the peasantry. "Our industry, which is the basis of socialism and the basis of our regime, rests on the home market, the peasant market," and, consequently, the party has to exercise "special attention and special care to the peasantry" (Stalin 1972, 190–91). At

---

* In Marxist terms, the value of a commodity is determined by the amount of "socially necessary" labor input (including indirect labor such as machinery and materials) used for its production. As a result of offer and demand, market prices fluctuate around the value or price of production and ensure an equal rate of return on capital.

the Fourteenth Party Congress in December 1925, advocating the centrist "party line," together with "ultra industrialization," Stalin equally refused the "agrarianist" concept, declaring that "this strategy would block industrialization and our country would never be properly industrialized, but would depend on the capitalist world" (Stalin 1947, 338–42).

Stalin's main comrade-in-arms in this debate was Nikolai Bukharin, a brilliant theoretician trained in Vienna and the ablest Bolshevik economist. Bukharin argued for the importance of developing the domestic market and denounced Trotsky's theory as "an attempt to destroy the domestic market" (*Pravda* 1924). He accepted the notion that industrialization was important and that domestic resources and industrial incomes were not adequate for the task. Bukharin declared that the peasant economy was a potential source of industrialization and that "siphoning off" its income to state accumulation funds and industrial investments was acceptable. But, in a Leningrad debate in July 1926, he questioned how far the limits of the exploitation of the peasantry could be pushed. In his view, rather strict economic and political limits existed and industrialization should not be attained at the expense of agriculture. A balanced interrelationship between the two sectors was, for him, the central prerequisite of rapid and sustained growth. Bukharin's views are summarized in his study *Zametki ekonomista* (Notes of an economist), in a debate with Trotsky and Preobrazhensky. "In their naivete the ideologists of Trotskyism suggest that a maximum yearly transfusion from the peasant economy into industry will generally ensure a maximum rate of industrial development. But that is clearly not the case. The highest rate can be *sustained* only . . . on the basis of a rapidly growing agriculture. . . . What the Trotskyists fail to comprehend is that the development of industry depends on the development of agriculture" (Bukharin 1982, 310). In the mid-1920s, Bukharin and the majority of the Bolshevik leadership were therefore still arguing along the NEP policy-line and stressed that "the more quickly accumulation occurs in our peasant economy, the more quickly will it occur in our industry. . . . Thus industry requires successes in agriculture" (Bukharin 1982, 242). Just as "superindustrialization" required the elimination of the market and the introduction of central planning, the concept of economic equilibrium and a mutual dependence between the main sectors of the economy demanded market relations, market prices, and profit incentives. According to Bukharin, the economic plan, the central will, or the "law of primitive accumulation" could not replace the market, but, as an instrument, could only help to achieve accumulation and development that would otherwise be spontaneously created more slowly by the market forces. Another leading economist and participant in the debate on the Bukharin side argued in the 1928 *Planovoye Hoziaystvo* (Planned economy) that "historical experience proves the importance of workers' interest in their work, moreover . . . , in the given circumstances only the market can automatically control whether an economic action is good or mistaken" (Bazarov 1928, 2). The concepts of balanced economic growth and of the interrelationship between agricultural and industrial development were linked therefore to the notion of combining market mechanisms with central planning.

During these debates, Stalin declared in a speech to the Fourteenth Party Congress in December 1925 that "we are staying and will stay behind Bukharin!" Even the Fifteenth Party Congress accepted Bukharin's position, which was repeated in Stalin's introductory speech. Stalin declared in December 1927: "It is incorrect to start with a demand for the maximum siphoning off of resources from the sphere of peasant economy into the sphere of industry, for this demand signifies not only a political rupture with the peasantry but also an undermining of industry's own raw material base . . . , its domestic market . . . of exports and the disruption of equilibrium in the whole economic system" (Stalin 1949, 299–313).

In the late twenties, however, Stalin and his majority in the Bolshevik leadership gradually and silently revised their policy. In December 1926, Stalin's close aid Kuybishev was appointed head of the Supreme Economic Council. In spring of the next year, construction began on the Dnieper hydroelectric power station, a highly debated, gigantic investment and a symbol of the a new industrialization drive. A plan of rapid industrialization was presented at the Fifteenth Congress, but it was rejected by the majority. Stalin, victorious against the Left Opposition and stabilized in power, cynically "borrowed" his victims' concept of industrialization and opened a new front, therefore launching a new attack, this time against a Right Opposition.

Merging "Socialism in One Country" and the Program of Forced Industrialization

Trotsky's and Preobrazhensky's concepts of forced accumulation and industrialization were thus rejected between the crucial years of 1923 and 1927, a period of struggle for power. A strong group of the most influential Bolshevik leaders blocked Trotsky's drive to replace Lenin. By 1923 and for another two years after Lenin's death, a triumvirate of rulers was formed by Kamenev, Zinovyev, and Stalin. A cult of Leninism was generated to denounce Trotsky and his positions in earlier debates with Lenin on the role of the unions, the Brest-Litovsk policy of compromise for peace, and the issues of the NEP and industrialization. A new campaign instilled party discipline and unity, and party members who formed "factions" were expelled. Lenin's will warned the party that the rivalry between Trotsky and Stalin could lead to a party split and suggested the removal of Stalin from the post of secretary general. Kamenev and Zinovyev, however, successfully defended Stalin and continued to attack Trotsky. In 1925, Trotsky was removed from the post of people's commissar for war. During the next year, he was discharged from the Politburo and then from the Central Committee; he was finally expelled from the party in November 1927. In the meantime, the triumvirate dissolved, split up by the confrontation between Stalin on the one hand and Kamenev and Zinovyev on the other. Zinovyev criticized Stalin's concept of "socialism in one country" and assumed the leadership of the Left Opposition. As a result, Zinovyev was also expelled from the party, and the Fifteenth Party Congress expelled seventy-five leading additional figures associated with the Left Opposition. Stalin did not hesitate to make his victory complete: Trotsky was deported to Alma Ata and Rakovsky to Astrahan. After a year, Trotsky was expelled from the Soviet Union and forced to flee to Turkey. Kamaniev and Zinovyev were also arrested and deported.

In his struggle against Lenin's closest comrades, Stalin enjoyed the cooperation of influential old Bolsheviks such as Bukharin, Rykov (chair of the Council of the Peoples' Commissars), and Tomsky (president of the Trade Union). He also scrupulously built his majority in the Politburo. The newly elected members of the leading body—Molotov, Kuybisev, Rudzutuk, Vorosilov, and Kalinyin—and the newly created candidate-membership of the Politburo—Kirov, Kaganovich, Andreyev, and Mikoyan—strengthened Stalin's position.

His independent-minded allies soon became a burden for Stalin, who was seeking absolute power. After the final defeat of the Left Opposition, a split became inevitable. The devastating new grain crisis and famine in early 1928 gave Stalin the excuse he needed to act. He turned against the liberal treatment of peasants under the NEP, focusing special attention on the kulaks. Simultaneously, he launched an attack

against the so-called Right Opposition within the party leadership—
that is, his influential rivals, Bukharin, Rykov, and Tomsky, who were
arguing for the continuation of NEP and seeking to hinder Stalin's an-
tipeasant campaign. But the struggle remained behind the scenes until
the end of 1928. Stalin repeatedly declared, even in October, that "in
the political Bureau there are neither Right nor Left deviations nor con-
ciliators toward those deviations" (Stalin 1976, 322).

On January 30, 1929, circumstances played into Stalin's hands:
Bukharin opposed the policy of the Central Committee in an open declaration. On February 9, Bukharin, Tomsky, and Rykov issued a joint
statement, which denounced "the policy of the feudal-military exploitation of the peasantry." Bukharin refused to withdraw the declaration, and in April 1929, the time ripened for Stalin's attack. He accused Bukharin of organizing a Right Opposition. Bukharin, Rykov,
and Tomsky were removed from their posts and dismissed from the leading bodies of the party. They saved themselves temporarily from further repression by severe "self-criticism." But their removal signaled the
end of both the struggle for power and Lenin's legacy. Stalin became
the unquestioned ruler of Bolshevik Russia. On December 21, 1929,
Moscow celebrated his fiftieth birthday with spectacular festivities.
Stalin's statues and photos appeared in squares, shop windows, and public buildings throughout the vast empire. A propaganda campaign began to brainwash the population with the idea that "Stalin is the Lenin
of today!"

Finally in possession of absolute power, Stalin made a radical policy
turn in 1928–1929. The expropriation of peasant lands was ruthlessly executed in a full-blown collectivization drive. "We have succeeded in
turning the bulk of the peasantry in a large number of regions away
from the old capitalist path of development," Stalin declared. In his
speech on agrarian policy in December 1929, he announced the policy
of "dekulakization": "Now we are able to carry on a determinant offensive against the kulaks, break their resistance, [and] eliminate them as
a class . . . Dekulakization . . . is an integral part of the formation and
development of [the] collective farm" (Stalin 1976, 474).

At the same time, citing the example of Peter the Great, who "built
factories and shops to supply his army," Stalin announced a program
of rapid industrialization. Industrial investments were increased by five
times during the summer of 1929. At the Sixteenth Party Congress in
June 1930, Stalin declared triumphantly: "We have arrived at the thresh-
old of being, instead of an agricultural, an industrialized country." In

that year alone, it was planned to increase industrial output by 50 percent. Stalin achieved superindustrialization and won the war against the kulaks so thoroughly and brutally that the Left Opposition's old idea of primitive accumulation at the expense of the peasantry now seemed a naive liberal concept. In February 1931, Stalin stressed passionately that the "tempo [of industrialization] must not be reduced! On the contrary . . . [it must] increase." He recalled the lessons of the past:

One feature of the history of old Russia was the continual beatings she suffered because of her backwardness. She was beaten by the Mongol khans . . . by the Turkish beys . . . by the Swedish feudal lords . . . by the Polish and Lithuanian gentry . . . by the British and French capitalists . . . by the Japanese barons. All beat her because of her backwardness. . . . We are 50 or 100 years behind the advanced countries. We must make good this distance in 10 years. Either we do it, or we shall go under. (Stalin 1976, 528–29)

The rhetoric on the goal of international proletarian revolution survived this onslaught, but the central aim behind the slogan of "socialism in one country" became one of national modernization with the goal of catching up with the West "in 10 years." What were the motives behind Stalin's dramatic turn? Arguments such as Maurice Dobb's suggest that the primary impetus for the adoption of the program of the former Left Opposition stemmed from a major change in international relations. The international revolutionary movement disappeared first in Europe, and then, after the massacre of 1927, in China. Consequently, the Soviet Union remained visibly alone and isolated. Furthermore, the capitalist world recovered from its postwar crisis and shifted noticeably towards the Right, thereby signaling new dangers (Dobb 1966). Stalin sought to be prepared for a new attack. His arguments in 1931 pointed to the military vulnerability of a nonindustrialized soviet state and set a deadline of ten years for catching up with the West. Stalin's framework eventually came to seem prophetic when the deadly military attack against Russia by the German Nazis was launched exactly ten years later, in 1941. In essence, the economic debate of the mid-twenties was delineated by military considerations.

The new grain crisis and famine that developed in the seventh year of the NEP also had a great impact on policy. Stalin's reaction was similar to the measures of "war communism": extreme pressure upon the peasantry, including "dekulakization," forced collectivization of agriculture, and the modernization of the country via industrialization. All these motives coexisted with a ruthless struggle for power, and various competing political views provided an outstanding background from which to create "deviators" and "traitors"—rivals to be eliminated.

The Stalinist model of a new modernization dictatorship became a bridge between two contradictory postwar revolts: the social (or class) revolution and the national revolution. In fact, the modernization dictatorship created during the late 1920s and early 1930s merged Russian social (proletarian) revolution with the national revolution. In several countries of the region, social problems and backwardness appeared as aspects of the national question and belated national revolutions offered a "national medicine" to solve them. In Stalin's Soviet Union, the national issue of coping with traditional Russian backwardness was transformed to become the essential goal of the social (proletarian) revolution. In several countries of the region, the primacy of the national question became the legitimizing factor for national dictatorships that rejected class struggle as that which divides and weakens a nation. But Stalin legitimized both his dictatorship and the central goal of soviet-national modernization by linking them with the class struggle. The Russian revolution, in consequence, stepped onto a new path.

9

Economic Nationalism and Its Consequences

Inflation and Despair

Politics and economy were closely connected throughout Central and Eastern Europe. As the region took the nationalist path, governments designed their economic policies to serve what they assumed to be national interests. In this manner, political considerations penetrated and colored matters of economy. The task facing these governments was tremendous. The long war had brought about economic exhaustion, general shortages, and chaos. By 1917 in the more developed Austrian half of the Austro-Hungarian Empire, economic exhaustion was nearly total. By 1918, it was obvious that the Austrian economy could not survive another winter of war. Agricultural production declined by half. Hungary, the traditional supplier of Austrian markets, could not meet its own demands and thus could no longer export. Most industries suffered from shortages of fuel and raw materials. Even war supplies and production were declining. During the winter of 1918, daily rations of bread and flour were only between 100 to 150 grams and milk consumption was at 7 percent of the prewar level. Other basic supplies were in as appallingly short supply, and lack of coal paralyzed the railroads. In the winter of 1919–1920, barely a quarter of demands for coal could be met. Only one-third of households managed to obtain a small quantity of rationed coal; others burnt fences and cut down trees. Industrial output was only slightly above one-third of prewar levels. The financing of the war with paper money had decreased the value of the

Austrian crown by 67 percent by the end of 1918, shortly after the Austrian Republic was set up. Where 3 billion crowns had circulated before the war, nearly 43 billion were circulated in 1918, and the figure reached 4,405 billion by 1922. The Austrian crown, at parity with the Swiss franc before the war, lost half of its value during the war, and, in 1922, 130 crown were equal to 1 franc.

The situation in Hungary was no better. Conscription and causalities — millions of men were killed, wounded, or held in prisoner of war camps for many years — and the military use of horses nearly crippled the unmechanized system of agriculture, the leading branch of the economy. Output was only one-third of prewar levels in 1919. Restrictions were so severe that in 1918, production of industrial consumer goods stood at one-third of the prewar level. Even the production of strategic goods such as iron and steel decreased by half. By the fall of 1919, industrial production declined even further to 15–20 percent of the 1913 level. The printing of more money to finance the war effort devalued the currency. By the end of the war the value of Hungarian crown had fallen by 60 percent, and by the summer of 1919 it had declined by 85 percent. The amount of currency in circulation grew at astronomical numbers from 17 billion in the summer of 1921 to 2.5 trillion in May 1924. Hungarian currency became worthless: having stood at par with the Swiss franc before the war, it declined to 2.7 to the franc by October 1918, 10 to the franc by summer 1919, and 18,000 to the franc by spring 1924.

Poland's economy was also affected by war. The new Poland had to build on ruins caused by some of the longest and hardest battles of World War I. Half of the railway bridges, stations, and repair shops had been destroyed, and in former Russian Poland scarcely any rolling stock remained. During the war, 1.8 million houses, 2.4 million hectares of forest, 2 million head of cattle, and 1 million horses were destroyed, and a great number of machines (8,000 electric motors and tools) were removed, mostly stolen by the occupying forces. Polish industrial production was one-quarter of the prewar level in 1919. Financial chaos was even worse because, at the time of the founding of the new state, several different currencies were circulating: three types of Russian ruble with different values, the Austrian crown, the German mark, and the so-called Polish mark. The total value of all currencies in circulation in the fall of 1918 was 150 million Polish marks, and by the end of 1919 it reached 5.3 billion marks. In 1920 the Polish mark became the only legal tender, but by the spring of 1924 it had lost virtually all its value:

9.3 million Polish marks brought 1 U.S. dollar. Where prices increased 14,000 and 23,000 times in Austria and Hungary respectively, in Poland they increased 2.5 million times between 1913 and 1924 (Berend and Ránki 1974).

Economic exhaustion and hyper-inflation caused hitherto unprecedented levels of poverty and starvation for the masses in Central and Eastern Europe. They also decimated exports, which were the mainsprings of the region's economic dynamism. In Romania, oil production fell from the prewar level of 1.9 million tons per annum to 0.9 million tons per annum in 1919. Annual wheat exports, which represented 8 percent of the world wheat exports before the war, declined from 3 million tons to 1 million tons in the postwar years. Hungarian wheat and flour exports, the major prewar exports of the country, dropped to 0.3 percent of their prewar levels and virtually disappeared in 1919–1920. Animal and meat exports also declined to 2 percent of their previous levels. Bulgarian exports in 1919 reached little more than a quarter of their prewar standard and were still at half that standard in 1920.

Besides the Austrian Republic, Hungary, and Poland, certain Baltic areas suffered the most during the war. The prolonged military campaigns and various German and Russian offensives and counteroffensives that lasted until the end of 1919 made the Baltic region a major theater of war. The Russian authorities evacuated most of the industrial installations to central Russia. Riga, a major port and industrial center, collapsed, as did other important industrial centers. Three-fifths of the Courland population and one-third of the Latvian population fled their countries after the German occupation. Allied interventions in Russia after the Bolshevik revolution and the blockade of 1919 caused additional damages. The lack of worthwhile currency contributed to postwar economic chaos. The German occupation currency, the *Ostmark*, remained in circulation during the first years of independence. In Lithuania, the *Ostmark* circulated until 1922. It wasn't until 1926–1927 that a stable national currency was introduced in Estonia, which otherwise suffered less than its Baltic neighbors.

Severe inflation and unbacked currency were not merely signs of postwar economic crisis and disorganization; they were also major factors in subsequent recovery. Inflation had a positive impact on reconstruction: the state made loans—virtually gifts, because they were paid back in worthless paper money—that financed rebuilding. In fact, between 1921 and 1924 a unique inflationary prosperity emerged with active investments, a situation that contradicted dominant economic theory and conservative fiscal approaches. Instinctive business sense and pragmatism led to an economic-financial policy that a decade later became theory when John Maynard Keynes discovered that controlled inflation can finance and generate recovery.

Economic Slowdown and Structural Crisis in the World Economy

This era was interpreted theoretically as a temporary postwar turbulence followed by recovery and a return to normalcy. In reality, however, when the countries of the region were finally able to cope with war-exhaustion and chaos, they found themselves faced with a dramatically changed world economy. World trade had slowed down. European trade had grown at an extraordinary rate from the mid-nineteenth century and had increased by 50 percent between 1900 and 1913, but in 1929, it surpassed the prewar level by only 1 percent. The per capita increase in world trade had increased by 34 percent between 1881 and 1913, but between 1913 and 1937 it grew only by 3 percent. European wheat consumption, which had increased by leaps and bounds in the nineteenth century and which, by virtue of the continuously expanding market, had continued to grow until the onset of World War I, stagnated in the interwar decades. In general, the role of agricultural products in world trade declined from 27 percent to 23 percent. In addition, although the export of meat, butter, and tropical products increased considerably, wheat export declined much faster than the average.

The significant slowdown in world trade was not accompanied by a similar decline in the level of world output. World industrial production stood at nearly 50 percent and 88 percent above the 1913 level in 1929 and 1936–1938 respectively, but world trade of manufactured goods increased only 12 percent by 1929 and, more surprisingly, dropped 8 percent below the 1913 level in 1936–1938. These figures illustrate the increasingly difficult market conditions, which created greater obstacles for weaker and less competitive countries than for more developed ones. Europe's position in world trade declined. The United States, Canada, and Japan doubled their exports, whereas Germany's industrial exports stood at 10 percent and 35 percent below the 1913 level in 1928–1929 and 1936–1938 respectively. The less developed exporters of agricultural products and raw materials experienced even greater decline. Whereas aggregate wheat exports of Argentina, the United States, and Canada jumped from 5.8 millions tons to 17.3 million tons between 1909–1913 and 1928, the traditional grain-exporting countries of Europe lost markets and suffered decreased trade. The percentage share of non-European countries in the world export of food stuffs and raw materials rose from 37 percent to 50 percent in the interwar decades. It is small wonder that grain prices sharply declined. The world market price for wheat nearly halved from $2.10 to $1.15 per bushel between 1925 and 1929. The gap between prices for agricultural products and raw materials and for industrial goods broadened dramatically, creating a price scissor. Between 1913 and 1921, this price scissor increased by 20 percent and 35 percent at the expense of agriculture and raw materials respectively (Kenwood and Lougheed 1971).

The majority of Central and Eastern European countries experienced major losses in addition to those caused by shrunken markets. Hungary exemplifies this situation. Whereas trade prices had been protected in the Austro-Hungarian Monarchy, they were not protected after the war, and there was a 10 to 20 percent decline in the terms of trade by the end of the twenties. The decline was not only an immediate postwar phenomenon but a permanent trend: terms of trade declined by an additional 8 percent between 1926–1927 and 1929. In 1929, therefore, Hungary had to export 10 to 20 percent more goods than in 1913 in order to pay for the same level of imports (Berend and Ránki 1985). In contrast, the advanced industrialized countries improved their terms of trade and compensated for their losses at the expense of the less-developed, agricultural regions of the world.

The years of economic slowdown and the decline of the relative position of agriculture were closely connected with dramatic technological change and structural metamorphosis. The old leading sectors of the economy declined spectacularly and new leading branches emerged in the postwar world economy. Not only grain production and traditional raw material extraction but also the leading branches of nineteenth-century industrialization—textiles, iron and steel, and engineering related to steam technology—faced a terminal crisis and declined. The market for these traditional sectors was pruned, firms and workplaces closed, and permanent unemployment climbed—in the mid-twenties, around 10 percent and 18 percent of the industrial workforce in Britain and Germany respectively was unemployed. Most contemporaries of the era, having witnessed the end of an age, looked back with nostalgia to the "golden age of peace."

What happened, however, was not a "general crisis" and decline of capitalism, as Leninist ideologists maintained. Behind these changes, a genuine renewal of technology, caused by a "whole set of technological innovations," was occurring. Large amounts of capital, technology, and labor were being transferred from the old to the new sectors. Several economic historians speak about the "fourth industrial revolution" that dramatically replaced the old technological regime with a new one.

The era's increase in energy consumption illustrates the character of this transformation. At first glance, it may seem that the transformation was slow: there was a leisurely 21 percent increase in energy consumption in Europe during the two interwar decades. But this aggregate figure masks the fact that a stormy structural change was taking place. The production of old energy sources declined and coal mining went into crisis, whereas electric energy generation jumped from 52.8 billion kilowatt-hours to 199 billion kilowatt-hours (nearly fourfold) in twenty years. Under a calm surface, a strong current of structural change transfigured the energy sector of the economy. The steam engine and coal were replaced by electricity; this renewed the technological base of industry, and electric motors penetrated areas of production previously not open to machinery. But the most significant effect, obviously impossible in the age of steam, was the electrification of households. In 1920, only 0.7 million households in Britain consumed electricity; by 1939, that figure had jumped to over 8.9 million. The constant expansion of the network, increases in capacity, and the construction of standardized systems allowed the use of electric lighting, water heaters, irons, electric stoves, heaters, vacuum cleaners, refrigerators, and last but not least, radios. Early broadcasts began in the United States and Holland in 1920, in Britain in 1922, and in Hungary in 1924. There were only 1,500 radio sets in Germany in 1924; by 1929, there were 3 million. Radios were a mass consumer good that lay within the reach of the average wage earner (Landes 1969); their purchase stimulated the economy. Because of the technical nature of the radio industry and because of the increased production and use of household appliances, a large industry developed to supply spare parts and extended services. All this aided the rapid development of modern telecommunications. During World War I, military demands spurred not only radio production but also the construction of more satisfactory telephone and telegraph networks, which, after the war, became widely used by the public.

During this era another revolutionary technological invention reached the public and conquered the market: the internal combustion engine. Although the process of creating this new industry began at the turn of the century, it was still in its infancy before World War I. In 1913, only 1.3 million cars were registered in the United States and 0.5 million in Europe. The war was the primary impetus for the expansion of the automotive industry, as for all new industries; it created the need for fast troop movements, for tanks, and for a fledgling air force. The European auto industry emerged triumphantly: in 1919, André Citroën created his famous A-1 model, the first popular French mass-produced car. By 1929, 10 million cars had been produced in Europe, and American carmakers had rolled out 57 million cars. The first civilian airplane service was inaugurated between London and Paris in the summer of 1919. As David Landes states:

It would be hard to exaggerate the significance of this growth for the overall expansion of the European economies. The motor car industry was beginning to play at this point a role analogous to that of the railroad in the mid-nineteenth century: it was a huge consumer of semi-finished and finished intermediate products . . . and components . . . ; it had an insatiable appetite for fuel and other petroleum products; it required a small army of mechanics and service men to keep going; and it gave a powerful impetus to investments in social overhead capital. . . . In the language of development economics, no other product yielded so rich a harvest of forward and backward linkages. (Landes 1969, 442–43)

Based on these spectacular changes in technology, new branches and leading sectors of the economy emerged. The share of the previously most important export items—textiles and traditional industrial consumer goods—fell from 52 percent to 38 percent of world trade between the wars. In contrast, the products of the electrical engineering and auto industries increased their shares from less than 10 percent to 17 percent, and the ratio of machines (including machine tools) in world exports increased from 20 percent to 30 percent. A major restructuring transformed the industry. In Britain, textile products declined from 26 percent to 8 percent of total industrial output between the two wars. In Germany and Holland, textile products dropped from 19 percent to 7 percent and from 16 percent to 5 percent respectively. Meanwhile, the products of the electrical engineering, machine tool, auto, and modern transportation equipment industries jumped from 32 percent to 48 percent of the capital goods in Britain, from 34 percent to 47 percent in Sweden, and from 20 percent to 50 percent in Holland (Kenwood and Lougheed 1971).

To use Joseph Schumpeter's term, the interwar period was the scene of a dramatic structural crisis characterized by "creative destruction" (Schumpeter 1976). Most of the striking crisis phenomena, including declining or slow growth rates and permanent unemployment, were the consequences of the destruction of the old. But these phenomena were accompanied by the gradual rise of the new, in which the foundations for rapid growth were being laid.

Central and Eastern European nations thus faced not only the difficult problems of adjusting quickly to new statehood and of coping with war exhaustion, inflation, and postwar economic chaos, but were challenged by structural economic crisis and by the demanding requirements of long-term adjustment to an age of new technology. Although short-term troubles seemed severe, highly visible and painful long-term adjustment mattered more and had the greatest impact in the long run.

Stabilization Efforts

The dawn of a new technological regime was not easily recognizable. The everyday economic problems experienced by the person on the street were seen as an effect of war and postwar disruption. For most people, the evident solution was to return to "normalcy" by restoring old institutions and equilibrium. The leading powers made persistent efforts to restore the prewar world economic order; for this purpose, they sought to bring back the gold standard and a free flow of capital. In retrospect, we can see that these efforts were bound to fail. The gold standard and the international monetary system alone could not create a well-functioning world economy. In fact, a stable international monetary system and the gold standard were based on and reflected a complex system of equilibrium. Convertibility of currency became an intolerable luxury when the values of currencies were uncertain and huge balance-of-trade and payment deficits existed. Conservative monetarists, however, did not recognize the change in conditions and forced the restoration of monetary stability and trade and payment equilibrium in a dangerously inflexible way.

Central and Eastern European governments viewed budget deficits and inflation as fever symptoms of the sick economy. Their therapy was similar to those doctors who concentrate on breaking a fever, hoping to cure the patient by doing so. The victorious great powers encouraged this view and assisted in its realization. They were worried that the virus of the Bolshevik revolution had become virulent in the environment of economic collapse and chaos, and wanted to stabilize Central and Eastern Europe before it succumbed to the same disease as its Soviet Russian neighbor. John Maynard Keynes, who was to become the most significant theoretician and economist of the coming period, created a stir with *The Economic Consequences of the Peace*, in which he realizes that " the bankruptcy and decay of Europe, if we allow it to proceed, will effect every one in the long-run" and that economic prosperity would provide "the only safeguard against revolution in Central Europe . . . [if] even to the minds of men who are desperate, revolution offers no prospect of improvement whatever." Keynes asserts that improvements could not be expected from internal automatic economic mechanisms. "It will be very difficult for European production to get started again without a temporary measure of external assistance. I am therefore a supporter of an international loan" (Keynes 1920, 296, 283, 287). In agreement with Keynes's suggestions, loans connected with internal monetary stabilization began to flow to both the allies and their former enemies. The first step was the visit of monetary experts from the League of Nations to Austria in 1921, followed by the signing of the Geneva Protocol in October of the following year. The protocol provided a loan of 650 million gold crowns for the purposes of abolishing the budgetary deficit and required that uncovered banknotes no longer be issued. The stabilization of the crown, equating one new gold crown with 14,500 paper crowns, concluded at the end of 1923. A new, gold-based currency, the schilling, was issued in January 1925.

The successful example of Austrian stabilization was soon followed in Hungary, which had failed in its attempt to stabilize its currency with internal resources. In 1923, the Hungarian government applied for loans. Instead of the desired 550–650 million gold crown loan, Hungary received 250 million from the League of Nations in June 1924. Stabilization was carried out in the same way as in Austria, with one new gold crown equal to 17,000 paper crowns. In approximately two years, the new gold crown was exchanged for a gold based currency, the pengö.

Using internal resources, Poland tried to stabilize its currency in 1921 and in 1924. The newly introduced and mistakenly overvalued zloty, maintained with deflationary measures, began to inflate because of renewed equilibrium problems. In 1926, the government finally achieved monetary stabilization with the help of American loans and an American group of experts led by Professor Kemmerer (Landau and Toma-szewski 1980).

A stream of loans began to flow to the countries of the region after 1922. Austria, Hungary, Czechoslovakia, Romania, and Yugoslavia alone accumulated more than $3.5 billion in foreign debts. The total amount of foreign assistance exceeded the prewar inflow of capital to the area. As a British analysis stated in 1937: "The foreign capital which was used for the reconstruction of Europe was . . . necessary, but the amount which in the end was sent to this area was more than the debtors could hope to repay . . . [especially because] it resulted in a rise in the standard of living . . . but did not increase the efficiency of their export industries . . . to enable . . . them to meet the full service of payments" (*Report* 1937, 279). The countries of Central and Eastern Europe fol-lowed the advice of the prominent German statesman, Gustav Strese-mann, who declared in 1925: "We should simply take on loans of such a size and borrow so much that our creditors will see themselves en-dangered if we as debtors go bankrupt" (Thimme 1957, 69). Conserva-tive monetary considerations were replaced by a new attitude: "Let the creditor's head ache!"

The ideal of monetary stability and the reconstruction of the gold standard was accompanied by the desire to restore free trade. The vic-torious great powers together with the League of Nations tried to break down the walls of protectionism. During the war, the free trade sys-tem, which had been endangered during the prewar decades, collapsed. Most economists and policy makers believed that the tariffs established during that period were only an extraordinary and temporary measure. After the war, the United States, France, and even the former cham-pion of free trade, Great Britain, kept the high protective tariffs, but they insisted that they were only short-term expedients. The new states in Central and Eastern Europe adamantly advanced the principle of free trade, and the Supreme Allied Council stated on March 8, 1920, that between the new nations there would be a need for friendly coopera-tion and trade without barriers. At Genoa in the spring of 1922, the Al-lies reiterated that "the changes in territories caused by the World War should effect the normal conditions of trade only minimally." The League of Nations prepared detailed studies for a conference at Geneva in 1927, where speakers spoke out against trade barriers. "All national-ist policies are harmful to that nation which uses them and to all oth-ers, and defeats its own purposes," declared the conference (Berend and Ránki 1974, 202). All participating nations, including the representatives of Central and Eastern European governments, unanimously accepted the declaration in favor of gradual reduction of protectionist tariffs and the return to free trade. Reality, however, didn't allow a return to free trade and showed a strong, persistent, contrary trend.

The Principle and Practice of Nationalist Economic Policy

In the years following the war, national economic policies throughout Europe departed markedly from the ideal of free trade. In the honeymoon years of their new, independent statehood, newly created states in Central and Eastern European sought to establish national identities in a form that included economic independence. "The flare-up of nationalist passions fanned by the war, the disintegration of the old empires and the emergence of new states . . . provided a fertile field for the cultivation of economic nationalism" (Berend and Ránki 1974, 201). One of the clearest expressions of economic nationalism was phrased by Kemal Atatürk, the leader of the postwar Turkish national revolution: "If the political and military victory cannot be crowned by an economic one, then its results will hardly be lasting. . . . To be able to crown our victory, creating and stabilizing our economic independence is essential" (Adanir 1979, 1–2). The Turkish Economic Congress of 1923 defined the economic content of the national revolution as follows: First, ethnic Turks should take over the positions of foreign investors and non-Turkish nationals (Greeks, Armenians, and Jews); second, protective tariff barriers should be raised against foreign imports in order to thwart competition and to aid the development of national industry; and third, a comprehensive industrialization program, with active state participation if necessary and with state financing in branches that lacked sufficient private investments, should be developed. It pays to note that Bolshevik economic policy rested on similar principles. These ideas quickly penetrated the European periphery, becoming orthodox in Central and Eastern Europe.

In Romania in July 1919, laws were introduced that prohibited the importing of competitive merchandise until 1924. In June 1924, additional tariffs were imposed, and in 1927, rates, already high, were raised to the ad valorem level of 30 to 40 percent. In Transylvania, Romanian economic nationalism also sought to ensure ethnic Romanian entrepreneurship by using paragraph 249 of the peace treaty to legitimize the nationalization of companies formerly owned by Austrians or Hungarians. Companies were not allowed to have headquarters abroad, and at least half of the board of directors had to be Romanian nationals. As a result, the 60 percent German stock ownership in the *Banca Generală Romană* (Romanian General Bank) was reduced to 20 percent by 1922. The national interest in the Romanian oil industry increased from the prewar level of 6 percent to 12–15 percent. The numerous Transylvanian branches of the Hungarian Commercial Bank of Pest were purchased by Romanian companies. In 1925, the most radical measure was taken when a new mining law sought to abolish foreign interests in Romanian natural resources. Articles 32 and 33 declared that new mining concessions could only be given to Romanian companies in which investment capital from foreign sources did not exceed 40 percent. The new law also applied to existing mining concerns, which were given ten years to comply. These stringent regulations, however, were abandoned after five years in favor of policies that wiped out the discrimination against foreign entrepreneurs (Constantinescu et al. 1960).

Protectionism was the universal "wonder weapon" of economic nationalism (Manoilescu 1931). As a result of the peace treaty, customs borders increased by four to five thousand miles in length. The twenty-six independent European economic units became thirty-eight, and, in the place of twelve currencies, twenty-seven independent currencies began to circulate. Seven independent customs units replaced the Austro-Hungarian common market. After the war, each of these independent "units" established or maintained existing warlike import restrictions. In Czechoslovakia, new laws prohibiting or restricting imports were enacted after the war and remained valid until mid-1923. Hungary enacted similar regulations between 1921 and 1924, and Yugoslavia followed suit in 1923 (Hertz 1947). In the Baltic countries, emergency economic legislation characterized the early years of independence; imports and exports were licensed and imports of nonessential goods were virtually banned. In addition, currency laws in Estonia and Latvia enforced arbitrary exchange rates that upset foreign investors. New customs laws were enacted in Bulgaria (1922), Romania (1924), Austria, and Hungary (January 1925), Yugoslavia (March 1925), and Czechoslovakia (1926). These new regulations were substantially more detailed than previous ones, sometimes containing several thousand tariff rates aimed at halting the importation of certain items and at preventing other items from receiving preferential treatment. The new rates were much higher than the previous ones. In contrast to the 20 percent ad valorem duty of the Austro-Hungarian Monarchy, the new Hungarian regulations levied an average 30 percent tax. Certain industrial consumer goods were hit with an average ad valorem rate of 50 percent, and, in special cases such as industrial consumer goods, textiles, and leather products, the tax ranged from 100 to 500 percent. The Yugoslav custom rates were increased from their prewar (Serbian) level of 10 percent to an average of 20 percent, but for certain industrial consumer goods, the tariffs were raised to 70 to 170 percent. It is difficult to speak of an average tariff level, since tariffs constantly changed. The new so-called battle tariffs were often set too high for tactical reasons: to achieve a better bargaining position and a good compromise with partner countries. Between 1924 and 1927, when most of the trade agreements were signed by the countries of the region, most-favored-nation status was given to all signatories, thus lowering the tariff barriers. Individual countries, however, increased and modified their tariffs and set ever higher barriers in the years thereafter (Pasvolsky 1928).

With these policies, the mainly agrarian countries of Central and Eastern Europe tried to change their status in the traditional European division of labor. They refused to play the role of food and raw material exporters any longer, but they remained importers of the manufactured products of the advanced, industrialized countries of the West. Behind the high tariffs, which aimed primarily at keeping processed industrial consumer goods out, lay the goal of abolishing previous structural inequities by adopting a strategy of squeezing out imports and establishing industries to produce these products at home. The nineteenth-century pattern of export-led modernization, in which growing exports of traditional food and raw material products increased export incomes, thereby allowing investment in other branches of the economy, was replaced by import-substitution (Szlajfer 1990). This new approach promised faster industrialization sustained by a protected domestic market. The nearly complete displacement of imports by domestic products—the declaration of economic independence—also provided a direct method for establishing economic equilibrium and balanced trade by eliminating the negative effects of the deterioration in their terms of trade. An increasingly competitive world market prompted these countries to counterbalance declines in their export branches by establishing industries to produce substitutes for imports, thereby turning backwardness to their advantage (Johnson 1967).

Before World War I, domestic demand for industrial consumer

goods was met primarily by imports. Even in relatively developed Hungary, 70 percent of textile consumption in 1913 was covered by Austrian and Bohemian products. The same held true for wood, paper, glass, and leather goods. Whereas 80 percent of exports were agricultural, 60 percent of Hungarian imports were finished industrial products. Reducing imports allowed domestic industrialization in many fields. In Yugoslavia, only 1,831 firms existed in 1918, whereas during the following decade, 1,262 new firms were founded. Food processing, textiles, and the lumber industry accounted for more than seven hundred of these new establishments. The industrial production of Yugoslavia increased by 40 percent between 1913 and 1929. The prime mover of industrial progress was "light industry"—textiles, leather, and clothing products. Their share in industrial output increased from 9 percent to 26 percent in the same period. Nonindustrialized Bulgaria followed a similar path. Domestic production of industrial consumer goods barely covered one-third of consumption before the war. During the war years, Bulgaria made impressive progress in industrialization: the number of factories increased by nearly five times, and the number of workers and the machine capacity (in horsepower) almost trebled between 1912 and 1922. During the first postwar decade, an investment of 3.3 billion levas was made, one-and-a-half-times the value of existing industrial capacities. With the help of import restrictions and tariff protection, this investment produced rapid growth: in 1929, industrial output exceeded the 1915 level by 80 percent. The annual increase in the textile and paper industries was 8 percent. By 1939, the output of light industries had increased between four and five times and could meet 85 percent of domestic consumption needs (Lampe and Jackson 1982).

Romanian production of industrial consumption goods covered only 25 percent of domestic demands before World War I. In the interwar decades, however, one-quarter of total investments was given to the textile and food processing industries. The number of workers in textiles increased from 7 to 25 percent of the industrial workforce, and textile output rose from 10 to 22 percent of total industrial production. The textile industry doubled its output by 1929 and then doubled it again by 1939, finally achieving the ability to meet domestic demand.

Estonia and Latvia, which in addition to agricultural economies had large manufacturing centers that delivered goods to the Russian market before World War I, turned in "the direction of greater economic self-sufficiency . . . building up manufacturing industry . . . geared to supplying local needs" (Hiden and Salmon 1991, 85). In the 1920s and

1930s, thirty-eight large textile works were established, making textiles the largest employer of industrial labor in Estonia. A huge cellulose and paper factory was opened in Tallin, and a plywood and furniture industry came into existence. In Latvia, woodworking, textile, and food-processing industries played the leading role in industrialization: the number of industrial firms increased from 1,430, employing 61,000 workers in 1920, to 5,700 firms with 205,000 workers in 1937.

Import-substituting industrialization had more ambiguous results in those countries that were relatively more industrialized before the war. Though they shut out imports, Hungary and Poland experienced a sharp decline in previously leading industrial sectors. Consequently, increases of industrial output were limited. In the case of Hungary (using the 1920 borders), production decreases in the traditional and export-oriented industrial sectors (especially food processing, which even its highest interwar level reached only 75 percent of its 1913 output) might have caused a general decline in industrial output. If the general decline did not happen, that was partly because developments in import-substituting sectors not only counteracted shrinkage in traditional branches but also produced moderate overall growth. Rapid development in new or previously weak industries began with the banning of imports and the establishment of protective tariffs. One-third of total industrial investment in Hungary was channeled into textiles during the interwar decades. Characteristically enough, textile companies were started by acquiring empty buildings in idle flour mills, by buying cheap, discarded English textile machinery sold at scrap metal prices, and by employing low-paid female labor. As a result, textile output doubled in the 1920s and quadrupled by 1938. The number of cotton spindles increased from 39,000 to 324,000, and the number of looms grew from 4,000 to 14,000. The paper industry experienced a similar rate of growth. Overall industrial production in Hungary grew slowly, surpassing the prewar level by 12 percent in 1929, and by roughly 28 percent in 1938 (Berend and Ránki 1985).

Poland, an agricultural-industrial country like Hungary, was one of the strongest industrial centers in the Russian Empire and benefited by exporting coal, iron, and textiles to the less developed Russian market. In 1913, 44 percent of industrial production in the prewar Polish Kingdom was contributed by the textile, leather, and clothing industries. Import-substitution therefore could not offer an effective therapy for the declining former leading branches. Whereas the other countries of the region had stimulated development by halting imports and establishing self-sufficiency in textile and other light industrial sectors, these industries already existed in prewar Poland and declined sharply after the war: their share in industrial output dropped from 44 percent to 16 percent between 1913 and 1939. In Poland, import-substitution allowed the development of food processing for domestic supply. The share of this branch in overall production increased from 18 to 31 percent between the wars. The demand of the domestic market, however, could not counterbalance the loss of Russian imperial markets, and Poland's economy—like the economies of Austria and Spain—could not attain even modest growth rates in the interwar period (Kostrowicka et al. 1966).

Overall, with certain exceptions, Central and Eastern Europe exhibited a rather uniform development pattern after 1918. The turn from export-orientation to self-sufficiency caused decline in established export branches, such as agriculture and food processing, but it generated rapid growth in light industries. Textile, leather, clothing, paper, and glass production increased by 200–400 percent contributing 20–25 percent of total industrial output and functioning as one of the strongest sectors in the economy. Food processing, which had represented the majority of output before the war, declined, but still contributed 25 percent of total industrial output.

Agricultural Protectionism in Central Europe

The identification of economic independence with self-sufficiency was not limited to the agrarian countries of the region. Industrialized Austria and Czechoslovakia also turned toward protectionism. The previously interrelated "Cislethanian" Austrian-Bohemian-Moravian region of the Habsburg Empire now separated, and each country followed an independent path, which produced the most absurd consequences of protectionism. The Austro-Bohemian textile industry, the strongest sector of the economy, had been organized with a special division of labor: spinning mills usually were located in Austria, and weaving was concentrated mostly in the Czech lands. After the dissolution of the monarchy, both newly independent countries ruled out economic cooperation. As a consequence, because of disruption in supply and demand, spinning capacities in Austria and weaving capacities in Czechoslovakia were reduced. (The number of weaving looms declined from 137,000 to 75,000.) Meanwhile, each country concentrated on investing in the missing sectors, the Czechs on spinning and the Austrians on weaving. Similar trends characterized the postwar development of the sugar and paper industries in these two countries. The prewar center of both industries had been located in the Czech lands. Postwar Austria restricted imports of these Czech products and, by protecting its market, stimulated its domestic sugar and paper industries. With a 235 percent and 123 percent increase in their respective outputs, these industries emerged as the fastest growing sectors in the Austrian economy. In Czechoslovakia, branches of food processing that had been located in Hungary gained new impetus because of market protection.

However, Austria and Czechoslovakia could not successfully use the method of import-substituting industrialization. Their strong industrial sectors were traditionally export-oriented and even at the end of the 1920s, Austria was still exporting 45 percent of its industrial output, and Czechoslovakia was exporting 70 percent. Both of these countries sought instead to become self-sufficient in food supply, in order to avoid the scarcities they had experienced during and immediately after the war. Shortages made the Austrian economy highly vulnerable and caused severe balance of trade and payment difficulties after 1919. The trend toward self-sufficiency gained a strong impetus in 1925 when Germany introduced the Bülow Tariff, a form of strict agricultural protectionism. Austria reacted immediately by imposing a moving scale tariff on previously duty-free wheat imports. In 1926–1927, tariffs were increased on sugar (40 percent), flour (66 percent), and cattle and hogs (100 percent). Tariffs on lard and bacon were increased by 300 percent. Czechoslovakia followed suit, and her flour tariff eventually rose 80 percent.

High tariffs were only a part of the story. Nations also introduced extremely severe, complicated, often unmanageable veterinary requirements and reduced the number of entry points for animal imports. Special milling regulations specified the permissible amounts of foreign wheat in finished products, some imports were banned entirely, and several other formal and informal obstacles to trade completed the picture. Concomitantly, the industrial countries of the region tried to increase their domestic agricultural output. In Austria, yield of grain and other main agricultural products increased 10–50 percent, vegetable yields rose by 50 percent, and industrial crop yields rose by 60 percent. Czechoslovak yields increased similarly. Wheat output grew by 75 percent between 1920 and 1938, and, as a most extreme example of agricultural import-substitution, the nation became a net wheat exporter during the 1930s. Similarly, hog production in both Austria and Czechoslovakia rose by 40 percent during the interwar period (Průcha et al. 1974).

The Decline of International Trade

In 1927, the Geneva Conference of the League of Nations unanimously resolved that tariffs should be reduced and free trade promoted. Reconvening in January 1931 in order to examine results, the conference discovered that none of the signatory nations had complied with the 1927 resolution. The British and Dutch delegates demanded an explanation and received a frank answer from Yugoslavian Minister of Foreign Affairs Marinković. The old laissez faire economists had expected the restoration of economic equilibrium and free trade, explained Marinković, "but how would that equilibrium come about? At the expense of the weakest." He said that, with free trade conditions, the agrarian countries could only have improved their competitive position if they had enjoyed production and net cost conditions similar to those of their overseas competitors. But this was impossible. True, the imposition of protective tariff barriers was irrational and even threatened to kill world trade, but did any other rational solution exist for countries in an emergency? He continued:

Last year, when I was in the Yugoslav mountains, I heard that the inhabitants of a small mountain village, having no maize or wheat on which to live, were simply cutting down a wood which belonged to them . . . and were living on what they earned by selling the wood. . . . I said to them: "You see that your forest is becoming smaller and smaller. What will you do when you cut down the last tree?" They replied to me: "Your Excellency, that is a point which worries us: but on the other hand, what should we do now if we stopped cutting down our trees?" I can assure you that the agricultural countries are in exactly the same situation. You threaten them with future disasters; but they are already in the throes of disaster. (Carr 1940, 58)

Marinković's parallel may well illustrate that nationalist economic policy, with its tariff wars and effort to create self-sufficiency, was an irrational product of an irrational situation. The pattern of constant tariff increases, retaliation, and restriction was highly destructive and dangerous. Nations undermined each other by developing nonexisting industries, destroying their previous trade partners' export possibilities, and consequently limiting their own foreign markets. If Yugoslavia purchased fewer industrial consumer products from Austria and Czechoslovakia, these two nations, in turn, purchased fewer agricultural products from Yugoslavia. Whereas two-thirds to three-quarters of Serbian prewar foreign trade had been with Austria-Hungary, in 1929 the share of imports from and Yugoslavian exports to the successor states of Austria-Hungary declined respectively to 41 percent and 28 percent of total Yugoslavian trade. The value of Austrian and Czechoslovak exports to Hungary, taking territorial changes into consideration, declined by 60 percent. In immediate postwar Czechoslovakia, 52 percent of the exports went to the Danube countries to the south and southeast of Czechoslovakia, but by 1929, this figure fell to 31 percent. Austria's share of exports to this area dropped from 42 percent to 34 percent. Unable to sell its machines in the region, Austria retaliated by reducing its wheat imports from the area. Before the war, two-thirds to three-quarters of the trade of the Danube basin countries occurred amongst themselves, but by 1929, this figure had dropped to one-third.

The decline of old trade connections was even more dramatic in those countries that had belonged to the Russian Empire before World War I. Nearly two-thirds of prewar Poland, the so-called Polish Kingdom, had been part of the Russian Empire before the war, and roughly 80 percent of Poland's exports had been channeled to Russian markets. Independent Poland, born in a war against Bolshevik Russia, virtually ceased its trade relations with the Soviet Union, dropping that trade to 1.5 percent of its total exports. The Baltic countries, which had also delivered most of their products to the Russian market, followed a policy similar to Poland's. Estonia reoriented its exports and imports so that its trade with the Soviet Union dropped from 22 percent of the total in 1922 to 3 percent in 1932. Latvian exports to the Soviet Union declined to 2 percent by 1927, and after a transitory increase to 15 percent following the trade agreement of 1927, fell back to 1 percent by 1933. Germany and Great Britain soon became the dominant trade partners of Estonia and Latvia. In Lithuania, foreign trade with the Soviet Union did not surpass one-tenth of the country's total exports and imports.

The isolationist policy of protectionism and import-substitution exerted a negative impact on world trade, which was also in decline. In light of the Central and Eastern European experiences, Arthur Lewis is mistaken when he states that "the decline in trade in manufacture was due neither to tariffs nor to industrialization of new countries. The trade in manufactures was low only because the industrial countries were buying too little of primary products and paying so low a price for what they bought" (Lewis 1949, 155).*

Success Stories of the Twenties

Although it was irrational from the point of view of world economy and long-term economic interests, import-substitution seemed to be right for countries trying to escape postwar economic chaos by stimulating growth. The countries saw this prescription as the only rational therapy for their ailing economies and as the single possible way to regain economic equilibrium and growth. Indeed, the countries of Central and Eastern Europe experienced visible economic success during the first decade of their reconstruction. One unqualified success was the fact that the area surmounted the shocks produced by the war and subsequent peace. A decade after mass starvation, declining output, never-before experienced inflation, and chaos, stable currencies backed by gold had been established, foreign loans were flowing, and a moderate prosperity had taken root. Levels of production, except in one or two unfortunate countries, surpassed their prewar peak. The Czechoslovak economy attracted foreign investments, introduced modern sectors, and grew 40 percent between 1913 and 1929 (Teichova 1974). The Balkan countries began a successful industrialization campaign: both Yugoslavia and Romania increased their industrial output by 40 percent, and Bulgaria enjoyed an 80 percent increase during the first postwar decade. The industrialized Central European countries, in turn, developed their agricultural output, reaching prewar levels in the late twenties and surpassing them by one-sixth in the next decade. Gross domestic product increased, though at a greatly varying rates (between 5 percent to 50 percent); the best results were in Czechoslovakia and Bulgaria, whereas the worst were in Austria and Poland. Generally, the countries of Central and Eastern Europe managed to resume a process of steady growth (Bairoch 1976).

* The author's concept is convincingly debated by David Landes (Landes 1969, 365–68).

The Lack of Technological-Structural Adjustment

Despite important short-term economic successes, the region failed to adjust in the long term to the transforming world economy, modern technology, and related industrial structures. The short-term achievements of import-substitution promoted relatively rapid growth in the textile and other light industries. But this road to industrialization produced systems that failed to incorporate the structural changes occurring in the already industrialized world. In reality, the two systems had opposite traits. The rising industries of Central and Eastern Europe were already declining in the industrialized West, whereas innovative leading sectors in the West—new branches of engineering and electrical industry—based on the achievements of the "fourth industrial revolution" were barely present in the East. Import-substitution was successful for the relatively backward and poor countries of the region because it allowed them to avoid deadly competition with the industrialized countries and to increase their output by using outdated technology. In the long run, however, these successes were transitory and ambiguous, and they failed to facilitate adjustment to the world economy. The new technologies and leading sectors, crucial for the future, were mostly absent. Therefore, the independent nations of Central and Eastern Europe could not close the gap with the West and were unable to change their peripheral position in the international economic system. The structure of their economies and the role of the region in the international division of labor hardly changed. The nonagricultural share of the labor force grew faster in the region than in the West, but still the agricultural character of the countries prevailed. Compared to the prewar years, the agricultural population of Romania declined from 80 percent to 74 percent of the total by 1930, still a majority. In Bulgaria the decline was roughly 2 percent, but 80 percent of the active population remained in agriculture. In Yugoslavia, the percentage of agricultural population remained unchanged at 79 percent in 1920 and 1930. Poland and Hungary represented a higher stage of industrialization and experienced a more rapid increase in industrial population, but even in Hungary, agricultural population (although dropped from the prewar 56 percent) was still 51 percent of the 1930 total labor force. In the Balkan countries, relatively rapid industrial growth could not absorb population increase: industry took in only one-quarter of the population growth (Kaser and Radice 1985). The gap between the West and the East—except in the Soviet Union—continued to increase. Figures for general construction and road building, expressed by per capita cement consumption, clearly illustrate this trend: compared to the 100 kilogram (roughly 220 pounds) Western average, Austria and Czechoslovakia used only 60 to 70 kilograms (132 to 154 pounds), and the other countries of the region used only 15 to 25 kilograms (33 to 55 pounds). Automobilization, with its revolutionary spin-off effects, remained in its infancy. The so-called motorization index, the number of cars in comparison to the territory and population of the country, showed an average 5.7 in Europe, but only 1.8 in Czechoslovakia, 0.5 in Hungary, and 0.3 in Poland, Yugoslavia, and Romania.

The developed West was shocked by the structural crisis, but the crisis's destructive impact was counterbalanced in the West by the construction of modern new branches. In Central and Eastern Europe, this did not happen. Recovery in these regions meant the reconstruction of prewar levels of output based on the development of outdated sectors. Agriculture remained the leading sector, and the structure of its output changed very little. Wheat remained the most important product, a development that ran counter to world market conditions, although this fact was concealed by the brief international boom in the late twenties. An unchanged nineteenth-century infrastructure did not suffice for twentieth-century structural changes, and the developing industries in Central and Eastern Europe represented nineteenth-century economic sectors not suitable for twentieth-century competition. In spite of their transitory success, protectionism and self-sufficiency divided markets into ever smaller segments. As markets diminished, conflict emerged, fed by modern technology and mass production that demanded larger markets and a well-developed international division of labor. After World War I, most of the countries of Central and Eastern Europe, despite partial modernization and national economic reconstruction, continued to lag behind the West and preserved their obsolete structures.

The postwar decade, however, was only the first act of the twentieth-century drama. In the second half of the 1920s, loans were still flowing, a temporary agricultural boom was under way, and the policy of import-substitution appeared successful. But the mirage was soon to disappear. By the fall of 1929, the short interval had ended, and the second, more shocking act of the drama had begun.

PART III

The Great Depression and Its Impact

Social Changes; The Triumph of the Right; The Art of the Crisis and the Crisis in Art, 1929–1939

Introduction

In spite of postwar exhaustion and uncertainty in Europe, the world economy soon recovered, because the war years had created industrial and agricultural opportunities for overseas countries that increased their capacities to meet economic demand. The United States emerged as the leading economic power in a changing world system, and Latin America and former "white colonies" such as Australia and New Zealand became important factors in the world agricultural market. After a few years in flux, Europe profited from a massive capital inflow and adjusted to a different technological regime. A new agricultural boom and the seemingly successful attempts to reconstruct certain basic institutions of prewar prosperity, such as the gold standard, heralded the return to normalcy. The existence of the League of Nations and the cooperation among the Western great powers signaled the restructuring of the former world system. Although Great Britain, the leading power in the nineteenth century, became the "sick man" of Europe, France flourished and Germany recovered spectacularly from defeat and hyper-inflation. In the United States, stock speculation boomed in the twenties. Stocks in prospering companies proved to be lucrative investments; during 1928 and 1929, at the peak of the boom, profits of up to 50 percent could be gained within a few months by buying and then selling shares in certain businesses. A magic cycle emerged and the economy improved steadily. In his annual State of the Union speech to Congress on December 4, 1928, the president of the United States said: "No Congress of the United States ever assembled, on surveying the state of the Union, has met with more pleasing prospect than that which appears at the present time. In the domestic field . . . the highest record of years of prosperity. In the foreign field there is peace, the good-will which comes from mutual understanding" (Galbraith 1961, 6).

In the light of events shortly to come, this view was absurd: the speech came less than a year before the onset of the worst world economic crisis in history. During this crisis, international relations deteriorated—first in the Far East, then in North Africa, and finally in Europe—bringing the world to the brink of a second great war. A few months after the proud presidential report, the orgy of speculation met with retribution: For whatever reason, the great crash exploded on October 24, 1929. Black Thursday on the New York Stock Exchange, with its spectacular consequences—suicide and financial collapse—signaled the opening of a stormy and unpredictable period. A fragile European prosperity was already endangered in 1929 when its largest creditor, the United States, started to recall loans and to restrict new credit: the net capital inflow declined from one billion to two hundred million dollars, one-fifth of the 1928 level. This event forecast unbridgeable financial difficulties because half of all foreign debts—in Germany as well as in Central and Eastern Europe—were short-term credits, usually repaid by means of new loans. Investments dramatically dropped; in Germany, they hit bottom in 1931 at 3 percent of the 1928 level. World production of coal, iron, and steel declined by 60 percent between 1929 and 1932. Demand plunged everywhere, and world trade dwindled rapidly. The value of world exports and imports—in 1934 gold dollars—fell in 1935 to an unprecedented one-third of its predepression level. World market prices followed; the prices of major agricultural commodities, such as wheat and meat, dropped by nearly 60 percent. Industrial output in the United States and Germany nearly halved, that in Canada and Holland dropped by roughly 40 percent, and France and Belgium witnessed a more than 30 percent decline. In 1931 alone, 2,290 banks filed for bankruptcy in the United States, and, in the same year, Germany declared insolvency and faulted on repaying its debts. Unemployment doubled in Britain, reaching 2.7 million. In Germany, 6 million were unemployed at the nadir of the Depression. Overall, 15 million people lost their jobs in Europe.

Special economic factors, severe policy mistakes, and human psychology contributed to the unprecedented economic and social drama of the Great Depression. Was it a consequence of irresponsible speculation during the late twenties? A mistaken reconstruction of the gold standard? An extreme version of "normal" economic fluctuation, a uniquely severe Juglar-cycle, which accompanied the rise of modern economy from the late eighteenth century and had its hits, as its mid-nineteenth century French discoverer described it, in each decade? Was it a special coincidence of two types of cycles, the down-turn of a medium-length Juglar-cycle and a long-term Kondratiev-cycle? Was it a combination of all these factors, accompanied by a dramatic Schum-peterian structural crisis? Several explanations exist for this catastrophic shock to the modern world economy. "On the whole," states John Kenneth Galbraith about the crisis in the West, "the great stock market crash can be much more readily explained than the depression that followed it. . . . Economics still does not allow final answers on these matters" (Galbraith 1961, 173–74). Paradoxically, it is easier to explain the depth and turbulence of the depression in Central and Eastern Europe.

10

A Distinctive Great Depression in Central and Eastern Europe

Moderate Industrial Decline

The Great Depression dealt a harsh blow to the leading powers of the world. Small wonder that the relatively poor countries at the periphery of the European and world economy suffered even more. The only industrialized countries of the region, Austria and Czechoslovakia, faced a situation similar to that in the Western countries: Declining market possibilities brought about a dramatic decline in output. Austria's exports decreased by 50 percent, which, in a nation where one-third of national income was obtained by means of foreign trade, in turn led to a 40 percent decline in domestic industrial production and an unemployment rate of 25 percent in the industrial workforce. Recovery was very slow; in 1936, industrial output was still 20 percent below its 1929 level. In Czechoslovakia, the traditionally export-oriented industrial consumer-goods industries plummeted: textiles dropped by 36 percent and glass by 52 percent. Three-quarters of the workforce in the latter industry became unemployed. The once strong iron and metal industries also declined, producing roughly two-thirds of their predepression output. Altogether, Czechoslovak industry produced 40 percent less in 1933 than in 1929 (Teichova 1988). Poland, an agricultural country that also possessed an export-oriented, relatively strong industrial sector, faced an overall 37 percent industrial decline, and in 1936 output was still below its predepression level.

Hungarian industrial decline was much more moderate. Although investment in the mining, construction materials, iron, and machine industries declined steeply, falling to only 52 percent of the 1929 level by 1932, industrial recession was less severe than in the industrialized countries. In agricultural countries, the relatively undisturbed development of consumer-goods industries partly counterbalanced the crisis in other branches. After a short, transitory setback, the textile, leather, and paper industries, the leading branches in import-substitution, continued to increase and by 1933 had surpassed their 1929 level by 10 percent. The overall average decline of industrial output in Hungary reached 24 percent in the nadir, but it surpassed the 1929 level by 3 percent in 1936 (Berend and Ránki 1974).

The agricultural countries in the Balkans and the Baltic region experienced even milder industrial decline. In Romania, output of investment goods decreased sharply—cement and construction timber by 40 to 50 percent, coal by 37 percent—but the total industrial output fell no more than 11 percent below the predepression level, even in 1932, the worst year. The reason for the moderate decline lay in the strength of the industrial consumer-goods sector: after a brief setback, it experienced a continuous increase. Oil extraction was also developed, in a government effort to compensate for severe losses in agricultural exports. In Yugoslavia, after a very short period of decrease, industrial employment began to increase. By 1933, it was already 10 percent higher than it had been in 1929. In Estonia, the industrial workforce fell from thirty-two thousand people to twenty-five thousand people (nearly 20 percent). But, the impact of this trend was moderated by two factors: first, the relatively high industrial unemployment touched scarcely more than 3 percent of the total labor force because industry employed just a little over 17 percent of the active population in Estonia; and second, unemployment disappeared by 1936. It should also be noted that industrial decline was much more serious after World War I. The industrial workforce was halved just after the war and remained at under 80 percent of the 1913 level until the onset of the Great Depression. Industrial decay during the depression was even less important in Latvia and Lithuania, where the fledgling industrial sector employed only 13 percent and 6 percent of the population respectively (Rauch 1987).

This pattern of moderate industrial decline in the primarily agricultural nations of Central and Eastern Europe did not mean that the Great Depression was less destructive in the region. On the contrary, relatively backward agricultural countries suffered much more than advanced nations. The Great Depression in the region was distinguished by three main characteristics: the unusual depth of the agricultural crisis and its consequences for the balance of trade and payments; the devastating debt crisis, insolvency, and impact on trade; and the lack of ability to adjust to the technological-structural challenges of the crisis.

The Agricultural Crisis
and Declining Terms of Trade

The agricultural "overproduction"—the production of more goods than were being bought—made the sale of agricultural products difficult, and it led to the accumulation of huge stocks and the collapse of food prices. The average aggregate agricultural price level in 1934 dropped to 37 percent of the 1929 level. Wheat prices dropped to one-third of their predepression level, and meat prices decreased to four-tenths of that level. Recovery did not come quickly. Agricultural commodity prices were stuck, fluctuating at one-third to one-half of their 1929 level, even at the beginning of World War II.

What happened in the world economy was highly paradoxical and bizarre: Food prices collapsed, yet food itself became increasingly more difficult to obtain. Millions of people suffered from starvation, while millions of tons of unsold food stocks were poured into the sea, burned, or wrecked. Though prices fell sharply and food stocks rose, farmers did not cut back on production; indeed, they often attempted to increase it. This apparent lack of rationality was, in fact, the only rational behavior for farmers and peasants with small plots, who were trying to counterbalance price declines: They could not afford to cut back their output as prices fell. Nowhere was land taken out of cultivation. Unlike most sectors in the economy, agricultural production did not respond to the normal market mechanisms of supply and demand; declining food prices failed to limit production, and, as a result, both producers and consumers suffered the results of overproduction.

Both domestic and world agricultural markets shriveled up. In the early thirties, Romanian livestock exports declined by 45 percent and wheat exports by 55 percent. Yugoslavian agricultural exports dropped by 54 percent. Bulgarian cattle exports, in the worst year of the depression, stood at only 14 percent of the precrisis level. Because of the steep decline in prices, export incomes fell far more than export volumes: 73 percent and 42 percent respectively. In Hungary, these figures were 60 percent (the decline of generated income) and 27 percent (the setback of the volume of export). The absurdity of market conditions is clearly expressed by the fact that, while Poland increased its agricultural exports by 28 percent, income from those exports fell by 56 percent.

Matters were even worse because of a price scissor between agricultural and industrial prices. Although all prices declined, the prices of industrial products used by the farmers and peasants fell much less than those of agricultural goods. In Romania, agricultural prices declined by nearly 56 percent between 1929 and 1934, whereas prices of industrial goods used in agriculture fell less than 19 percent. In the same period, the gap between industrial and agricultural prices was 33 percent and 22 percent in Yugoslavia and Poland respectively. In Hungary, industrial prices rose 6 percent more than agricultural prices between 1913 and 1928, but, by 1933, the gap had increased to 70 percent. It caused an unbearable extra burden for the peasantry. Peasant incomes declined 58 to 59 percent in Romania and Poland and 36 percent in Hungary (Kaser and Radice 1985).

Because most Eastern European countries were overwhelmingly agricultural, the trauma experienced by the peasantry shocked the entire economy. The negative effects were transmitted by declines in the countries' terms of trade. In the dictionary of foreign trade economics, *terms of trade* refers to the difference in dynamics of the import and export prices of a country. In Yugoslavia, for example, because export prices declined more steeply than import prices between 1929 and 1933, the terms of trade deteriorated by 25 percent. In the case of Romania, the price level of imported goods declined 34 percent but that of export prices fell 60 percent, and thus the country had to export nearly 25 percent more for the same quantity of imports. Hungary was seriously affected as well: taking the 1925–1927 period as a base, the terms of trade declined by 8 percent by 1929, by 15 percent by 1931, and by 19 percent by 1933. However, compared to prewar price relations, the terms of trade dropped by 30 percent (in other words, Hungary had to export almost one-third more agricultural products for the same amount of industrial goods).

All these trends hurt agriculture badly. Adaptation to the worsening market conditions would have been possible only if production costs were diminished and structural changes made (technical modernization, greatly increased yields, and crop diversification away from wheat, the hardest hit, into more intensive cultivation of products with better sales potential and market prices). Because of declining peasant incomes and the price scissor that was increasing at the expense of agriculture, it was impossible to make technological improvements such as the mechanization of agriculture and more extensive use of chemicals. Investment in agriculture came to a halt and the use of new technology not only ceased but actually declined. In Yugoslavia, where agricultural machinery was not produced, the import during the thirties of threshing-machines dropped to 2 percent, mechanical harvesters to 8 percent, and sowing machines to 3 percent of the level of the late twenties. Mass unemployment made it necessary to substitute men for machines. This situation probably influenced the Yugoslav government's decision to ban the use of tractors in the thirties. Only two-thirds of the existing tractors were used in Hungary during these years because low wages made the use of tractors cost ineffective. The same happened with fertilizer: although use had increased impressively (it trebled in Yugoslavia and quadrupled in Hungary) during the 1920s, the process stopped in the thirties. In Hungary, instead of 21 kilograms of fertilizer per hectare in the late twenties, only 2.6 kilograms per hectare were used in 1933, and 7 kilograms per hectare in 1938. In Poland and Yugoslavia, the use of fertilizers in the thirties was half that in predepression years. In comparison with the Western European nations where fertilizers were used at a rate of 100 to 300 kilograms per hectare, Central and Eastern Europe virtually gave up their use.

With a few exceptions, productivity in agriculture stagnated or declined. The yields of wheat per hectare during the period from 1935 to 1938 were 20 percent and 4 percent below levels in the years 1910 to 1913 in Romania and Poland respectively. Sugarbeet yields declined between 5 and 15 percent in Poland, Bulgaria, Hungary, Romania, and Yugoslavia. Corn yields dropped by 20 percent in Romania. Even though these declines were partly compensated for by increased yields in other products such as rye and potatoes in Romania (9 and 4 percent respectively), wheat and potatoes in Bulgaria (28 and 58 percent respectively), and wheat and corn in Hungary (12 and 20 percent respectively), the relative position and competitiveness of Central and Eastern European agriculture did not improve. The average yields of the seven main crops were 85, 74, and 63 percent in Hungary, Poland, and Romania respectively in comparison to the European average level during the 1930s, and the average productivity level of agricultural workers in the Balkans was scarcely one-half that of the European average (Berend and Ránki 1974).

Most countries in Central and Eastern Europe tried to introduce structural changes in traditional agricultural output to meet the changing market requirements. Meat and dairy products experienced better market conditions than grain, and higher incomes could be gained by substituting the production of oilseeds and vegetables for grains; therefore, output shifted in these directions. Poultry farming increased significantly in Hungary, doubling poultry exports between the mid-twenties and the end of the thirties. Butter exports increased from between one and two thousand quintals to between fifty and sixty thousand quintals, and wine exports increased tenfold in the same period. In spite of these spectacular increases, the basic structure of agricultural output and export remained relatively unchanged: the total value of livestock, animal products, butter, and wine exports only increased from 27–28 percent to roughly 33 percent of all agricultural exports. Grain production continued to dominate. The Baltic countries turned toward the Scandinavian pattern, developing high quality dairy and meat production for the British and German markets. Estonian and Latvian butter, eggs, pigs, and bacon and Lithuanian poultry, geese, pigs, and processed food were exported to Britain, which absorbed 42 percent and 37 percent of Latvian and Estonian exports respectively in 1938.

Some modern structural changes occurred in all agrarian countries of the region. The share of vegetables in Yugoslavian agriculture increased from 1 to 6 percent during the twenties. In Bulgaria, the land area devoted to growing vegetables and fruit increased from 3 to 5 percent of all land under cultivation, and that devoted to industrial crops increased from 1 to 7 percent. The country's wine exports increased from two hundred thousand hectoliters in 1928 to six and a half million hectoliters in 1932. Because of the almost unlimited labor supply in Poland, Yugoslavia, and Romania, labor-intensive branches of cultivation advanced. Compared to the mid-twenties, the areas sown with hoed and root crops increased by 40 to 50 percent in these countries, and the area given to corn nearly equaled that of wheat in Yugoslavia and Romania.

In most of the countries, however, the amount of land devoted to wheat cultivation far exceeded that devoted to all other crops combined. In Bulgaria, it even increased from 71 to 72 percent of all arable land between 1920–1924 and 1935–1938. In Hungary, it decreased by 3 percent but still occupied two-thirds of all arable land.

In the absence of a radical overhaul, the nations of the region continued to produce traditional agricultural products. Moreover, they attempted to counterbalance the severe price decline by producing more goods, which, in turn, were sold at even more depressed prices. This overproduction is reflected in the fact that the output of the traditional seven main crops in Central and Eastern Europe surpassed the 1909–1913 level by 17 percent in the years between 1934 and 1938. All in all, the countries of the region could not adapt to the changing market conditions of the thirties either by reducing costs or by making structural changes in production. Institutional, cultural-educational, and economic obstacles were too strong. Most practices continued as before; people only hoped for some miracle in market conditions that would end the seven lean years. This particularly harsh agricultural crisis and the associated deterioration in the terms of trade caused a heavy additional burden for the agricultural countries of Central and Eastern Europe. The region shared the destiny of the agricultural peripheries of the world (Maddison 1985); although they were an integral part of the world system, they occupied a niche that caused them to suffer more than the West during the depression: "The agrarian countries of the periphery were strongly integrated into the world market during the twentieth century, however, together with integration, a parallel trend of polarization . . . [hit] the agricultural countries[,] . . . [which] were trapped into the dependence of traditional social structure" (Rothermund 1983, 13).

The Debt Crisis and the Golgotha of the Debtors

Besides experiencing this peculiar agricultural crisis, caused in part by their position as peripheral areas, the Central and Eastern European countries also suffered from the additional burden of a debt crisis. During the first years of the slump, international money and credit markets still functioned, albeit more clumsily than before. With the new short- and medium-term loans that were made available, payment conditions and production capabilities could still be improved and foreign trade was still possible. But the repayment abilities of debtor countries, negatively affected by the depression, became increasingly endangered, and creditors, consequently, grew more cautious. The two leading lender powers disbursed almost one and a half billion dollars of credit in 1930, but in 1931 and 1932 the figures were only thirty million and thirty-two million dollars. The breaking point occurred in the spring of 1931, when the leading Viennese bank, the *Creditanstalt*, collapsed. This Austrian bank was not only one of the largest banking companies in Europe but also a cornerstone of the Rothschild empire, itself a symbol of solidity; it owned or controlled two-thirds of Austrian industry and played a traditionally important role throughout Central and Eastern Europe. When the *Creditanstalt* went bankrupt on May 11, 1931, the entire international financial world was dumbstruck to learn that the losses for the bank equaled its capital. These losses trebled by the end of the month, because most foreign funds were immediately withdrawn. The National Bank of Austria, in an effort to stop the landslide, assisted the *Creditanstalt* by discounting its bills. As a result, the value of bills held by the National Bank jumped from 70 million Austrian schillings to 450 million schillings by the end of the month. Payments outdrew heavily on the gold and foreign exchange reserves of the National Bank. By October, more than half of the gold and foreign exchange reserves had been paid off, and by the summer of 1932, the reserves had dropped from 930 million to 114 million schillings. The gold base of the schilling became endangered; it decreased from nearly 87 percent in early May, 1931, to 25 percent at its lowest point. In a few months, one billion schillings of foreign loans were recalled. The Austrian money and credit system was on the brink of collapse.

The mushrooming financial panic quickly dragged down the heavily indebted Weimar Republic, which had half of its ten-billion-mark debt in short-term credits. In a matter of six weeks, the German *Reichsbank* lost two billion marks in gold and foreign exchange. German depositors stormed the banks to demand their money, and the *Darmstädter- und Nationalbank*, one of the three largest German banks, collapsed in July. Within forty-eight hours, all of the banks were forced to close. The banking system, the citadel of the German economy, collapsed. The government announced a compulsory bank holiday on July 13. The landslide became unstoppable, burying everything in its path. The heavy indebtedness of the Central and Eastern European countries allowed no room for maneuvering and resistance. New loans were stopped and credit was no longer available on the international financial market. For the debtor countries of the region, this situation amounted to insolvency. Because of irresponsible credit practices in the twenties and the failure to make investments in productive export branches that would have strengthened national finances, the countries of the region were unable to make payments on their debts without new loans. The Hungarian example clearly illustrates this situation. Between 1924 and 1931, 40 percent of all loans to the country went to service outstanding debts; in 1929, all credits opened went to service debts.

Another debt problem that plagued even the more developed nations of Germany and Austria was the high percentage of short-term loans in the debt stock. Such loans were at least 50 percent of the total debt stock, and their recall put the debtors in an untenable situation. During the speculative boom in the late twenties, when credit was abundant, these short-term loans had often been used irresponsibly in areas for which they were not designed (such as long-term investment). In the new financial situation, this practice produced a series of spectacular insolvencies, such as that of the Victoria Milling Concern in Hungary. As foreign creditors withdrew in the spring and summer of 1931, a large number of industrial firms and banks in Central and Eastern Europe became insolvent. To aid these companies and to fulfill their debt-servicing obligations, the central banks of these countries depleted their already small gold and foreign exchange reserves. Between May 1 and July 13, 1931, the Hungarian National Bank paid out two hundred million pengö in gold and foreign exchange, an amount that exceeded the value of its holdings of precious metal and foreign exchange at the end of April (Berend and Ránki 1985). Poland repaid nearly one billion zloty of short term loans. The 1.8 billion lei paid by Romania toward short-term loans eventually dried out its gold and foreign exchange reserves. Nearly half of the banks in Yugoslavia became insolvent because of the repayment of thirty million dollars in loans and the withdrawal of five billion dinars in deposits. The economic collapse in Central and Eastern Europe was total, and international economic ties were broken (Berend and Borchardt 1986).

Lack of Adjustment to the Structural Crisis

In addition to the special burdens associated with being agricultural and debtor nations, the Central and Eastern European countries had to contend with a third aspect of the Great Depression: the necessity of responding adequately to the challenge brought on by the technological-structural transformation of the world economy. It was not an easy task even for the advanced, industrialized powers, but the countries of Central and Eastern Europe faced a particularly difficult situation. It must not be forgotten that these countries had been denied an appropriate period to adjust to dramatic postwar changes. All of these countries—newly independent and either enlarged or reduced in territory—struggled with the tremendous task of building up independent national economies. The Great Depression intensified their need to adjust to nationhood and the changing world economy—but how were they to cope with all the obstacles in the depth of history's most severe depression? Was President Roosevelt's famous aphorism from his first Inaugural Address on March 4, 1933, "The only thing we have to fear is fear itself," valid for Central and Eastern Europe? To some extent, yes. The degree of fear, especially in this part of the world, was ominous. It gave bad counsel and sometimes contributed to desperate and even suicidal actions. More often, it fueled devastating, murderous mass movements and governmental adventures. But in this region, it was not fear alone that was frightening.

In the West during the depression, a constructive process of technological-structural change produced progress. Thus the depression and economic creation were not mutually exclusive, antagonistic categories. Viewed from this standpoint, the Great Depression did not bring on an entirely new situation but rather made painfully manifest the emerging structural crisis of the postwar world economy. The emergency situation of the depression provided a new impetus to the process of adjustment and thereby helped to construct a new foundation for a renewed prosperity. The essential issue became not merely to recover from economic decline, negative growth, and record unemployment, but to successfully adjust to emerging technologies, establish new, competitive export branches, and replace obsolete sectors by restructuring the traditional economy.

Did the only solution for the Central and Eastern European countries lie in creating new automobile and aircraft industries, or in establishing modern electrotechnical, chemical, or similar pioneering branches? By no means. The relative market competitiveness of traditional branches could have been improved by technological innovations and cost-reducing and quality-improvement measures. Canada and Japan, countries that achieved noticeable increases in their share in world trade, did not accomplish this increase by developing the most modern economic and product structures. On the contrary, between the two world wars, Canada and Japan increased their share in world exports from 0.7 to 5 percent and from 2.5 percent to nearly 8 percent respectively by exporting traditional industrial consumer goods such as textiles, export items that generally were being forced into the background of world trade. Canada and Japan countered this trend by making these sectors increasingly competitive. Denmark, too, preserved its traditional export structures; in the Danish situation, which superficially resembled the situation in the agricultural countries of Eastern Europe, more than two-thirds of exports consisted of traditional food products. Behind this seemingly traditional export structure, however, lay factors such as high productivity and low production costs, the consistent creation of high quality products, and high rates of processing based on an existing food processing industry, all of which gave Danish agricultural products an unequaled competitiveness.

The prerequisites for successful adjustment, whether in pioneering fields or in traditional ones, were a modern infrastructure, developed research, high levels of education, a quickly retrainable workforce, sufficient capital formation and investments, and a traditional entrepreneurial attitude. Yet most of these factors did not exist in the majority of Central and Eastern European nations. On average, capital accumulation in the region during the interwar decades did not surpass 6 percent of the gross domestic product (with the exception of the Czechoslovak rate of 14 percent). This low rate of accumulation was accompanied by a dearth of capital inflow to the area. Foreign investments had always played a role in financing these economies. During the half century before World War I, foreign sources accounted for 25 to 50 percent of investments and played the leading role in building railroads, in developing modern banking systems and mining, and in establishing up-to-date industrial plants. Between the wars, foreign investments and loans were available for only a couple of years in the latter half of the twenties. Social conditions, including a rigid social hierarchy, an extremely weak middle class, and the absence of an entrepreneurial mentality in both gentry and peasants, did not create a social environment able to respond to the international economic challenge. The same was true regarding the educational system. In some countries, mass illiteracy existed, and secondary education, still highly elitist and exclusive, had not adopted modern structures. Thus, the school system was not producing graduates with the skills needed in the changing world.

In spite of these obstacles, partial achievements appeared in almost each country. Electric power generation doubled in Czechoslovakia between 1929 and 1938, and new modern branches of the chemical industry, partly introduced by the *Spolek Work*, increased production in the chemical industry by 50 percent. Czechoslovakia's export structure changed significantly because of advances in mechanical engineering and the metal industry. The *Škoda Work* played an important role in this process. The share of machines, tools, cars, and instruments in total Czechoslovak exports increased from 3.8 to 6.3 percent, and that of iron and metal products from 11.6 to 18.9 percent between 1929 and 1937 (Teichova 1974). In Bulgaria, the rapid development of tobacco and cigarette industries created new export possibilities. Yugoslavia trebled its copper and bauxite production, and Romania doubled its oil production in the thirties (Lampe and Jackson 1982). In Hungary, new branches of food processing such as fruit and vegetable canning and especially the production of tomato puree concentrate opened up export markets and increased exports twenty-fold. Bauxite mining and oil extraction promised new possibilities as well. The Jendrassik-type diesel train produced at the Ganz factory won several international competitive bids and entered the Latin American and African markets. Krypton gas-filled tungsram bulbs helped to double the production of *Egyesült Izzó* (United Bulbs Co.) and to increase exports by 40 percent (to fifty-three countries) in the thirties (Berend and Ránki 1985).

A long list of partial successes in each country could be made. To it should be added description of progress made in modernizing infrastructures, including the construction of a new leisure infrastructure (cinema chains and sports stadiums), a health-care network of hospitals, and an extensive system of schools. These changes, however, failed to meet the need for suitable modernization of the infrastructure and for essential changes in technology, competitiveness, and industrial structure.

All of these factors combined to prevent changes in the macrostructure of exports from Central and Eastern European countries. The only marked exception to this pattern was Czechoslovakia, where the role of the traditional leading export branches—textiles, glass, leather, and sugar, which together represented more than 60 percent of the country's exports in 1929—dropped to 43 percent by 1937. (The share of textiles declined from nearly 35 percent to less than 22 percent.) In contrast, the share of capital goods—metal, engineering, and other "heavy industrial" products—increased from 39 to 57 percent in the thirties (Průcha et al. 1974). The agricultural countries of the region could not achieve such success. The ratio of traditional agricultural products and raw materials in Hungarian exports declined only from 60 percent to 59 percent between 1929 and 1938. In Polish exports, the share of food products and raw materials remained unchanged at 76 percent between

1928–1929 and 1937–1938. The same can be said for Yugoslavia and Romania, where food and raw materials made up 96 percent and 83 percent of exports respectively. In Romania, the share of the five traditionally most important export products in overall exports remained at 86 percent in 1925 and in 1937. In Yugoslavia, the five leading export items' role even increased from 50 to 56 percent. In Hungary, this portion reflected a wider export diversification and was significantly lower—34 percent—but remained unchanged during the thirties. In Poland, the leading export items' role somewhat decreased (by 5 percent) but remained at 42 percent of total exports. Only Bulgaria achieved a more significant restructuring of exports: the five most important export products represented roughly 75 percent of total exports in the twenties but declined to 61 percent by 1937 (Kaser and Radice 1985). The agrarian countries of the region, even given the few exceptions that hardly modified the overall picture, could not adapt to the extremely demanding conditions in the world market. The Great Depression in Central and Eastern Europe was thus not only deeper and more devastating because of the agrarian character and indebtedness of the region's countries, but, most significantly, was not accompanied by technological-structural renewal, a fact that determined the long-term destiny of the area by conserving its peripheral status in Europe.

From the Great Depression to Nazi and Stalinist Isolationist Autarchy

Emergency Measures to Avoid Financial Collapse

Though appropriate adjustment to the transforming world economy was nearly impossible in Central and Eastern Europe, the magnitude of the impending economic catastrophe did not allow delays in emergency actions. The countries of the region could not find a path (long-term transformation) toward future prosperity, but they did discover an emergency exit (short-term measures) from the frightening depression. Many excellent ideas were suggested to avoid an immediate economic collapse. Above all, it was necessary to prevent the bankruptcy of state finances and banking systems. In most cases, the countries of the region followed the German pattern by temporarily closing all banks on July 13, 1931. The Hungarian cabinet was the first to do so, introducing the same measures the next day. The Polish government was the last, closing banks only in the spring of 1936. Protected by the shield of the emergency "bank holiday"—the three-day break when all debt repayment and bank transactions were halted—the governments introduced appropriate emergency measures. Among them, the most important were the foreign exchange restrictions, first introduced by Germany and soon followed by all countries of the region. Both the gold standard and currency convertibility were abolished and all foreign exchange transactions were placed under the control of the national banks. These measures stopped the further outflow of gold and foreign exchange from the indebted and insolvent countries. As a consequence, only small amounts of interest and principal were repaid in the thirties. When payments became due, the debtor countries deposited in their national banks and in their own currencies the amount of the installments owed. But because of the existing foreign exchange regulations, creditors could not repatriate these funds. Lender countries could do nothing but accept the freezing of their funds. In many cases, lenders actually signed intergovernmental agreements acknowledging the suspension of payments for one to three years. Again, the pattern was set in Germany, and in the summer of 1931 the Hoover Moratorium sanctioned the solutions that been introduced by the German government. The Lausanne Conference formally ended the payment of war reparations (Berend and Ránki 1974).

Avoiding bankruptcy, of course, was not enough. Because governments and private firms could no longer count on new loans, the restoration of the balance of trade became a focal point of economic intervention. Because exports could not be increased, the only viable solution for restoring trade equilibrium lay in drastically reducing imports. Not a novel idea, this approach was a revitalization in more extreme form of postwar emergency measures. In addition to import reduction, other familiar policy tools and tested methods coalesced into a coherent policy in which each component amplified the others, forming a theoretically sound system. Import tariffs and restrictions, used extensively for a few years after the war, now reappeared, and protectionism became a leading trend between 1930 and 1934. The importation of products that could be produced domestically was successfully halted. Czechoslovakia and Austria increased wheat and other agricultural tariffs by threefold and twofold respectively, and Hungary implemented strict import bans on all finished industrial products in early 1933. Exemptions could be obtained only with special government permission. In addition to tariffs, the use of the quota system became widespread and effective. By means of quotas, governments had the power to decide what quantities of various items would be allowed into their nations. Bulgaria, for example, set her import quotas at 50 percent of predepression import levels (Kofman 1990).

Another important weapon in import restriction and export incentive was the hidden devaluation of currencies. All Central and Eastern European nations with the exception of Czechoslovakia and, for a while, Poland, implemented hidden devaluation. Devaluation made export goods cheaper for foreign buyers. Even though an increase in exports was crucially important for debtor countries, they could not follow the example of the creditor countries, the great powers such as the United States, Britain, and France, which openly devaluated their currencies by roughly 30 percent. For debtor countries, open devaluation would have acted as a double-edged sword. What they would have gained by improving their trade balances, they would have lost as their debts increased (devaluation would have increased the amount of foreign exchange needed, by the percentage of devaluation, to repay debts). Therefore, the debtor countries of Central and Eastern Europe did not openly devalue their currencies but maintained their previous official exchange rates. Yet these debtor countries did not want to miss out on the advantages offered by devaluation; they needed devaluation both to make their products cheaper for foreign buyers and to raise the prices of imports.

The problem of simultaneously eating and keeping the pie, of taking advantage of devaluation while, at the same time, avoiding its disadvantages, seemed unsolvable. The solution finally adopted completely disregarded the traditional economic system. Following Germany's example, the debtor countries of the region maintained official exchange rates, thus preventing an increase in their debts. Actually they achieved more: as their creditors devalued their own currencies by about one-third, their debtors' debts decreased by this amount. But the debtor countries also could not afford to lose in the area of foreign trade. Therefore, in conjunction with keeping their official exchange rates, they also introduced a hidden currency devaluation, valid only for foreign trade. The invention was a special premium-price system, involving the introduction of two or even more exchange rates. Beside the official exchange rate, countries set up a devalued exchange rate for foreign trade transactions. Such action was possible because the international exchange system had broken down and currencies had been declared nonconvertible. Consequently, all foreign exchange transactions, including export and import deals, could be channeled to national banks, which had the power to approve or reject any proposal. This situation made it possible for central banks to use variable exchange rates. For financial transactions (including debt repayment), they used the official exchange rate, but for foreign trade, they introduced different commercial exchange rates. In the case of export to Western countries that paid in hard currency, the Yugoslavian or Hungarian national banks paid 40 to 50 percent more to a Western buyer than the official exchange rate (an export premium) when exchanging currency. In effect, this set up a lower exchange rate for foreign trade transactions. In this manner, the countries of Central and Eastern Europe devalued their currencies by 30 to 40 percent and made their products cheaper for foreign buyers. Hidden devaluation allowed flexible maneuvering so that the most advantageous exchange rate could be established for each foreign currency. Needless to say, lower commercial exchange rates, in addition to promoting exports, also created obstacles for imports by effectively raising their prices. These rather unusual, sometimes complicated government measures helped economic survival by isolating the Central and Eastern European countries from the world economic system, allowing them to create unique new rules (Kaser and Radice 1985).

Government Interventions and Self-Sufficiency

The gold standard and laissez faire were dead in Central and Eastern Europe, but strong, interventionist states were emerging. Governments assisted agriculture in overcoming the collapse of prices and instituted price supports for grain and other agricultural products. High levels of internal debt were forgiven for farmers, and tax rates were lowered to ease the burden on agriculture. In all of these countries, partially or totally state-owned purchasing and sales organizations were created. The *Prizad* state monopoly, the seller of row crops in Yugoslavia, was founded in 1930. It purchased 4.6 million quintals of wheat for 965 million dinars and sold it for 621 million dinars between 1930 and 1933 — in other words, it provided a 36 percent price support to wheat growing peasants. In Romania, the state-owned trade organization, created in 1930, paid an export subsidy of ten thousand lei or sixty dollars for each freight car load of exported wheat. After 1934, two major state-owned cooperatives in Hungary, *Futura Ltd.* and *Hangya* — 70 percent state-owned — monopolized and subsidized nearly 85 percent of agricultural exports.

With the assistance of the national banks, national governments helped to destroy another major obstacle to foreign trade, the scarcity of hard currency incomes and reserves. In 1931, at the Prague conference of the national banks, the president of the Austrian National Bank suggested the introduction of a "currencyless" trade agreement, the so-called clearing system. In this rapidly accepted scheme, the export of one country to another was determined by the import of the same country: deliveries were not paid by currency but by other deliveries. This was a trade-in-kind system where only the differences in the value of deliveries among partner countries were paid in currency at the end of the year. The first clearing agreement was sign by Yugoslavia and Austria in January 1932. Germany signed similar agreements with each of its six Southeastern European trade partners in the same year. By 1935, 63 percent of Hungary's trade was based on clearing agreements, and by 1938—as in the case of Bulgaria—this share increased to nearly 85 percent. At the same time, nearly 78 percent of the Yugoslavian and 75 percent of Romanian foreign trade occurred within the boundaries of clearing agreements. This meant that trading among Central and Eastern European countries, as well as Germany and Italy, was governed by barter and clearing agreements. Naturally, this agreement system could not exist without total state control of foreign trade.

State interventionism penetrated the general economy of the region. One of the most telling episodes illustrating that interventionism was in the air was recalled by Michael Kalecki, the well-known Polish economist. He was asked to visit the head of the military junta during the post-Piłsudski era (the late thirties) and ordered to explain the Keynesian theory, of which "the whole world was talking." After thinking for a short while, this is how Kalecki answered: "Colonel, I cannot undertake to explain this complicated economic theory in a few sentences. But let me tell you a story that will illustrate the essence of Keynesism. In the mid nineteenth century, a New Yorker went to the Wild West. When he arrived in the saloon of a small dusty town and saw several suspicious looking characters, he recognized the danger of his adventure. So in a raised voice, for everyone to hear, he turned to the saloon keeper and said: 'Sir, I'm going to travel this area for many years and I don't want to take my money on this dangerous trip. I've five hundred dollars and all of it I'm going to give you for safekeeping.' Then he left. After the traveler had been gone a year, the saloon keeper thought to invest the money rather than keeping it in cash. First he had the saloon painted, then he had an addition built. For this, he employed workers. These received wages and started to buy new furniture and even to build or to enlarge their own homes. They needed materials, and new stores opened in the town to supply them. When, after four years, the traveler safely returned, he barely recognized the neat and bustling town with its new buildings, streets, shops, and booming industry. He entered the saloon, which had become a hotel and casino. The owner recognized him, opened the cash register, and returned the five hundred dollars. To the saloon keeper's great surprise, the traveler folded and then put a match to the money and lit his pipe with it. 'They are counterfeit notes,' he explained. 'I left them here to let everybody know that I had nothing worthwhile to steal.' Shocked, the saloon keeper looked around and thought, this bustling town of ours was founded on five fake bank notes? You see, Colonel," Kalecki said as he ended his story explaining how to create additional demand by printing paper money, "this is the true essence of Keynes's theory."

There can be no doubt about the attractiveness of Keynesian theory to leaders in the region. As the Kalecki anecdote illustrates, the junta in Poland wished to revitalize the economy by means of bold state interference; in fact, Poland advanced farther down the path of government planning than its neighbors did. The colonels decided to further industrialize by establishing a central industrial triangle consisting of Warsaw, Kracow, and Lvov, where state investments would build modern industries (Landau and Tomaszewski 1982). In Hungary in 1938, partly as preparation for the impending conflict, the government introduced a job-creating Five-Year Plan that called for investing one billion pengö to modernize transportation and create new industrial capacities. Central and Eastern European government planning and investments programs mostly copied the Nazi-German pattern, Hjalmar Schacht's *Neuer Plan*, a four-year plan of economic preparation for war.

By separating themselves from the international economic system and turning toward a state-regulated economy, the countries of Central and Eastern Europe committed themselves to import-substituting industrialization, a policy associated with the years immediately following World War I. In the 1930s, the depression gave this policy new incentive. In Hungary, for example, the importation of finished industrial goods, which declined from 62 percent to 40 percent of total imports between 1913 and 1929, dropped to 27 percent by 1937. The single most promising path out of the depression seemed to be the possibility of impressive growth in the domestic consumer goods industry at the expense of imports. The conquest of the domestic market would lead to a significant further decrease in imported finished industrial products, but it would increase the importation of raw materials need for domestic industrial output: cotton, the raw material for textile production, would be imported instead of more expensive finished textiles. The price of raw materials and semifinished products, as an average, declined in the same dramatic way as agricultural products. In other words, the change in the structure of imports profoundly improved terms of trade, and consequently, it also helped to rectify the balance of trade and payments. The share of raw materials and semifinished goods in Hungarian imports was 38 percent in 1913; it increased to 60 percent by 1929 and reached its peak (73 percent) in 1937. The terms of trade, which deteriorated in the early thirties because of a 58 percent decline in Hungarian export prices versus a 36 percent decrease in import prices, found parity at the end of the decade; the changed structure of imports produced a decline in import prices as measured against the decline in export prices. Eventually, the terms of trade improved and reached their predepression level. In Poland, the share of finished industrial consumer goods in imports declined from 25 to 10 percent. In Romania, domestic production supplied only 25 percent of textile consumption in 1929, but that figure rose to 40 percent by 1938. In Bulgaria, the share of industrial consumer goods dropped from 46 to 20 percent of imports, whereas the importation of machinery and other investment goods rapidly increased. In the less industrialized countries of the region, import-substitution generated increased imports of machines and industrial equipment. For this reason, the share of finished industrial products in Polish, Romanian, and Yugoslavian imports did not diminish, comprising 53, 86, and 75 percent respectively (Berend and Ránki 1974).

Central and Eastern European countries thus achieved impressive successes that helped consolidate their crisis-ridden economies by the latter half of the thirties. They found a way to escape the virtually hopeless economic situation of the Great Depression and halt the advance of economic disaster. But the results that were achieved, although by no means negligible, were ambiguous: the developments in infrastructure, technology, and industry were not those actually needed for twentieth-century success, because they preserved obsolete structures. In the industrialized West, the worldwide economic depression prompted the demolition of unviable and obsolete structures: to use an ancient Greek parallel, the unviable was thrown down from the Taigethos, and the promising, healthy newborn was carefully nursed and grew up tall and strong. In contrast, in Central and Eastern Europe the success only nursed the ballast of the obsolete.

In order to escape from world competition, the countries had to do more than isolate themselves from the world market by building national protectionism within the national borders. None of the small or medium-sized Central and Eastern European countries was able to realize self-sufficiency. They could not manage without imports; consequently, they had to export. The maintenance of the traditional economic and export structure obviously would not have been possible without the creation of a larger economic region in which the participating countries separated themselves from the rest of the world by setting special prices, excluding foreign exchange payments for trade, and ensuring export possibilities for obsolete, noncompetitive old branches. Such a self-sufficient regional economic unit was established in the mid-thirties in Central and Eastern Europe. Its initiator and organizer was Hitlerite Germany.

The Creation of a German-Led, Isolationist, Regional Agreement System

Shortly after the Nazi seizure of power, Nazi economic policy broke away from the previous German policy of self-sufficiency and agricultural protectionism. Between 1934 and 1938, it began to develop toward a German *Grossraumwirtschaft* (large-area economy) to build a large, self-sufficient economic area in concert with several Southeastern European countries in Germany's backyard. Under the direction of Hjalmar Schacht, the *Neuer Plan* provided the economic preparation for the war. Nazi Germany rejected previous foreign trade norms and sought to create a parallel world market with its own rules. "Now that internal German economic space has been established according to plans, which was the most important task in the first year of the national socialist government," stated Hans Ernst Posse, deputy minister of the Hitler cabinet, in 1934, "the time has come for attainment of *Grossraumwirtschaft* to become our most important economic policy goal" (Posse 1934).

The Southeastern European countries possessed surplus foodstuffs and several important strategic raw materials, indispensable for a German war economy and attainable by means of safe, blockade-free overland routes. In addition, trade connections with the region would serve German economic expansion, the first stage toward a Nazi-ruled Europe. On February 21, 1934, a German-Hungarian trade agreement was signed, the first of its kind; it would serve as a model for German trade agreements with other countries of the region. In the Hungarian agreement, the German government undertook an obligation to accept large grain deliveries (125,000 tons of wheat and other grain in 1934), live-stock (6,000 head), pork (3,000 tons), and pork products (3,000 tons of lard and 1,500 tons of bacon) by establishing import quotas for these products. The German government also guaranteed a partial repayment of high agricultural tariffs. To this end, a government fund was established in Berlin. Export subsidies were also added to the quota system. The Hungarian government would pay a price subsidy for all exported commodities, in the case of a quintal of wheat, four to six pengös and in case of a quintal of lard, seventy-four pengös. The Hungarian government would pay up to twenty-two million pengös (more than five million dollars) in export subsidies per annum, which would then be repaid by the German government. (To finance Hungarian subsidies, Germany used the German assets that were "frozen" in Hungary as a consequence of foreign exchange regulation and were paid by the Hungarian debtors in pengös to an account at the Hungarian National Bank.) As a result of this agreement, prices for Hungarian agricultural products on the German market were higher than those on the world market.

The German-Hungarian agreement was based on clearing or barter trade. Hungary guaranteed export quotas for German industrial products and a 20 to 30 percent tariff deduction. Hungarian agricultural deliveries were thus paid for by German industrial goods. The agreement, however, ensured that only 90 percent of Hungarian exports would be paid for with German industrial deliveries. The remaining 10 percent could be used by Hungary to buy raw materials and other goods of strategic importance, including transit goods from countries other than Germany that were available only for hard currency. A fixed amount, two million Deutsch marks, was available for the Hungarian National Bank to buy hard currency (Berend and Ránki 1985).

The German-Hungarian model agreement had spectacular results: Hungarian agricultural exports more than doubled in a single year. Butter exports increased threefold, cattle exports sevenfold, and lard and bacon exports more than twentyfold. The German share in Hungarian exports increased from 11 to 22 percent between 1933 and 1934.

Within a few weeks, in May 1934, a similar German-Yugoslavian trade agreement was signed, which was followed by a German-Bulgarian agreement later in the same year (*Bulgarsko* 1972). In March 1935, a German-Romanian agreement was also signed. Southeastern Europe thus established strong economic ties with Germany. Between 1929 and 1937, whereas Austrian and Czechoslovak trade with Germany declined (from 28 to 15 percent and from 25 to 15 percent respectively, in part for political reasons), Germany's share of total Bulgarian exports rose from 30 to 43 percent, and its share of Yugoslavian exports rose from 9 to 22 percent. Meanwhile, Germany was the source of 25 to 50 percent of all imports to the region's countries other than Austria and Czechoslovakia. Southeastern Europe played an important role in German supply: 37 percent of wheat, 35 percent of meat, 31 percent of lard, 61 percent of tobacco, and 62 percent of bauxite imports by Germany originated in these countries (Kaiser 1980).

German interest in the Baltic area was also strong. Germany had played a leading role in Baltic trade since the close of World War I. In 1920, Germany provided nearly 20 percent of Latvia's and 30 percent of Estonia's imports, and within two years, this share increased to 48 and 40 percent respectively. At the end of the decade, Germany monopolized nearly half of the Lithuanian market. In the thirties, however, the Baltic became a theater of British and German competition. After the British abandoned the gold standard and introduced tariff protection in 1931, they commenced a program of bilateral trade agreements, concluding commercial treaties with the three Baltic states in 1934. Consequently, the economic position of Britain in the Baltic strengthened: its share in imports increased from 10 to 19 percent in Estonia, from 8 to 20 percent in Latvia, and from 9 to 37 percent in Lithuania between 1929 and 1935. Germany's economic offensive in the second half of the thirties was also rather successful. Except in Lithuania, where its predepression positions could not be recovered, German trade dominated the Baltic region. Between 1934 and 1938, the German share increased from 21 to 31 percent in Estonia and from 25 to 39 percent in Latvia. In the Baltic countries, as in the Southeastern European area, the German economic position grew in strength (Rauch 1987).

Hermann Gross was right when he stated in 1938 that "Germany was the only industrialized state to give generous aid to the Southeastern European agrarian countries, with preferential treatment and an increased acceptance of products from these countries" (Gross 1938, 18). The Nazi economic-political goals were clearly expressed in then-secret documents. "Germany's intent with the agreement," states a January 1934 government document, "is to link the Hungarian economy strongly and inseparably to the German one by increased trade" (Deutsches Archiv 1934). As David Kaiser concludes in his analysis of

German economic penetration into Southeastern Europe in the thirties, the West lost the "first battle of World War II" when it followed a shortsighted noncooperative policy and allowed Hitler to incorporate the region into his Lebensraum (Kaiser 1980).

In a significant part of Central and Eastern Europe, a new isolationist regional economic system was formed with Nazi Germany at its center. This system, based entirely on bilateral agreements with Germany, operated according to trade mechanisms and price levels different from those of the world market. On the one hand, the new system offered an exit from the trap of the Great Depression for the crisis-ridden countries of the region. On the other hand, it created an even more dangerous trap. In the framework of the isolationist system, regional self-sufficiency, impossible within narrow national boundaries, became achievable. The challenge of the world market was brushed aside and the obsolete traditional agricultural structures of the participating countries were safeguarded. Recovery from the devastating effects of the depression came quickly. The short-term advantage of the new system was spectacular. With this achievement, however, the incentive to adjust and to modernize was also cleared away. The backward countries of the region were incorporated into the German "living space," contributing to Hitler's war preparation and thus endangering their national independence. The German-led regional economic system prepared the road for Nazi political and military penetration and domination in Central and Eastern Europe.

In 1935–1936, the agreement system transformed into a forced economic cooperation. Hermann Göring was appointed to direct a four-year plan for war preparation. The policy of "cannons instead of butter" combined with bad harvests to create meat and grain shortages in Germany. The policy of "generous aid"—that is, of opening the German markets to the agricultural countries of Central and Eastern Europe—was replaced by overt blackmail and pressure intended to force these countries to meet German demands. In the years between 1933 and 1937, agricultural world market prices significantly increased: 70 percent for wheat, 150 percent for corn, and 100 percent for meat. The world market began to offer better deals than the German market. "Grain export," stated an internal memo of the economics department of the Hungarian Ministry of Foreign Affairs in the spring of 1937, "is much more favorable to other countries than Germany. Italy pays 70 percent hard currency for wheat, [and] deliveries for Switzerland are met 25 percent by convertible currency" (Hungarian Archive 1937). By the mid-thirties, the Hungarian government sought to refuse German demands for increased deliveries. "As far as the assumed German demand of increased wheat deliveries is concerned," decided the economic cabinet, "the resolution is to step aside. Each quintal of wheat delivered to Germany diminishes our possibilities to increase our hard currency incomes" (Hungarian Archive 1935). Poland adopted strict measures in the fall of 1936, and Yugoslavia in March 1937, to curb German trade and eliminate increasing export surpluses. Romania began to pay special subsidies for grain exports to other countries than Germany and limited her oil export to Germany to a maximum of 25 percent of total oil exports. In the fall of 1936, Göring traveled to Hungary and demanded increased Hungarian agricultural deliveries. "Hungary must not leave Germany high and dry in this situation," declared Göring. The Hungarian trade officials asked permission from the minister of foreign affairs to make a statement during the trade discussion with Germany that Hungary, on principle, "rejects German dictates on the quantity of grain deliveries" (Hungarian Archive 1935a). The new trade agreement of 1937, however, significantly strengthened the German trade position. Hungarian exports to Germany increased by nearly 25 percent in one year. For the first time in the history of Hungary, Germany became its number one trade partner. Meanwhile, the formerly advantageous trade terms noticeably deteriorated. Moreover, the price level was no longer higher than world market prices. Hjalmar Schacht declared in the summer of 1935 that the agricultural countries were selling their products in the German market because they "have to, therefore they have to accept German prices and adjust to German measures" (Hungarian Archive 1935b). Germany refused or silently sabotaged payments in kind. Increased Eastern exports were covered less and less by German industrial deliveries, and at the end of 1936, nearly five hundred million marks had accumulated in German clearing debts to its Southeastern European trade partners. In addition, Germany failed to fulfill its obligation in raw material deliveries: instead of the more than 22 percent demanded by agreement terms, raw materials represented barely 13 percent of German deliveries in 1936 and less than 7 percent in 1937. The isolationist regional agreement system was under strict German control and the participating countries were forced into great dependency on Hitler as the thirties came to a close.

Isolationism and Self-Sufficiency in the Stalinist Soviet Union

On January 7, 1933, a triumphant Stalin proudly reported the results of his first five-year plan to the Central Committee of the Bolshevik Party:

Whereas by the end of 1932 the volume of industrial output in the USSR rose to 219 percent of the 1928 output, the volume of industrial output in the USA dropped during the same period to 56 percent, in Britain to 80 percent, in Germany to 55 percent, [and] in Poland to 54 percent. What do these figures show if not that the capitalist system of industry has failed to stand the test in competition with the Soviet system, that the Soviet system . . . has all the advantage over the capitalist system. (Stalin 1976, 597)

As Stalin's report reflects, the Great Depression bypassed the Soviet Union, which switched to the highest possible gear of economic growth in 1928–1929. As the depression hit the West and the backward European agricultural areas, the Soviet Union initiated its first five-year plan, history's boldest modernization and industrialization endeavor. The plan was initially prepared in March 1925 by a committee headed by the old Bolshevik, Pyatakov. At the end of the year, the Planning Office took over the task and, in March 1926, Strumilin presented a first and rather moderate draft of the plan to the party leadership. Spurred by the emotional debates on industrialization in the mid-twenties, new versions of the plan in spring 1927 suggested a much faster industrialization drive. After the Fifteenth Party Congress and the defeat of both the Left and the Right opposition, Stalin changed his centrist line and became the most ardent advocate of the previously rejected superindustrialization.

In 1928, a new plan reflecting Stalin's new line was prepared and introduced in the 1929–1930 economic year. According to the overambitious plan, the Soviet Union would more than double its national income and would increase agricultural output nearly twofold, gross industrial output more than twofold, and the production of capital goods threefold by 1932–1933. In this "second revolution," a "breakthrough in the world's history comparable in significance to Lenin's October," Stalin targeted as goals "the construction of socialism in one country" and the modern industrial transformation of peasant Russia, "a revolution from above" (Tucker 1990, 8–9). The ethos of forced industrialization and a hysteric fear of a new "imperialist attack" pushed industrialization efforts toward the impossible. "We could not know just when the imperialists would attack the USSR," explained Stalin in 1933, "but they might attack us at any moment. . . . The Party could not afford to wait. . . . It had to pursue the policy of accelerating development to the utmost" (Stalin 1976, 599–600). As a consequence, the plan indicators were modified again in December 1929, by accelerating growth indexes for the first year of the five-year plan period; then, after a few days, a new slogan was phrased: "Five-Year Plan in four years!" For the second year of the plan, new and more fantastic growth targets were set: instead of a genuine doubling of the production of capital goods, the new goal was an increase of more than threefold; instead of increasing engineering production by twofold, the new target was a fivefold increase; instead of more than doubling its output, the electrotechnical industry had to increase its production nearly sixfold. Textile and other consumer good industries preserved modest 20 to 60 percent growth targets.

On February 4, 1931, Stalin declared that in strategic industries the plan would have to be fulfilled in three years. Astonishing targets were set: crude oil extraction was to be increased from 11.7 million tons in 1927–1928 to 50 million tons, instead of to the original target of 21.7 million tons. Iron production was to grow from 3.2 million tons to 16 million tons, instead of the original goal of 10 million tons. Trotsky and Preobrazhensky had never dreamed that their notions of superindustrialization would be taken to such extremes and result in the ruthless "dictatorship of industry" that Stalin realized in the early thirties (Nove 1992).

Ruthless dictatorship was required to subordinate and exploit agriculture, the economy, and the entire population—to enforce the tremendous human suffering and sacrifice necessary to achieve Stalin's monomaniac industrialization goals in an extremely short period. There was no place for the "invisible hand" of spontaneous market rules. The strongly visible iron hand of the state introduced the dictatorship of central planning. The industrialization debates of the early mid-twenties were connected to the controversy over the relative merits of the market or of planning. Whereas Bukharin argued for a balanced development in which market mechanisms regulate the economy, Preobrazhensky suggested destroying the market and market prices and introducing state regulations and redistribution by central planning in their place. The concept and practice of superindustrialization led to the victory of an overcentralized planning system. The debate on the so-called genetic or teleological planning—the controversy over whether to set targets on the basis of existing economic sources, or, instead, on the basis of ideal goals or political requirements—was also ended. Stalin declared in February 1931: "In 10 years at most we must make good the distance that separates us from the advanced capitalist countries. . . . That depends on us. Only on us! . . . It is time to put an end to the rotten line of non-interference in production. It is time to adopt a new line, one corresponding to the present period—the line of *interfering in everything*" (Stalin 1976, 530).

The plan indicators became compulsory orders; their fulfillment was sanctioned by drastic regulations and laws. The failure to fulfill the plan was interpreted as sabotage and crime. Market and profit motivates were totally eliminated. The personal interest of managers and workers was consciously linked to the fulfillment and overfulfillment of centrally-set plan indicators. State-owned firms, instead of selling their products, delivered them to other state-owned firms according to the plan: the market was replaced by a system of central distribution. Retail and wholesale "trade" were similarly organized. In 1929, strict rationing of food and consumer goods was introduced. Money scarcely played a role in exchange. Economic targets and plan indicators were set in physical terms, in tons and square meters. The central Planning Office worked out national material and product balances. A compulsory sowing and delivery system regulated agriculture, prescribing what to produce and how much to deliver to the state. Since delivery was compulsory, the state could pay unrealistic prices, often at and sometimes even below the cost of production. The price scissor and the exploitation of the peasantry (the bulk of the population), which had been suggested by Trotsky and Preobrazhensky in the early twenties and rejected by Stalin at that time, was ruthlessly realized in the thirties in a most extreme manner.

"The events of 1929–34 constitute one of the great dramas of history. They need much more space than they can possibly receive here, and a more eloquent pen than the author's to describe them" (Nove 1992, 159). Indeed, Stalin's revolution was the bloodiest and most insane, but also, in certain respects, the most successful modernization revolution in history. His plan targeted the impossible, and the Communist Party and the Soviet state mobilized millions. A modernization euphoria was generated, accompanied by deliberately shock-producing efforts. Millions of people were killed or imprisoned; others were frightened in cruel and inhuman ways. Millions more were uprooted and sent to uninhabited, wild areas in order to build new industrial centers. The creation of a new center of iron, steel, and engineering in Magnitogorsk in the Ural region, construction of the Dnieper hydroelectric power station, the establishment of a mining industry in Kazakhstan and of an engineering industry in Georgia, and other major projects and symbols of Soviet modernization required the mobilization of 11.5 million new industrial and construction workers, and thus women and peasants were hastily trained. Several major projects, such as the Volga-White Sea Canal, were completed with forced labor. The number of workers in the traditional peasant country grew by more than 100 percent, far surpassing the original goal of a 33 percent increase. Sleeping Central Asian and West-Siberian areas were linked by the "Turksib" railroad to the growing Soviet economy. The introduction of cotton production created a domestic raw material basis for a textile industry, and the virtually unlimited resources of the huge empire were hurriedly mobilized for use in an import-substituting industrialization scheme.

Besides millions of new workers, billions of investments were also needed. Central planning, the destruction of the market, and the ruthless exploitation of the peasantry and the entire population, propped up by the practice of mass terror, produced an unprecedented rate of accumulation in the backward, peasant economy. In 1932, forced accumulation at the expense of the peasantry and curbs on living standards transferred 30 percent of the national income into the state accumulation fund. Although the extreme goals of the plan were not fulfilled, industrialization was achieved: national income doubled and industrial output more than doubled, while the production of capital goods, including engineering, more than quadrupled.

The other central factor in Stalin's revolution was the collectivization of agriculture. This policy had roots in late-nineteenth-century Marxist theory, according to which peasant agriculture, unlike other sectors of the economy, would not be nationalized but rather, by means of deliberate cooperation, would be structured on socialist rather than private property lines. Although he stressed voluntary compliance and gradualism, Stalin engulfed the countryside in cruel pressures and ruthless terror, thereby forcing the peasants onto cooperative farms (*kolhozi*). Stalin's motivations lay partly in finding protection against repeated famines, partly in controlling and centrally directing the agricultural sector, and partly in making agriculture less labor-intensive so that large numbers of peasants could be forced into growing industry. In some regions, brutal forced collectivization began in the summer of 1929. On

June 28 in Russia, and on July 3 in the Ukraine, agricultural products were impressed. Compulsory delivery was imposed on entire villages and unequally charged to households, burdening the kulaks and well-to-do peasants disproportionately. This began the infamous "dekulakization" program, in which kulaks, who could not fulfill the extremely heavy delivery plans, were severely punished (Conquest 1968). Their land was confiscated, and they were arrested and deported. Frightened "middle-peasants," who were easily denounceable as kulaks or "kulak accomplices," hurried to join collective farms in order to avoid this fate. In the November 1929 session of the Central Committee, a report announced a "spontaneous turning point" in collectivization: the poor and middle-peasants were joining collectives en masse. Whereas in June only about one million people lived on the cooperative farms, by October, this number had doubled. Kulaks, however, were not allowed to join. During the summer of 1930, three hundred thousand kulak families (roughly one and a half million people) were expropriated and deported. The next year, this number increased to one million households and four and a half million people. The remaining kulak farms were required to deliver 70 percent of their products to the state. Anyone who could not or would not fulfill that obligation was accused of "anti-Soviet activity" and deported.

The fate of millions of unfortunate peasants, killed in this inhuman and extremely brutal collectivization campaign, belongs to the darkest chapter of Soviet history. According to inaccurate and varying estimations, between ten and fifteen million people (probably as many as three million families) were victims of dekulakization, mass terror, and famine. It should be added that Stalin was not satisfied by the "elimination of the kulaks as a class," meaning the expropriation of their property. In 1932, he announced a crusade against kulaks who attempted to find jobs at construction works or in industry and ordered these "discredited" people "swept away" from state-owned firms. "State terror is triadic. One element of the triad," notes Robert Tucker, "is a political leadership determined to use terror for its purposes. The second is a minority chosen for victimization in so frightful a form that the third element, a far larger body of people, seeing what happens to the victims, will be motivated to fulfill the leadership's purpose" (Tucker 1990, 174). Millions of unfortunate, victimized people, the "chosen minority" of kulaks and kulak accomplices, the target of a murderous hatred, faced total humiliation, loss of subsistence, and death.

By February 1930, half of all peasants had joined the collective farms.

The deadly campaign was ended in the spring that year, following several local uprisings and demonstrations (in the first days of March, forty-five cases) that signaled the unbearable tension in the countryside. In his hypocritical manner, Stalin stressed the voluntary character of collectivization and harshly criticized or punished "local despots," who became "dizzy from the successes." Within a few weeks, more than half of the collectivized peasants had left the cooperative farms: The percentage of collectivized peasants dropped from 58 to 23 percent. During the next year, however, forceful methods were reinstated and the entire peasantry was compelled to join: in 1931, the percentage of peasants on collectivized farms again reached 53 percent; in 1932, it increased to 64 percent, and in 1936, to 90 percent, occupying 96–98 percent of all arable land.

Upon joining a collective farm, peasants were required to give up their animals to the collective. As a result, slaughtering animals, an expression of resistance, emerged as a natural side effect of collectivization. In Kazakhstan alone, the number of sheep and goats dropped from 19.2 million to 2.6 million. Cattle stock in the Soviet Union declined from 71 million in 1928 to 38 million in 1933. Pig and sheep stocks decreased from 26 million and 147 million to 12 million and 50 million respectively. Animal stock, in short, was halved and in some cases even cut to one-third of precollectivization levels. The demoralized, expropriated peasantry turned against collective ownership by stealing everything possible. Punitive laws attempted to halt this practice: paragraph 58 of the penal code of 1932 severely punished any act that harmed collective assets. The minimal punishment was a ten-year imprisonment, but in serious cases, capital punishment was ordered. A great number of peasants who joined the Bolshevik Party also resisted. In the North-Caucasus, for example, 43 percent of party members were expelled from the party during the collectivization drive.

The collective farms were required to follow a uniform pattern: they could not own machinery, and their members received income according to the number of "work units" fulfilled. Each family was allowed a small private plot for growing food for the household, but marketing was strictly limited. The mechanization of agriculture began with leaps and bounds: the state machine stations received tens of thousands of tractors and combines. After the nadir of output in 1932–1933, and at the cost of murdering or bringing suffering to tens of millions of people, a gradual modernization of agriculture practice began to yield moderate increases in production. Grain production reached ninety-six million tons in 1937, compared to seventy million tons in 1932. The value of the gross agricultural product increased from thirteen billion rubles to twenty billion rubles but remained far behind the planned increase to thirty-six billion rubles (Nove 1992).

With modernization, the Soviet Union took gigantic strides forward. The country could no longer be called a "sleeping giant." In the place of backward *muzhik* parcels, modernizing large estates began to employ modern agricultural technology. Green field investments created new industrial centers and transformed the agricultural economy of the country into a modern industrialized one. Even though this transformation was accompanied by unprecedented conflicts and turmoil, the Great Depression bypassed the Soviet Union. Stalin drew the conclusion that because the socialist Soviet economy curbed and eliminated capitalist market anarchy and introduced central planning, it therefore would be free of economic crises. Certainly in the period of the devastating Great Depression, the Soviet Union achieved its greatest prosperity and fastest growth. "The USSR stands out like a rock," Stalin noted in his victory report at the Seventeenth Party Congress in January 1934. "During this period, the USSR has become radically transformed and has cast off the aspect of backwardness and medievalism. From an agrarian country it has become an industrial country. New industries have been created. . . . Thousands of new, fully up-to-date industrial plants have been built. . . . New large towns, with large populations, have sprung up in what were almost uninhabited places" (Stalin 1976, 672, 694–95).

The unprecedented economic expansion and modernization in the Soviet Union presented a sharp contrast to the devastating crisis, decline, and absence of structural change in Central and Eastern Europe. Yet are the two performances, indeed, so extremely contrasting? From the point of view of growth rate, employment, and industrialization, they certainly are, but with respect to their modernization policy, much less separates them. Central and Eastern Europe as well as the Soviet Union turned down the path of import-substituting industrialization. Whereas the Soviet Union concentrated its efforts toward building up its own capital goods and heavy industries—the second stage of import substitution—the other countries of the region sought self-sufficiency in consumer goods and light industries—the first stage of import-substitution. Their policies were actually similar, because import-substituting industrialization required an isolationist, protectionist shield, with high tariffs, quotas, and other restrictions, and the abolition of the gold standard and of currency convertibility. All of the countries in Central and Eastern Europe introduced these measures by curbing and limiting markets and strengthening state intervention. Because the Soviet Union went the farthest, completely destroying its market economy, it was able to introduce the most consistent measures. The other nations abolished their self-regulated markets, replacing them with regulated market economies and, at the end of the thirties, introduced some state planning, but their policies could not be entirely consistent. They were unable to achieve total isolation and self-sufficiency, and they sought, therefore, to reach their goals within the framework of the German-controlled regional agreement system. Instead, they became more dependent on Nazi Germany. The Soviet Union, in contrast, one-sixth of the world's territory, was large enough to accomplish this goal alone.

The Soviet Union moved ahead full steam to establish economic independence. A *Pravda* editorial on the goal of self-sufficiency in the production of capital goods stated in 1927: "This is an absolutely right policy, guaranteeing us economic independence; and it is being carried out . . . in spite of the fact that it postpones somewhat the abolition of the shortage of consumer goods" (Carr and Davies 1974, 867). The Sixteenth Party Congress stated that overambitious development targets in engineering were the way to eliminate dependence on foreign countries. Consistency in economic policy that aimed at establishing economic independence fueled the harshness of the Stalinist dictatorship. The other countries of the region, although dictatorial, never developed this consistent and cruel form of dictatorship, and, as a result, they remained less self-sufficient.

In its unfailing, deliberate, but also imposed isolationism and self-sufficiency, the Soviet Union did not have to adjust to the world economy and its competition. Foreign trade became marginal and did not influence domestic economic trends; the latter diverted significantly from international trends and escaped the fluctuations of the world market. Since the Soviet economy was explicitly responsible for defending the country from a hostile Western attack, it became highly militarized. Forced industrialization, as debates in 1928 stressed, served "the needs of defence to the maximum," and "the forced rate of industrialization . . . [has increased] as much as possible the defence capacity of the country" (Carr and Davies 1974, 866).

Stalin's explicitly expressed motivation for his actions was his firm belief in an unavoidable war. He spoke about an "unavoidable war in a few years" in January 1925, at the session of the Central Committee, repeated his conviction that the world was shifting toward war at the Sixteenth Party Congress in the summer of 1930, and repeatedly warned of the same in the thirties. Did he "beat the war drums" in order to stir up support for high-speed industrialization and collectivization and create an underpinning for his political goals? Did this rhetoric serve his oversized ego and appetite for power, helping him reach his "supreme goal: fame and glory" by launching a "second revolution," his "own October" (Tucker 1990, 3, 74–75)? His psychological motivation to emerge as the "Lenin of today" certainly contributed to his drive. Yet one could not argue that the danger of war was nonexistent and that his warning was an empty threat. His preparations for war could be evaluated as astute political foresight. After all, others realized at Versailles that the peace after World War I might only be an "armistice for twenty years," as Marshal Foch noted, and that war would probably resume. By the early thirties, war had broken out in some areas. Preparedness would thus have seemed to be eminently sensible.

In fact, the Stalinist industrialization drive, framed as a preparation for a possible or unavoidable war, was not senseless at all. The entire Soviet economic policy of the thirties can be seen as nothing other than a hurried war preparation. The Soviet Union did not search for a response to the challenges of change in the old technological regime and of consequent structural crisis. Neither did it seek to compete in the world market. What Stalin forced was the production of as many strategic materials and products as possible. His industrialization drive was based on the technological-structural requirements of the early twentieth century and sought to increase the production of coal, iron, steel, oil, tractors, and some traditional engineering products, all required for wartime self-sufficiency. This centralized, isolated war-type economy was less vulnerable to the Great Depression and, in fact, generated rapid growth. This did not mean, however, that the Soviet economy created the appropriate technological and structural basis for the 1930s and beyond. Stalin's model of modernization was not a model of modern adjustment to the world economy. In this respect, the spectacular Soviet performance was not so different from the rest of Central and Eastern Europe's nonadjustment escape from the depression. The similarities in the economic endeavors in the entire region during the thirties were striking and became more so by the end of the thirties, when self-sufficient war economies were already markedly in the making.

12

Social Changes

New Forces and Factors

World War I and the Great Depression had a tremendous impact on Central and Eastern European societies. The masses were mobilized and learned their own strength, but they were also humiliated and learned the strength of powerful states. Large groups were uprooted and traditional hierarchies were both attacked and defended. The nineteenth-century society that characterized backward peasant countries began to transform.

The Peasantry

In spite of its developing differentiation and the existence of a small, well-to-do layer, the nineteenth-century peasantry in Central and Eastern Europe remained excluded from the wider society as a sort of underclass. Social and economic discrimination arose partly as a consequence of the survival of large estates, which kept more than half of the peasant population nearly or entirely landless. The lasting value system of the former "noble societies," the village lifestyle, low levels of civilization and culture, mass illiteracy, and the absence of sociopolitical emancipation all had equal impact. The road toward social elevation—to embourgeoisement, white-collar lower-middle-class positions, and urbanized skilled worker status—remained mostly blocked (Hanák et al. 1993). At the turn of the century, there was no genuine peasant political party or representation in any of the overwhelmingly peasant countries. Even in the Balkan countries, which lacked native ruling classes, the peasants were similarly downtrodden. The poor "minifundia" of the region kept large families living at subsistence levels. Village communities lacked market orientation and social mobility and were plagued with a paralyzingly poor education system and overwhelming illiteracy; these conditions held the peasants back and made them easy victims of the uneducated but nouveau-riche peasant-merchants and the bureaucratic-military elite. Even though peasants made up two-thirds to three-quarters of the population, they could not become an independent social and political factor in these countries (Stavrianos 1963).

This situation began to change at the turn of the century, and after World War I, the rate of change accelerated. Social and political emancipation of the peasantry, a basic characteristic of modern society, became a tenet in modernization policy. This emancipation was facilitated by the growing economic power and influence of a commodity-producing, market-oriented stratum of the peasantry. In addition, the revolutionized, semiproletarian, lower peasantry began revolting against existing regimes before the war, and their coordinated harvest strikes and bloody spontaneous uprisings signaled the coming great transformation. After the war, the peasants applied the lesson of World War I: to organize and use weapons against their enemies. After their harsh four to five years of "apprenticeship" in open trenches, the revolutionized peasant masses of Russia became the decisive factor in defeating the old regime during the Bolshevik revolution. These events in Russia and the turmoil in postwar Bulgaria and Hungary made change throughout the region more urgent. Even the ruling elite recognized that they could no longer afford to exclude the peasantry; instead, various groups began to compete for peasant loyalty. The war had one additional major consequence in the arena of social change. Nationalism, in victorious and vanquished countries alike, whether expressed in belated national revolutions or in ethnic hostility and confrontation, required the mobilization of the bulk of the population, the peasant masses. National interest demanded that the body of the nation be strengthened with this now emancipated and newly included social force.

Land reform, one of the most important and visible consequences of social change, became a number one issue on postwar sociopolitical agendas throughout the region. "Just distribution of land" entered common parlance as both a social and national slogan. It called for granting land to the landless and small landholders by destroying or severely limiting large estates. Such radical social change, a taboo before the war, became part of government programs even in highly conservative regimes. The methods and results of these land reforms varied. In several cases, they were motivated and accelerated by nationalist, antiminority measures. In Yugoslavia, land reform gained political preference as early as the end of 1918 in the first manifesto of the Royal Regent and was formalized by decree in February 1919; this far-reaching land reform, which parceled out estates over fifty hectares, wiped out the large estate in the formerly Austro-Hungarian land. In Croatia, Voivodina, Bosnia-Herzegovina, and Macedonia, large estates, which occupied roughly 40 percent of the arable land, disappeared; nearly two and a half million hectares of land were redistributed among 650,000 families. The radicalism of the Yugoslav reform originated in part in the egalitarian Serbian land tenure practice that was adopted throughout the new nation. Another major factor contributing to radicalism in Yugoslavia was the ethnic-national composition of the landowner class in these formerly Austro-Hungarian territories. Land redistribution weakened the former Hungarian and Austrian landed-aristocratic ruling elite and thus served a central national-political goal (Kaser and Radice 1985).

Nationalism also contributed significantly to the land reform movement in Romania, where reform was announced in December 1918 at the Alba Iulia assembly in Transylvania and passed as a law within two weeks. The upper limit for estates varied between one hundred and five hundred hectares, depending on the area in question. The most radical reforms were executed in Bessarabia and Transylvania in order to eliminate Russian and Hungarian landownership. All lands owned by non-Romanian citizens who resided outside the country were confiscated. Altogether, 6.3 million hectares were distributed among 1.4 million peasant families. Peasant farming became predominant and, after the reforms, estates over one hundred hectares occupied only 14 percent of the arable land in Romania.

National and political considerations radicalized land reform in the Baltic countries as well. Estonia and Latvia had the most unequal land distribution before World War I: large estates occupied 58 percent and 48 percent respectively of all agricultural land. In Estonia, where two-thirds of the rural population was landless, reform became a question of life or death during the fight for national independence; when all large estates were confiscated and redistributed in Bolshevik Russia, the

Estonian government recognized that it was of crucial national interest to ensure the loyalty of the peasantry. Consequently, in October 1919 a radical expropriation law was enacted in Estonia that affected nearly 97 percent of the large estates and even the summer houses of the landowners. From the more than one thousand expropriated estates, fifty-six thousand small peasant holdings were created, and the number of Estonian peasant farms more than doubled. In Latvia, nearly one-quarter of all arable land was redistributed among landless peasants, making peasant farming predominant. In Lithuania, the March 1922 land reform act maximized the size of private holdings at 150 hectares and caused large estates virtually to disappear (Rauch 1987).

It was not only the "immunization" of peasantry against the Bolshevik virus that motivated the radicalism of reforms. National revolutions also sought to eliminate a supposedly alien landowning class. In Estonia, only fifty-seven large estates belonged to ethnic Estonians, whereas the bulk of the more than one thousand expropriated estates were held by Baltic Germans. In Lithuania, the landowning class was mostly Polish or Russian. The destruction of old, alien ruling classes and the rise of a new indigenous landed peasantry thus became inseparable parts of Baltic national revolutions (Hiden and Salmon 1991).

The national factor played a more moderate but nonetheless significant role in Polish and Czechoslovak land reforms. Whereas the upper limit for landed estates was set at three hundred hectares for the area of the former Polish Kingdom, it was often reduced to sixty hectares in areas that were formerly part of the German and Austrian empires and where much land belonged to German and Austrian landowners. Similarly, the otherwise usually moderate Czechoslovak reforms radically reduced the Hungarian big estates in Slovakia. In neither of these countries, however, was the large estate eliminated.

Polish land reform law was quite radical—it ordered that estates over sixty, and in certain areas over three hundred, hectares be parceled out—but its implementation was extremely slow, and, in the end, only one-quarter of the large estates were expropriated; 20 percent of the land remained in the hands of the traditional landowning class. The 2.65 million hectares parceled out during two decades of reform affected only roughly 10 percent of the arable land but created more than 730,000 new peasant farms. Nearly 860,000 additional, existing peasant holdings were increased by distributing 5.4 million hectares among them. Land reform in Poland could not compensate for the growth in the peasant population: the 133,000 hectares annual distribution of land could not match the annual agrarian population increase of 250,000.

The implementation of the Czechoslovak land reform affected only 16 percent of the arable land. Here too, implementation was extremely slow: ten years after the promulgation of the land reform act, the large estates had lost only three hundred thousand hectares, and estates over five hundred hectares were still predominant, possessing over 40 percent of the land. After the parceling out was speeded up (1.3 million hectares had been distributed by 1938), the share of arable land still in large estates declined to one-sixth of the total.

Land reforms in Hungary and Bulgaria were even more moderate, affecting a smaller percentage of land. In Bulgaria, large estates did not exist, but the left-wing populist Stamboliski government, led by the ideal of an egalitarian peasant society, set the upper limit for land holdings at fifty hectares and parceled out 6 percent of the arable land. In contrast, Hungary announced a land reform in 1920, mostly for political reasons. The counterrevolutionary Horthy regime sought to gain the loyalty of the peasantry and to exploit the major mistake made by the Hungarian Councils' Republic, which, instead of parceling out the land, created state-farm cooperatives. The character of the regime, however, created strict limitations: the preamble of the land reform bill stated that its goal was not to abolish large estates but to "improve land distribution." No upper limit was given for landed estates, and only 6 percent of the land was distributed among the quarter million landless peasants (one hectare each). Some viable, well-to-do peasant farms were strengthened, and politically loyal peasants who joined Horthy's "national army" gained larger plots. In the mid-thirties, as a consequence, more than 41 percent of the land still belonged to large estates (Berend and Ránki 1974).

To varying degrees, then, land reforms destroyed or reduced large estates in Central and Eastern Europe and strengthened peasant holdings. The peasantry became stronger as property owners and gained political power and influence.

The changing role of the peasantry was connected to important progress in education. Compulsory, tuition-free elementary education was widely established throughout Central and Eastern Europe during the interwar decades. Concomitantly, illiteracy was largely eradicated. In Hungary, illiteracy rates dropped from 35 percent in 1910 to 8 percent just before World War II. The Baltic countries made impressive progress. Lithuania, the most backward of these nations, introduced compulsory, free elementary education in 1931. The national student body increased from 15 per thousand to 116 per thousand, and illiteracy rates dropped sharply, even though they remained higher than the Latvian rate of 14 percent and the Estonian rate of 4 percent in the thirties. Illiteracy still characterized 30 percent to 40 percent of the population in the Balkans but was increasingly confined to the older generation. A narrow path to secondary and even higher education was opened as well, and the peasant-intellectual appeared in the early thirties. Enthusiastic first-generation, peasant, white-collar workers, teachers, and writers became, for the first time, members of the intellectual elite in these countries. The leading groups in the emerging populist movement were recruited from their ranks. Burning problems—the humiliating remnants of the past and the backwardness of the peasant life—were discovered and openly presented to the public. Students began to visit the countryside, collecting the requisites of traditional peasant life. Peasant songs and dances became popular and were considered expressions of national character. A cult of rural-peasant values, viewed as a source of national purity and health, emerged.

Social changes triggered a great transformation in the political role of the peasantry. Before 1914, peasant parties did not figure in the politics of Central and Eastern Europe. After the war, strong, influential peasant parties emerged and, in several cases, became part of governing coalitions or ruling parties. In 1920, the Smallholders' Party was founded in Hungary and gained the majority of the votes. After two years, the party lost its peasant character, having been "hijacked" by count István Bethlen, the prime minister of Hungary who entered the party and transformed it into a quasi-monolithic united government party. But during the thirties, the party regained some of its genuine peasant character (Balogh 1985).

Peasant parties appeared in the political arena in nearly every country. The strongest and by far the most genuine was Stamboliski's Bulgarian Agrarian Union, which tried to topple the bureaucratic-merchant elite by means of a peasant revolutionary program. The coup against and murder of Stamboliski put an end to the influence of the party in 1923, but it regained ground during the trying years of the Great Depression. In Poland, peasant parties failed to emerge after World War I, but in 1931, a moderately radical Peoples' Party was formed and enjoyed broad popularity.

In newly independent Estonia and Latvia, the political arena was confused—in small Latvia, 39 political parties were represented in the parliament during the twenties—and peasant parties emerged as leading political forces. The Homesteaders's and Farmers's parties, which merged and formed the Agrarian Union in Estonia, and the Peasant Union and the new Farmers in Latvia were created as representatives of both the "old" peasantry and the new peasantry that had been established by the radical land reforms. In both nations, however, the peasant parties became moderate right-of-the-center political forces, representing nationalist political trends. The Estonian Agrarian Union supplied half of the prime ministers of the country and leading politicians such as Päts and Laidoner. The Latvian New Farmers' League was represented in each of the country's governments and provided twelve prime ministers out of eighteen. In Lithuania, the peasant masses were recruited by the Christian Democratic Party, a sort of people's party (Hiden and Salmon 1991).

In several cases, peasant parties lost their genuine character. Parties that expressed the interests of peasant masses were incorporated or transformed at times, becoming national parties. Ironically, the Czech Agrarian Party became the strongest party in that industrialized country, but it was peasant in name only and actually represented the middle class. This party participated in almost every government of the country and sometimes governed alone. The Romanian Peasant Party, founded by Ion Michalache after the war, also lost its peasant character after its merger with Maniu's Transylvanian National Party in 1926. The new party, called the National Peasant Party and now led by Maniu, became a middle-class national party that pressed for nationalist economic policy. The Radić brothers' Croatian Peasant Party, a genuine representative of the peasantry, soon became a Croatian national party in the struggle against Serbian centralism and lost its original character under Maček, the successor to the assassinated Radić (H. Seton-Watson 1967).

During the stormy thirties, political polarization and splits occurred in the various peasant parties. Some, such as the Slovak movement, shifted toward the protofascist political camp; others, such as the Bulgarian peasant movement, turned toward the radical left. The independent peasant parties were seldom able to preserve their genuine peasant traits and programs and eventually represented divergent trends across the political spectrum. Their politics sometimes merged with those of the bourgeois middle class, other times supported nationalism and separatism, and also occasionally merged with extreme right-wing or left-wing positions. Nonetheless, the important political role of the peasant parties clearly expressed the social changes that had taken place. The peasantry had grown strong and had discovered their own worth, provided sufficient political force to support these political changes.

The Emergence of a Confused Lower Middle Class

In the industrialized nations of the Western world, new lower middle classes appeared in the last third of the nineteenth century. The Central and Eastern European countries, still rural and peasant in character, could not follow this trend. During the interwar years, however, growing numbers of a new lower middle class signified a new and characteristic social trend in the region. The occupational structure of industrialized Austria and Czechoslovakia began to resemble that in the Western countries: the independent self-employed and their families accounted for 37 percent of Austria's population. In both Austria and Czechoslovakia, nearly half of the population belonged to the lower middle class, to the white-collar worker strata and intellectuals. Their numbers grew not only in response to modernizing trends that rapidly increased opportunities in these occupations but also as a consequence of the postwar recession and the depression of the thirties, which halted industrial development and decreased industrial employment. People were, ironically enough, forced into white-collar and independent occupations. Whereas roughly one-third of gainfully employed people were industrial workers, and one-quarter to one-third belonged to the peasantry, the largest sector of the population belonged to the lower strata of the middle class, including the well-to-do upper layer of the peasantry.

The urban lower middle class gained ground in Poland and Hungary as well. One of the most rapidly increasing social strata were the urban self-employed and small proprietors of services in Hungary. The overall urban population reached 38 percent of the total population, and the number of small independent proprietors grew to between three and five million people (an increase of one million persons, or roughly 40 percent) during the interwar period, thus becoming the largest single group in the population after the peasant majority. The percentage share of intellectuals increased from 4 to 5 percent in the rapidly growing Polish population (in two decades, the population grew by 27 percent). The same increase was true for the share of clerks in Hungary.

The Baltic states made a great effort to create an indigenous professional class. The number of medical doctors almost trebled in Estonia, the number of primary and secondary schools more than doubled in Latvia, and the number of school teachers nearly quadrupled in Lithuania between the wars.

Paradoxically, the growth in size of the middle strata was, generally speaking, accompanied by a loss in stability and certainty. The increase in déclassé intellectuals and insolvent independent shopkeepers, a general déclassé middle class, became a characteristic social phenomenon. One of the first salvos in this process—one with a tremendous social and political impact—was triggered by the disbanding of a segment of the vast wartime officer corps, an act enforced by peace treaty on the defeated countries. Migrant people, uprooted by postwar territorial changes, enlarged the déclassé elements (Arendt 1966). Many of the déclassé individuals belonged to the bureaucratic-administrative and intellectual elite of territories that were given to neighboring countries by the Versailles peace treaty. For example, tens of thousands became déclassé after having moved from Transylvania to Budapest.

The growth in the size of the urban lower middle class and its loss of economic stability provided the social backdrop and breeding ground for institutionalized, political anti-Semitism. In Poland, Hungary, Romania, and Lithuania, increased competition and the uncertainty of the lower middle class heightened awareness of the traditional "overrepresentation" of Jews in trade, banking, self-employment, intellectual pursuits, and white-collar occupations. In the Poland of the thirties, 40 percent of all artisans and 25 percent of university graduates were Jewish. In Romania, three-quarters of bank officials, two-thirds of commercial clerks, and one-quarter of medical doctors were Jewish. In Hungary, half of all lawyers and clerks in commerce, one-third of medical doctors and journalists, and one-quarter of actors and actresses were Jewish. An expanding but confused and scared lower middle class angrily turned against the Jewry. Jewish aggressive resourcefulness was accused of causing job scarcity and economic uncertainty for "indigenous" intellectuals and white-collar workers. The Jews "occupied" positions and were "overrepresented" five-to-tenfold in comparison to their percentage share in the population (Silber 1992). As one of the Nazi-Austrian political slogan stressed, "500,000 unemployed, 400,000 Jews—the solution is easy!"

The "Jewish question" became an inseparable part of the nationalist agenda. The newly independent countries launched ambitious attacks against the "nonindigenous" elite and sought to replace them with new, mostly gentry-bureaucratic-military elite and new peasant intellectuals. A "change of guard" was demanded explicitly by the Hungarian gentry-military groups and by the enlarged Romanian political elite. The new "indigenous" Baltic political elite sought to eliminate all German, Russian, Polish, and Jewish elements in the old socioeconomic elite. Nationalist political efforts were linked to movements of belated political modernization and to attempts to enlarge the social base for belated national revolutions. Nationalism was part of the process that weakened the positions of the old aristocratic, land-owning political elite in the former "noble societies" and reinvigorated the bureaucratic-military elite of the Balkans. The breaking of the political hegemony of the aristocracy and large landowners after the war allowed the modern middle class and its parties to gain political power. The Czech Agrarian Party, the Romanian Liberal Party, and the Austrian Social Democratic Party replaced the outdated aristocratic ruling elite. Yet the stratum who benefited the most from this change of guard was not the modern urban-middle class but the gentry-bureaucratic-military elite, which earlier had stood only on the second and third echelons of the hierarchy. Their experience and position in the army and state bureaucracy allowed their role in the power structure to increase significantly during the war, and they found their stronghold in the regular army and the private armies, the paramilitary organizations. As Heiden states regarding the German gentry-bureaucratic-military elite, "The war was their home, the civil-war their homeland" (Heiden 1944, 100).

The establishment of independent statehood with its associated expansion of public administration and government apparatus had a similar consequence. Protectionist economic policies, strong state interventionism, and preparations for war gave further impetus to the process. The military, including the various associations of retired and reserve officers, became main actors in the political arena and often played the leading role in political changes in Poland, Bulgaria, Hungary, Austria, and Yugoslavia, even though the military acted differently in each case. The establishment of a public sector in industry and banking in Poland, the involvement of the military elite in the Polish state sector, and the role of the Hungarian gentry in taking over semistate cooperatives, foreign trade monopolies, and well-paid managerial positions in the thirties created strong and lucrative business connections, unthinkable for the nineteenth-century noble-gentry elite, which shunned business as an "ungentlemanlike" activity. The gentry, which had historically been part of the feudal middle class, became a catalyst in regrouping the ruling elite. A great part of the new lower middle class and peasant intellectuals were strongly attracted by and copied the attitude and behavior of this "historical middle class" (as they often called it) and its representatives, long-standing families and bearers of "historical names" (Szekfü 1922). They sought to be part of a new national elite that would lead in the struggle against external and internal enemies—neighbors, Jews, Germans, Poles, Hungarians, and communists—in order to purify the nation.

The New Strata of Workers and Humiliating Unemployment

The development of the working class, whose members increased impressively in number and whose political influence grew, became a major factor in social change. Whereas 35 percent to 45 percent of the active population in the West had become workers in the latter portions of the nineteenth century as a consequence of the industrial revolution, the industrial working class in the Balkans and Central and Eastern Europe represented only a small minority (1 to 17 percent) of the population before World War I. Social modernization increased this stratum of society. In Austria and Bohemia, where social democratic movements had a long and strong tradition, one-third to two-fifths of the active population belonged to the rank and file of a modern working class before World War I. In the interwar years, this working class became increasingly homogeneous. The second and third generation of the hereditary working class preserved its position and its trade and political organizations. The Social Democratic Party, in a situation unthinkable only a few years before, formed the government and determined the president of the republic in postwar Austria. "Red Vienna" became a stronghold of the socialists. In Czechoslovakia, the Communist Party used its strong following in the industrial centers and among intellectuals to gain enough votes to acquire a position in the parliament. Throughout the region, the working class steadily increased its political influence.

The size of the industrial working class also increased throughout the region in the interwar period. In Hungary, Poland, and Estonia, it encompassed roughly 20 to 25 percent of the population, and in the Balkans and Lithuania, it represented roughly 10 percent of the total. In an immobile sea of peasant society, Belgrade rapidly developed a modern, mobile, working- and middle-class society (Marković 1992).

The maturing of a whole new generation of workers after the war and the convulsions of revolutions brought great changes in the composition of the working class. In the new social and political atmosphere, uncertainty acted as a decisive psychological factor in this transformation. Permanent unemployment, which began to appear even during the relatively prosperous second half of the 1920s (when unemployment reached 10 percent), jumped to unprecedented levels (33 percent) during the early 1930s. Although unemployment hit the entire workers' community, it had the most devastating impact on the younger generations. It often hindered their integration into the society and created large humiliated groups of déclassé people. This change was accompanied by disappointment in the labor movement. In Hungary, Bulgaria, and some of the Baltic countries, where postwar revolutions or revolutionary attempts failed and generated harsh repressions, most of the new generation of workers remained isolated from the traditional workers' organizations and labor movement. In addition, in the nonindustrialized countries of the region, a great part of the relatively small working class worked not in big industry but rather in small-scale handicraft shops. In Hungary, only half of the industrial workers and one-tenth of the population worked in manufacturing industry. In Bulgaria and Lithuania, nearly two-thirds of the workers were employed in small-scale industries. The hereditary stratum of workers constituted a minority of the young working class: even in relatively more industrialized Hungary, it represented only one-third of the workers, and this percentage was smaller in the Balkans. Because interwar import-substituting industrialization produced its most rapid growth in the textile and other consumer good industries, new workers were recruited from unskilled and semiskilled groups; as a result, the relative size of the traditional, highly organized, and skilled workforce declined. The portion of the working class represented by unorganized, unskilled or semiskilled workers increased from one-sixth to one-quarter in Hungary and was even higher in the less industrialized countries.

This trend was accompanied by corresponding growth in the employment of female labor. Whereas previously only one in five workers in Hungary was a woman, by the end of the thirties the figure had risen to one in three. The overwhelming presence of a newly recruited female workforce was even more characteristic in the Balkans. In most of the Balkan countries, the industrial working class was only in its formative stage.

In Yugoslavia, the industrial workforce accounted for one-tenth of the active population, whereas factory workers represented a mere 4 to 5 percent. In Bulgaria, the industrial workforce was even smaller, accounting for 8 percent of the population and for only 2 percent of factory workers. In Romania, the number of industrial workers increased somewhat more rapidly and grew by 50 percent. "Unlike other countries in Central and Eastern Europe, in Romania," notes Vladimir Tismaneanu, "the modernization shock did not lead to the development of working class parties but rather to some resentments and ruralist nostalgia manipulated by the extreme Right" (Tismaneanu 1995, 27). In this mostly new working class, peasant in origin and now expanded by the large segment of female labor absorbed in the formidable textile industry (which employed more than one-quarter of the Romanian workers), the role of transitional, semipeasant workers was especially significant because tens of thousands of peasants worked in the food processing industry as campaign workers, often no longer than a few months in a year, then went back to their villages (Lampe and Jackson 1982).

Between the two world wars, various social strata drifted into insecurity and a new urban déclassé class emerged. The déclassé layers were far from a homogeneous social grouping, and the individuals swept into the periphery from various social backgrounds must not be treated as part of a single entity. They differed considerably—ranging from unemployed career officers and noncommissioned officers in the vast wartime armies to déclassé white-collar workers or déclassé intellectuals, to unemployed young people who could not enter the working class. Yet despite their differences and vastly dissimilar goals, they had much in common. They emerged as a new social factor between the wars, desperate and ready to act.

13

Political Impact

The Dirty Torrent of Dictatorships

The economic and social decay of the early 1930s had direct and immediate political repercussions. The political consequences of the Great Depression revitalized fears of turmoil, revolution, and war, which had almost been forgotten in the relatively peaceful and prosperous years of the late twenties. Lionel Robbins, professor of economics at London, expresses the general European mood in the concluding chapter of his 1934 book on the Great Depression:

What, then, are the prospects of enduring recovery? It is clear that they are not bright. . . . There is a danger of war and civil disturbance. These dangers may not be mature. It may be that the next two or three years (or even longer) may be years of comparative revival. But it is impossible to feel any confidence in a continuance of stability. (Robbins 1934, 195)

The shock caused by the Great Depression, the misery and hopelessness of the early thirties, gave rise simultaneously to various and confronting political trends throughout the nations of Central and Eastern Europe. Revolutionary hopes were reborn, and the revolutionary political struggle, having been defeated at the end of the war, recommenced. The Politburo of the German Communist Party stated on June 4, 1930, that the hope was to "destroy . . . [capitalism and] establish the dictatorship of the proletariat[,] . . . creating a Soviet-Germany" (*Geschichte* 1955, 275). Most people, however, plunged into a deep political apathy rooted in the everyday struggle for survival. Some people, déclassé or frightened at the prospect of losing their economic and social status, sought to restore or ensure their standing and to guarantee "law and order"; they welcomed the idea of right-wing revolutions, or—as Fabri, the Italian revolutionary anarchist called the triumphant Italian fascism in the early twenties—"preventive counterrevolutions." Fabri's analysis of postwar Italy is applicable mutatis mutandis to the Central and Eastern European region in the early thirties: a dangerous political vacuum had been created by the spectacular disintegration of the old regime, a danger that was exacerbated by the weakness of left-wing revolutionary forces. A political vacuum in such a situation may be filled by groups willing to use brute force to accomplish a preventive counterrevolution. The early thirties, like the immediate postwar years and early twenties, saw desperate, chaotic, revolutionary and counterrevolutionary political turmoil. In the place of the Weimar Republic, history's most frightening system of terror was installed. Almost immediately, the new regime began burning books and later turned to killing its opponents as it prepared for the war that was intended to extend its power throughout the world. The one-hundred-eighty-degree political turn in Germany was striking, even though all its factors were inherent in previous political processes. In most Central and Eastern European countries, similar political developments—an almost uniform "right face!"—occurred: dictatorship became the rule. The changes differed from those in Germany only by being less daring and more organically linked to the political trends of the twenties.

All of these dictatorial regimes shared certain characteristics. They were antiparliamentary, anticommunist, antisocialist, and antiliberal authoritarian systems that had elements, organizational structures, and even symbols of fascism but lacked a fascist party behind the ruling government. In quite a few countries, powerful Nazi-fascist mass parties emerged, but they mostly acted as an extreme-right voice, opposed even to the existing right-wing governments; with their strong influence and desire for power, they pushed the governments toward the extreme Right. The ruling elites and governments chose not to mobilize the fascist mass parties but rather to base their power on the army, state bureaucracy, exclusive elite organizations, and paramilitary forces. All the regimes followed extreme nationalist economic policies, with state-run modernization programs that tended to exclude ethnic-national minorities and to treat neighboring countries as adversaries. Several countries followed territorial revisionist policies that demanded radical border changes to accommodate national visions (Vago 1975).

Despite these similarities, the right-wing dictatorships in Central and Eastern Europe also differed from each other and can be categorized into three main types: the conservative-authoritarian regimes typified by Austria, Hungary and Poland; the "royal dictatorships" characteristic of the Balkans; and the "presidential dictatorships" associated with the Baltic countries.

Engelbert Dollfuss: A Compromise between Political Catholicism and *Heimwehr* Fascism

Between 1929 and 1931, an ailing Austria moved to the brink of civil war. Powerful private armies fought each other, and the government was powerless to control the situation. On August 18, 1929, a Social Democratic Party celebration in St. Lorenz was attacked by two thousand fascist *Heimwehr* storm-troopers, led by the Styrian *Heimwehr* chief Reuter (later Gestapo chief in Holland). Three people were killed and two hundred were wounded in the violence. Two days later, a similar fatal attack occurred in Vösendorf, a township near Vienna. Despite the fact that the Social Democratic Party acquired a substantial base of power and became the largest party in the parliament when it captured seventy-two seats in the November 9, 1930, elections, it could not govern alone and failed to form a coalition government. The actual balance of power in Austria was decided outside the parliament. The fascist *Heimwehr*, which gained only eight seats in the parliament, turned to force in order to obtain power: Walter Pfrimer, the newly appointed leader of the private fascist army, launched a coup d'etat in Styria followed by a *marcia su Wien* (march on Vienna) in which his army attempted to occupy the capital. Having begun earlier than originally planned, this poorly organized putsch failed to gain unquestioned support even among *Heimwehr* organizations, which were divided over the question of *Anschluss*, the unification with Germany. Traditional Austrian informal joviality, the characteristic *Schlamperei*, affected fascists and putschists alike. They were both frightening and at the same time ridiculous, a claim illustrated by an incident that occurred in the course of a heated parliamentary debate in 1932. A *Heimwehr* deputy threw a heavy ashtray at one of the socialist deputies, but instead he hit the only *Heimwehr* member of the government. Pfrimer, the self-appointed "half-day dictator," as he was called by his enemies in the press, glorified youth and military virtue but was himself a fat, bald man who was hard of hearing and a poor orator.

The rival extreme-right pro-*Anschluss* Austrian Nazi party was actually a branch of the German Nazi organization. It failed to win even a single parliamentary seat in 1930, but with its typical fascist methods, it contributed significantly to creating an atmosphere of civil war. In the troubled winter of 1931–1932, the political arena was characterized by a growing number of Nazi brownshirt attacks, anti-Semitic atrocities, bombings, acts of vandalism that damaged bridges, roads, and telephone networks, and local skirmishes with paramilitary units associated with the Social Democrats. The Nazi offensive was counterbalanced by an "increasing radicalization of the Left," as Kurt von Schuschnigg, the later chancellor, writes in his memoirs: "And when here and there armed conflicts took place the same farce was always repeated: the one side would accuse the other[,] . . . both would accuse the police and the authorities of giving protection to the other side, and both would sneer at the weakness of the Chancellor, who was unable to cope with the witches' sabbath of unleashed political passions" (Schuschnigg 1938, 177).

Schuschnigg and many others believed that the "two extremes"—the Austrian Nazis and the Social Democrats—reinforced each other and threatened the very existence of Austria. Against these extremes and on behalf of law and order, an Austrian nationalist-authoritarianism gained ground. This political force emerged in the twenties, but during the difficult years of the Great Depression, it seized power as the guarantor of order and stability and as the savior and reformer of an independent Austrian fatherland.

In May 1932, Engelbert Dollfuss was appointed chancellor. Born an illegitimate child in a peasant family, the talented young Dollfuss obtained a doctorate with the help of the bishop of St. Pölten. He served in the war and, afterward, established the *Landbund* peasant organization. A deeply religious man who lived in a harmonious marriage, he became popular in the rural areas of Austria. He was extremely short—his opponents called him "Millimetternich," combining the term *millimeter* and the name of the famous Austrian abolitionist politician of the early nineteenth century—and rather ambitious. He opposed the idea of *Anschluss* and rejected all forms of Nazism, socialism, social democracy, and even parliamentary democracy. During the interwar years, when powerful groups of both the *Heimwehr* and the Austrian Nazis advocated the *Anschluss*, Dollfuss created a position that combined Austrian nationalism with fascist authoritarianism. His friend, Ernst Karl Winter, called the new regime "a compromise between political Catholicism and *Heimwehr* fascism" (Rath 1971, 34). Dollfuss, whose party held a parliamentary majority by one vote, gave three key government positions to fascist *Heimwehr* leaders. Moreover, in May 1933, when he established his monolithic *Vaterländische Front* (Fatherland Front), a mass organization beyond parties, the post of vice president was given to Prince Ernst Rüdiger Starhemberg, the *Heimwehr*'s dashing leader. Major Emil Fey, the *Heimwehr* chief of Vienna, became vice chancellor.

As a symbolic celebration of this alliance, a *Parteitag* (Party Day) was organized in the garden of the Schönbrunn Palace. Forty thousand uniformed men of the *Heimatschutz* (Fatherland's Defense) and thousands of civilians marched behind a huge wooden crucifix, led by Dollfuss on horseback wearing his war uniform and by Starhemberg and Fey, also on horseback. A mass was celebrated, and Starhemberg announced that in the interest of Austrian independence, he would place his strength at the chancellor's disposal. Dollfuss declared the abolition of the old party and parliamentary system, claiming that both traditional liberalism and capitalism had ended and that national unity was in the making. The symbols and institutions of fascism and Nazism were enthusiastically borrowed: the idea of the corporative state; the salute "Heil Dollfuss!"; the *Neues Leben* (New Life), an organization of the Fatherland Front, modeled on Mussolini's *Dopolavoro* (After Work) and Hitler's *Kraft durch Freude* (Strength through Pleasure) movements that sought to organize and control leisure activities and cultural events; and, last but not least, ceremonies "which hardly differed from those in Germany." As Ernst Hanisch rightly stated: "'People grew accustomed to a public life which was adorned by symbols and forms of fascism'" (quoted in Binder 1991, 70).

The face of "Austro-fascism" gradually took shape during 1933 and 1934. First, the parliamentary system was eradicated (Kitchen 1980). On March 4, 1933, a parliamentary crisis arose regarding the measures to be taken against striking railway workers. Renner, the Social Democratic speaker of the House, and his two deputies resigned. Using this crisis as a pretext, Dollfuss declared the "self-dismantling" of the parliamentary system. He announced over the radio the institution of government by decree, with appropriate modification of the constitution. On April 30, 1933, at 10:35 A.M., a brief session and an official announcement concluded the short and ambiguous history of Austrian parliamentarism. By 10:50 A.M., the new constitution was enacted. Although a mere apologia, Schuschnigg's memoirs correctly state that "in many other countries as well the authority of parliament had been for a long time badly shaken. . . . Austria, unlike England, or even Hungary, had not the tradition of parliament" (Schuschnigg 1938, 81).

Under the new constitution, the chancellor acted as a dictator. Mussolini's Italy, which Dollfuss visited in the spring and fall of 1933, provided the model. Dollfuss sought to merge the fascist Italian corporative model with Christian ideology, a goal that was made clear in proclaiming the new constitution: "In the name of God, the Almighty, from Whom all justice derives, the Austrian people receive this constitution for their federal state based on Christian, German and corporative principles" (Rath 1971, 25).

The *Österreich-Idee* (Austrian Ideology) stressed "an Austrian mission to create a new 'Holy Empire' with an 'organic and corporate' structure . . . ,[and] reshape Central Europe, from the Baltic to the Black Sea" to bring the peoples "at last into the sphere of German culture." Although anti-Semitism never became an official government policy, the fact that German-inspired Nazism provided an ideological foundation for the Austrian regime ensured that the "Jewish question" would become a political issue (Kienzl and Prokop 1989). A meeting of the leading officials of the *Heimwehr* in September 1936 announced that "the Jewish question . . . is the main problem" and that they had to fight against the "Jewish mentality . . . [of] materialism, Marxism, Liberalism, and the like." Leopold Kunschak published a draft bill in early 1936 that had been prepared originally in 1919. The bill suggested separating the "Jewish nation . . . [from the] German majority . . . [and introducing a] quota system . . . in public service, certain professions and business enterprises, limiting entry for Jews to their proportion of the total population" (Staundinger 1991, 1–2,7,17–8).

Another fundamental characteristic of the regime was its harsh antisocialist stand. Although the Social Democratic Party offered to ally with Dollfuss against the threat of Nazism, he firmly refused. Socialist paramilitary forces, prominent newspapers such as the *Arbeiter Zeitung*, and the May Day celebration were banned. The *Heimwehr* component of the regime went even further than that. During Dollfuss's visit to Budapest on February 8, 1934, Major Emil Fey took things into his own hands by ordering a search and ransacking of the Social Democratic Party headquarters and the arrest of both party leaders and the commanders of the *Schutzbund*, the party's private army. Even the mayor of Vienna was arrested. The actions in "Red Vienna" were repeated in Linz on February 12.

In reaction, the Social Democratic Party declared a general strike, and for several days Vienna was embroiled in civil war. Army and *Heimwehr* divisions besieged the working-class residential districts, whose residents fought back. Artillery was used in the siege of socialist residential quarters, *Engelshof* and *Karl Marxhof*, and after hand-to-hand combat, these quarters fell. Julius Deutsch, commander of the social democratic *Schutzbund*, stated after the first day of fighting, "We stand with our backs to the wall: we must fight or capitulate. There is no other way" (Kreissler 1970, 227). After a few days, only capitulation was possible: official reports listed 314 dead and 718 wounded, whereas unofficial estimates suggested casualties of two to three thousand. Days after the fighting, dead bodies still floated in the Danube. A manhunt was staged by the government, and Koloman Wallisch, the socialist mayor of Bruck an der Mur, was hanged after his capture. Karl Renner was arrested, and Otto Bauer, Julius Deutsch, and other socialist leaders fled to Czechoslovakia. Between spring 1933 and the end of 1934, over thirty-eight thousand people were arrested for political reasons and over one hundred thousand houses were searched. Social democracy was defeated.

However, the Austrian nationalist-fascists had won a Pyrrhic victory, because the Social Democrats had been their only potential allies against their primary political enemies, the Austrian Nazis. Since 1933, the Austrian Nazi Party had organized thousands of terrorist actions. Attacks on "Jewish-looking" people in the streets, vandalism of cafes and shops, and the explosion of bombs in thoroughfares (in February 1934, some forty bombs exploded every day in Austria) became common events. The Austrian Nazi-leader, Alfred Proksch, openly advocated the overthrow of Dollfuss. The government endeavored to fight a battle on two fronts, against both socialists and Nazis. Two thousand Nazis were arrested and German agents were expelled from the country. Nazi organizations and the wearing of their uniform were banned.

The actions of Dollfuss's fascist-authoritarian regime are often explained as an attempt to erect barriers against *Vollfaschismus* (full fascism). Ernst Hanisch, for example, rejects Otto Bauer's interpretation of the Dollfuss regime as a "coalition between clerico-fascism and *Heimwehr*-fascism." According to Bauer, political Catholicism, the Austrian Catholic Church, and the Vatican, which began a "new offensive, a new crusade for a new counter-reformation" and a struggle "against the non-religious forces," fully supported the Dollfuss regime. The Church's position was stated as early as December 21, 1933, at a meeting of the Austrian bishops in Hirtenbrief. But Hanisch argues that although political Catholicism and the Church itself were associated with the authoritarian regime, they also acted as a strong anti-Nazi force. The *Christliche Ständestaat*, or Christian Corporative State, of Dollfuss was the lesser evil and the most acceptable alternative to both Nazism and Bolshevism (Hanisch 1984, 53–54, 59).

Karl Renner, the Social Democratic leader, drew a different lesson from history. He stated in 1933 that "in Austria two forms of fascism . . . are at war with each other" and that the self-defensive anti-Nazi "Austrofascism" could not succeed; indeed, he added in 1945, Austrofascism prepared the soil for Hitler. "Robbed by clerico-fascism of their rights . . . the working class turned sadly against their own state, and reached the conclusion that, if fascism was unavoidable, then better the German version. . . . This meant that the main body of the work force . . . blinded by Hitler's initial successes, accepted without resistance the annexation which followed four years later" (Binder 1991, 75–76). Nazism and German nationalism had struck deep roots in Austria. After 1934, they even penetrated the armed forces and police, a fact illustrated by the arrest of Dr. Steinhäusel, the chief of criminal police, who was sentenced to seven years imprisonment for Nazi conspiracy. Hitler actively cultivated Austrian Nazis by extending open support and money. Austrian national *Heimwehr*-fascism was not strong enough to defeat the Nazis. Thus, the attack by Dollfuss's regime against the socialists "shifted more and more workers, especially the young generations, into the Nazi-front." Dollfuss's "twin-fronts against the 'Red' and 'Brown' danger" was a hopeless attempt that relied on a small minority of people to defeat movements that appealed to three-quarters of the Austrian population (Goldinger and Binder 1992, 225–26).

At 12:53 P.M. on July 25, 1934, trucks carrying men in police and army uniforms simply drove through the gates of the Ballhausplatz Chancellery, and Otto Planetta got out of a truck, walked into the chancellor's office, and fired two shots at Dollfuss. Before he died, the fatally wounded Dollfuss asked his deputy to recommend his family to Mussolini's protection. Meanwhile, Austrian Nazi units stormed the Vienna Radio studio and announced the resignation of the government. The putsch failed, however, when the advocates of an independent Austria, including the bulk of the *Heimwehr* forces, loyal government police, and army units, defeated the putschist Nazis. Schuschnigg, Dollfuss's friend and confident, succeeded to the chancellorship. On All Soul's Day, November 1, 1934, Arturo Toscanini conducted Verdi's *Requiem* at the Vienna Opera. Fixed over the stage was Dollfuss's death mask, and the exclusive audience, dressed in black, felt deep emotion for the murdered chancellor and their Austria as they listened to the chorus: *Et lux perpetus luceat eis* (Let perpetual light shine unto him). Too soon, their Austria would be raped: in the spring of 1938, an ecstatic crowd would welcome the arrival of Hitler.

Gyula Gömbös and His Planned "Radical Operations": Hungary Shifts Further to the Right

The labor movement in Hungary was incomparably weaker than in Austria. It had been humiliated, decimated, and forced partly underground after the Communist revolution of 1919. Even a decade after Horthy's "white terror," it had not recovered. Despite the striking decay and poverty caused by the Great Depression, no radicalization of the masses occurred in Hungary. A trade union demonstration in September 1930, the only one to occur in the period, did not signal a reawakening of labor. The right-wing gentry-military elite, which had played a leading role in the repression of the Communist revolution and the establishment of the Horthy regime between 1919 and 1921 but had been pushed aside by count István Bethlen in 1921, now remobilized. An advocate of harsh dictatorship and open anti-Semitism, this group regarded the regime's government and institutions as insufficient; in the group's opinion, the situation in the early thirties revived the threat of revolution. The Hungarian elite sought to exploit the situation in order to regain the power that they had lost to Bethlen. Endre Mecsér, a typical representative of this group, warned in a letter to Miklós Kozma, the former comrade-in-arms and close confidant of Horthy:

We are fast heading towards the abyss, where only social issues dominate. The middle parties are usually ruined by this, even the United Party [of Bethlen]. The Christian Socialist Party is not a powerful enough club against Marxists, it smells far too much like consecrated water for that. Thus today there is no viable anti-Marxist political party with mass backing in Hungary. What will become of us? . . . I feel that *radical operations are needed*. (Hungarian Archive 1932)

The right-wing gentry and military elite now sought to return to its program of 1919–1920; they urged that the Horthy regime become more authoritarian, that "Jewish" capitalism be regulated, and that "the guard" be changed to give themselves the leading economic positions in Hungary. István Bethlen's ten-year-long government fell in the depth of the crisis in 1931. On October 1, 1932, Horthy, who himself originated from this dissatisfied group and was surrounded by its representatives, appointed Gyula Gömbös, the "strong man" of the gentry-military elite, as prime minister of Hungary. Gömbös had been a leading figure in the post-1919 counterrevolution and head of the right-wing paramilitary organization *Magyar Országos Véderö Egyesület* (Hungarian National Defense Association) and was a close associate of Horthy. He had served from 1923 to 1928 as head of the *Fajvédö Párt* (Race Protecting Party), the right-wing parliamentary opposition to the Bethlen government. He seemed the ideal person to undertake "radical operations." As Miklós Kozma noted in a personal letter to Endre Bajcsy-Zsilinszky, another leading representative of the gentry-military elite, Gömbös "can overcome disorder with iron hands, even in a brutal way if needed" (Hungarian Archive 1932).

Gömbös and a new group of young right-wing politicians, the so-called reform generation, initiated a fascist renewal in Hungary. With his close aides, Sándor Sztranyavszky and Béla Marton, Gömbös began in October 1932 to reorganize the traditional ruling party into a mass party. Renamed the Party of National Unity, it was based on the *Führer-Prinzip* and established an active nucleus of so-called vanguard fighters. Gömbös also announced the reform of existing capitalism by "cutting off its aberrations" and regulating "selfish cartels." Using typical fascist rhetoric, he spoke of a "united Hungarian public spirit" and the creation of a "self-contained nation-state" that would realize the "interests of the united nation." By the fall of 1934, a plan was put forth to introduce a corporative system. Modeled after Mussolini's *Carta del Lavoro* (Charter of Labor), it proposed creating various vocational chambers where representatives of both employers and employees would handle all labor issues and negotiate collective contracts. Strikes and lockouts would be banned, and disputes would be decided by the labor court. "If I integrate the Hungarian workers into the body of the national community," Gömbös stated, "the socialists will be out of politics in Hungary" (Gömbös 1932, 46). With his theme of national unity, Gömbös attracted populist writers and peasant intellectual groups, who supported his "ninety-five points reform program" and were ready to join his right-wing intellectual movement, the New Spiritual Front. In January 1935, during a personal talk with Ferenc Szálasi, leader of the

Hungarian Nazis, Gömbös noted that "he himself had intended to build up a mass movement from below, but in Hungary a movement may be organized only from above." Gömbös offered Szálasi an increased pension and suggested that the Hungarian Nazis link themselves to his government party (Szöllösi-Janze 1989, 103).

An important and broadly popular element of Gömbös's course was his nationalist foreign policy. Having announced a "peaceful border revision," he intensified the connections between Hungary and fascist Italy. He admired Mussolini and modeled himself after the Italian dictator; Gömbös was proud, and often mentioned in intimate circles, that his chest measurement was identical with the Duce's. "I am convinced," he wrote to Mussolini in the first days of his premiership, that "if Rome and Berlin, Budapest and Vienna would form a stronger alliance, they could play an important role in European politics" (Balogh 1985, 177).

A major turning point occurred in January 1933, when Hitler seized power in Germany. Within twenty-four hours, Gömbös sent a letter to the Hungarian ambassador to Berlin, ordering him to visit Chancellor Hitler as soon as possible: "On my behalf, pass my best regards and wishes. . . . Recall that ten years ago, on the basis of our common principles and ideology, we were in contact via Mr. Scheubner-Richter. . . . [Tell Hitler] my firm belief that the two countries have to cooperate in foreign and economic policy" (Hungarian Archive 1933). In April 1933, Gömbös sent a letter to Hitler urging cooperation between the two countries, which he described as *"alte rassenschützlerische Kameraden"* (old race-protector comrades) who shared the same *Weltanschauung*. Acting on the personal invitation of Hitler and the German Nazi Party, Gömbös was the first foreign head of government who, as a "private person," visited Hitler after he became chancellor. In the fall of 1935, during a second visit to Berlin, Gömbös, in a secret face-to-face talk to Göring, guaranteed that he would introduce a German-style totalitarian system in Hungary within two years. Miklós Kozma, an old friend and member of Gömbös's cabinet, noted in his diary: "I discovered without any doubt that Gömbös and Göring made a far-reaching agreement, without the knowledge of anybody. . . . This agreement covered the political system, totalitarianism, and the Jewish question" (Hungarian Archive 1935c).

In the spring of 1935, Gömbös provoked a political crisis and convinced Horthy to dissolve the parliament. In the new elections, which were accompanied by brutal violence in the countryside, Gömbös's party gained an absolute majority of 170 seats out of 245. István Bethlen, the former prime minister, stated in an interview: "The danger has arisen that the institutions of our thousand-year-old constitution, our political and economic system, are going to be guinea pigs for immature, bizarre, imported foreign ideas. We shall witness increased flirting with national socialism, party totalitarianism, and the establishment of SS and SA units" (Reggel 1935).

Gömbös's actions generated a strong resistance in the conservative wing of the traditional ruling elite. But Gömbös became seriously ill in the spring and died in a hospital near Munich on October 6, 1936. The imminent danger of a constitutional coup vanished with his death.

Although this attempt to introduce a Nazi-fascist dictatorship failed, the Horthy regime itself shifted rapidly further to the Right. The process gained impetus in 1935 in response to the founding of the Party of National Will, a genuine fascist mass party under the leadership of Ferenc Szálasi, a retired major and a charismatic lunatic. In the fall of 1936, Szálasi began to unite many small, Nazi-fascist organizations— among them the Race Protecting Socialist Party of László Endre and the National Socialist Hungarian Workers Party of Zoltán Böszörményi—and in October 1937, at a mass rally, he announced the foundation of the Hungarian National Socialist Party, more commonly called the Arrowcross (*Nyilaskeresztes*) party after its symbol. Before that event, according to Miklós Lackó, "the membership of the party hardly surpassed one or two thousand, [and] Szálasi's movement was comparable to the characteristic military-bureaucratic-gentry-middle class right-wing organizations of the early thirties" (Lackó 1966, 63). However, Szálasi's Hungarian Nazi Party soon became a genuine Nazi urban-populist workers' party, attracting young workers and the lowest stratum of the middle class. Szálasi declared his intention of building a Hungarian national socialist state,

[a] united socialist community of the workers . . . [that] divides the profits . . . between the factors of production . . . [and] abolishes money capitalism and the hopeless misery of the working class. . . . A single leading political idea directs the community[, and] . . . the worker . . . will fight to bring victory to the ideology. . . . The purpose of our movement is to win over the Hungarian working class to the Hungarian national socialist ideology. (Szálasi 1964, 158,162)

Szálasi's Arrowcross party appealed directly to workers, promising "the liberation of workers from the yoke of feudal-capitalistic and social-democratic-communist Jewry . . . and to integrate them into a nation that loves workers" (Szöllösi-Janze 1989, 109). The success of this appeal is illustrated by the fact that the Hungarian Nazis were able to build a mass party of about a quarter million members in 1939, one of the two largest fascist parties of the region. In 1940, they organized a coal miner's strike, the only general strike that occurred in Hungary during the Horthy regime.

Advocating the imitation of Hitler's program and using extreme anti-Semitic propaganda, Szálasi gained one-fifth of the entire vote in the 1939 elections. His party gained noticeable ground among the young generation of blue-collar workers; Miklós Lackó and György Ránki have convincingly documented this trend. The Social Democratic Party lost its influence in a dramatic decline. It had won nearly 40 percent of the vote in Budapest in 1922 but captured only 22 percent in 1935 and 12 percent in 1939. The Arrowcross success in the workers' districts of Budapest was striking: in districts three, nine, ten, and fourteen of the capital, where one-third to one-half of the population was blue-collar, Arrowcross won 30 to 33 percent of the vote. In the so-called Red Suburbs, a traditional socialist "fortress" of thirty-two industrial-worker residential settlements around Budapest, where the Social Democrats had won more than 33 percent of the votes as late as 1935, the Hungarian Nazis won nearly 42 percent in 1939: the Social Democrats, in contrast, garnered only 17 percent of the vote. The well-known black uniform, boots, green shirt, Nazi salute, and uninhibited demagogy made the Arrowcross party popular and influential. Szálasi clearly announced that the party's goal was to gain power: "We declared unambiguously and several times," he stated at a party "round robin" in February 1936, that "the party is organized in order to seize power and that it seeks to take over" (Szöllösi-Janze 1989, 105).

During the second half of the 1930s, the Hungarian prime ministers who succeeded Gömbös—Kálmán Darányi, Béla Imrédy, and Pál Teleki—attempted to stem the right-wing tide by occasionally banning right-wing parties and even arresting their leaders. (Szálasi was arrested three times during these years.) Horthy's authority was significantly strengthened by extending his veto rights over parliament actions, a constitutional reform designed to provide guarantees against a political landslide by any party in the parliament. He was also given more power to issue decrees. According to a 1937 law, the governor was no longer responsible to the parliament. Moreover, he gained the right to "suggest" his successor—Horthy's younger son István was soon appointed his deputy-governor—so that a dynasty could be established.

Though these measures blocked a fascist takeover, the Horthy regime continued to shift toward the Right. The government began a suicidal race to take the wind from the sails of the radical Right by adopting more and more elements of its program. For example, the Arrowcross party was banned and several of its leaders interned on February 26, 1939, the day that debates in the parliament began on the second anti-Jewish law. This pattern of paired actions continued throughout the second half of the thirties.

Although politics in this period were characterized by hesitation and flux—a stop-and-go process—the advance of fascist elements proved unstoppable. It was continuously strengthened by the reconsideration of Hungarian border claims, the primary goal and permanent dream of the Horthy regime from the time of its foundation. Now, because of the consolidation of Hitler's power and the creation of the Berlin-Rome axis, it seemed that the dream could shortly become reality. Horthy and his officials were ready to realize that dream by strengthening Hungary's German orientation. From time to time, they expressed reservations, but room for diplomatic maneuvering shrank. As the former American ambassador John F. Montgomery saw it, Hungary was a "reluctant satellite" of Nazi Germany (Montgomery 1947). Reluctance could slow down the process of subordination and adjustment to Nazi demands, but it could not stop the trend. The one-billion-pengő rearmament plan was initiated in the fall of 1937 and announced in the west Hungarian city Győr in March 1938. The first anti-Jewish law outside of Germany was issued in May 1938; in the name of "the more effective ensuring of the equilibrium of social economic life," the law introduced discrimination and restrictions against Jews. The events at the end of that year, following the Hitler-Chamberlain pact in Munich in September, decided Hungary's destiny: in November 1938, the first Vienna-award revised the Trianon peace treaty of 1920 and returned a southern, mostly Hungarian-populated strip of Slovakia—nearly twelve-thousand square kilometers of territory with more than one million inhabitants—to Hungary. That same month, the Nazi organization *Volksbund der Deutschen in Ungarn* (National Association of Germans in Hungary), a fifth column of Hitler, was allowed to establish itself in Hungary and recruit members among the German minority. A second anti-Jewish law soon followed; instead of religious discrimination, the law introduced racial discrimination according to the Nazi pattern. Anti-Jewish atrocities were launched in the streets, and Jews were attacked physically in the universities. The main synagogue on Dohány street in Budapest was bombed—a bloody anticipation of the murderous violence to come. In January, Hungary joined the German-Italian-Japanese "anti-comintern pact." With the permission of Hitler and Mussolini, Hungary continued its border corrections by occupying north-eastern Sub-Carpatho-Ukraine, a twelve-thousand-square-kilometer territory with six hundred thousand inhabitants (only forty thousand of whom spoke Hungarian as a mother-tongue) that was then part of Czechoslovakia (Balogh 1985).

By 1941, the process was complete. Thus, before the outbreak of World War II, Hungary had already incorporated elements of Nazism and had joined Hitler's aggressive war alliance. The destiny of the nation was sealed.

Jósef Piłsudski and the Dictatorless Dictatorship in Poland

The Horthy regime was born in a bloody counterrevolutionary military dictatorship and, after a decade of moderation and liberalization, returned to that starting point and gradually shifted further to the authoritarian Right. The Piłsudski regime in Poland had a different chronology yet a strikingly similar conclusion. Piłsudski's regime was born in a national revolution that sought to establish a Western-style parliamentary democracy. The hardships of the twenties, however, caused it to depart from the concepts and practices of democracy: Piłsudski's coup d'etat in 1926, his subsequent effort to create a quasi one-party system in 1928, and, most of all, the infamous "Bržešč incident" of September 1930, when opposition leaders were arrested, virtually destroyed parliamentary democracy in Poland.

The events of the thirties moved Poland much further down this road, and a gradual shift to the Right characterized the entire decade. As elsewhere in Central and Eastern Europe, labor unrest revived in the thirties. Spontaneous peasant strikes engulfed the countryside, and solidarity strikes in urban centers soon followed. In 1936, the one-million-member-strong trade unions organized a series of strikes in Kracow, Łodz, and Upper Silezia. The peasants refused to supply the cities in the summer of 1937, and the government sent police to use brute force in order to suppress resistance. In the resulting armed conflicts, a number of peasants were killed: government reports noted forty-two fatalities. Frightening signs of mass dissatisfaction appeared everywhere. One of them was the surprise victory of the socialists in fifty-two townships at local elections. After the "Bržešč incident," left-of-center groups founded the *Stromnictwo Ludowe* (People's Party), which attempted to organize a union of all democratic forces including the socialists. The party's youth organization urged radical reforms along a left-wing populist line and turned against the traditional gentry-military elite that included the ruling military leaders; the youth organization demanded radical land reform and appropriate peasant participation in the exercise of power.

The Right's fear of left-wing movements was strong, and right-wing response was forceful. The National Democratic Party of Dmowski, a party of the traditional extreme Right in Poland and one of the first parties in Europe to advocate anti-Jewish measures and dictatorship, dropped the misleading *Democratic* from its name, strengthened its anti-Semitic and antisocialist propaganda, and organized anti-Jewish pogroms. The party became particularly strong in Poznan, Pmorze, Kielce, and Łodz but also had centers in Warsaw, Vilna, and Lwow. The most radical group of the younger generation in the National Party was not satisfied even with this conservative-right-wing action and left the party. In 1934, these youth established the National Radical Camp, which adopted a genuine Nazi program. The "Falanga" faction of the National Radicals (named after Franco's Falange Party), headed by Boleslaw Piasecki, a talented and reckless figure, embraced fascist terror and violence. Falanga's mass rally in 1937, with its Nazi-fascist relics, uniforms, boots, and oath of allegiance, was connected with preparations for a fascist coup. But the Polish government would not tolerate this extreme-right opposition: on October 25, 1937, eighty Falanga leaders were arrested (Rothschild 1977).

As in Austria and Hungary, while fighting against the explicitly Nazi-fascist extreme-right opposition, the Piłsudski regime itself was pushed by its rival toward the Right. The traditional competition between the Dmowski and Piłsudski camps continued. To cite Cat-Mackiewicz's insightful observation, Dmowski "was certainly satisfied to see Poland governed by his opponents who were implementing his program in all respects" (quoted in Wynot 1974, 29).

After Bržešč, Piłsudski decided to go further in establishing his authoritarian rule. He first sought to implement changes by using legal parliamentary procedure to modify the constitution. The November election of 1930, which was accompanied by ruthless police actions against the opposition and the arrest of roughly five thousand people, brought a more than 46 percent majority for Piłsudski's "Nonpartisan Bloc," but this figure fell far short of the two-thirds majority required for constitutional changes. Still desiring legal change, Piłsudski declined "to decree a new constitution by fiat . . . [and] had his paladins maneuver a new constitution through the legislature by utilizing an extended series of parliamentary tricks and formal casuistries. This exercise in sharp practice," concludes Joseph Rothschild, "was politically and morally at least as demoralizing as straightforward dictation would have been" (Rothschild 1977, 69).

A new constitution was finally enacted in 1935. It established presidential rule by allowing the presidential veto to limit the power of parliament and asserting the president's right to dissolve parliament and dismiss the government. The president also gained the right to appoint one-third of the senators and to issue decrees with the force of law. The president was responsible only to "God and History," not to parliament. With other legal and administrative changes, central power became extremely strong. The courts were subordinated to and controlled by the government, provincial governors and prefects were nominated by the minister of the interior, and the prefects gained the right to veto the election of town mayors. The constitution was tailored to make Piłsudski a popular and "democratic dictator" who was beyond social strata or interests and would use his exceptional power to bring about a balance between the antagonistic Right and Left for the good of the nation. Ironically, the constitution came into effect in April 1935, but Piłsudski died on May 12, 1935.

After the death of the founder of the state and the new authoritarian regime, Poland remained a dictatorless dictatorship. The succession was smooth because control passed to the "junta of the colonels," Piłsudski's closest associates from the legion and always pillars of his regime. They attempted to continue Piłsudski's "lawful dictatorship" by holding new elections in September 1935. However, they also sought further guarantees against opposition; therefore, by new electorial regulations, they restricted the franchise and attempted to create a nonpartisan parliament, which, they believed, would stabilize their power. The opposition boycotted the elections and the percentage of voter turnout dropped from 75 percent in 1930 to less than 47 percent in 1935. The opposition lost its institution base and the parliament became a rubber stamp for the military junta. After the election, Piłsudski's former party, the Nonpartisan Bloc, was also dissolved. Although the military clique was thus secure in its power, it lacked an unquestioned charismatic leader and soon disintegrated into rival groupings.

One faction, headed by Colonel Walery Sławek, the founder of the Nonpartisan Bloc, the closest confident and associate of Piłsudski, and the main architect of the new constitution, wanted to restore the early-Piłsudski coalition and worked for an alliance of the colonels with the early "legionary" socialists. Sławek believed that a coalition between the Left and the military would guarantee the continuation of Piłsudski's policies. However, his secret maneuvering for such a coalition failed; in the ensuing political scandal, Sławek committed suicide.

Another faction drew a different conclusion and sought to secure power by shifting toward fascism. To curb both social tension and right-wing opposition, Colonel Adam Koc and his group tried to strengthen authoritarian rule. In 1937, he founded the Camp of National Unity (*Ozon*) and its youth organization, the Union of Young Poland, both based on the blueprint of fascist mass parties and ready to compete with Piasecki's fascist Falanga. Koc's program imitated Mussolini's corporative system by trying to set up a state-sponsored employee-employer triangle. Although the program did not call for the extermination of Jews, it announced as its goal the "Polonization" of industry and commerce. A crusade of "cultural self-defense"—as the program was entitled—advocated "the solution of the Jewish question" by encouraging mass emigration (Marcus 1983). Like Dmowski, Koc rejected the idea of Jewish assimilation and believed that the rapid suppression of the Jewish intelligentsia was a particularly urgent task. "Ghetto benches" separated the Jewish students from others at universities, and limits were placed on their number. Boycotts of Jewish businesses were organized with silent assistance from the state. One grotesque "solution" suggested that Poland should acquire a League of Nations colonial protectorate in Madagascar and resettle its Jews there. Koc was ready to unite his youth movement with the Falanga and made extremely enthusiastic statements to this end after having visited Falanga's secret training camp near Pilica.

A third faction called *Zamek* (Palace), organized around President Ignacy Mościcki, advocated a more pragmatic, technocratic regime, focusing on modernization and state intervention as symbolized by the Four-Year Plan of 1936 and the Three-Year Plan of spring 1939. Marshall Edward Smigly-Rydz, who succeeded Piłsudski in the decisive post of chief of the army, joined this faction and gradually gained control of Polish politics after 1936.

In spite of these inner conflicts, power struggles, and intrigue within the ruling military junta, the military dictatorship remained unchanged after the death of Piłsudski. Hugh Seton-Watson sarcastically notes, "The truth was that the fundamental question in Polish politics was not 'Freedom or Authority?', 'Democracy or Leadership?' or 'Strong Government or Popular Rule?' but 'Which gang shall rule the rest?'" (H. Seton-Watson 1967, 166). This certainly was partly true. Nevertheless, in addition to strengthening its own power, the ruling military group made efforts to modernize the country and to enhance its defense. It sought to balance the various social forces locked in domestic power struggles and to maneuver safe passage through the gathering international storm. Continuing Piłsudski's foreign policy legacy (Piłsudski signed a nonaggression agreement with Hitler in 1934), the Polish government attempted to keep good relations with both Nazi Germany and the Western powers. As a result, German political organizations increased their destructive activities in Poland (Grünberg 1970). Cultivating its German connections, the military junta even was ready to participate in Hitler's action against Czechoslovakia. In October 1938, Polish troops joined the resurrectionist action and, taking revenge for the 1918–1919 conflict that had led to Czech rule in the debated area, occupied the Czieszyn region in Lower-Silesia. In spite of these actions, the Polish leaders rejected Ribbentrop's demands in October 1938 and April 1939 regarding Gdansk and the Danzig-corridor. This first refusal of Hitler's piecemeal expansionism led to a dramatic policy change: in April 1939, Britain signed a guarantee with the Polish government, and Hitler canceled the 1934 German-Polish nonaggression agreement. Maneuvering between Hitler and the West became impossible, and Poland joined the Western alliance.

Presidential Dictatorships in the Baltic Countries

As in Austria and Poland, parliamentary democracy was challenged during the years of the Great Depression in the crisis-ridden Baltic countries. Their "democratic institutions . . . as operated during a period of parliamentary government . . . never functioned properly, from the time of their inception until their abrogation. . . . Each [of the countries] started with an ultra-democratic constitution, and each has passed through a phase of dictatorship" (*Baltic States* 1938, 41, 43). In Estonia and Latvia, as many as thirty parties competed for parliamentary seats, and fragile coalitions could not form stable governments. Between 1919 and 1933 in Estonia, the average lifetime of governments was eight months and twenty days, and it often took between thirty and fifty days just to form these short-lived governments. It was small wonder that democratic experiments in the Baltic soon ended. The first democracy to disappear was in Lithuania in 1926, when a putsch established the so-called Voldemaras dictatorship.

Right-wing, extremely nationalist authoritarian forces were highly active in the region. In Estonia, veterans of the war of national liberation of the late 1910s founded several small organizations in the midtwenties and merged them into the Association of Estonian Freedom Fighters in 1929. A strongly anticommunist, antiliberal, and antiparliamentary movement under the leadership of Major-General Andres Larka and the reckless demagogue lawyer Artur Sirk, the association developed into a well-organized mass party with all the fascist symbols: the green-gray shirt and black-and-white armbands with the emblem of a hand clutching a sword, party-cell organization into companies and sections, and violent street activities. The Freedom Fighters first acted within the law and pushed through a referendum for constitutional reform that gave absolute power to the president. The revised constitution became law in January 1934, and following democratic rules, a presidential election was called. The Freedom Fighters launched a massive electoral campaign and gained an absolute majority in most large Estonian cities.

Major-General Larka had a good chance to be the first president under the new constitution, but instead, prime minister Konstantin Päts, one of the leading nationalist politicians of the country, carried out a preventive coup with the help of the army. Päts, who was born into a peasant family and worked as a newspaper editor, had been sentenced to death by the Russian tsarist court and had emigrated to Switzerland. He participated subsequently in building an independent Estonia and served as prime minister five times in the twenties and early thirties. He introduced a state of emergency after seizing control, banned the Association of Freedom Fighters, and arrested nearly five hundred of its leaders and activists, including industrialists who were financing the movement. Päts also played a role in the mysterious death of Artur Sirk in a hotel in Luxembourg. Because the danger of a takeover by the fascist Freedom Fighters was quite real, the parliament approved Päts's actions, and a socialist newspaper proclaimed, "In the defence of democracy even the use of force is justified" (*Baltic History* 1974, 214).

The parliamentary approval and the socialist endorsement of Päts's actions were premature. As in many other nations of Central and Eastern Europe, the real political struggle was between two types of dictatorial extremism. The Estonian parliament soon was dissolved, and parties and trade unions were banned: the president began to rule by decrees. In an effort to gain popular support, the government sponsored *Isamaaliit* (the Fatherland League) as a party beyond parties and an expression of national unity. A fascist corporative system was introduced with the formation of chambers of labor, commerce, and culture. Altogether fifteen chambers in various fields were responsible for creating social peace by integrating disaffected strata into the society; the state authority was to act as a judge and balancing force. A paramilitary "defense league" was also established. The ideals and patterns of the Baltic right-wing movements were a combination of models used by Piłsudski, Dollfuss, and most of all, Mussolini. In 1938, however, Päts decided to strengthen the quasi legal-parliamentary character of his authoritarian regime and held a referendum on a new constitution, in which it was proposed to construct a bogus bicameral parliament with an elected state assembly and an appointed state council.

A similar authoritarian trend, with similar motivation, prevailed in Latvia just a few months after the Estonian coup. Right-wing nationalist extremists began a harsh antiparliamentary campaign; they accused the Left of demagogy and urged a Mussolini-type solution for Latvia's ills. The campaign was followed by a proposal for constitutional reform to strengthen presidential power. Ironically, the weak and inefficient parliamentary system in Latvia was opposed by both the Right and the Left: not only was the political Right a strong and violent antiparliamentary force, but the Latvian Social Democratic Party warned of the example of Germany, where the Weimar constitution—the model of the Latvian constitution—had made it possible for Hitler to gain power. In such a climate, right-wing takeover was in the air. A series of Nazi-fascist parties appeared in the political arena. The National Revolutionary Workforce sought to eliminate communists, socialists, and Jews and to introduce a planned economy. The Latvian National Socialist Party and the Economic Center were both modeled after Hitler and introduced brownshirts. The Association of Legionaries followed the Polish pattern of Colonel Koc. And, in 1933, the *Perkonkrusts* (Thunder Cross) was established by Gustav Celmiņš. Thunder Cross was the most powerful and frightening of the Nazi organizations; it introduced the Hitler salute and greeting (*Kampf Heil*) and a uniform of gray shirts and black berets. However, despite these similarities to German Nazism, the highly anti-Semitic and extremely nationalist Latvian Nazi movement was anti-German.

Following the Estonian pattern, Karlis Ulmanis, the head of the Peasant League who was appointed Latvian prime minister in March 1934, thought the time ripe for action. Ulmanis had a background strikingly similar to that of Päts. He came from a peasant family and, as a lawyer and ardent Latvian nationalist, had to emigrate to the United States during the last period of the oppressive tsarist regime. He then emerged as one of the founders of independent Latvia and served as one of its first prime ministers. On the very evening that he assumed the reigns of government, Ulmanis declared a state of emergency, suspended the parliament, banned all political parties, arrested several right- and left-wing opponents, and declared his intention to govern by decrees. He also established the Fatherland League and extended the Italian corporative system. The new administrative structure of Latvia was based entirely on Mussolini's model: a National Economic Council, Cultural Council, and other chambers were formed whose members were appointed and played only an advisory role. The state sector of the economy was enlarged, also following the Italian fascist pattern. The state-owned Latvian Loan Bank was established and took over several previously private companies. State-controlled companies gained special privileges. Ulmanis took over the Latvian presidency in 1936 and held two posts—president and prime minister—simultaneously. Until 1938, the state of emergency continued and power was based in the army, headed by General Balodis, and in the paramilitary organizations (Hiden and Salmon 1991).

The series of Baltic coup d'états, which began in Lithuania in 1926, also concluded in Lithuania in the summer of 1934. The Voldemaras dictatorship of 1926–1929 gradually shifted toward the extreme Right. The *Tautininkai* (Nationalist Party) and the fascist, paramilitary "Iron Wolf" organization of Voldemaras gained increasing power. Although neither ideologically nor politically alien to President Antanas Smetona, the emergence of extreme right-wing parties generated a rivalry in government: the president asked Voldemaras to resign and arrested him when he refused to do so. Smetona then appointed his brother-in-law as prime minister and established his own dictatorship. A one-party system and youth organization and restrictions on human rights and freedom of press were introduced. The Nationalist Party was reorganized along the Nazi pattern and Smetona became *Tautos Vadas*, "Der Führer" or "Il Duce" to the people. Following a new law, "crimes against the Republic" were ruthlessly punished. A new constitution was enacted that further strengthened presidential power. Corporative professional chambers were founded, and a large part of the economy was taken under state control.

The Baltic nationalist-right-wing "presidential dictatorships" were extremely hostile to minority groups. In Lithuania, "after the establishment of the Voldemaras dictatorship . . . nationalist feeling ran higher than ever, and forty-eight Polish schools were shut." Bloody pogroms were launched against Jews in Kaunas, Slobodke, and Shanz in 1929 and repeated in 1934. In Latvia, "under the dictatorship established in May 1934 the privileges of the minorities sustained a fresh series of assaults." Lettish became the sole official language, and the German Educational Board was abolished along with the "German guilds which had existed for some 700 years" (*Baltic States* 1938, 32, 35–36).

The three Baltic dictatorships, similar in political structures and institutions, implemented elements of fascist and even Hitlerite regimes, but as ardently nationalist systems, they also sought to safeguard their recently regained independence and wanted to distance themselves from Nazi Germany. Although Germany became one of their main economic partners and German economic influence was strengthened during the thirties, the Baltic countries tried to maneuver among the rival great powers. But all the major plans to form international alliances failed — fruitlessly, Jan Tönisson dreamed in 1917 of creating a Scandinavian-Baltic Bloc of thirty million people, the 1922 Warsaw Accord proposed a Finnish-Polish-Estonian-Latvian collaboration, and Piłsudski planned a Polish-Lithuanian-Ukrainian confederation. As a result of these failures, the small Baltic countries remained insecure. The Estonian-Latvian defense alliance of 1923 did not create security even after its extension and enlargement in the spring of 1934 when a bilateral alliance system was formed, nor was security ensured by the so-called Baltic Entente of September 1934 that bound the three Baltic countries together for defense. In April 1935, searching for guarantees against the danger from Germany, the Soviet Union offered bilateral agreements of mutual aid in the case of aggression but was refused by all three Baltic governments. By mobilizing its troops, Poland forced Lithuania to reestablish diplomatic connections with Poland in March 1938; moreover, Poland was ready to collaborate with Nazi Germany against Lithuania, as it had in the case of the Czeczyn incident against Czechoslovakia. In December 1938 and January 1939, the three Baltic countries all adopted neutrality laws, but these were powerless to save them. Danger emerged openly in March 1939 when Hitler issued an ultimatum, one week after he invaded Bohemia, demanding that Lithuania hand over the Klaipeda region to Germany. The German fleet arrived off Lithuanian shores ready to act, and the Lithuanian government quickly signed the forced agreement.

Long before World War II began, Hitler sought to localize the future conflict against Poland by signing a nonaggression agreement with Lithuania. Earlier agreements, genuinely desired by the Baltic nations, had been signed in the twenties, and then again in the early summer of 1936. In 1939, however, the pacts were forced: having brought Lithuania into line by brute military pressure, Hitler offered the same treaty to both Latvia and Estonia. They signed on June 7, 1939.

These steps, which were sometimes interpreted as the acceptance by Hitler of President Roosevelt's suggestion that nonaggression treaties be signed with neighboring states, were in reality a careful preparation for German expansion and war. As von Weizsäcker learned from the German ambassador in Rome, Hitler noted in April 1938 that "the Baltic area is . . . our aim." In August 1939, Hitler clearly explained to Ciano, the Italian foreign minister, that "the East and Northeast, that is, the countries on the Baltic Sea, have been Germany's indisputable sphere of interest since ancient times." As Rolf Ahmann concludes, "There can be no doubt that ultimately, Hitler was aiming to occupy the Baltic states"(Ahmann 1989, 344). Hitler's treaties in the Baltic region were merely hints of the deadly aggressive conflicts that were to come. In an effort to gain the time needed to realize his expansionist goals, Hitler offered a deal to Stalin, who immediately accepted it because of the failure of a proposed tripartite alliance with Britain and France and the refusal by the Western powers to guarantee the Soviet Union and the Baltic states against German aggression. "On 22 August, it was announced that the Russo-German talks had led to full agreement. . . . [Next day] Ribbentrop . . . signed a ten-year Pact of Non-aggression and consultation with Molotov in the presence of Stalin" (Pick 1946, 158). In September, during Ribbentrop's second visit, the spheres of German and Soviet interests in Poland and the Baltic region were carefully separated. The secret protocol of the Ribbentrop-Molotov Pact recognized "vital Soviet interests in the Baltic area." The nonaggression treaty provided more time for Stalin to prepare for war, arranged for the partition of Poland, and gave Russia a free hand in the Baltic area. Shifting the Soviet borders toward the West seemed to serve Soviet security interests, especially because Stalin followed traditional Russian military doctrine and sought to create as large a buffer zone as possible against a potential German invasion. The pact allowed Stalin to continue the old tsarist expansionist policy and to regain territories that had been lost after the Bolshevik revolution. Thus Stalin did not hesitate to act on the terms of the pact: on October 31, 1939, he forced the Lithuanian government to sign an agreement of "mutual assistance" that sanctioned the establishment of Soviet military bases in the country. On June 14, 1940, Molotov handed an ultimatum to the ambassador of Lithuania, demanding that "an unlimited number of the Soviet troops be admitted into Lithuania" (*Report* 1972, 335). Within two days, the Estonian and Latvian ministers received similar ultimatums from Moscow. The Baltic countries were invaded and incorporated quickly into the Soviet Union. The Baltic area subsequently became a playground for the neighboring great powers, and the influence of domestic politics in the incorporated nations waned.

In summary, between 1934 and the time of the Soviet occupation, authoritarian regimes—so-called presidential dictatorships—were established in all of the Baltic countries. Although they suppressed their right-wing, unquestionably Nazi-fascist opposition, they themselves absorbed major elements of fascism. However, like most of the other Central and Eastern European authoritarian regimes, they also attempted to balance the Left against the Right, and, in suppressing these two extremes, they began to follow the fascist-authoritarian pattern. Although they certainly belonged to the "mildest dictatorships" of Europe (Vardys 1978), and although they sought to prevent clear-cut Nazi-fascist putsches, the Baltic dictatorships were definitely not "authoritarian democracies" (Rauch 1987, 154), as they were misleadingly called, but rather were classic examples of the right-wing dictatorial regimes that characterized Central and Eastern Europe.

Royal Dictatorships in the Balkans

Whereas the Baltic regimes were presidential dictatorships, Balkan authoritarian power took the form of royal dictatorship. Postwar Balkan national revolutions were also connected with attempts

Baltic presidential dictators: Konstantin Päts and Karlis
Ulmanis

Jan Tönisson

Hitler's welcome in Vienna

Hitler's army enters Prague

General Ion Antonescu
(right), with the father
of Codreanu

Hungarian Nazi mob in the street

Deportation of Jews in Hungary

Victims in Dachau

Cultural control: Stalin (lower left) and his politburo at a theater

The beginning of ruthless purges: Stalin (front right) with the ashes of Kirov

THE ARTS OF RESISTANCE
AND OF THE DICTATORSHIPS

Joseph Síma: *The Return of Theseus*

Lajos Vajda: *Dark Vision*

Frantisek Musika's painting: *From the Czech Paradise*

Hristo K. Stanchev: *On the Field*

Gyula Derkovits: *Generations*

Béla Bartók (by Ferenczy)

Latvian heroic nationalist realism: *Chainbreakers*

Hungarian heroic
nationalist realism:
irredenta statue
commemorating
the lost western
territories

Estonian heroic nationalist realism: *Those Who Won Freedom*

The School of Rome: Pál C. Molnár's Madonna

The School of Rome: Jenö Medveczky's nonerotic painting

Paris's Judgment—the Nazi cult of the healthy body

In Good Hands—the Nazi cult of the motherland and the large family

Falsified history: *The Leaders of October*

Falsified present: A. A. Plastov's happy *Kolhoz Feast*

Stalinist socialist realism: Muhina's statue of 1937, *Worker and Kolhoz Woman*

Falsified history: *The Leaders of October*

Falsified present: A. A. Plastov's happy *Kolhoz Feast*

In Good Hands—the Nazi cult of the motherland and the large family

Nazi propaganda mural in a public building

Hitler's Visit to Frankfurt—the Nazi cult of the Führer

The first piece of Nazi architecture: The House of German Art in Munich

I. I. Brodsky's *Lenin Speaks in the Putylov Work in May 1917* — the Soviet cult of the leaders

A. M. Gerasimov's *Stalin Addresses the Sixteenth Party Congress*—the Soviet cult of Stalin as "the Lenin of today"

A. M. Gerasimov's *J. V. Stalin and K. J. Voroshilov in the Kremlin*

to establish Western-type parliamentary systems, but the political elite in this region soon encountered the difficulties of governing according to democratic rules. The perplexing ethnic-national conflicts, economic difficulties, and countless obstacles to modernization all demanded solutions. Parliamentary efforts were frustrated by the Great Depression, when economic and social hardships coalesced and threatened the fragile political stability. After the first decade of the parliamentary experiment, if not sooner, most of the governments of Central and Eastern Europe turned toward authoritarian rule to address their problems. Like a thin skin, democracy was peeled away from the Balkan regimes. The first nation to experience this process was Albania, followed by Yugoslavia, then by Bulgaria, and finally by Romania.

"Albania's brief turbulent experiment with democracy," states Edwin Jacques, "seemed to offer little promise of a solution to her problems. It appeared to some that only strongly centralized government . . . could bring things under control" (Jacques 1995, 386). Modern political institutions and tribal social structures confounded attempts to consolidate the political and economic situation in independent Albania. Coup and countercoup followed each other during the early twenties. Absolute rule was required in order to stabilize power, a lesson learned well by Ahmet Zogu, the ambitious warrior-chief of the mountaineer Mati clan. Forced to flee to Yugoslavia by a political coup in 1924, Zogu returned in December of the same year and led a successful countercoup, by which he seized absolute power. Shortly afterward, he combined administrative and presidential authority: as prime minister of the country, he was "elected" president in January 1925, and he kept both posts until 1928. At a convention near Tirana in June 1925, the tribal chiefs of the Shkodra, Kosova, and Dibra mountains pledged their loyalty to Zogu. To strengthen his personal power, Zogu established a dynasty with "proper" constitutional legitimization. As a result he became "Zog I, King of the Albanians" in September 1928.

The new Albanian constitution established a constitutional monarchy with a parliament and other related institutions. In reality, however, the kingdom was ruled as an absolute monarchy. Representatives were chosen by the ruling clique around the king, Zogu enjoyed absolute control of the army, and restrictions were placed on the electorate, all of which provided important guarantees for the first royal dictatorship in the Balkans. Zogu could also count on the absolute loyalty of his special paramilitary troops, the armed Mati and allied clans; all other tribes were disarmed. Opposition of any kind was ruthlessly suppressed. Zogu smashed the 1926 Yugoslavia-assisted uprising in the north and halted the series of local uprisings and armed conflicts that accompanied the first half of the decade. Political opposition was not tolerated: in the "Tragic March" of 1925, Zogu had two of his most prominent opponents, Luigj Gurakuqi and Bajram Curri, assassinated. Zogu also banned "harmful publications which attack national sentiment, hinder the . . . consolidation of national unity, or . . . [are] contrary to morality . . . [and] the state regime of Albania" (Jacques 1995, 394). In an effort to modernize Albania, Zogu established "law and order," prohibited polygamy and the veil for Muslim women, outlawed blood feuds, and introduced the use of family names. New office buildings and the parliament building, as well as the elegantly paved "Boulevard Zogu the First" in Tirana, the first such avenue in Albania, symbolized the modernizing vision of the royal dictator.

Zogu's regime was closely linked to that of Mussolini in Italy through the Tirana Pact of "friendship and security" in November 1926 and the second Tirana Pact, a treaty of military alliance, that put the Albanian army under Italian control. Mussolini's expansionist interests were served by the *Societá per lo Sviluppo Economico d'Albania* (an Italian-established Society for the Economic Development of Albania), the founding of the Albanian National Bank by Italian investment, and Italian loans to Albania. Zogu, however, did not share his mentor's ideology. Partly to overcome tribal separatism, Zogu had worked to create a modern Albanian nationalism. Nevertheless, despite resemblances between his ideas and those of fascist-extreme nationalism, full-blown fascism had little appeal: it was too dangerously modern and revolutionary.

In his relationship to fascist Italy, Zogu exploited Mussolini's interests in order to serve Albanian modernization. When Mussolini presented bills in 1932 and 1934 that suggested the foundation of a customs union and demanded concessions that would have curbed Albanian independence, Zogu refused to renew Albania's treaties with Italy, and Mussolini consequently withdrew the Italian military mission and loans from Albania.

The threat of an Italian invasion led to a liberalization of the dictatorial Albanian regime—a liberalization made possible because Zogu's firm stand against Mussolini increased his popularity and legitimacy in the country. In particular, Zogu gained supporters among younger intellectuals who had been part of his more enlightened democratic opposition. In spite of these developments, Zogu could not outsmart Mussolini, who on March 25, 1939, conveyed an ultimatum demanding a protectorate over Albania and the stationing of Italian troops in the country. When this ultimatum was refused, an Italian army of one hundred thousand men landed in Albania and, after four days of fighting, occupied the country.

Like Albania, Yugoslavia turned to dictatorship in an effort to overcome its ethnic-national divisions and increasing internal confrontations. The continuous Croatian-Serbian political skirmishes of the twenties exploded into open hostility after the assassination of Stjepan Radić, the head of the Croatian nationalist Peasant Party, in June 1928. Political solutions to the tension became impossible, especially as parties moved increasingly to the Right. In Croatia, an extreme nationalist-separatist force emerged, led by Ante Pavelić, the new leader of the old Croatian Party of Right, who combined separatism with Italian-style fascism and formed a violent, terrorist fascist party in 1928. In this critical situation, with the survival of Yugoslavia at stake, King Alexander, who was brought up in the Russian tsarist court and was a strong believer of absolute royal power, assumed dictatorial omnipotence. On January 6, 1929, the king suspended the democratic *Vidovan* (St. Vitus Day) Constitution of the country. The parliament—the scene of Radić's assassination—and all political parties were abolished. As an absolute ruler, the king concentrated all power in his own hands, which left him responsible to no authority but God. Among other things, the king now assumed the powers to appoint the prime minister and to form his own government, to select public servants and army officers, and to declare war. King Alexander appointed General Pero Zivković, a former officer of the Royal Guard, as prime minister. He also suspended freedom of press and association and moved to halt the ethnic-national conflicts that were shaking Yugoslavia. Alexander reorganized the administration of the country, abolishing the many small administrative territorial units and, instead, dividing the country into nine huge counties. He took meticulous care to see that the administrative units did not coincide with traditional nationality lines. To underline his support of unity, King Alexander renamed his country: instead of the Kingdom of Serbs, Croats, and Slovenes, it was to be called Yugoslavia. Efforts were launched to generate a kind of Yugoslavian nationalism, and with this goal in mind, the king advocated an anti-Bulgarian campaign and supported the Great Yugoslavian nationalist, paramilitary Organization of Yugoslav Nationalists (formed in 1921).

The Yugoslavian Action—a new, strictly antiparliamentarian, anticommunist organization—was established in 1930; it advocated a planned economy and the introduction of a corporative system along fascist lines. An Association of Veterans of Yugoslavia was also created. Although the royal dictatorship of Yugoslavia sponsored these new organizations, the dictatorship sought always to stand above political parties and to base its power on the army and the state bureaucracy. When various right-wing organizations moved too far toward extreme fascism, the government did not hesitate to ban them. Both Yugoslavian Action and the veteran organization shared such a fate. The Yugoslavian dictatorship functioned as a Bonapartist balancing power and was seen as the savior of the country. Certain groups of Croatian nationalists regarded the establishment of the dictatorship as the first step toward the fulfillment of their demands, and the Serbs welcomed the protection the dictatorship provided by uniting various ethnic groups into a single nation. Given this ability to appeal to factions with disparate points of view, the royal dictatorship enjoyed relatively broad popular acceptance (H. Seton-Watson 1967).

The only resistance to the dictatorship came from the extreme Left. The Central Committee of the Communist Party immediately issued an appeal for an armed insurrection, an adventurous action that was bloodily suppressed by the king.* An ardent anticommunist, the king acted to decimate the Communist Party and to arrest and execute both Djuro Djaković, its secretary, and Pajo Marganović, the leader of its youth movement.

Although his dictatorship was popular, King Alexander nevertheless sought to "legalize" it. Thus, in September 1931, a new constitution set up a nationalized, uniformed, fascist trade union and a bicameral parliamentary system. From the beginning, this system was crippled by structural flaws: representatives were elected by universal male suffrage, but the use of the open ballot guaranteed strict government control and victory. Furthermore, the king rather than the parliament exercised control over the national administration, and the king possessed strong legislative veto rights. Parties were allowed to exist, but highly ethnic and religious parties were banned, and measures were introduced to control the central list of candidates. Electoral fraud, including falsification

---

* "People have been inclined to interpret the call to an armed uprising as a highly sectarian and adventurous act which only brought harm to the movement," Josif Broz Tito stated later. "I think . . . that it was partly so. The decision . . . was unrealistic, to be sure, because conditions for it did not exist." And yet, Tito points out, the heroic, self-sacrificing struggle against the dictatorship enhanced the reputation of the party and later contributed to the maturing of a broad alliance and the successful anti-Nazi struggle (Tito 1977, 40).

of results, was institutionalized. Consequently, the November 1931 elections were easily won by the regime. King Alexander's dictatorship was moderated not only by these formal efforts at gaining legitimacy but also by the replacement of General Zivković with the much more "European" Vojislav Marinković, a well-educated diplomat. An effort was made to create a unity party called the Yugoslavian Radical Peasant Democratic Party, which borrowed and merged programmatic elements and names of earlier Serbian and Croatian leading parties—the historic Serbian Radical Party and the Croatian Peasant Party.

During the second half of the decade, another unity party, Milan Stojadinović's Yugoslav Radical Union, dominated the political arena. But in the mid-thirties, the greatest impact was made by the banned, openly fascist, paramilitary Croatian organization called *Ustaśha*. Ante Pavelić, the head of the party, fled to Vienna when King Alexander established his dictatorship. Pavelić settled in Italy, set up headquarters, and from there effectively organized a terrorist army dedicated to the cause of an independent Croatia. Although an uprising planned for 1932 was never realized, other successful terrorist actions were carried out. Training camps in Italy and the Hungarian Jankapuszta prepared the *Ustaśha* terrorists to carry out assassinations, bombings, and anti-Jewish atrocities. Ideological similarities and the goal of destroying Yugoslavia provided the basis for cooperation between Pavelić's party and the IMRO (Inner Macedonian Revolutionary Organization), a Bulgarian right-wing terrorist organization. Their most successful joint action, the assassination in Marseilles of King Alexander and of Barthou, the French minister of foreign affairs, during the king's state visit to France, shocked the world on October 9, 1934. The Yugoslavian royal dictatorship now lacked its dictator.

In his will, Alexander had ordered that his cousin Paul act as prince regent. This prince, an art collector who had been educated in Britain and had mostly lived abroad, hated politics and uneducated Yugoslavians equally. Consequently, he lacked Alexander's pro-Serbian bias and was ready to compromise with the Croatians. Maček, the Croatian peasant leader, was released from prison, and the more educated Slovenes gained positions in public offices. An agreement was reached by the leading Serbian and Croatian parties to resolve their national conflicts.

The main actor in Yugoslavian politics between June 1935, when he was appointed prime minister, and February 1939, when he was dismissed, was Milan Stojadinović, a banker and financial expert. A protégé of Pasić, Stojadinović served in Pasić's government in the early twenties. The Stojadinović government not only worked on a compromise with Maček's Croatian Peasant Party but also concentrated on easing the unbearable burdens of the Great Depression by fostering vigorous state intervention in the economy. An aggressive peasant policy, designed to revitalize ailing Yugoslavian agriculture, halved the huge amount of peasant indebtedness and introduced a moratorium on repayments, while intensive diplomacy in search of appropriate export alliances led Yugoslavia toward rapprochement with Nazi Germany and fascist Italy. Stojadinović secretly accepted Italy's position in Albania in advance and was helped by the *Volksdeutsch* (German minority) votes, which Hitler ordered Yugoslavian Germans to cast for Stojandinović. This orientation had its internal impact: Stojadinović organized a fascist youth movement that incorporated the uniform green shirt, the Hitler salute, and the rhythmical ovation, "leader-leader." Following a visit to Rome in December 1937, the Italian foreign minister Ciano noted in his diary, "King Alexander had only force, he [Stojadinović] observed, but he himself would make the dictatorship popular" (Hoptner 1962, 86–87).

As a conclusion of this policy, Yugoslavia joined the aggressive, German-Italian-Japanese "Tripartite Pact" on March 25, 1941. The prince regent, like leaders of neighboring Hungary, Romania, and Bulgaria, walked into Hitler's trap; in return, Hitler offered special guarantees and privileges for Yugoslavia.

But this agreement proved the last straw for the Serbian military-bureaucratic elite, because they saw the alliance with Hitler as a betrayal of national interests. On the night of March 26–27, 1941, General Borivoje Mirković and General Dušan Simović carried out a successful military coup, in which they forced the prince regent to resign and proclaimed young Peter the King of Yugoslavia. Enthusiastic Serbian demonstrations engulfed the streets of Belgrade, welcoming the coup and expressing readiness to fight for independence—shouting *Bolje grob nego rob* ("better the grave than a slave") and *Bolje rat nego Pakt* ("better war than the pact") to make their point (Rothschild 1977, 265). In a few weeks, indeed, the war and the grave were their only option.

The next Balkan country to turn toward royal dictatorship was Bulgaria. The Great Depression severely hit its backward and fragile economy, causing social decay and accelerating uncertainty and confusion. The postwar decade was characterized by bloodily suppressed peasant and communist revolutionary attempts and subsequent continual right-wing nationalist terror. Every day, murderous attacks and killings oc-

curred, including terror against various factions within the terrorist organizations. The Macedonian terrorist organization experienced internal war. Established government was hopelessly impotent.

The decline of the early thirties mobilized the defeated Left and large
groups of the lower social strata. Dissatisfaction with the status quo
emerged in the parliamentary elections of 1931, when a coalition of opposition parties led by the Agrarian Union gained an absolute majority. This victory by the opposition coalition—a rare political event in
interwar Central and Eastern Europe—posed social and political threats
to the ruling elite, particularly because clear signs of a communist revival also appeared in the political arena. In local municipal elections,
the Bulgarian Labor Party, the legal front for the banned Communist
Party, attained only 11 percent of the votes in November 1930 but gained
absolute majorities in two city councils and large delegations in ten others at the end of 1931 and early 1932. In September 1932, the party also
achieved an absolute majority in the Sofia city council. This shift toward the Left could also be seen in the government's willingness to allow old and respected associates of Stamboliski to return from exile.
These radical leaders reformulated their demands for extensive reforms
to improve the situation of the peasantry and to introduce democratic
political institutions.

A cruel wave of terror followed these elections in the early thirties.
Macedonian terrorists arrested and killed communists, including Hristo
Traikov, the advocate of the eight-hour workday. The mandates of la-
bor representatives in the Parliament were invalidated. Lawless attacks
against the government went unchecked by the seemingly powerless
Bulgarian leaders.

The shift to the Left on the part of the masses and the uncontrolled,
seemingly unstoppable terrorist actions by the extreme nationalist
Right mobilized the leading Bulgarian military clique, which was led
by Colonel Damian Velchev, the organizer of the 1923 coup d'état against
the Stamboliski government. The civilian wing of the former putschist
group of 1923 had reorganized itself in the late twenties around their
Zveno (Link) organization. Their program advocated "law and order"
and a nonpartisan policy of national reconstruction, to be led by a strong
government. In the spring of 1934, an unimportant cabinet crisis accompanied by right-wing demonstrations provided *Zveno* leaders with
an excuse to act. On May 19, 1934, Colonel Velchev and a group of
young colonels and officers carried out his second coup and occupied
Sofia. They formed a new cabinet consisting of several officers, Zveno

group intellectuals, and Velchev's friend Colonel Kimon Georgiev, whom they appointed prime minister. An antiparliamentary dictatorship was introduced, political parties and trade unions were banned, and nonpolitical corporative institutions were created. Economic measures to assist in the consolidation of insolvent peasant farms were also introduced, and most important of all, severe actions were taken to reestablish law and order. The most impressive result of these actions was the cleansing of the country by defeat of the terrorist IMRO. Until that point, IMRO had functioned as the uncrowned ruler of interwar Bulgaria, and all attempts to destroy their power had failed. This time, the headquarters for the terrorists was occupied by the army and thousands were arrested. Ivan Mihailov, the unscrupulous young terrorist leader, fled to Turkey. In connection with the introduction of dictatorial order, the military regime began to reorient the country's foreign policy by restoring diplomatic relations with the Soviet Union and building friendly relations with Yugoslavia. Both policies entailed giving up traditional territorial claims.

A conflict within the ruling military clique gave the Bulgarian Tsar Boris the opportunity to assert his own power. He introduced his own dictatorship on January 22, 1935. The army was depoliticized and lost its independence. From then on it acted as an obedient pillar of the royal dictatorship. The Georgiev government resigned and Colonel Velchev, the éminence grise of interwar Bulgarian politics, was forced into exile in the summer of the same year. When he returned illegally in the fall, he was arrested, accused of treason and conspiracy against the monarchy, and sentenced to death. Although the sentence was commuted to life imprisonment, Velchev and his military circle effectively lost their dominant political role. The new royal dictatorship continued nonparliamentarian rule and strictly blocked paths that might have allowed a revitalization of the terrorist movement. As an iron-handed Bonapartist monarch, Tsar Boris efficiently eliminated all mass movements. When he decided to moderate his dictatorial rule by allowing a parliamentary election in 1938, the representatives were elected as individuals, forbidden to represent parties and interest groups. Those elected who were affiliated with opposition liberal (*Pladne*) circles and left-wing groups were immediately discharged.

Although the tsar did not modify the dictatorial regime, he radically reoriented Bulgaria's foreign policy. Conciliation with Yugoslavia continued and was formalized in the Eternal Friendship Pact of 1937, but a marked shift toward the Axis powers moved the country more strongly into the Hitler-Mussolini camp. Boris's German father and his marriage to an Italian princess in 1930 provided personal motivation for his foreign policy, but the real cause behind this reorientation was exactly the same as it had been in several other countries of the region. Like Hungary, Bulgaria walked into the Hitlerite trap, lured by promises of economic cooperation and border revisions.

During the second half of the thirties, Bulgaria was the country most dependent economically on Nazi Germany. Boris's ambition to revise the Neuilly Treaty was as strong as Horthy's desire to eliminate the Trianon Treaty. To achieve his goals, Boris allowed Hitler to use Bulgarian territories as a base for his aggression against Greece and Yugoslavia and cooperated in the occupation of these countries in order to enlarge Bulgaria. For the reward of several small territories, he was ready to declare war on Hitler's side against the Western powers. Bulgaria's destiny, therefore, was linked to the fate of Nazi Germany by the royal dictator, the champion of nonpartisan national interests. The country set off down a tragic dead-end road.

King Carol II of Romania was the last king in the Balkans who introduced a royal dictatorship before World War II. Although this happened a decade later than in Albania and Yugoslavia, the origins of this dictatorship lie in the Great Depression. During that era, both the ruling Liberal Party and the rising Peasant Party suffered devastating defeats. The Liberal Party was destroyed by its political failure, by its incompetence in financial and agricultural policy, and by rapidly worsening corruption. The radicalization of the late twenties had significantly strengthened various peasant parties and culminated in 1926 in the formation of the National Peasant Party, a merger of the former Transylvanian and *Regat*, the former kingdom's peasant parties, with other groupings. Other populist groups acted as strong political forces. The ideas of peasant democracy and radical land reform advocated by Ion Michalache, the viciously anti-Semitic and anticapitalist demagogy of Octavian Goga, and, last but not least, the nationalist Transylvanian concept promoted by Iuliu Maniu proved a powerful combination of forces. They could not, however, gain ground in the twenties, for, as Hugh Seton-Watson remarks, their violent language and program "alarmed King Ferdinand . . . [who looked upon Michalache] as something not much better than a 'Bolshevik'" (H. Seton-Watson 1967, 201).

The situation changed radically after the death in 1927 of King Ferdinand and Ionel Brătianu, the pillars of postwar Romanian conservative quasi-democracy. The National Peasant Party emerged as a leading political factor that the Regency Council, acting on behalf of the young King Michael, could not reject any longer. A major peasant demonstration, the symbolic "march on Bucharest," led to the appointment of Iuliu Maniu, the Transylvanian leader of the party, as prime minister. New elections in 1928 produced a landslide victory for the National Peasant Party, more than 78 percent of the vote, distorted by a corrupt "bonus" regulation that cast votes to strengthen the showing of the victor. The victory, however, was Pyrrhic. The National Peasant Party lost virtually all of its peasant character and became a traditional national, middle-class, bourgeois party that continued the traditional Romanian way of governance. Lack of expertise, a deflationary policy that exaggerated the economic decline, social insensitivity, and extreme arrogance and brutality in the exercise of power combined with the heritage of Ottoman-Balkan corruption in a counterproductive fashion during the trying years of mass peasant insolvency and general decline caused by the Great Depression. The bloody military suppression of the coal miners' strike, the discovery of a military plot against the government, the foundation of a paramilitary peasant guard, an assassination attempt against the minister of the interior, and the resulting excessively brutal retaliation all signaled the increasing political instability. By failing to keep its promises and honor its myth, the National Peasant Party discredited itself quickly in the early thirties, just as its predecessor, the Liberal Party, had done in the twenties. The election of June 1931 brought a devastating defeat: a rejected and fragmented National Peasant Party won approximately only 9 percent of the vote.

Accidental factors, or, perhaps, behind the scene conspiracy and intrigue, led the exiled Prince Carol to return to Bucharest in June 1930. He had been living in France since 1926, after he was forced to give up his right of succession because of his marital "irregularities." Upon Prince Carol's return, his nine-year-old son Michael and the Regency Council resigned, and Carol declared himself king of Romania. From that time on, King Carol and Madame Lupescu, his extremely ambitious mistress, advisor, and coconspirator, worked to establish his unquestioned absolute power. His method did not involve military takeover but rather relied on intrigue and maneuvering. King Carol bided his time. He played an important role in destroying the weakened National Peasant Party by dividing it. His operation was helped by the resignation of Maniu as a protest against the King's return. "The break . . . between Maniu and the monarch, regarded by most historians and politicians of Rumania as the end of the 'democratic experiment' and a stepping stone to totalitarianism," states Fischer-Galati, "was a consequence of the clash between parochial and 'modern' authoritarianism rather than between democratic and anti-democratic forces. . . . [The king refused] to take a back seat to the Prime Minister" and sought to reestablish his "dynastic authoritarianism" (Fischer-Galati 1991, 46–47). Carol refused to replace Maniu with Michalache, the party's candidate. From the mid-1930s to the end of 1933, eight cabinet crises were provoked. The quasi-monolithic National Peasant Party began to split: Iorga, the ambitious conservative academic, was lured away from the party, and Vaida-Voevod left to found an anti-Semitic radical right-wing party, the Romanian Front.

In this atmosphere of political flux and rapidly increasing distrust, a growing part of the disappointed masses turned toward the promises proffered by fascist programs. Corneliu Zelea Codreanu founded his Legion of the Archangel Michael in 1927, proclaiming the need for moral resurrection and the creation of a "new type of man." He believed that only "true" Romanian-peasant-Orthodox values could supply the basis for reforms to overcome the effects of modernization and corruption, both of which he believed were rooted in alien values. He also advocated liberating the nation from "Jewish influence" (Ioanid 1990). Codreanu's party participated in its first elections in June 1931 but gained less than 2 percent of the vote and thus failed to earn a place in the parliament. By July 1932, the Legion began profiting from the general popular dissatisfaction and gained five parliament seats. Five years later, the Legion had an impressive sixty-six seats, representing 16 percent of the voting electorate.

Traditional Romanian political parties sought to oppress their increasingly popular rival. In January 1931, the minister of interior ordered a search of Codreanu's headquarters and of the homes of several prominent leaders in his movement. Codreanu, Banea, and others were arrested. In December 1933, the newly appointed prime minister Ion Duca ordered a major roundup, in which eighteen thousand Legion members were chained and arrested. Yet brutal repression, torture, and even the killing of Legion supporters could not stop the movement's momentum. In less than three weeks, Codreanu took his revenge: three of his men, known from their initials as *Nikadori*, gunned Duca down on the platform of Sinai railway station.

Although it overstates the case to say that "a long period of classic liberalism and civility in Romanian politics ended with the assassination of . . . Duca" (Georgescu 1991, 196), authoritarian rule was definitely strengthened. Censorship was introduced in 1934, and government by decree was instituted.

Despite the measures taken against the Legion, rumors maintained that royal circles were pleased with and perhaps even indirectly involved in Duca's assassination. The assassins were not punished, and Duca's death helped King Carol to divide the Liberal Party. Furthermore, Codreanu's movement was financially assisted by the court via two political oldtimers, Tatarescu and Inculets.

In 1934, Codreanu organized a new political party called *Totul pentru Ţara* (All for the Fatherland), but it was most often called the Iron Guard. The party was, as Codreanu noted in 1936, "a school and an army," militarily organized, uniformed in green shirts, and arranged in basic units or "nests" consisting of a few guardists. The number of nests increased from 4,200 to 34,000 between 1936 and 1937. Iron discipline was demanded in accordance with "eight commandments" that were laid down by Codreanu. The first commandment required "moral purity," and the second called for the elimination of personal gain and total submission to the community. This "didactic moralism," as Eugen Weber notes, sought to create a new elite—"honest, responsible, industrious, reliable, above all correct" (Weber 1966, 106)—all virtues lacking among then-contemporary Romanian leadership. According to Codreanu, a guardist had to learn "to fight, in order to learn how to be brave and strong; to work, in order to learn the habit of working[;] . . . to suffer, in order to steel himself; to sacrifice, in order to get used to transcending his own person in the service of his people" (Codreanu 1976, 320).

The elitist, anticommunist, antidemocratic Iron Guard was a mixture of mystic and religious nationalism, populist egalitarian purism, and fascist demagoguery—a mass fascist party unusual in Central and Eastern Europe. Its leaders, although centered in urban areas, came from peasant families or from families of teachers and priests with peasant roots. As radical revolutionaries, they declined to join in moderate compromises in striving for power. Their rhetoric of fierce social criticism, denunciation of the corrupt political order, and egalitarian demands found ready listeners among the masses, who were drawn to and mobilized by the Iron Guard's social program, encapsulated in the slogan *Omul si Pogonul* (one man, one hectare of land).* That program included the special Workers' Corps founded in 1936, the Mota-Marin Corps for

---

* *Pogon* is an old, traditional Romanian unit of land.

schoolboys and students set up in 1937, and the welfare organization where the poor in the Predeal hospital were treated for free and others paid according to their conscience. The program also included a ruthlessly violent crusade against "Judeo-Bolshevik" enemies. Murder and other anti-Jewish atrocity became a common political weapon and a means of self-expression. The *Echipa Mortii*, the kamikaze-like death commando group, bloodily revenged any actions that they perceived as contrary to the interests of the nation and to the Iron Guard: Jews, rival politicians, and other "traitors" were killed with impunity. Even disaffected Iron Guardists were vulnerable: when Nicolae Stelescu attempted to leave the Iron Guard in order to set up an independent organization, ten Guard members, the *Decemvir* (using the classic Latin term for a group consisting of ten people), shot and dismembered him in a hospital ward. It was this Iron Guard that emerged as the largest fascist party in Central and Eastern Europe with 270,000 members in 1937 and nearly half a million votes in the December elections of that year (Nagy-Talavera 1970).

The strength of the extreme Right and the potential for a right-wing revolution was intensified by the existence of the conservative-fascist National Christian League (LANC, the *Liga apărării national-creştină*), established by the merger of Aleksandru Cuza's Christian National Defense League and Octavian Goga's National Agrarian Party in 1935. This extremely anti-Semitic, antiliberal, nationalist organization, which used the swastika in its badge and adopted a blue shirt, openly admired Hitler; Cuza and Goga even visited the Führer and won his support. The LANC paramilitary terrorist units (the *Lancieri*) conducted more pogroms and terrorist outrages in Romania between 1935 and 1937 than the Iron Guard and gained 9 percent of the national vote in 1937.

Challenged by the strongest fascist parties outside of Italy and Germany, the traditional Romanian ruling parties failed to maintain power in the late thirties. The 1937 elections yielded results that made it possible for King Carol to appoint a fascist Goga-Cuza government on December 28, 1937. This act was viewed as a formal approval of fascist violence. Within weeks, Romania slipped into total chaos: Jew-beating became an everyday phenomenon, tens of thousands of *Lancieries* launched open attacks in the streets, and gang warfare replete with fatal clashes between the gangs and rival Iron Guard units became a common occurrence. Shops were closed and the stock exchange collapsed. The Western powers protested. The country seemed on the brink of civil war. To end the chaos, King Carol dismissed Goga on February 10, 1938, suspended the constitution, proclaimed the parliament and parliamentary government unviable, and cast himself as the savior of the nation. A royal dictatorship was introduced. A referendum approved the new authoritarian constitution (nearly 4.3 million votes for versus 5,483 votes against), and all democratic institutions were abolished. Advocating change in the form of government, whether in speech or writing, was banned, and disruption of the public order was punishable by death. The basic principle of democracy—separation between executive and legislative roles—was abandoned, and the two functions were united in the person of the king. Carol appointed the Romanian Patriarch prime minister, banned political parties, and replaced them with his Front of National Revival. Within a few weeks, this new organization had three and a half million members because membership in the party was a prerequisite for any career. Compulsory social work for students was introduced, in the form of a compulsory year of agricultural labor: the goal was to familiarize young people with peasant life. The king's youth organization, *Straja Ţarii* (Guard of the Fatherland), with its compulsory membership, uniform, and Nazi arm-salute, sought to provide a counterbalance against the strength of the extreme right wing. Furthermore, a volume of wise *Royal Sayings*, nearly three hundred pages long, was published in 1939.

King Carol no longer need the populist-fascist force, and therefore Codreanu, who was preparing to emigrate to Italy, was arrested and sentenced by a military court to ten years forced labor. In the early morning of November 30, 1938, Codreanu and thirteen other Iron Guard leaders were transported from the Rîmnicu-Sarat prison to Jilava; following royal orders, they were garroted, and it was announced that they had been "shot while trying to escape."

Romania's shift toward the Right and the introduction of the "balancing" Bonapartist royal dictatorship were accompanied by continuously increasing German economic influence. Like all the other agricultural countries of the region, Romania became dependent on Hitler after its naive attempt to maneuver between the West and Hitler collapsed in 1940. Romania was pushed into a corner by three disastrous political blows. The first was launched by Stalin, who was working intensively to shift his borders toward the West. In the summer of 1940, he sent an ultimatum to King Carol demanding Bessarabia and Northern Bukovina, the territories that Romania seized after World War I and the Bolshevik revolution. "We are requested to evacuate these territories in four days, and the occupation of the cities of Cernăuţi, Chisinan, and Cetatea Alba begins tomorrow at twelve o'clock," noted King Carol in his diary. "I am for resistance, but Gigurtu cannot see how" (Buzatu 1991, 41). Hitler "suggested" that Carol accept the ultimatum. Because Romania wanted Hitler's support in its conflict with the Hungarian irredenta, Tătărescu accepted Hitler's advice and rejected the 1939 Anglo-French guarantee of Romanian borders. An openly pro-German government of Ion Gigurtu stepped out from the League of Nations and joined the Axis.

These measures in July 1940 did not prevent the second, even more devastating blow, when Hitler decided to divide Transylvania between his two allies and give northern Transylvania back to Hungary. This so-called second Vienna Award cut off from Romania more than forty-three thousand square kilometers of territory and nearly two and a half million inhabitants (including one million Romanians). Within a few weeks, the third blow came with the Treaty of Craiova, in which Romania lost to Bulgaria the highly contested, mostly Bulgarian-populated southern Dobrudga. One-third of the territory and population (more than six million people, half of them ethnic Romanian) of Great Romania, founded after World War I, was thus lost.

King Carol's dictatorship collapsed after these setbacks; he abdicated, barely escaped alive, and settled in Portugal. Meanwhile, the Iron Guard recovered from the loss of its leaders. Under the new leadership of Horia Sima, it continued its terrorist actions—highlighted by the assassination of Prime Minister Armand Calinescu in 1939—and revolted against the perceived national humiliation of Romania. The Iron Guard's leadership stirred up fears of a "Judeo-communist conspiracy. . . . Most of [Carol's] followers joined the Guardists, and his son, now King Michael, entrusted power to the Iron Guard and the pro-Guardist military leaders headed by general Ion Antonescu. A new crusade, anticommunist, anti-Semitic, and anti-all opponents of the Guard, was initiated" (Fischer-Galati 1991, 61–62). In September 1940, in a proclaimed National Legionary State, the Iron Guard was declared the single legal political party. Romania thus became the only country outside Italy and Germany where a fascist party assumed control without direct foreign assistance. In October, however, Nazi troops arrived in the country. As these events illustrate, the political trends embodied in populist-fascism and royal dictatorship, following their internal logic, carried the nation to the extreme Right.

The Iron Guard leader, Horia Sima, now vice prime minister, "chosen by God . . . as resolute as a rock . . . [and] bigger than the mountains," launched a bloody revenge. He ordered the murder of "sixty-four former dignitaries and officers . . . for their involvement in the assassination of Codreanu. . . . Nicolae Iorga and Virgil Madgearu were also murdered. . . . Offenses became daily occurrences" (Georgescu 1991, 213).

General Antonescu, a "law and order" soldier who himself sought to be the unquestioned "*conducător* (leader, or Führer), and who spoke of himself only in the third person," visited Hitler on January 14, 1941, and was informed of the details of Operation Barbarossa (Georgescu 1991, 213). In return for his cooperation, he "was also given a free hand to eliminate his rivals." When he took action, however, an armed rebellion erupted in Bucharest on January 21. Iron Guard units occupied the National Radio headquarters, built barricades, launched pogroms in which 120 Jews were killed, and engaged in street fighting. With his army, Antonescu defeated the Iron Guard and restored order by the evening of January 22 (Buzatu 1991). Antonescu's new government consisted almost entirely of generals. In describing these events, Vlad Georgescu concludes that Antonescu's regime was a military dictatorship and that Antonescu "was primarily a good soldier . . . not a Nazi, a fascist, or even pro-German, but as a soldier he came to expect a German victory" (Georgescu 1991, 215). This argument was repeated in Romania during the debate and process of rehabilitation of Antonescu in the early 1990s, but it is undermined by the facts. Antonescu joined Hitler's war and led the Romanian troops deeply into the Soviet Union. In the summer of 1941, deadly pogroms took place in Iasi. Jews were executed after Romania seized Bessarabia. By June 1942, 150,000 Jews had been deported in inhuman conditions (Georgescu 1991, 215). According to Fischer-Galati, "Antonescu's dictatorship . . . differed from that of his predecessors' and from contemporary European counterparts in significant respects . . . [, and although it] enjoyed the overwhelming support of the Rumanian nation for his military activities against the Soviet Union . . . [, it was] a fascist military dictatorship" (Fischer-Galati 1991, 63–64).

The Characteristics of Fascism and the Authoritarian Regimes in Central and Eastern Europe

Fascism emerged in Central and Eastern Europe in the 1930s. Violent paramilitary organizations, classic Nazi-fascist programs and pogroms, corporative systems, nationalized trade unions, one-party states, anti-Jewish legislation, Nazi-fascist symbols, and uniforms appeared in every nation. In a few countries of the region, large, powerful fascist mass parties were organized and gained broad popularity and parliamentary representation. In certain transitory periods, and in some countries, one out of every four or five people voted for these parties. Interwar regimes in the area, as Bela Vago summarizes, can be called "clerico-fascist" in the Austrian and Slovak cases, "monarcho-fascist," in the Balkans, "authoritarian-fascist-type," or "fascistoid," in Hungary and Poland, and "pre-fascist" or "semi-fascist," as Andreas Hory and Martin Broszat suggest in connection with Croatia (Vago 1979, 245–48). Several historians paint the permanent shift to the Right as a "fascization" (to borrow George Barany's term) of the countries. But fascism and Nazism did not triumph in the region in the thirties. Rather, fascist-inspired mass parties remained the right-wing opposition to the ruling regimes until the outbreak of the war. These regimes, however, turned to authoritarian rule, in part because of the competition posed by the powerful fascist opposition and in part because of economic difficulties that resisted solution while engendering severe ethnic-national conflicts and other social upheavals. Parliamentary systems that had been innovations after the war failed throughout the region, with the single and partial exception of Czechoslovakia. Authoritarian rule, either in its Austrian-Hungarian and Polish forms or in the Baltic and Balkans presidential or royal dictatorships, borrowed the rhetoric and other elements of fascism but remained, nevertheless, distinctively different from true fascist and Nazi dictatorships. The Central and Eastern European forms adopted the classic Bonapartist strategy, seeking to balance power among the conflicting layers of societies by launching a struggle on two fronts against the Left and Right extremes. These regimes did not build their power on monolithic mass parties, as was the practice in Italian fascism and German Nazism, and their effort to establish various national fronts and unity parties — mass organizations designed to back the ruling regimes — was more a formality and stage setting than reality. It was the army (assisted by paramilitary units of reserve officers and noncommissioned officers) and the state and local bureaucracies that served as the bastions for Central and Eastern European authoritarian regimes. Consequently, the social structure supporting these regimes was not dramatically changed: the lower strata and traditional pillars of the former archaic "noble societies," such as the lower middle class and the gentry-military-bureaucratic elite, remained crucial to the new authoritarian governments. In the Balkans, where a native gentry did not exist, the "historic middle class," as the Hungarian gentry liked to refer to itself, was replaced by an *Ersatz Klasse* (substitute class) consisting of a new military-bureaucratic elite with its roots in the peasant society.

The argument that the lower middle class played a dominant role in bringing about fascist regimes has been advanced ever since Giovanni Zibordi and Luigi Salvatorelli first voiced this claim in 1922 and 1923. Zibordi argues that the *piccola borghesia* (lower middle class) launched fascism "as their own revolution." Salvatorelli goes even further by stating that "the petit-bourgeois element not only predominates numerically, but in addition is the characteristic and directing element. . . . Thus fascism represents the class struggle of the lower-middle class which exists between capitalism and proletariat as the third [group] between the combatants" (Carsten 1979, 458). This view of fascism, as the revolution (or counterrevolution) of the "little men," is widely accepted among historians of the phenomenon. "The fascist," maintains Wilhelm Reich in analyzing the mass psychology of the trend, "is the sergeant of the vast army of our profoundly sick civilization, the civilization of industrial society" (Reich 1971, 17).

However insightful this argument may be, it is not applicable to Central and Eastern Europe. Quite evidently, it is impossible to speak of a "civilization of industrial societies" in the region, and the metaphor of the "fascist as the sergeant" of the vast army of this society also breaks down. It would be more appropriate to speak about the "dictatorship of the colonels" of the army in semimodernized, nonindustrial societies: the regimes of Colonel Koc, Colonel Velchev, reserve officer Dollfuss, Admiral Horthy, and Captain Gömbös neither turned to the masses nor sought seriously to mobilize them. In the place of a mass fascist party, these leaders were satisfied with the assistance of an obedient army, police force, and bureaucratic state machinery, all alienated from the population. In this manner, the status and power of the elite was preserved in an environment that was hostile to all radicalism, whether in the form of proletarian revolution or fascist revolution.

The dictatorship of the colonels was certainly motivated by the fact that the mass fascist parties of the region manifested a highly populist, peasant, and working class character. Especially in Romania and Hungary but also in Slovakia and Croatia the parties attracted large numbers of peasants and workers in addition to the usually noted lumpen elements—lumpen intelligentsia and uprooted people from whatever social strata. It should not be forgotten that the modern middle class and lower white collar worker strata were extremely weak in these peasant societies, and, therefore, the lower middle class could not be a leading force in the region. Eugen Weber, challenging stereotypes on revolution and counterrevolution, speaks of "fascist revolution in Italy" and "Nazi revolution in Germany" and suggests that "we should abandon the notion of one revolution, identified with only one direction or theme; replace the question: 'what is revolution?' by the question: 'what kind of revolution is it?'" (Weber 1979, 503). For King Carol of Romania and Admiral-Governor Horthy of Hungary, the danger of different kinds of revolution was quite evident. They chased, imprisoned, and murdered communists as archenemies, but they also only reluctantly tolerated and more often oppressed, imprisoned, banned, and sometimes even murdered parvenu fascist leaders and their revolutionary, subversive mass movements. The royal and presidential dictators and the ruling military juntas introduced authoritarian regimes that borrowed several elements of fascism and Nazism and mixed these elements with their native conservative systems in order to guarantee law and order and fight communism as well as all expressions of plebeian unrest. Most of these regimes not only were counterrevolutionary, offering a conservative defense of the ancien régime, but also represented a cautious "national revival" and a gradual, revolutionary transformation of their backward economies and archaic societies. Most of the authoritarian regimes of Central and Eastern Europe emerged in the course of belated national revolutions that restored or established national independence. As latecomers, these nations turned against the established values and rule of the Western great powers. They searched for, and in several cases found, alternative patterns associated with revolt against the West—patterns that promised them successful modernization within a new European order. Nazi-fascist relics and trappings were not only a facade but also elements of these cautious, conservative modernization dictatorships. These regimes and contemporary fascist movements enjoyed relative success in spite of having borrowed Italian and German elements, because they had a native base stronger than the imported foreign elements. Lucretiu Pătrăşcanu—the Romanian communist and later victim of the Stalinist purges—emphasizes this aspect of the Romanian Iron Guard and LANC in his book (Patrascanu 1945).

Antiparliamentary dictatorships took over almost everywhere in the area during the early thirties. The peculiar form taken in the region by the Great Depression played an important role in these takeovers. According to Karl Polanyi, "The true significance of fascism became apparent [after 1929]. The deadlock of the market system was evident. Until then fascism had been hardly more than a trait in Italy's authoritarian government. . . . [Fascism] now emerged as an alternative solution of the problem of an industrial society. Germany took the lead in a revolution of European scope" (Polanyi 1964, 243). The collapse of the backward market system was nowhere so evident and painful in Europe as in Central and Eastern Europe. But, as Peter Sugar, the editor of a compendium of essays on fascism in Central and Eastern Europe, rightly notes in the concluding chapter of the volume: "Most of our authors of the studies on Eastern Europe (but not all), reject such standard explanations for the rise of fascism as economic dislocation and the depression" (Sugar 1971, 153). Analyzing Austrian events, Fritz Fellner makes a similar statement regarding that nation: "The economic depression might have helped in pushing certain social groups toward radicalism, but when a social analysis of the Nazi following is finally undertaken, the results . . . will show that the greater bulk of the unemployed did not join the Nazi ranks" (Fellner 1971, 17).

The rise of fascist mass parties and the establishment of various kinds of dictatorial regimes were certainly connected to the Great Depression, which shocked these societies and turned huge groups toward right-wing radicalization and dictatorship. The fear of a new revolution from the Left during the Great Depression, the failure of the postwar parliamentary systems, and the search for new ways also shaped political responses. But the programs of the Arrowcross and Iron Guard parties and of the various authoritarian regimes in the region reflected much older and deeper structural problems that had originated before the Great Depression. The political trends of the thirties were rooted in Central and Eastern European economic backwardness, archaic social structures, and semifailed modernization. In the final analysis, the profound trauma experienced by the capitalist market system gave rise to revolutions and revolutionary attempts only in the backward regions of Europe. In the industrialized, advanced West, to borrow Eugen Weber's true and witty metaphor, the "consumer society consumed the revolution" (Weber 1979, 524). Although the depression struck some of the most advanced countries with extraordinary force, it was only in the relatively backward peripheral region—or in countries that were pushed or believed themselves pushed back to the periphery—that the Great Depression intensified the process of right-wing dictatorship to a politically decisive extent, so that dictatorships and fascist trends spread and grew in strength. These right-wing trends undoubtedly were intensified but certainly not generated by economic crisis. Rather, the failure of the modernization attempts during the late nineteenth and early twentieth centuries and the preservation of peripheral backwardness prepared the soil for right-wing growth. The basic issues facing these regions, in other words, were the same in the early thirties as they had been at the end of World War I. During that earlier era, several forms of revolts and revolution occurred as responses to the historical challenge. Most of these revolutionary forms failed, including the most characteristic form of all, the national revolution. Consequently, revolts against peripheral backwardness were subsequently channeled, with an exaggerated extremism, into authoritarian, right-wing courses. Authoritarian modernization and right-wing revolution would lead, in the end, to the bloodiest tragedy yet experienced in these countries.

From Bolshevik Revolution to a Deformed Party-State Dictatorship

Like other revolutionary experiments and national movements that attempted to break away from backwardness and establish a respectful, modern national status, the Bolshevik revolution gradually deformed into a ruthless dictatorship. Indeed, the Bolsheviks began their revolutionary march under the banner of a dictatorship. Lenin constantly stressed that the revolutionary dictatorship and its spontaneously founded support institutions, the soviets, embodied the revolutionary power of the majority of the proletarian, semiproletarian worker, and peasant masses. The dictatorship directed against the minority bourgeoisie and the tsarist military-bureaucratic elite declared itself the democracy of the majority of the population.

After the fire of the early revolutionary days burned out and the young soviet state began transforming during Stalin's "second revolution" into an imperial modernization dictatorship, terror and despotism, once directed solely against the elite, were turned against the entire population. Forced industrialization and the brutal collectivization drive were carried out by a bureaucratic, constitutional, legally-institutionalized party-state dictatorship. Its decisions and actions were not subjects of doubt or criticism. The pathetic revolutionary lawlessness intended to destroy the ancien régime was replaced by daily bureaucratic terror, sanctioned by bloody laws, and executed by entitled authorities in the name of the people against the bulk of the population.

This performance was staged in front of the backdrop of revolution. The victory of the modernizing communist-led Soviet nation was celebrated at the Seventeenth Party Congress in January 26, 1934, where Stalin proudly announced:

The USSR has become radically transformed and has cast off the aspect of backwardness and medievalism. From an agrarian country it has become an industrial country. . . . From an ignorant, illiterate and uncultured country it . . . is becoming a literate and cultured country. . . . How was it possible for these colossal changes to take place in a matter of three or four years. . . . Was it not a miracle? . . . It cannot be described as a miracle if we bear in mind that this development took place on the basis of . . . socialist construction. (Stalin 1976, 694, 696)

Against this backdrop, despotism was relentlessly institutionalized during the 1930s. In February 1935, the Central Committee announced plans to revise the 1924 constitution, declaring that a united Soviet society had been created. The principle of people's representation, as the new constitution phrased it, was thenceforth combined with "direct democracy," people's participation in power. In reality, a consistently centralized, monolithic power structure was established, a peculiar party-state that became the vehicle of Stalin's personal tyranny. Paragraph 126 of the constitution adopted in November 1936 formalized the "leading role of the Communist Party." Party and state were declared inseparable, and the party was depicted as the leading force behind all types of organizations, social and state alike. The soviets, once a spontaneously elected organ of the people, became bureaucratic organizations directed by the professional party apparatus. A formally "democratized" electoral system, which eliminated previous restrictions against class enemies and the open ballot, now guaranteed universal suffrage and the secret ballot, but in reality, elections became a centrally organized festive mass demonstration of party power in which voters were presented with only one candidate, picked by the party apparatus, for a given seat.

The first elections based on the new constitution, held in December 1937, set a pattern: 96.8 percent of the voters participated, and 98.6 percent of them accepted the official candidates. "Alone in the entire world, only our elections are really free and democratic," stated a triumphant Stalin. The highest legislative authority was granted to the

Supreme Soviet, whose members were elected for four-year terms by direct elections. The Supreme Soviet, in turn, elected its Presidium and assigned it all the power, including the right of appointing the government, the supreme court, and the chief prosecutor between the sessions of the Supreme Soviet. The All Union Council, consisting of one elected delegate for every three hundred thousand inhabitants and the representatives of the various nationalities in a bicameral legislature, was powerless in reality and offered only an empty framework of democracy. A Soviet textbook euphemistically described the system as follows: "Because of the political and moral concord of our people and, consequently of their representatives in the supreme legislative bodies, all the laws are always accepted by unanimous vote" (Kareva 1948, 206–7). The role of both legislative bodies was, indeed, formal. Only two short sessions of a few days each were held in each year. Between these brief sessions, the Presidium Council of the Supreme Soviet, a kind of collective head of state, was authorized to enact laws and decrees and even to declare war. People's representation was, thus, substituted by central power. All state and social organizations were subordinated to and directed by the "vanguard" party. Trade unions and the state councils acted as conduits between the party and the people. All associations, one of the basic elements of Western-style democracy, were strictly banned and the "bourgeois principle" of the separation of powers was rejected. Legislative, executive, and judicial powers were all assigned to a single leading authority, the Communist Party, which selected, appointed, and controlled all representatives and officials at every level of power.

In this centralization of power, the party itself functioned primarily as a rubber stamp subservient to its leaders. The confrontation between views that had characterized the early postrevolutionary years was not tolerated after Stalin consolidated his power. His elimination of both Left and Right opposition leaders erased all differing "platforms," all debates and doubts about party policy, and even the features and elements that had marked the party as spontaneous mass movement. The often mentioned principle of "democratic centralism" camouflaged the unquestionable centralization of power in the hands of Stalin, who transformed the party into an obedient instrument capable of mobilizing and controlling the masses.

Between 1933 and 1936, while he was establishing absolute personal power and "domesticating" the party, Stalin initiated new waves of party purges, the *chistka* (cleaning) and the *proverka* (verification of party documents), and issued new party cards. The decision to "unmask and annihilate the enemy" and to get rid of the "ballast" of recently enrolled, "passive" and "unsteadfast" elements was announced by *Pravda* in an article of April 1933, issued in the name of the Central Committee. This party cleansing program was followed by the massive buildup of party membership, which between 1930 and 1933 had added six hundred thousand new members to its ranks. A "revolutionary vigilance" was declared necessary to eliminate the elements of the defeated class enemy who had allegedly gone underground and infiltrated the party. Prior to 1933, two major purges — in 1921 and in 1928 — had expelled 25 percent and 11 percent of party members respectively. The new wave of cleansing during the first half of the thirties forged an obedient party. Roughly 18 percent of party members were expelled by centrally organized *chistka*, but a large number of deliberate withdrawals and "disappearances" raised the total attrition to 33 percent. The *proverka*, which was carried out by local party organizations, and the change of party cards expelled an additional 10 percent of the party members.

As Arch Getty proves, besides stimulating the action "from below" deemed necessary to revitalize the over-bureaucratized, poorly-organized party, the purges unleashed a power struggle between center and local organizations, with serious consequences for party structure and function (Getty 1985, 49–90). The party apparatus was enlarged by appointing new cadres whose members were most enthusiastic and obedient in carrying out the purges. From that time on, the apparatus functioned as a real power center (Getty 1985, 56).

The party now became the embodiment of "truth" and thus, with its military-style discipline, required unquestioned loyalty from its members. A permanent Control Commission, established in 1934, with a vast network of local bureaus, punished every disloyalty and deviation from the party line. By the end of the 1930s, an army of nearly four million party members, who lacked real power to influence party policy and participate in decision making, acted as the obedient executor of Stalin's will. Despite its formal omnipotence in the party structures, the Central Committee lost its decision-making and policy-forming powers. Its 139 members (up from fifteen members in 1918) merely rubber stamped the decisions of the powerful politburo and secretariat, both themselves the creatures and obedient followers of Stalin. As an idol, the infallible source of truth, and the charismatic despot revered as the leader of a cult, Stalin was feared, hated, respected, loved, and elevated to near Godlike status just as the tsars had been in prerevolutionary Russia. This Stalin phenomenon would be unrealizable with-

out both the ruthless oppression and successful modernization that uprooted and massacred millions but elevated other millions.

In the monolithic Stalinist party-state, cruel despotism was accompanied by a legalized permanent terror. The search for and unmasking
of enemies, fabricated accusations, and spectacular show-trials became
common phenomena in the Soviet system in the thirties; the resulting
atmosphere has been chillingly evoked in the masterful novel, *Darkness
at Noon* (Koestler 1941). Economic and technical experts, old leading
Bolsheviks, and close aides of Lenin were accused of spying for imperialist powers, of preparing and executing sabotage actions, and of
killing revolutionaries with the intent to undermine Soviet power. During well-prepared show-trials, these individuals were forced to plead
guilty to incredible crimes and accusations.

The series of purges began almost at the same moment that Stalin
assumed absolute power in the late twenties. In March 1928, Soviet journals reported that the OGPU (*Obedinennoe gosudarstvennoe politicheskoe
uprevlenie*, or Association of State Political Administration), the secret
police, had unmasked a major sabotage action by sixty engineers in the
Shakhty coal mines of the Donbass region. It was alleged that these
"bourgeois experts" had ordered inappropriate machines from the
West, destroyed other machines, and flooded the mines in order to slow
down output. Between May and July 1928, a widely broadcasted trial
was arranged. Of the fifty-three defendants, eleven were sentenced to
capital punishment, and five of the eleven were executed. The case provided a signal: Krylenko, the prosecutor in the Shakhty case, warned
that what happened there was "not an exception. . . . If it could happen in the coal industry, then why not in the oil industry . . . in the railways . . . in construction?" (Lampert 1979, 40). Stalin himself warned
at the Sixteenth Party Conference in April 1929 that "Shakhtysts are present in each and every branch of industry." At the end of the year, reports were published on a widespread campaign to arrest experts in the
engineering, chemical, defense, and shipbuilding industries. A major
trial of industrial experts was organized in November 1930, and a trial
of Mensheviks (the former minority of the Russian Social Democratic
Party that did not join the Bolshevik majority and continued the social
democratic line) followed in March 1931. A bloody offensive against
"bourgeois experts," who were allegedly sabotaging socialist construction in the service of former owners and foreign agencies, led to the arrest of somewhere between two thousand and seven thousand people.

These arrests began a new period of "constructed" trials. As Abdurakham Avtorkhanov documents, the Shakhty case was initiated by J. G. Yevdokimov, a local OGPU chief (Avtorkhanov 1953). Yevdokimov's "evidence"—confiscated letters from abroad that he said contained secret, coded messages—was not accepted by Menzhinsky, his superior in Moscow. Consequently, Yevdokimov turned personally to Stalin, who authorized further action. At an extraordinary session of the politburo, Menzhinsky, Kuibyshev, and Rykov opposed the action, but Stalin went ahead. On May 18, 1928, a highly publicized trial presided over by Andrei Vishinsky—a kind of dress rehearsal for the show-trials of the thirties— began in the Trade Union Palace in Moscow. The evidence presented consisted of confessions obtained from the defendants. The organizers, however, were inexperienced: two German engineers pleaded not guilty at the trial and were acquitted; and, although the prosecutor demanded twenty-two capital punishments, only eleven defendants were executed.

The second wave of this campaign, the trial of the Industrial Party, purged several leading experts of the *Gosplan,* the Planning Office (including professor I. A. Kalinnikov, vice chairman of the Department of Production) and the Supreme Council of National Economy (including its deputy president S. D. Shein) who had openly opposed overambitious industrialization plans. "Evidence" consisted of confessions extracted from the accused. In February 1930, Kuibyshev stressed the "inseparable tie . . . between the work of wreckers and our lack of fulfillment of economic and production plans" (Bailes 1978, 126). Suspicion and fear ruled. Industrial accidents, delays in deliveries, failures to fulfill plans, and calls for caution or warnings about difficulties might be evaluated as sabotage. Atrocities against engineers and old experts became an everyday phenomenon. "Everyone is afraid of everyone else, no one trusts anyone," a report stated on the *Donbass* region, "sabotage is seen in every mistake, no one dares to give a final answer" (Bailes 1978, 132). The management of firms was virtually taken over by party organizations and local OGPU agents.

After this three-year-long terror campaign, which purged experienced experts and caused chaos in the economic sphere, a secret order of the Central Committee urged that the reputation of the technological intelligentsia be reestablished. Secret police searches, unless directly requested by a firm's management, were banned. Actions by local party organizations "to change, correct or delay the operative orders of the directors of the factories" were prohibited, and the "presence of official representatives of OGPU in the enterprises" was declared unnecessary (Bailes 1978, 152).

The series of show-trials between 1928 and 1931 created precisely the atmosphere of fear and suspicion required for a "command economy" and for a forced program of industrialization. "Vigilance" and the search for enemies during this period of "sharpening class struggle" paved the road for the paranoid despotism of Stalin. The essence of despotism is fear, as Montesquieu recognized, and the creation of such an atmosphere in the Soviet Union was calculated and pragmatic.

The industrial show-trials, however spectacular, were only the prelude to the bloody wave of unprecedented terror that occurred in the thirties. According to several interpretations, the signal for the onset of terror was given when a bullet from a gun shot by Leonid Nikolaiev in the corridor of the Smolny Palace killed Sergei Mironovich Kirov on December 1, 1934. As the popular party chief of Leningrad, Kirov was a dangerous rival of Stalin's. At the Seventeenth Party Congress in early 1934, three hundred ballots were cast against Stalin's candidacy for the secretary-general, whereas only three were cast against Kirov. Kirov's assassination was, as several sources supposed, initiated and exploited by Stalin, who used it to justify the elimination of all rivals, antagonists, or independent-minded critics of his policy and to institutionalize a state of permanent purges in which hundreds of people were executed and thousands deported to Siberia.

Stalin's conspiracy to kill several birds with one stone—getting rid of his dangerous rival Kirov and subsequently attacking opposition within the party by means of purges (1934–1939)—was challenged. As Arch Getty argues, the party "leadership had been unprepared. . . . *Pravda* did not know whom to blame for the killing. Rather than moving forcefully against key leaders of the opposition, the regime lashed out at White Guards. . . . Radicals did make a halfhearted and unsuccessful attempt to incite the party against the opposition as the December arrest of Zinovyev and Kamaniev demonstrated." At their trial in January 1935 in Leningrad, however, they accepted "the moral responsibility" for the Kirov assassination but denied the other accusations. "It seems clear that the wave of repression following the Kirov assassination died out by the spring of 1935" (Getty 1985, 113–15).

A second wave of purges began in mid-1936, based on "newly discovered evidence." A July 29, 1936, letter from the Central Committee Secretariat to the party organizations accused the Trockyist-Zinovyevist Counterrevolutionary Bloc of planning and instructing terrorist actions, including the murder of Kirov. "Witnesses" and confessions "proved" that a "conspiracy of the terrorist center" had existed since 1932 and intended to follow Trotsky's orders to assassinate Stalin and other Soviet leaders and to build a direct connection with Hitler's Gestapo in order to undermine and destroy Soviet power. After a spectacular show-trial in August 1936, Zinovyev and Kamaniev, having plead guilty and confessed to unbelievable crimes, were executed on August 25, 1936. Unlike previous party cleansing, which mostly targeted petty enemies, bureaucrats, corruption, and passivity, the new purge campaign was openly directed against the opposition within the party.

The series of show-trials continued, when, in January 1937, the case of a "parallel Trotskyist center" was staged in Moscow. The main defendants were Radek, Piatakov, Sokolnikov, and Sherebrjakov, old Bolsheviks (party members before 1920), and people's commissars who were accused of working directly for Trotsky to undermine Soviet power, of spying for fascist governments, and of organizing terrorist and sabotage actions. Most of the defendants were either executed or sent to concentration camps. In March 1938, the trial of "a rightist Trotskyist bloc" continued the spectacle of constructed show-trials. The defendants— Nikolai Bukharin, the leading Bolshevik theoretician; Rykov, the successor to Lenin as president of the Council of Peoples' Commissars; and Yagoda, the bloody-handed secret police chief and primary organizer of the Zinovyev-Kamaniev trial—were all accused of high treason, of conspiring with the Nazis, and of preparing to abandon the Soviet front in case of a German attack. As Vishinsky, the chief prosecutor, "proved" and the defendants confessed, they all had conspired to destroy Soviet power and had ordered the murder of Gorki and Kuibyshev; moreover, they had worked for the tsarist secret police before the Bolshevik revolution. Most of the accused in this case were executed in March 1938. On the eve of World War II, the Red Army was rendered leaderless when most of the officers' corps, including generals and colonels, became victims in the Tukhachevsky case. The old guard of the Bolshevik Party was liquidated. In the closing act of the pageant, Lev Trotsky, the legendary leader of the Bolshevik revolution, was assassinated in his study in Mexico. Some 80 percent of the delegates to the Seventeenth ("Victors") Party Congress were executed. Consequently, the percentage of old Bolsheviks in the Eighteenth Party Congress of 1939 was only 19 percent, down from 80 percent at the previous congress.

Debate continues about the reasons for and motivations behind the Stalinist mass terror. Several authors maintain that Stalin was the "master planner and active organizer of a well-laid plot," that he masterminded, ordered, and commanded the endless waves of purges (Conquest 1968, chapter 4). Psychohistorical argumentation emphasizes the personal motivation of a man who grew increasingly paranoid, spurred on by a neurosis that intensified after the suicide (or murder) of his wife, a death for which he was responsible. To avenge himself against imagined enemies, he fabricated conspiracies, believed his opponents were attempting to kill him, and demanded confessions from his victims as proof that he was right (Tucker 1990, 217, 219, 475). Others argue that Stalin was not always in command and that several groups were engaged in power struggle: moderates versus radicals, and Moscovites against local leaders. In this view, the archaic practice of vendetta and personal revenge as well as the use of the secret police to eliminate antagonists generated an "avalanche-effect": "political violence has a logic and momentum of its own" (Getty 1985, 126–36). Stalin certainly did not have a coherent plan for the purges, and his role "in many areas could have been little more than occasional intervention, prodding, threatening, or correcting. . . . He was an executive, and reality forced him to delegate most authority to his subordinates" (Getty 1985, 203). Stalin was not a creator of the huge apparatus which steamrolled the party but, as Trotsky stated, the creature and personification of it (Trotsky 1972, 277).

All these explanations, of course, do little to alter the terrible image of the bloody Stalinist dictatorship. In fact, knowing that this regime was the consequence not only of the acts of an evil, neurotic man but also of the essential structure of the regime makes the spectacle even more frightening. Indeed, the great purges represent only the tip of the iceberg of terror. Several legal forms of harassment also victimized people during the 1930s. The bloody penal codes of August 1932 and June 1934, dealing with the "defense of socialist public property" and with high treason, legitimized terror against the public at large. At the session of the Central Committee on January 7, 1933, Stalin painted "legalized terror" as the main weapon in the class struggle:

The last remnants of the moribund classes—the private manufacturers and their servitors, the private traders and their henchmen, the former nobles and priests, the kulaks and the kulak agents, the former Whiteguard officers . . . all sorts of bourgeois intellectuals . . . have been thrown out of their groove . . . [but] scattered over the whole face of the USSR, these "have-beens" have wormed their way into our plants and factories . . . government offices and . . . collective farms. They have crept into these places and taken cover there, donning the mask of "workers" and "peasants." . . . These gentlemen are no longer able to launch a frontal attack against the Soviet regime. . . . Hence, the only thing left them is to do mischief and harm to the workers, to the collective farmers, to the Soviet regime. . . . They set fire to warehouses and wreck machinery. They organize sabotage. They . . . inject plague and anthrax germs into cattle on the collective farms and . . . organize mass theft and plundering of state property. . . . To permit theft and plundering of public property . . . and to ignore such counter-revolutionary outrages means to aid and abet the undermining of the Soviet system. . . . It was on these grounds that our Soviet Government passed the recent law for the protection of public property. . . . A strong and powerful dictatorship of the proletariat—that is what we need now in order to scatter to the winds the last remnants of the dying classes. (Stalin 1976, 623–26)

In absence of economic and market incentives, the new panel codes, using the concept of class struggle, sought to make fear the driving mechanism for the economy. For example, paragraph 728 of the Russian penal code punished the production and marketing of bad, substandard products with five to eight years of imprisonment. Theft of public property, a counterrevolutionary action, was punished by seven to ten years of imprisonment, and in "serious cases" committed by groups, the punishment was extended to ten to twenty-five years of imprisonment. Even omitting to report such cases was punishable by two to seven years. Paragraph 107 of the penal code forbid the buying and selling of food products by private persons, calling such actions "speculation" and prescribing five to ten years of imprisonment for offenders. And being twenty minutes late to work twice in two months was punishable by "correction work" for up to six months.

The "laws" of the dictatorship provided the basis for the possible arrest and imprisonment of virtually any Soviet citizen. Almost everyone was standing with "one foot in Siberia," not only in the abstract but also in reality. In addition to the ten to fifteen million victims of dekulakization and famine estimated by Roy Medvediev, roughly four to five million people were the victims of political retaliation, and one out of ten of them was executed (Medvediev 1989). According to Dmitrij Volkogonov, between four and five million people were arrested, and nearly nine hundred thousand people were sentenced to death (Volkogonov 1991). The camps and prisons held three to four million people in 1937–1938 alone. The exact number of arrests during the "witch hunts" of the thirties, suggests Robert Tucker, is not known (Tucker 1990, 474).

Reprisal for political crimes, treason, diversion, and terrorist actions included not only capital punishment but also the deportation of offenders' family members to Siberia for five years. Family members of military personnel who fled illegally abroad, according to paragraph 58 of the law of 1934, might be imprisoned for five to ten years. The loss of a classified document could bring an imprisonment of four to ten years. In 1928, thirty thousand people, and in 1931, roughly 2 million people were sent to prisons or to the infamous "correction" camps of *Gosudarstvennoie Upravlenie Lagerej* (State Administration of Camps, or the gulag). It is estimated that before the outbreak of World War II, as many as twenty to twenty-five million people went to the camps.

The Stalinist dictatorship sought more than to eliminate a few million people; it also sought to control minds. Therefore, all forms of culture—such as art, music, and writing—were purged and subordinated to the goals of the regime. Art trends and individual artists deemed unworthy or dangerous were wiped out. The revolutionary Bolshevik intelligentsia, the artists' collective, as well as cultural institutions of the revolution were virtually eliminated, replaced by a subservient brainwashed new guard.

The purge in the social sciences targeted institutions such as the Communist Academy and the Institute of Red Professors, which had been established after the revolution to replace traditional "bourgeois" institutions such as the Academy of Sciences and universities. Leading Bolshevik social scientists such as Abram Moisejevich Deborin—editor of *Under the Banner of Marxism*, a journal of Marxist philosophy, and head of the philosophy department of the so-called Red Professorship—was harshly attacked as an idealist Menshevik deviator who was passive in the struggle against Trotskyist-Zinovyevist treason. A young journalist from the countryside, P. F. Yudin was appointed to accomplish the "Bolshevization" of the science of philosophy. The old Bolshevik theoretician, D. B. Ryazanov, founding director of the Marx-Engels Institute, was expelled from the party and arrested in February 1931 on the charges that he was seeking to create a "third force" between the party and its enemies and that he had established an asylum for Menshevik deviators at his institute. The doyen of Marxist historians, M. N. Pokrovsky, was attacked in June 1930.

The "Bolshevization" of the history profession was led personally by Stalin, who, in an October 1931 letter to the editorial board of *Proletarskaia Revolutsia* (Proletarian revolution), accused the journal of publishing an article of "rotten liberalism." He called its author, Slutsky, "a hopeless bureaucrat" and an "archive rat" because the innocent historian had dared to note an absence of documents to support Lenin's attacks against the "centrists." Deeds and not archive documents and declarations, stated Stalin, are the test of a party. Stalin charged *Proletarskaia* with "smuggling Trotskyist ideas" into historiography and with the "falsification of party history" (Barber 1981, 129). A consistent, critical reevaluation of Soviet historiography began in 1931. A group of 130 young Bolsheviks analyzed historical publications in Moscow. Kaganovich, Stalin's henchman, argued in November 1931 that *Partiinost* (party loyalty) required linking "the history of yesterday with the general line of the party, with those grandiose tasks which stand before us today" (Barber 1981, 134). Several leading historians were expelled from the Institute of History and the Historical Association.

Similar attacks were launched against the Institute of Law and Economics, and all academic institutions were reorganized under new leadership. Pokrovsky died in the spring of 1932. His school was blamed for anti-Marxist deviation, and most of its leading figures—Gorin, Fridly, Lukin, Zaidel, and others—were purged. The Institute of History of the Communist Academy was closed in February 1936.

These devastating attacks against the leading 1920s Bolshevik institutions of social sciences were accompanied by the revitalization and purging of the old "bourgeois universities" and the Academy of Sciences. In the Academy of Sciences, 128 members were expelled, and the secretary general, S. F. Oldenburg, an orientalist who had been a member of the provisional government, was dismissed in 1929. The renowned historians Tarle and Platonov were arrested. All "Communist" and "Red" research institutes were merged into the Academy of Sciences and placed under the direction of a group of young Stalinist guards.

The natural sciences shared the same destiny. A devastating attack was launched against Vavilov, an Academy member who was arrested for spying and died in prison. His younger brother, who had been ready to denounce him, later was appointed president of the academy. Applied research rather than basic research gained preference and ensured careers for a group of ruthless and ambitious young guards. Searches and purges decimated all the scientific fields. The Statistical Institute was shut down and its leading members were arrested in 1930. The *Pravda* reported "sabotage actions of the enemy" in astronomy in 1937. Science became the servant of politics, and Soviet scholarship was hermetically sealed off from contact with the West. During the 1920s, Soviet scholars worked regularly in Western institutions and laboratories and participated at international conferences. Avram F. Yoffe worked in the Röntgen Institute each summer and lectured at the University of California. As a Rockefeller fellow, Vladimir A. Fok worked in Göttingen, while Jakov I. Frankel lectured in Minnesota, and Andrei P. Kapica was a fellow at Cambridge. In 1935, all these avenues of contact were closed. When Kapica returned to Russia for a visit, he was not allowed to go back to Britain. Soviet scholars disappeared from international conferences. International contact became life threatening.

Although committed to liberating humankind and creating a democracy of the majority, the Bolshevik revolution degenerated and was deformed into a cruel despotism. This tragedy of the Russian Revolution, the "darkness at noon" in Moscow, undermined any merger of progressive forces against nationalist, fascist dictatorships. The various revolts and modernization attempts in Central and Eastern Europe, whether nationalist, right-wing, or left-wing, all deformed into dictatorships—Nazi, royal, presidential, military, and Stalinist—during the 1930s.

14

The Art of Crisis
and the Crisis in Art

In their attempts to destroy the hated ancien régime and create a new, just and prosperous society, revolutionary utopian political activists shared a common goal with turn-of-the-century avant-garde artists who denied old ideals and created new values with which to redesign the world. But both utopian activists and avant-garde artists were severely challenged by the growing crisis during the 1920s and 1930s. As cruel dictatorships engulfed Central and Eastern Europe, along with an unparalleled depth of depression and associated poverty, artists were eventually forced to return to a more direct representation of reality: the art of crisis.

The art of crisis acted in part as a warning — a cry of an endangered humanity, a protest against the humiliation of people — expressed with sometimes shocking documentary realism. The art of crisis, however, also became a crisis of art, when extremist political trends and ruthless dictatorships forced it into a straitjacket as the servant of politics. Collectivist dictatorships sought to use the arts as propaganda to advertise their goals and to persuade or brainwash people. Certain art trends, chosen for their political utility, were lavishly subsidized, whereas others were banned and perished. The art dictatorship was enthusiastically assisted by antimodernist artists who, as representatives of traditional forms declared out-dated by their avant-garde colleagues and antagonists, were intent on seeking revenge. Triumphant political authoritarianism was, therefore, assisted by an artistic counterrevolution in the 1930s.

Back to Reality: Protest against a Dadaist World

While avant-garde artistic trends replaced each other with extreme rapidity, culminating in constructivism and surrealism, an elemental reaction involving a return to reality began to emerge in the twenties.

As a natural reaction to avant-gardist attempts to redesign the world, the *Neue Sachlichkeit* sought a new objectivity. Disappointed artists, horrified by the war and its consequences and disillusioned with rootless utopian visions, returned to basic questions about existence, about the conflict between the permanent and the transitory. Some artists equated reality with ugliness. Sharply defined, sarcastic caricatures and distorted, emaciated bodies with pendulous shapes were used to display with a grotesque, disturbing naturalism the obnoxiousness of human being. Others—painters and musicians alike—returned to neoclassical forms.

In the new historical situation, when feverish enthusiasm and high hopes collided with tenacious resistance and bloody counterattack by destructive forces, the request for truth and reality acquired an elemental urgency: it seemed to provide a way of defending fundamental, endangered human and social values. As György Bálint, the Hungarian writer stated in 1936, "The would-be rebel" in Central and Eastern Europe, where reality is drowning in irrationalism, "can now rebel against a Dadaist reality only in the name of common sense" (Bálint 1961, 232). The journal edited by Lajos Kassák, the leading avant-garde writer-painter-editor, expressed this view in an even more direct way in 1932: "We want to create literature, and we are silenced by politics. Then let us engage in politics to liberate literature from the politics of betrayers of the spirit" (Kassák 1972, 307). Several artists and intellectuals in Central and Eastern Europe echoed Louis Aragon, who announced: "I proclaim the return to reality, for the transformation of this reality!" Why mock or destroy the old painting's ideals of beauty when pictures were being burned and statuary smashed in the courtyard of the Berlin fire-brigade? What a poverty of imagination to reject literary forms such as the old novel and poetry by gluing together unfinished texts or words drawn from a hat, when the wild slogan of the futurists—"Burn the libraries!"—was becoming reality in the strictest sense of the word? The pyres of books and paintings and the deportation and killing of artists were the real denial of art and the new reality. Employment created by preparations for war and the destruction of food stocks, or payment of government subsidies to reduce production in a time of mass starvation, transformed Dadaism into reality.

The turning of art to realism was thus an important manifestation of direct social action, a fight for hearts and minds, resembling a political rally. The realistic presentation of human degradation, abject poverty, empty fear, and the threat of war—in writing, on film, and in paintings—in the increasingly depressing world and narrowing defensive space of Central and Eastern Europe acted as a front line of political struggle in the thirties. Artists turned back to reality to warn of and protest against a frightening disaster.

Documentarism became a leading trend in Polish and Czechoslovak movies. The films of the Polish START group—the Society of the Friends of Artistic Cinema established by Cehalski, Jakubowska, Wohl, and others in 1929—addressed social problems, highlighting poverty in the cities and the realities of people's lives. A series of movies in the early thirties, such as *The Pulse of the Polish Manchester* (1930) by Aleksander Ford, introduced audiences to the dreary world of the factories. The *Street Legion* (1932) portrays the lives of Warsaw newspaper deliverers, and the *Awakening* (1934) presents the striking reality of unemployment. Franciszka and Stefan Themerson's *Europa* (1932) warns of the growing threat of fascism and war. The Czechoslovak cinematic documentarism produced films with telling titles: *Such Is Life* describes the workers' world and activities: shoveling coal, washing clothes, eating their lunch in shabby, tiny apartments, and enjoying even shabbier entertainment. Gustav Machatny's social critique *From Saturday to Sunday* (1931) presents the simple life of salesgirls. In Josef Rovensky and Otokar Vavra's *Innocence* (1937), a girl sells her body to pay her lover's medical bills.

This passionate social sensitivity combined with the goal of direct political agitation in Romanian and Czechoslovak documentarist graphics. This powerful, highly politicized art form drew on placard language to create modern, highly distilled, immediately effective, didactic messages. Examples of Romanian "sociographics" include Aurel Jiquidi's *Mass of Workers Singing the International* (1932), the futureless desolation of *Apprentices* (1935), and the nursing mother with hollow breasts sitting by the gutter in Gheorghe Labin's *Poverty* (1935). The Slovak Koloman Sokol's *Hunger* (1931) and *The Terrorized* (1934) follow the same path with their exceptionally expressive and tense political commitment.

Explicit political messages and realistic forms of expression were supremely manifest in Gyula Derkovits's synthesized modernism. In the last half decade of his life, this Hungarian painter, plagued by tuberculosis, combined the symbolism of expressionism, the lyrical perspective of postimpressionism, and the classic method of compositions to create a unique individual language of image and color, "reminiscent of the altarpieces of the trecento" (Németh 1973, 167). The bitter conceptual contents of his paintings, portrayed in a muted metallic color of faded pink and silver, lift the compositions into an ecstatic world of spirit. *Hungry People in Wintertime* (1930), *For Bread* (1930), *Execution* (1932), and *Bridge in Winter* (1933) all exhibit poverty and oppression. *Generations* (1932) might be considered his *ars poetica*. In the foreground, a stern-faced worker—a self-portrait—reads a book bound in red; in the mirror behind him a mother is reflected as she nurses her child, while a photograph on the wall shows a bearded grandfather—unmistakably Marx. This modern classical and classically modern painting exhibits a peculiar play on time: the present is represented by the reading worker, an international symbol of the awakening proletarian; the past is depicted by the book and Marx's portrait, both symbols of revolutionary theory; and the future is portrayed by the child.

In Hungary, a circle of intellectuals and peasant-born writers produced a series of documentary "sociographic" books, *Discovery of Hungary*, during the thirties. Gyula Illyés's *The People of the Puszta* (1934) accurately describes the condition of agricultural workers on a manorial estate, their lives marked by a moral enslavement more wicked than their physical misery. In a striking episode, a peasant women humbly undresses before the gentleman (master) from the city, accepting her defenselessness as the natural course of things. This dispassionately passionate chronicle indicts the then-still-extant medieval system of manorial landholding in which peasants remained landless and defenseless. Géza Féja's *Stormcorner* faithfully describes the eating habits of the various strata of the peasantry and the poor peasant children's daydreams about food. In this powerful series, Zoltán Szabó, Ferenc Erdei, and others uncover and describe the life and destiny of the peasantry in the fossilized social structure that characterized various regions of Hungary under the Horthy regime.

Tragic-grotesque literature, one of the most characteristic artistic expressions of the area and of the era, followed a different path. The grotesque always served to negate something: circa World War I, an irrational grotesque was used to deny the rationality of a detestable reality. The situation was reversed in the thirties: the rational, almost realistic grotesque became the negation of historical irrationality, of mad politics.

Masters of this genre appeared during the thirties. The Croat-Yugoslav Miroslav Krleža, a cultural institution in his country, created a hitherto nonexisting plebeian folk poetry and transformed the nineteenth-century novel of realism and naturalist drama into a "realistic grotesque" when he published the first two volumes of his *Banquet in Blitva* at the end of the thirties. The imaginary model state of Blitva is made up of Croatian, Hungarian, Polish, Baltic, and Balkan historical and sociopolitical elements. A condensation of typical Central and Eastern European characteristics, described from a peculiar outside perspective, makes the satire biting and reality grotesque. As the writer of this fictional history explains,

The sovereign and independent Republic of Blitva was created when the legionaries of Colonel Barutanski proclaimed Blitvan independence. . . . The peace treaty . . . created the independent Blitva for 1,700,000 Blitvans but did not solve the Blitvan problem because 1,300,000 Blitvans remained in the newly created Blatvia. . . . The unsolved Blitvan irredentist problem brought about the second coup d'etat by Colonel Barutanski in December 1925. . . . He had no other choice but to ruin Blatvia by war. . . . Blitvanen will declare war on the Blatvian Vajdahunen, while Vajdahunen, joined by Hunnia, Kobilia and Ingermanland will set fire to and destroy Blitvanen, whereupon Blitvanen will start a new fight to free Blitva[,] . . . and this new irredentism results in a sequence of new European wars . . . [that] come to an end at a new emergency armistice in the Blatvian Kprivnyak in 2048. (Krleža 1979, 7–8)

In Blitva, "it was a national disgrace to wear a decoration, whereas ending on the gallows became a poetic ideal." If "someone outgrew the local Blitvan limitations, he had to flee abroad, or else . . . he became dull, broken, mired in the mud." "Blitva has no constitution . . . no judges, no legal security . . . the jails for preliminary detention are torture chambers, suspects are shot while trying to escape . . . Blitvans drink . . . they denounce one another, the network of informers pervades everything." The invented hostile Blatvia "developed over the centuries the peculiar Blatvian traits of unreliability, distrustfulness, and suspiciousness. . . . The Huns and Blatvians . . . built their political views, ideals, and convictions on mutual rejection" (Krleža 1979, 13–14, 319, 324–25). Krleža's trilogy, burdened by lengthy monologues, is presumably not the most enjoyable reading but is certainly the most expressive and urgent parody of the "Central and Eastern Europeanness" of the era.

Karel Čapek, a successful Czechoslovak political writer and author of science fiction and psychocriminal literature, turned to "realistic grotesque" in his 1936 book, *The Battle with the Salamanders*. Mercilessly mocking the self-deluding Czech mentality, the book presents Mr. Povandra, a man of the street who does not believe that the salamanders can reach Czechoslovakia and Prague even though they have already conquered half of the world and are standing before Dresden. Povandra puts his trust in the impenetrability of the Czechoslovak mountains, ignoring, as a "different matter," the fact that the salamanders have "in Guatemala sunk an entire mountain range under the water." He realizes his mistake only when, fishing in the Vltava river, "exactly in front of the National Theater," he glimpses his first salamander—in Prague.

Witold Gombrowicz created Polish antinovel and antidrama in his stories, novels, and dramas—*Teenage Memoirs, Ivonne, Princess of Burgundy*, and *Ferdydurke*—which confront the lies of a daydreaming society with harsh realities. His grotesque point of view attacks the psychic attitudes concomitant with "Polishness."

The bitter reality depicted by the grotesque style that flowered in Central and Eastern Europe during the thirties was a mirror image of the society, born of helplessness, fear, and the awareness that the endangered society needed a wake-up call. Karel Čapek observed that his *Salamanders* was not a humorous speculation or utopia but "a picture of our days[,] . . . the mirror image of the circumstances among which we live" (Zádor 1961, 212). As the Czech artist Vitežsval Nezval said at the opening of an exhibition in 1931, this art was "the presentation and at the same time the denial . . . of an era . . . so unacceptable, exacerbating its contradictions to such an extent that it stands at the brink of universal catastrophe" (Bojtár 1977, 113).

Indeed, the premonition of universal catastrophe permeated the art of Central and Eastern Europe in the thirties. Whether surrealist painters, poets of classic hexameters, documentary filmmakers, or writers of grotesque antiliterature, the artists of the region rang the alarm-bell to warn of the approaching danger. In various fields, poets, writers, and artists alike developed the themes and forms of a new trend that may be called "catastrophism." The paintings from the thirties by the Romanian Victor Brauner express a surrealistic vision of helplessness and defenselessness on the part of a people, tortured and terrorized. Brauner's apocalyptic environment of giant mushrooms, enormous insects, and intermingled human, animal, and mineral elements suggest a catastrophe to come. The black-and-white ink and charcoal

drawings of the Hungarian Lajos Vajda also conjure up a vision of apocalyptic catastrophe. His frightful apparitions and huge-winged creatures
are a "tragic scream," an expression of the feeling that "the drama was
nearing its denouement" (Körner 1963, 59). In his poem "The First of
May" (1932), the Czech poet Vilém Závada speaks of sweet-smelling
flowers and miraculous breezes laden with pollen, but the pleasures are
abruptly interrupted—"Suddenly, in the park, under the grass, as if there
was a corpse somewhere"—by a sense of anguish. His compatriot, Fran-
tišek Halas, entitled an entire volume of poems *The Cock Starlets Death*
(1930) and in "Old Women" (1936) describes the gradually advancing
death symbolizing the passing away of an era. Czeslaw Milosz was inspired by premonitions of cataclysmic war and of the destruction of Europe. His poems "Poem about Frozen Time" and "The Three Winters"
(1936) sound the alarm with particular artistic power.

A tragic representative of this generation, the Hungarian Miklós Radnóti instinctively felt the presence of death. The death motif appears
constantly in his poetry of the mid-thirties:

> Oh this garden too is going to sleep, to die
> unloading its fruit before a heavy fall.
> It is growing dark. Around me a belated
> blond bee navigates its death-drawn circle.
>
> And for you, young man! what kind of death?
> Will a bullet come flying, with an insect sound,
> or will a noisy bomb plow into earth,
> so that, your flesh torn, you will fly about?
>
> (Radnóti 1963, 115)

Despite this instinctive apprehension of death, Radnóti asserted: "Still,
I write, and I live in the midst of this mad-dog world, as that oak lives:
it knows they'll be cutting it down; that white cross on it means that
tomorrow the woodcutter will saw down the region; calmly it waits for
that fate, yet it sprouts new leaves in the meantime." György Bálint, a
critic and contemporary of Radnóti, concluded correctly that this was
not the fear of death, but "simply the consciousness of death." It appears within the world of objects, sounds, and plants, in the total harmony of reality and vision. "We were condemned to death, we were
granted reprieve; until then, anyhow, we live as we are able to," commented Bálint. "Sometimes we even think of the future, which evidently
will not belong to us, but no doubt will come to pass. . . . Let us walk
around, as long as we can. We know we may not do it for long, but this

should not discourage us. . . . The shorter the time while we may, the more worthwhile it is" (Bálint 1961, 279–80). The validity of these lines is a thousand times multiplied by the fact that, retrospectively, both the critic and the poet about whom he wrote were, indeed, already "condemned to death" by history, both of them, indeed, had merely received a reprieve: eight years later, in 1944, the sentences were carried out.

The tragic overture to the approaching catastrophe was created by Czechoslovak, Russian, Austrian, and Hungarian composers. The striking late works of Janácek and the impressive young talents of the Schönberg school equally express choking fear, anguish, unexpectedly erupting passion, human struggle, hopelessness, and despair. In *Moses and Aaron*, completed in 1932, Arnold Schönberg portrays the conflict between the two brothers as a contest between Truth and Beauty, Ideal and Life. Schönberg composed the only opera in existence in which the principal character, Moses, representing Truth and Ideal, is unable to sing. He only talks and, therefore, cannot reach the people: his song can be heard only in a brief moment of despair, in the misery caused by the downfall of the Word.

Béla Bartók's great compositions of the thirties condense the fears and swirling anxieties of the era. Music is not translatable into pictures, words, or thoughts but may express all of these along with the hidden inner emotional world of human fear and happiness. The *Music for Strings, Percussion, and Celesta*, which premiered on January 21, 1937, provides a kind of "musical accompaniment" to this historical period. Few works of music are able to create a realm of tonality more artistically polarized, in which timpani building to a fortissimo that expresses catastrophe and elemental explosion contrast dramatically with the otherworldly delicacy of the celesta. The dancing folksong-like melody-world of the nevertheless menacing timpani, the piano solo, sounding softly at first, then becoming unexpectedly harsh, the fearsome accompaniment of rumbling drums in the background, all conjure up the era. The real contrast, however, lies in the sudden transformations from tranquil, harmonious, folksong-like careless episodes to compulsive, wildly erratic distracting rhythms evoking wild pursuit, and back again to lines representing resolution and rebirth. The sobbing melodies, the terror of themes dying with the breaking of strings, and the writhing forces of the dancing melodies finally dissolve in the persistently recurring leading motif and in the reverent hymn of the conclusion.

Bartók, the sensitive and withdrawn artist, confessed his credo in a letter sent to Bucharest: "My true guiding ideal . . . [is] the evolving brotherhood of peoples, brotherhood in spite of all wars and conflicts. This is the ideal that I am endeavoring to serve . . . in my music" (Bartók 1976, 397). A man of principle, who changed his vacation plans in order to avoid setting foot in fascist Italy, passed a harsh judgment on the future of Hungary: "How I can then continue to live . . . [and] work in such a country," wrote Bartók in a letter in the spring of 1938, "is beyond the imagination. . . . The 'educated' Christian people are almost all in the Nazi camp: I am truly ashamed of having come from this class" (Bartók 1976, 581–82). In protest, he left his homeland in 1940 as a voluntary exile. Artists who sought to save their integrity and their human and artistic values could no longer exist in Central and Eastern Europe.

The Straitjacket of Arts: Nazi-Fascist "Retro-Garde"

In Central and Eastern Europe, the actions of authoritarian, bloody dictatorial regimes produced a deep crisis in the arts and intellectual life in the thirties. Intellectuals and artists were forced to work within the straitjacket of government-dictated "healthy," "optimistic," and "patriotic" political propaganda. The logic of dictatorship, whether exercised by the Right or the Left, demanded the subordination of the arts to politics, the degradation of free artistic expression, and the harnessing of artists to didactic roles in the service of specific political goals. The arts had to function as merely one more propaganda weapon, bombarding the populace with messages easily understand by anyone.

Berthold Hinz, the historian of Nazi art, states,

There is a widely held view that similar governmental systems will produce similar art. Nothing could be further from the truth. Futurism, for example, achieved significant cultural standing in fascist Italy. In Germany, however, an allied country with a similar political system, Futurism was banned. In Fascist Spain, art was little affected by domestic policy and therefore remained relatively free. . . . These differences can be traced back to traditions in art ideology that vary from country to country. (Hinz 1979, 1–2)

Variations, indeed, were endless, and accidental factors as well as traditions played an important role in art policy in each of the authoritarian regimes.

Despite these variations, the *Gleichschaltung* (forcing into line) of the arts was a general trend in European authoritarian systems. Even though the *Gleichschaltung* occurred at differing paces and with varying degrees of radicalism, it exhibited several fundamental, readily discernible similarities in fascist Italy, Nazi Germany, and Bolshevik Russia. Whether a comparison is made of Soviet, Nazi, fascist, and Maoist art trends (Golomshtok 1990), or of Nazi, Soviet, Italian, and Austrian arts (Tabor 1994), one finds art forced to serve the state. "The officially condoned art in the Third Reich," asserts Susanne Deicher, "was a propaganda instrument of power politics" (Deicher 1988). If architecture always has a "function of representation," this role, as Chatrine Brice argues, became extremely strong in totalitarian regimes, where architecture serves "a political liturgy." It is required to illustrate "the legitimacy and greatness of the regime based on its architectural achievements." The image "developed by the regime on itself," of the role of the strong state and almighty party, was expressed "by new ministries and other public buildings." Indeed, the party headquarters became architectural "self-references." The architecture of fascist-authoritarian regimes is thus "characterized by a considerable megalomania and 'monumentomania" (Brice 1989, 103–4, 106). This analysis applies equally not only to Italian *Novecento* art and Soviet socialist realism, but also to nationalist-authoritarian Bulgarian art and Estonian conservative academism and classicist monumentalism (Lehmann-Haupt 1954).

Although Italy and Germany are outside the scope of the area under discussion here, their art policies and art trends must be briefly reviewed as direct influences on and the sources of ideal patterns followed in Central and Eastern Europe. Mussolini's *Marcia su Roma* (march on Rome) had an immediate impact on arts: in 1922, the year of the fascist takeover, the *Novecento* group was established, and its practices soon entered the mainstream of Italian fascist art. Its first exhibition was held in the Galleria Pesaro in Milan in 1923. Successive exhibitions in 1924 and 1926 — during the first and indirectly fascist period of *Novecento* art — clearly initiated a return to order, the rejection of the disintegration of forms, and the rehabilitation of drawings. Unlike the *Neue Sachlichkeit* in Germany and the *Valori Plastici* (Plastic Values) in Italy, both of which had direct connections to and shared several common features with *Novecento*, the *Novecento* attempted to return to the "old harmony" that had been so passionately rejected by the revolutionary avant-garde. The *Sachlichkeit* of *Novecento* was not accompanied with the representation of the unpleasant and ugly that was typical in *Neue Sachlichkeit* social critiques.

This first and rather pluralistic era of *Novecento* art attempted to create a balance between avant-garde modernism and traditionalism. Futurism exerted a strong influence on *Novecento* works and was itself enjoying a honeymoon of sorts with the fascist regime. In 1922, Ardengo Soffici, a former Italian avant-garde artist, argued in Mussolini's journal that the "old" avant-garde was outmoded, and he advocated a "recall to order" to a "retro-garde" art able to assist politics. That the avant-garde

discredited and repudiated . . . principles [of moral and social order] might have been . . . an act of recklessness, a tremendous mistake . . . an error owing to a certain immaturity of judgement . . . a wily desire to appear courageous and extraordinary. . . . Fascism . . . aims not at a transvaluation of values but rather at their clarification; it does not admit anarchy or arbitrariness but, on the contrary, wants to restabilize and reinforce the law. (Soffici 1993, 246–47)

Soffici and the early fascist artists sought to find a compromise, a fascist art that would be "neither reactionary nor revolutionary since it unifies the experience of the past with the promise of the future" (Soffici 1993, 248).

During the second period of *Novecento*, the attempt to balance modernity with conservativism was replaced by a strong romantic historicism, a kind of rigid Latin-Italian neoclassicism accompanied by conservative megalomaniac monumentalism. Avant-garde futurist elements gradually lost ground in the mature second period of *Novecento*. This transformation of *Novecento* art emerged after the Matteotti assassination during the period of Mussolini's second revolution. Just as parliamentary pluralism was being abolished, so, too, artistic pluralism was rejected after 1926. Eventually, the *Premio Cremona* (the Cremona award, and the name of the "advanced," fascist, openly propagandistic art trend in Italy) emerged as a form of state-sponsored art (Bottai 1940). *Premio Cremona* sought to create "nondegenerate," "healthy," "traditional," and politically useful works of Italo-German iconography. A specific fascist party cultural policy, advocated by Roberto Farinacci, secretary general of the Fascist Party, shaped both forms and practices through the experience of state patronage. The result was a system that side-stepped market mechanisms in the arts.

The gradual and far-reaching shift in Italian *Novecento* had no counterpart in Nazi Germany, where immediate, dramatic change was introduced by central orders from above. Adolf Hitler, a third-rate, un-

successful painter himself, declared the subordination of arts to politics only a few weeks after he assumed control of the government. "Simultaneously with the political purification of our public life, the government of the Reich will undertake a thorough moral purging," Hitler
stated in his speech before the Reichstag on March 23, 1933.

The entire educational system, the theater, the cinema, literature, the
press . . . must all serve the eternal values present in the essential character
of our people. Art will always remain the expression and the reflection of
the longings and the realities of an era. . . . Heroism in progressing will in
the future shape and lead political destiny. It is the task of art to be the expression of this determining spirit of the age. Blood and race will once more
become the source of artistic intuition. (Hitler 1969, 568)

A few months later, at the 1934 Party Congress in Nuremberg, Hitler
explicitly excluded cubist, futurist, Dadaist, and other "artistic sabo-
teurs" and "charlatans" from National Socialist art. "They will see that
the commissioning of what may be the greatest cultural and artistic projects of all time will pass them by as if they had never existed" (Hinz
1979, 35). On the occasion of the opening of the House of German Art,
the first demonstrative architectural achievement of Nazi art, in Munich in July 1937, Hitler condemned the formerly dominant view of art
as an "international experience" and a "phenomenon of its time" that
speaks of a general "modern art" and thus denies the existence of German and French arts. Modern art, according to Hitler, reduced art to
the level of fashion: "something new every year." That was the slogan,
Hitler maintained, of impressionists, futurists, cubists, and perhaps
even Dadaists. For Hitler, these new "periods" of art would be comic,
were they not tragic. They made people unsure of their judgment and
silenced many who would have liked to object to this "cultural Bolshevism." True art, Hitler claimed, is eternal and remains eternal; it does
not follow fashion. The Nazi solution to modern art was extremely
simple: the "Herostrati of culture," as Hitler stated, were committing
criminal acts and "consequently all personal debate with them must be
concluded by either imprisoning them or locking them up in mental
institutions." Just as killing in order to protect one's personal freedom
cannot be permitted, Hitler reasoned, so the "murder of the souls" of
a people for the sake of "artistic freedom" is unacceptable. In a Munich
speech, he proposed abolishing modernism with self-assured aesthetic
judgment: "What do they fabricate? Deformed cripples and cretins,
women who inspire nothing but disgust, human beings that are more

animal than human." Hitler condemned artists who are determined to perceive "meadows as blue, skies as green, and clouds as sulphur yellow. . . . [I]n the name of the German people I mean to forbid these pitiable unfortunates, who clearly suffer from visual disorders, from attempting to force the results of their defective vision onto their fellow human beings as reality or, indeed, from serving it up as 'art'" (Hinz 1979, 42). On the occasion of the opening of the second Exhibition of German Art in July 1938, Hitler laid down the rules for following "eternally healthy and eternally beautiful" artistic ideals: "The German people of the twentieth century represent a newly-awakened affirmation of life, full of admiration for Strength and Beauty and therefore for that which is healthy and vigorous . . . The artist in this century must dedicate himself to this century" (Hitler 1969, 605).

Hitler's pronouncements were translated into actions. Under his orders, a five-member committee headed by Professor Ziegler started a nationwide tour to collect all "base and degenerate" works from German museums. Altogether, 15,997 paintings and sculptures by 1,400 artists were confiscated, including more than one thousand paintings by Emil Nolde, a member of the Nazi party. Works from 112 of these artists were displayed at the *Entartete Kunst* (Degenerate Art) exhibition in 1937. The paintings were organized in various galleries: the first gallery displayed the "barbaric method" by which form and colors had been destroyed; using expressionist works, a second gallery showed the "immorality" of modern art, the view of the world as a bordello; the third illustrated attempts to destroy racial awareness; and the last depicted modernism as the "art" of mental illness. Some of the confiscated works were locked away and some were sold abroad for hard currency. Finally, and most symbolically, 3,825 paintings and statues were burned in the central yard of the Berlin fire department on March 20, 1939, in an act that, like the infamous book-burnings, set the tone for the future.

In the same year, the House of German Art in Munich initiated its first showcase exhibition, laying down guidelines for German art. In response to the exhibition call, fifteen thousand works were submitted, and nine hundred of them were exhibited. Hitler himself participated in the preliminary selection process and personally eliminated eighty works as "unfinished." The sign, "Bought by the Führer," appeared under 144 paintings and sculptures at the exhibition. Hitler dictated taste as he dictated the country.

What were the main characteristics of the fine arts during the Nazi period? Above all, the "finished" look, the lifelike imitation. The style borrowed heavily from the genre paintings of the early nineteenth century, which, although considered examples of true Germanic tradition, were in fact themselves inspired by seventeenth-century Flemish art. In addition, a neoromantic trend that employed unambiguous symbolism presented the Nazi nationalist message with a heroic monumentalism.

The public buildings of the Nazi regime stood as the most expressive cultic monuments of Nazi art. With their impressive size that dwarfed individual human beings, Nazi public buildings were designed to set in stone the superiority, omnipotence, and immortality of the Nazi Reich, the future conqueror of Europe. Hitler, the fanatic who dreamed of power transfigured through art, made sketches for rebuilding Berlin as an imperial capital in the twenties. Although it remained on the drawing board, his plan was a clear expression of his imperial megalomania: it focused on a five-kilometer-long avenue, thirty meters wider than the Champs-Elysées in Paris, and crowned by a monumental *Arc de Triomphe* three times as large as Napoleon's. At the end of the avenue, there was a new central railway station with four traffic levels. In front of the station was a huge square, three hundred meters wide and one hundred meters long, modeled on the road leading from Karnak to Luxor and framed with captured enemy arms. At the other end, the avenue terminated in an assembly hall designed to accommodate 150,000 people, several times the size of St. Peter's Cathedral in Rome. The avenue was lined with dozens of ministries, theaters, and twenty-one-story hotels.

A young and talented architect, Albert Speer, was appointed to realize the dreams. "Your husband is going to erect buildings for me," said Hitler to Speer's wife during a dinner in the spring of 1934, "such as have not been created for four thousand years" (Speer 1970, 58). In early 1934, Speer was instructed to design a permanent building in Nuremberg for the annual Nazi party congresses. The size of the Nuremberg project was breathtaking. A field more than four kilometers long was framed by rows of steps twenty-five meters high and topped by a long row of pillars that imitated the altar at Pergamon. The parade ground, with an area of sixteen square kilometers, was surrounded by a gallery that seated 160,000 people and contained twenty-four towers, each over forty meters tall. Over the dignitaries' boxes rose the huge figure of a woman, twenty-five meters taller than the statue in the Capitolium of Rome erected by Nero and fifteen meters taller than the Statue of Liberty in New York. It was the largest statue of its kind to be erected anywhere and anytime in the world. In the plans, a road paved with heavy granite slabs led almost two kilometers to the four-hundred-thousand-seat Great Stadium. The stadium, in classical style, would have exceeded the size of the pyramid of Cheops by nearly three times. Hitler was present when the foundation stone for the Nuremberg stadium was laid on September 1937. "He wanted the biggest of everything," wrote Speer while he was in the Spandau prison "to glorify his activities and to increase his pride." Then he cited Hitler, who had explained his attempt in 1939: "'Why always the biggest? I do this to restore to each individual German his self-respect. . . . I want to say . . . We are not inferior; on the contrary'" (Speer 1970, 69).

The erection of another important public building, the new *Reichskanzlei* (the German Reich Chancellery), was ordered in January 1938. The date for completion of the building was set at January 10, 1939! The clearing of the Voss Strasse in Berlin to make space began immediately. Even the tapestry factory had immediate orders to make tapestries for the building. Enormous efforts ensured that on January 10, 1939, Hitler was able to receive the members of the diplomatic corps in his new chancellery. Not unexpectedly, the chancellery was gigantic, twice the size of Nero's Golden Palace. Guests reached Hitler's reception hall through a gallery illuminated by filtered light; the gallery was twice the length of the famous mirrored corridor at Versailles. They also passed through rows of richly decorated rooms. "On the long walk from the entrance to the reception hall," Hitler remarked, "they will get a taste of the power and grandeur of the German Reich!" (Speer 1970, 103). The "imperial architectural megalomania," as Speer later called it, with its cold, rigid classicism and its aggressive conservatism, attempted to build "bridges of tradition" leading into the future.

Hitler's personal history and his concept of his role as Führer shaped Nazi architecture. Between 1910 and 1914, he posed as an artist in the streets of Vienna and Munich, painting naturalist watercolors, in some cases from picture-postcard models. He meticulously "photographed" every cobblestone of the road, the individual stones of the buildings, and the crumbling plasterwork of the houses, as well as the texts of the posters on the walls. As Sergio Salvi rightly notes, "Hitler's watercolours are a revelatory and coherent prelude to the official painting of the Third Reich that appeared twenty years later " (Salvi 1984, 13).

Hitler's conservative dictates concerning art coincided with a spontaneous artistic counterrevolution by large numbers of mediocre conservative artists. In 1930, no less than a quarter of a million artists joined the *Führerrat* (Leader's Council) of United German Art and Cultural Alliances. Within weeks of Hitler's seizure of power, this *Führerrat* published a five-point manifesto entitled "What German Artists Expect from the New Government!" It requested "one guideline for action . . . , a philosophy drawn from a passionate national and state consciousness anchored in the realities of blood and history!" It also demanded a "spiritual battle" in which "Bolshevist nonart and nonculture will be doomed to destruction," and it urged the government to destroy Bolshevist works, to use them "as fuel for heating public buildings," and to ban Marxist and communist artists by implementing the principle of "an eye for an eye" and by purging public areas of modernist statues and buildings. The doors, stated the manifesto, should be opened to "artists loyal to the German tradition. . . . Our powers are waiting to be called into life . . . [and freed] from the nightmare of the past years . . . [from] the terror of artistic Bolshevism" (Hinz 1979, 27–28).

Thus began a bloodthirsty campaign of revenge by conservative, mediocre artists. The fifteen thousand works submitted for the first Nazi exhibition of contemporary German art clearly showed the strength of the revitalized traditionalist trend. What happened on the cultural scene "was not something new but something old, indeed, something antiquated. The claim that German fascism created its own art . . . can no longer be taken seriously," states Berthold Hinz. "All it did was reactivate those artists who had been left behind by the developments of modern art . . . and who seized the opportunity to move into the vacuum once modern art had been liquidated" (Hinz 1979, 15). This mass support and Hitler's strong personal motivation undoubtedly strengthened the totalitarian drive to "standardize" public views, ways of thinking, and tastes. Arts were required to be devoted to Nazi values and aggressive nationalism and to serve the cult of the charismatic, infallible leader and the myth of racial-based national unity. These crucial goals were effectively accomplished by government authorities who exercised merciless censorship, even physically eliminating those slow to adjust, and who administered a lavish system of patronage, commissions, and opportunities for artists who embraced the desired values and forms.

The Stalinist Cultural Dictate: Mandatory Socialist Realism

When the Bolshevik revolution was transformed into a militarized ruthless imperial modernization dictatorship under Stalin, the logic of the new regime created a spectacular split between the regime and, as Hitler characterized it, "Bolshevik cultural anarchy," the revolutionary avant-garde still genuinely connected to the revolution. Although he used a rather different ideology, Stalin, like Hitler, sought to create social unity and collective society. Therefore, the *Gleichschaltung* of the arts and their subordination to explicit, simple propaganda tasks was as important in Stalinist Russia as in Nazi Germany. Like Hitler, the dictatorial Bolshevik regime set up a centralized party-state mechanism to articulate its goals, which included controlling the activity of artists by means of strict censorship and a nonmarket patronage system (Grois 1992).

Unlike the Hitlerite system, the formulation and introduction of Stalinist art policy occurred over a decade. In July 1925 in a resolution on literary policy, the Central Committee of the Bolshevik Party declared the importance of cultural pluralism and rejected cultural monopoly. Announcing solidarity with "proletarian writers," the Central Committee rejected the "literary ukase of communist literary critique" and declared the need for "free competition" among various literary groups.

Between 1928 and 1932, the years of Stalin's "second revolution," when the first purges hit the intelligentsia and decisive action was taken to mobilize and to "educate" the masses according to Stalinist ideology, an art dictate was introduced. Clear signals of Stalin's intentions were given in the 1929 campaign against two excellent "fellow-traveler" writers, Boris Pilnyak and Evgenij Zamyatin. Pilnyak's *Mahagony* and Zamyatin's *We*, both published abroad, were condemned as "anti-Soviet" and hostile to the regime. With the help of Gorki, Zamyatin left the country. Even though Pilnyak attempted to rewrite his book according to government requirements, he was eventually arrested and murdered. Voronski, the former *Polruk* (political leader) of literature who had advocated collaboration with the "fellow-traveler" writers, was accused of supporting "bourgeois humanism" and betraying the class struggle, and he was deported to Siberia. The *Perevel* (Pass) group was criticized as "Bergsonian idealists," and one of its members, Platonov, was labeled a "kulak agent" by his fellow-writer Fadyajev. Most of the members of the group—Ivan Katayev, Zarudjin, Kluchkov, Guber, and others—were soon arrested and killed.

As in Nazi Germany, the exercise of central control was aided by a mass movement, organized as an extreme left-wing association, the so-called RAPP (Russian Association of Proletarian Writers). The totalitarian party-state used this group successfully at the beginning but soon turned against it. In seeking to "nationalize" literature, the government annihilated this spontaneous, independent left-wing organization, accusing it of harboring "Trotskyist fascist agents." The *Proletkult* (proletarian culture), a strong postrevolutionary trend that used certain elements of modernism in its direct propaganda art, was also eliminated. During these years, Vladimir Majakovsky, one of the founders of Russian futurism and a living bridge between avant-garde art and the Bolshevik regime, committed suicide (or was killed?). The last remnants of the short-lived marriage of avant-garde and communist revolution were, thus, liquidated.

A Central Committee resolution in 1932 ordered the dissolution of all existing proletarian artistic organizations—which, according to *Pravda*, "dictated illiterate literature" (*Pravda* 1932)—and decreed the foundation of a single Writers' Union. Spontaneity was no longer tolerated, and literary and artistic life were thenceforth centrally organized. In August 1934, at the first congress of the newly established Writers' Union, Stalin's chief ideologue Andrei Zhdanov outlined a new set of mandates for writers. The heroes of literature were to be workers, peasants, and party officials, and Soviet literature was to embrace an optimism that would reflect the life of the society in its revolutionary development rather than in its objective reality. Furthermore, literature was to assist in educating the population and in creating an ideological unity. Zhdanov advocated "partisan revolutionary romanticism": an evocation of the future that existing reality was preparing, linked always intimately with the presumed readers, the proletarian masses (Zhdanov 1988, 293–94). The first congress of the Writers' Union also denounced modernism and formalism as expressions of bourgeois decadence.

The Writers' Union became an obedient executor of official party policy. It must not be forgotten that the year of its establishment, 1934, was also the year of the Kirov assassination that initiated the subsequent orgy of accusations and purges. In one of its editorials, the literary monthly *Oktyabr* (October) denounced "the enemies of the Party who have infiltrated the Writers' Union, editorial boards, and publishers" in order to realize their hostile, destructive goals. "The Soviet writers unanimously denounce the Trotskyist agents who have infiltrated the literary life, and cast them out from their ranks," continued the editorial; it then named a number of "literary traitors" and "graphomaniac Trotskyists": Tarasov-Rodyonov, five members of the *Perevel* group, Ter-Vaganyan (a "Trotskyist-terrorist"), Friedland (a "degenerated counterrevolutionary"), and others (*Oktyabr* 1936).

As political dictates further penetrated cultural policy, the ultimate literary criticism became arrest and murder. Isaak Babel, Osip Mandelstam, Nikolai Kluyev, Boris Pilnyak, and dozens of other Soviet writers were arrested and executed. Vsevolod Mayerhold, the pioneer of avant-garde theater, shared the same destiny. His theater was closed in January 1938 because, as the resolution stated, "it could not get rid of its deep bourgeois formalism, hostile to Soviet arts" (*Tyeatr* 1938). Mikhail A. Bulgakov, another giant of literature and theater of the period, was banned and excommunicated from Soviet culture.

Like a choral conductor, the previously-quoted *Oktyabr* editorial unambiguously signaled for a new song: its last paragraph stated that "all of the emotions and thought of our people are devoted to the Father of the Soviet Union, the shining sun of mankind, the greatest genius of our time, to our dear Stalin" (*Oktyabr* 1936). Evgenij A. Dolmatovsky, Stefan Shchipachev, and Aleksei A. Surkov wrote odes, indeed hymns, praising Stalin in this tone. Prokofiev composed his "Stalin Cantata." Dozens of painters portrayed "the great leader," whose portraits began to appear in offices, shop windows, and homes. Novels, presented in the form of conflict between "old" and "new," between enthusiasm and treason in the ruthless class struggle, spread word of the successes of the Five-Year Plan and of the great forward leap brought about by grandiose construction works. Compulsory clichés engulfed literature: conservative peasants, hostile former white-guardist officers, saboteur engineers, self-sacrificing workers, and communist heroes crowded the new Soviet novels and plays. Leonov's *Sot*, for example, portrays the story of the construction of a huge paper mill in the remote countryside, and Fedor Gladkov's *Energia* (Energy), Marietta S. Shaginyan's *Gidrocentral* (Hydroelectric power station), and Valentin Katajev's *Vremja, vperjod!* (Time, forward!) present the technological details of construction and production. Odes on the collectivization and the transformation of peasant life became another central topic embodied especially in the writings of Panjorov and Sholohov. Monumental historical novels by Sergeiev-Lenski, Solovjev, and Alexei Tolstoy on the Crimean War, Kutuzov, and Peter the Great, respectively, served the new party line of Soviet nationalism. A purged Soviet cinema joined the chorus. The formalism of Eisenstein and the avant-garde characteristics of early Soviet film were eliminated, and cinematographers were required to produce epic films dealing with the heroic past. Vsevelod Pudovkin's *Victory, Minyin and Pozharski*, and *Suvorov* and the entire series of historic tableaus on Ivan the Terrible, Peter the Great, and Alexander

Nevsky fueled Russian-Soviet patriotism. Historical films, such as the series on Lenin, the Maxim trilogy, and the exemplary film by the Vasiliev brothers on Chapaiev, spread official Party views. "The entire population is watching *Chapaiev*," stated *Pravda*. "It has become a political phenomenon. The reaction of the audience proves that the people have united with the Party" (*Pravda* 1934). In all these ways, Soviet literature, theater, and film during the thirties became the servants of party-politics and propaganda, fulfilling and sometimes more than fulfilling Stalin's requirements.

The Bolshevik attack on avant-garde painting began almost immediately after the 1917 revolution. Lenin conceived the task of painting as that of producing "monumental propaganda," and Lunacharski, as early as 1918, called for revitalizing "so-called old," realistic painting with a "new content." The Central Committee of the Bolshevik Party published a letter in 1920 that chastised "certain intellectual groupings [that] under the shield of *Proletkult* imposed [bourgeois values and artistic ideas] on the vanguard working class" (*Vestnik* 1920). In July 1922, *Pravda* harshly attacked the exhibition of "unfinished [paintings], which were more rough outlines than paintings" (*Pravda* 1922). Central government initiatives mobilized conservative artists, who had been pushed to the periphery of the arts by the earlier landslide victory of the avant-garde. These conservatives sided with the Party in urging realistic, understandable art based on traditional Russian genre-painting and in attacking cosmopolitan, sterile modernism.

In 1922, the *peredvizhniki* (itinerants), the traditionalist successors to nineteenth-century Russian realism, organized their forty-seventh exhibition, the first in many years. Of 396 exhibited paintings, 85 were presented by N. A. Kasatkin, a painter who had scarcely exhibited since 1907. This last relic of nineteenth-century Russian realist art won a prestigious state award and was celebrated as an exemplar. A group of conservative painters turned to daily socialist life for their themes, attacking modernism harshly. I. I. Brodsky, a member of the old Repin school, exhibited his monumental painting *The Festive Opening of the Congress of the Comintern* in 1924 and followed it with *Execution of the Twenty-Six Peoples' Commissar in Baku"* and *Lenin Speaks in the Putylov Work in May 1917*. The old school, with its epic realism, was thus rehabilitated and revitalized, and the road was opened for a successful artistic counter-revolution. Wassily Kandinsky and Marc Chagall moved to Munich and Paris, whereas other modern artists fought a rear-guard action by advocating that socialist topics merge with an accessible modernism and by rejecting, as J. Tugenhold phrased it, the "jump into the past." However, Kuzma S. Petrov-Volkin, Petr P. Konchalovski, Alexandr A. Dejneka, David P. Sterenberg, and many others who attempted to preserve modernist expression in paintings on revolutionary topics were harshly criticized as "incomprehensible expressionists" who produced "unfinished" paintings.

On March 11, 1931, a resolution on painting from the Central Committee of the Bolshevik Party clearly expressed the mandates for socialist realism. The socialist transformation of Russia and the processes of collectivizing and industrializing the countryside had to be presented in the early nineteenth-century style of classic Russian paintings. Representative Soviet exhibitions of the thirties presented examples of socialist realism according to various themes: the "Socialist Industrialization," "The Twenty-Years-Old Communist Youth Organization," "Stalin and the People of the Age of Stalin," "The Fifteen-Years-Old Red Army," and other exhibitions embodied the Party edicts on socialist realist painting. Thousands of painters joined enthusiastically in the movement, some to contribute to the socialist education of the people, others to achieve easy success and profitable careers. Some were scared and hoped that conforming would enable them to continue painting, whereas others religiously believed in the superiority of traditional Russian painting. The latter group painted the "socialist-genre paintings" that were ordered by the party-state. T. G. Gaponenko, transubstantiating the bloody process of forced collectivization of agriculture with its uprooted, deported, and murdered peasant millions, depicted a happy and enthusiastic countryside. His *Kolhoz Peasants Are Going to Work* in 1932 and *For Lunch to the Mothers* (1935) lie about a "happy new life." A. A. Plastov, who finished his studies before the revolution and remained outside artistic life during the 1910s and 1920s, emerged as a mature socialist realist in the second half of the thirties. His *Kolhoz Feast* was celebrated as the presentation of the "reality of the rich and happy kolhoz life" in 1937.

In a most paradoxical but nevertheless logical way, Stalin's archenemy, Hitler's Nazi Reich, organized strikingly similar exhibitions of didactic propaganda art, ordered thematically. "The Glory of Work" exhibition in Berlin in 1936 was dedicated to praising heroic industrial work on behalf of the fatherland. Peasant themes such as sowing, tilling, and harvesting were painted in an idealized traditional way, without showing any modern technology. *Völkisch*-Nazi national unity was depicted in Hans Schmitz-Wiedenbrück's *Workers, Peasants, and Soldiers,* a tryptic reminiscent of classic altar paintings. The center panel shows three soldiers, who represent the three main branches of the armed forces, the right-hand panel depicts two miners, and the left panel portrays two peasants leading a cow.

A similar parallel emerged in the "realism" of Nazi and Stalinist art. Stalin's most celebrated "court artist," A. M. Gerasimov, depicted Stalin standing in white uniform at the pulpit of the Sixteenth Party Congress in 1932–1933 while the entire Politburo sat in the presidium of the Congress. Gerasimov's main conceptual invention involved presenting Stalin at a speaker's pulpit, behind which towered a white marble statue of Lenin. The unambiguous visual message of this "natural background" to Stalin was "Stalin is the Lenin of today!" In 1937, Gerasimov exhibited his *J. V. Stalin and K. J. Voroshilov in the Kremlin*. "When the international situation became pregnant with the danger of war," Gerasimov explained, "I sought to symbolize the inseparable unity of our people and the undefeatable Red Army. In my painting our people is represented by Stalin, our Red Army by Voroshilov" (Nykoforov 1953, 140). Similar paintings—Jefanov's *Unforgettable Meeting*, Segal's *Leader, Teacher, and Friend*, and Magalashvili's *Stalin Talking with Peasants*— served party-state agitprop goals. In the end, this socialist realism obscured reality; it paraphrased and falsified history, transforming it into relentless propaganda about the "happy life" of the Soviet people and the greatness of the infallible demigod, Stalin.

Nazi art, too, was fond of large, didactic panel-paintings. A perfect example and a parallel to Gerasimov's huge panels is Georg Poppe's *The Führer at the Frankfurt Medical Association*, in which Hitler stands with a long gown romantically draped over his shoulders. The painting is filled with the most important motifs of the Reich. Behind the doctors in their white gowns stands an army of workers with shovels and swastika armbands. In the background, an *Autobahn* (highway) is being built on concrete pillars. In the right-hand corner, a young mother holding a child leans toward the Führer. In the opposite corner a peasant girl struts with a blond, determined-looking *Hitlerjugend* (Hitler Youth). Behind the Führer, uniformed figures representing the various armed services stand in close ranks. Such "heroic realism," so well-captured in Poppe's work, was the fundamental duty of art.

Sculpture served Stalinist "monumental propaganda" even more than painting. Statues of Lenin and Stalin, modeled on the monumental conservative traditionalism of S. D. Markuzov's works on the bank of the Moscow Canal in Moscow, towered in the main squares or main streets of every Soviet township. The robust bronze and stone figures of Lenin with raised arm pointing ahead and of Stalin in poses that embodied tranquillity, stability, and strength copied the mandatory heroic classicist pattern found in Muhina's *Worker and Kolhoz Woman*, whose symbolic double figures holding up the hammer and sickle graced the Soviet pavilion at the Paris World Exhibition.

As directed by state commissions, Soviet architecture avoided the formalist revolutionary avant-garde. The dreams of avant-garde architects remained only plans and blueprints; commissions were given instead to the old generation of traditionalists who sought to "preserve Russian architecture from the destructive influence of modernism . . . [and] constructivism." "The struggle against reactionary [meaning modernist] trends," announced M. Gopenko, the chronicler of socialist realist architecture, "culminated in 1930–1932 and ended with the total defeat of formalism" (Gopenko 1949).

The decisive turning point toward socialist realism in architecture occurred with the construction of the Palace of the Soviets. The guiding commission, chaired by Molotov, Stalin's right-hand man, declared that although it used modern technology, the building must nevertheless express a monumental simplicity according to the principles of classic architecture. Public buildings of the thirties—the Palace of the Council of Ministers, the Theater of the Red Army, the Hotel Moscow, and the Lenin Library—all were built in a neoclassical style using series of pillars.

Like Hitler, Stalin aspired to leave a rebuilt Moscow as his life legacy to Russia. A ten-year reconstruction plan designed to transform the sleepy, quasi-rural city into a modern, impressive capital was adopted in July 1935. Part of the newly constructed Moscow-Volga canal crossed the city and, together with the symbolic metro network, provided the backbone for the reconstruction. The main streets were broadened from a normal width of between six and fifteen meters to a grandiose width anywhere between twenty-four and seventy meters. Long avenues were built and eventually lined by five hundred seven-to-nine-story apartment buildings. Three main metro lines were built, under the personal direction of Kaganovich, another henchman of Stalin, who ambitiously sought to create not only an excellent public transportation system but also a symbol of the "construction of communism." The metro stations, with their lavish marble decorations, statues, and paintings, became "Stalinist cathedrals" for preaching the gospel of communism and the superiority of the regime. "Some of the stations have a traffic of one hundred thousand passengers per hour. What could be better to realize the concept of Lenin's 'monumental propaganda,'" reported the historian of the Stalinist arts, "than a metro station heralding the greatness, beauty, and happiness of the emerging epoch of communism" (*Architectura* 1949).

The straitjacket of mandatory socialist realism was forced even onto the most abstract artistic activity, music. During the 1920s, the young Soviet state was a center of modern music. The cultural tsar of early Bolshevik Russia, Lunacharski denied the existence of "class characteristics" in music and maintained that an "imperialist march" might equally serve revolutionaries, and that the "Marseillaise," with a changed text, might become a hymn to monarchy. "Music is music, not ideology," naively stated N. Roslavets, the chief editor of *Muzikalnaia Kultura* (Music culture). "If one crosses out the title of Beethoven's quartet Opus 132 . . . and renames it as 'Hymn of the Red Army' . . . it won't change the content of the quartet" (Schwarz 1988, 54). These men were dead wrong.

In April 1932, the Central Committee issued a resolution to found the Association of Soviet Composers. The association's new periodical, *Sovietskaia Muzika* (Soviet music), declared in its first issue "a continuous struggle against modernist music, which neglects the people and expresses the decline of bourgeois culture." Composers were forced to return to late-nineteenth-century Russia for models. The compulsory "jump into the past" was characterized by the use of folk songs and folk melodies, adapted to Soviet topics. Accidental factors, such as Stalin's personal aversion to "boring" symphonic and chamber music (as his daughter, Svetlana noted, his only recordings at home were of Russian, Georgian, and Ukrainian folk songs) led to the condemnation of some musical forms as antidemocratic. But his attraction to theater extended to opera and ballet, and these forms were declared the most important musical genres for delivering propaganda messages.

Besides dictating what general forms would be favored, Stalin personally criticized some works and praised others. In January 1936, accompanied by Molotov, he attended the performance of Ivan Dzherdzhinski's opera, the *Silent Don*. The next day, *Pravda* reported the conversation that Stalin and Molotov had with the creators of the opera and the leader's view on the "possibility of creating our own, classic Soviet opera," which would be emotionally inspiring, popular, and understandable by everyone (*Pravda* 1936). A few days later, Stalin heard Dmitry Shostakovich's *Lady Macbeth of Mtsensk* and found it too harsh, chaotic, and morbid—everything but his imagined ideal of Soviet opera. Stalin left the performance before its end. Shortly thereafter, *Pravda* published a devastating editorial titled "Chaos in Place of Music." It characterized Shostakovich's opera as "deliberately dissonant, chaotic . . . inarticulate cries. It is hard to follow this so-called music and absolutely impossible to memorize. . . . Passion is expressed by noise. . . . This music is the denial of the principle of the opera. . . . [It is a] tasteless petit-bourgeois formalist attempt to serve the perverse taste of the bourgeoisie . . . and sacrifice good music that could move the masses" (*Pravda* 1936b). Modern music was silenced.

"Understandable," political, propaganda opera and music gained ground. In Hrennikov's *In Tempest*, Lenin appeared for the first time as an operatic character, although his character did not sing. Moreover, when he spoke, even the orchestra was silenced. Several third-rate mass-operas engulfed the stages with heroic choruses and popular songs.

The greatest loss, however, was the music that composers did not compose, the ballet music never written by Shostakovich after the devastating critique of his *Golden Age* in 1936 and the works that Prokofiev might have produced had he not returned to the Soviet Union in 1933. Instead, Prokofiev obediently produced his "Stalin Cantata," based on folk songs of various Soviet peoples, to celebrate Stalin's sixtieth birthday. "Our fields were never so green, our life never so happy" roars the chorus, and Aksinia, the reward worker on her way to a Kremlin-reception, sings, "Thank you, Joseph Stalin!" Such degradation of music, literature, and arts is humiliating.

Several great works, such as Prokofiev's *Romeo and Juliet*, Shostakovich's Fifth Symphony, and other jewels by Shostakovich, Prokofiev, Kabalevski, and Miaskovski composed during the thirties, do not contradict the fact of the generally devastating impact of the cultural dictatorship. These outstanding works—as trees and flowers rooted in a small crack in a dead cliff nonetheless grow toward the sky—proved the strength of life and the immortality of great talent. Geniuses could still create masterpieces in an age of triumphant mediocrity, when all around them ambitious, talentless "court artists" rapidly rose to the top under the banner of "artistic democratism" and the communist cultural mission of educating a "new type of communist people."

Several talented composers, writers, and artists made severe compromises, following the dictated path because they were terrified by the fate of those who, having resisted, were silenced and even physically annihilated. Alexei Tolstoy once told a close friend, "I am flatly a cynic . . . [,] a mortal person who seeks to live. I will write what they order me to write" (Schwarz 1988, 129). Some, however, even in these circumstances, could realize their artistic goals and principles without major compromise and found the situation stimulating. Prokofiev, Gorki, Shostakovich, and others embraced the opportunity to speak to the masses of people and to discover a "new simplicity." Prokofiev found great satisfaction in composing good film music. But such exceptional accomplishments could not, in the end, counterbalance the devastating effects of the art policy dictated during the Stalinist era.

Conservative Academism and the Impact of Fascist Art

Centrally dictated and uniform artistic trends in fascist Italy, Nazi Germany, and the Bolshevik Soviet Union represented the most extreme versions of what one might call totalitarian art. The nations of Central and Eastern Europe did not accomplish such a total *Gleichschaltung* of literature, art, and music. Most of these regimes remained distinctively different from mass-mobilizing Nazism and Bolshevism: they did not even develop central ideas and complex policies on the arts. Nevertheless, censorship and political pressure brought about the banning or exclusion of everything "hostile" to fundamentalist nationalism. "Cosmopolitan" modernism, if tolerated, was forced to the periphery of artistic life. Governments and official institutions in these regimes gave artistic commissions only to representatives of conservative art trends whose work fueled nationalism and romanticized a heroic historical past.

Classicism and conservative, realist "academism" engulfed the entire region. In some cases, this development was assisted by the passing of an entire generation of artists. How symbolic it was in 1918 when the Habsburg Empire collapsed and most of the leading personalities of prewar Austrian art who had made Vienna a world cultural center—Otto Wagner, Gustav Klimt, and Egon Schiele—also passed away.

Progressive scholars, philosophers, and avant-garde artists left the countries of national fundamentalism and counterrevolutionary conservatism. The "Sunday Circle" of prewar Budapest with world-class social scientists such as Karl Mannheim, Arnold Hauser, and George Lukács, and internationally renowned avant-garde artists such as László Moholy-Nagy, Marcel Breuer and many others left Hungary. Lajos Kassák, the leading Hungarian avant-garde writer-painter-editor stated, "With the emigration of *MA* [(Today), an avant-garde journal,] . . . the continuity of the avant-garde ceased to exist in Hungary. The few . . . who remained, and others [who] joined . . . [could] not establish a united movement. . . . Academism regained its hegemony" (Kassák 1972, 283). The "Vienna Circle," a famous group of scientists and philosophers such as Neurath, Schlick, Carnap, and Hahn, who were in close contact with Ludwig Wittgenstein and had developed the school of positivist logic, attempted to work in interwar Austria but were paralyzed during the thirties. Schlick was shot dead by a right-wing student at the university of Vienna, and Carnap, Feigl, Neurath, and Frank left the country. Authoritarian regimes decimated scholarship and art that were not ready to serve or acted against their political interests.

In its desperate situation, Austria "lost not only a war and the bulk of its former territories," as Wieland Schmied notes, "but also its self-esteem" (Schmied 1983, 685). Waves of emigration decimated the artistic and literary life of the country between 1918 and 1938: Wolfgang Paalen, Rudolf Wacker, Johannes Itten, Albin Egger-Lienz, Emmanuel Fohn, Wilhelm Thöny, Oscar Kokoschka, Fritz Wotruba, Gerhart Frankl, Georg Merkel, and Anton Kolig left for France, Germany, Spain, Switzerland, and Britain. As Hans Tietze remarked in 1921, "Austria became hermetically insulated from any kind of fresh breeze" (Schmied 1983, 686).

A triumphant conservative academism filled the vacuum left by mass emigration. In the overheated political atmosphere of poverty, revolutions, counterrevolutions, political retaliations, rising racism, and war preparation, large groups of intellectuals and artists attempted to escape by "cultivating their own garden." The "spiritual pressure is so strong," Eva Körner noted, "that painters take refuge in the artificial safe heaven of classicism" (Körner 1963, 15). One could even speak about a kind of "internal emigration"—of artists turning inward, attempting to create an internal balance and peace. The Hungarian József Egry, who displayed obvious social commitment in his 1912 painting of a dock worker as the expression of a search for a new social order, dramatically changed his subject after 1919, becoming a painter of Lake Balaton's many moods, colors, and special lighting. The artist escaped to the shores of the lake and to a quiet peasant society, withdrew from the political reality of his nation, and created his own, personal, liberated inner world. As a critic of the landscapes by István Szönyi stated in the mid-thirties, "The modern Hungarian landscape actually depicts an internal scenery. . . . They are floating in the soul. . . . What is the cause of such introspection, such withdrawal from reality?" (Bálint 1961, 261–62). In the new political situation of strengthened authoritarianism, classicism thus sometimes reflected an escape from reality and an "emigration to the internal landscapes of the soul."

Several other forms of artistic escapism characterized the 1930s. In 1934, in the midst of the depression, 70 percent of Polish feature films were "cheap comedies and farces," replete with songs and music and a few excellent actors such as Adolf Dymsza. Also popular were melodramas such as *The Leper* (second version in 1936) and *Medicine Man* (1937), which depicts love between lower-class women and upper-class men (Janicki 1985). Three-quarters of the 132 movies produced in Hungary between 1931 and 1938 were comedies with music and happy endings. *Meseautó* (Dream car), for example, illustrates the corporative principle by depicting love and eventual marriage between a company director and his secretary.

Well-written Hungarian comedies and light "boulevard plays" entertained the middle class, which was scared and sought to forget its troubles. These comedies were popular not only in the Budapest theaters but also in fascist Italy. In "answer to the challenge and offensive of the Hungarian theater," Italian playwrights such as Aldo de Benedetto wrote so-called white-telephone plays—comedies that frequently used a white telephone, the symbol of middle-class modernity (Pedulla 1994, 219–20).

Operetta had its second blossoming in Vienna and Budapest. Staged works by the Hungarians Ferenc Lehár, Pál Ábrahám, Imre Kálmán, and Szabolcs Fényes—the *Ejféli Tangó* (Midnight tango), *Hotel Kikelet* (Hotel dawn), *Lila Akác* (Lilac acacia)—and operetta movies by Austrians—*Walzerkrieg* (Waltz war) and *Der Kongress Tanzt* (The congress dances)—offered images of a happy, isolated dreamworld (Bender and Schorske 1994). In *The Operatta*, a play written after this period, the Polish playwright Witold Gombrowicz speaks of "the monumental daftness" of operetta and the operetta world in contrast to the drama of reality. But to the many writers, composers, and artists, and to the majority of the frustrated and scared public, operetta offered a much-desired escape from the frightening reality of the thirties.

The logic of dictatorship and the requirements of authoritarian governments, although they could not and even did not want to completely control the cultural sphere, led to the emergence and spread of several typical features of fascist art and literature throughout Central and Eastern Europe. Authoritarian governments discovered means to initiate and encourage preferred conservative art trends: art critiques, state-organized exhibitions, official art journals, government-run propaganda papers, and official rhetoric created an atmosphere in which avant-garde artists were stifled. Newly founded state institutions were effective instruments for influencing literature and art. An excellent example was the foundation of the official *Staatspreisen für Literatur, Musik, und bildende Kunst* (State Award for Literature, Music, and Fine Arts) in authoritarian Austria in the mid-thirties. The award was given to writers and artists who, according to the government-appointed committee's evaluation, successfully propagated the *Österreichische Idee*, Austrian Christian nationalism, and represented the "durable values . . . of the *deutschösterreichisch* [Austrian-German] culture . . . in form and content" (Aspetsberger 1980, 3). The *Bundeskulturrat* (Federal Cultural Council), an appointed committee of thirty to forty members who were drawn from the Catholic Church, various religious organizations, and established writers and artists, gained the right to define principles and values for state-assisted literature and arts. The awarded writers—who included Karl Heinrich Waggerl, Erich August Mayer, and Johannes Freumbichler—represented the required values. The *Jahr des Herrn* (Year of the Lord), a novel on peasant life that was Waggerl's principle work, was a *Heimatroman* (fatherland novel) on the unspoiled fatherland and the law of nature and presented a "liturgy of the peasant life" (Bayr 1948). In Waggerl's words, "The peasant and the land, his house and courtyard together, [are] a single unit of life in the hands of God . . . in its undisturbed order" (Gutwenger 1967, 36, 38–39). Heinz Friedrich compares Waggerl to the Norwegian Knut Hamsun as his "brother in soul from the Alps." The myth and reality of the countryside and peasant life described in the realistic and valuable writings of Waggerl fit nicely with the ideals of the regime because "the myth of blood and land was a state religion" in which peasants were treated as symbols of "healthy blood" and an unspoiled race (Friedrich 1967, 24, 28–29).

Josef Wenter's *Im heiligen Land Tirol* (In the holy land Tyrol) was an even more pointed landmark in the genre of "holy fatherland" novels. The last sentences of this novel state with pathos-steeped sentimentalism that "this holy land is a jewel in the holy empire of the German nation, the thousand-year-old 'Ostmark': Austria" (Wenter 1937, 80). In emphasizing the land, this genre of Austrian literature showed a striking parallel with a typical trend in Nazi art. Landscapes were depicted in 40 percent of the paintings in the Munich Nazi showcase exhibition of 1937, which attempted to set patterns for required topics and styles, and several thematic exhibitions were organized to inspire the painting of pictures of the fatherland: "The Forest" in Berlin in 1937; "Pictures of the Homeland" in Oberhausen in 1938; and "German Peasant-German Landscape" in 1938. Landscape, with its simple symbolism, represented the soil and *Heimat* (home), the essentials of the Nazi fatherland. Both pro-Hitler and anti-Nazi, "Dollfussist" Austrian art copied this pattern.

The *Österreichische Idee* was propagated in the most direct and didactic way in a work by Leopold Andrian, in which four men discuss ideological questions and advocate the official ideology of Austrian Christian authoritarian nationalism. Franz, the twenty-eight-year-old *Heimwehr* officer, explains that Austria is the real representative of German culture. "More than half of the German Reich today belonged to Slavs and barbarians whereas Austria was a land of German culture." He also speaks about "the spring of a new age . . . [when the] old and corrupt institutions of the nineteenth century such as democratic parliamentarism" disappear and new forms are created. Erwin, the fifty-five-year-old poet, stresses the uniqueness and superiority of the "Austrian language" and its special rhythm and melody, whereas Gabriel, the forty-nine-year-old Jesuit priest, announces that "our Austria, Austria in 1935, has its own culture, or at least the opportunity to develop it." The discourse directly advocates an "independent Austrian state," the prerequisite for the survival of *Österreichertum*, the Austrian nation, urging against the idea of *Anschluss* and for the *Österreichische Idee* associated with chancellors Dollfuss and Schuschnigg (Adrian 1937, 20, 25, 47–48, 401).

A group of racist writers and Nazi sympathizers—Josef G. Wenter, Karl H. Strobl, Mirko Jelusich, and many others—turned to direct political propaganda. Jelusich, who published an article in the Austrian Nazi paper *Die Braune Woche* (The brown week) with the title "Mein Weg zu Hitler" (My path to Hitler) on June 17, 1933, became a bestselling writer with his novels *Caesar* (1929) and *Cromwell* (1933). According to his statement in an interview, both books express an "idea of the present. . . . I embodied in the figures of Caesar and Cromwell strength, will, genius, and all that I admire in the Führer" (Sachslehner 1985, 69). The officially recognized writers served the goal of "spiritual transformation . . . a radical change in one's . . . view of the world: 'Literature has set all this in motion. . . . The statesman has completed the venture'" (Amann 1991, 194). Small wonder that the "Jewish Vienna literature" by Schnitzler, Hofmannsthal, Werfel, Zweig, and Kraus was radically eliminated and replaced by propagandist historical novels, World War I literature, and the so-called Blood and Soil nationalist writings.

Governments helped to popularize literature and art forms that served their political goals and interests and strengthened their leading ideology. One of the most important vehicles for accomplishing official goals was the erection of public monuments. All major commissions were given to conservative artists, and government requirements virtually imposed classicist academism on sculptors. "Monuments," states Jan Stanislaw Wojciechowski, speaking of the postwar Polish experience, "were an instrument of the state authorities' cultural policy" (Wojciechowski 1984, 75). Wojciechowski's statement is equally valid for the Central and Eastern European region in general. The fascist cult of heroic-monumental memorials provided a model, setting the pattern with Zocchi's robust soldier figure in Sienna (1923) and his romantic soldier-hero in a flying gown in Modena (1925), Pancera's and Guerrisi's multifigured baroque-monumentalist war-monuments of Catanzaro and Monza (1926, 1932), and Arturo Dazzi's statue of the *Era fascista* (The fascist era) in Brescia (1932), with its young nude male figure, peering self-confidently into the future with a clenched fist that symbolized strength and will (Cresti 1986). It should be added that monuments and sculptures were also regarded as the most important art forms by Hitler. Monumentality, greatness, power, and eternity: the didactic expression of these ideals is seen in Arno Brecker's vacuous bronze athletes, allegories of the Party and the *Wehrmacht* that stood in the courtyard of the Reich Chancellery. The sculptures for the chancellor's new palace were created in Joseph Thorak's more-than-fifty-feet-high studio, a personal gift from Hitler, who often dropped in to visit his favorite artist, refresh himself, and talk of the importance of accessibility in art.

Hundreds and thousands of statues and war memorials were erected in the main squares and streets of Bucharest, Warsaw, Sofia, Belgrade, and Budapest. In one of the main squares of Budapest, a series of heroic-romantic allegorical sculptures symbolized the territories that were "stolen" by the Trianon peace treaty. Kisfaludy-Strobl's *North*, and Sidló's *West* equally served nationalist propaganda goals, expressing their messages in the most didactic terms. The "heroic realism" of the young, dying, wounded men—symbols of the lost territories and of the strong tribal solders ready to defend and revenge—reflected a romanticized historicism and a mobilizing nationalist idea. Tranquil heroes, strong and enthusiastic fighters, all the numberless public monuments of these regimes displayed the most conservative academic style.

The style espoused by the authoritative regimes was even more characteristically expressed by newly erected public buildings. The *Foro Mussolini* (Mussolini Square), the fascist architecture of public buildings and reconstructed squares, the classicist-monumentalist buildings of Piacentini, Fosci, and Michelucci, and the numberless public buildings of fascist Italy provided a model for expressing greatness and modernization, an attractive pattern to signal and symbolize the mission of the regimes (Cresti 1986, 52–53, 56–57). Nationalist authoritarian regimes in the newly established independent states of the region, with their explicit program of national revival and conservative-modernization goals, demanded a visible and educative form of self-expression. John Kenneth Galbraith speaks about three types of economic modernization in the post–World War II historical context. Among them is "symbolic modernization . . . [, which] is designed to give the developing country the aspect, though not necessarily the substance, of development. There are certain things the modern state must have. Any claim to nationhood requires . . . a capital with pavement, some impressive buildings of state. . . . Effective national leaders have always known the importance of the concrete and visible expressions of national being" (Galbraith 1964, 4).

Symbolic modernization that aimed at expressing the greatness of a country and its regime inspired the copying of "imperial" style, the expressions of grandeur exhibited by Nazi-fascist architecture. The connection in some cases was direct: Gherardo Bosio's plans for the center of Tirana, with a monumentalist Scanderbeg square, the *Casa del fascio* (House of Fascio), and cold fascist neoclassicist buildings around the planned Littorio Square brought fascist architecture to vassal-occupied Albania. Bosio also prepared plans for the *Casa degl' Italiani* (House of Italy), a prototype of "Mussolinist" architecture for Bucharest.

Tsar Boris's attempt to plant symbols of his dictatorial modernization drive in backward Bulgaria can be seen in the spread of classicist-monumentalist architecture. The new post office buildings in Varna, Rusz, and Plovdiv (1929 and 1930), the neoclassical facade with a row of columns of *Sdebnata* palace in Sofia (1936), the Italian-style agricultural faculty (1928) and military academy (1937) in Sofia, the *Sofijskata Popularnaja Banka* (People's Bank of Sofia) (1938), Ovcharov's and

Popov's hospital buildings in Sofia and Plovdiv (1935 and 1937 respectively), the new ministerial buildings built by Ovcharov and Zagorski in Sofia (1936–1937), and Zlatev's and Koev's Institute of Epidemiology and Microbiology (1932) are excellent examples of the use of classicist-monumentalist public buildings as a form of symbolic modernization in a poor country (*Kratka* 1965, 500–47). Another poor Balkan state, Yugoslavia, followed the same path: Dimitrije Leko's Ministry of Social Policy in Belgrade (1932–1934) is an example (*Srbska* 1973, 16). The same style also appeared in Poland. Although most of interwar Polish architecture followed a more modern trend, "after 1918," notes Brian Knox, "the official style became the sort of stripped classical all too familiar elsewhere, Piłsudski Populist" (Knox 1971, 148). Kazimierz Skorewicz's parliament building (1925) and Bohdan Pniewski's court building (1935) exhibited this phenomenon.

Belated nationalist romanticism and heroic realism became the leading artistic trends in the region. An outstanding and typical example is contained in the work of the Bulgarian painter Emanuil Rakarov, whose postwar political messages were expressed between 1918 and 1921 on powerful posters against poverty and war. The most telling depictions were a dragon-slaying worker—the symbol of struggle against exploitative speculators—and a pietá-like mother crying over her son killed in the war. During the 1930s, however, Rakarov turned to heroic national topics, creating symbolic historic tableaus on the birth of the Bulgarian nation, the adoption of Christianity, and the struggle against the Turks. In his romantically conceived paintings of the years 1935 to 1938, weather-beaten national heroes search for their slain comrades and battle with the Turkish besiegers, assaulting the enemy bastions under skies laden with dark clouds. Three paintings—depicting the coronation of 1204, the Cyrill and Method, and the baptizing of Boris I, the warrior who rejects paganism with the missionary looming tall behind him—clearly exemplify the artistic fashions of the age.

The style of photographic representation associated with romantic nationalism was also powerfully served by Bulgarian films. Romantic-heroic realism was the leading genre in films such as Vasil Gendov's *The Mutiny of the Prisoners* (1933) and Alexandr Vazov's *Hill* (1936), which portray the struggle for independence against the Turks.

Historical movies were also commonly produced by the interwar Polish film industry. Ryszard Ordynski's *The Men from the Pawiak Prison* (1931) and Jósef Lejtes's *Hurricane* (1928), *Young Forest* (1934), and *Kosciuszko at Raclawice* (1937) recalled heroic battles and gave a dramatic account of famous episodes from late-eighteenth-century to early-twentieth-century anti-Russian national struggles. Historical movies such as *Barbara Rodziwillowna* (1936), set in the sixteenth century, advocated strong central power.

The authoritative regimes and the atmosphere of the thirties in Central and Eastern Europe revitalized nineteenth-century genre painting and arts. What became dominant was far from new, representing instead the continuity of the obsolete. Nothing expressed it better than the Austrian *Lukasbund* (Lukas Society), which was established in 1809 by six young painters in Vienna. Silently and totally forgotten, six generations of such painters worked in an unchanged style, even during the years of dramatic changes and rotating trends of avant-garde. The Nazarenes, as they were later called, slavishly followed the *Altdeutsch* (Old-German) painters' guilds to create a "new-German religious-patriotic" trend. Their ideals were Raphael and Albrecht Dürer and late-medieval Christian painting, which they copied unchanged for a century-and-a-half. A timeless religious-national moral was expressed by the continuity of their "eternal" topics and style. The authoritarian Austrian government, expressing its artistic ideal, decorated the last Nazarene, Ludwig Ritter zum Thurn und Goldenstein, with the Knight's Cross, First Class in 1935.

After a short Cubist experiment in the first half of the 1920s, Estonian art returned to realism and neoclassicism in the late twenties. The Cubist group disintegrated, and "some of its members retreated from the principles adopted previously, recurring to a more natural manner" (*State* 1982, 42). Classicism, sometimes with remnants of French postimpressionism or German expressionism, became dominant in the thirties.

Several traditionalist artists provided a link between late-nineteenth-century and interwar arts (Korsakaite, Latse, and Solomykova 1981). Nikolai Triik represented the "original character of national art . . . , themes of folklore and ancient legends." Together with Raud and Laikmaa, he "was attracted by national romanticism" (*State* 1982, 30). After his start as a national-romantic painter, Triik was highly influenced by *sezession* and German expressionism. In the late twenties and during the thirties, however, his portraits of Hugo Randsepal (1932), Voldemar Evaldi (1935), and Jaen Kärner (1938) exhibited a return to conservative realist painting, and he directed the painting studio "Pallas" along this line from 1921 until 1940 (Pihlak 1985, 56, 58–59, 67). Triik's contemporary, Adamson-Eric, consistently painted traditional realist still lifes and summer landscapes during the thirties. Kaarel Liimand's *Autumn* (1934),

Andrus Johani's *In the Kitchen* (1935), Eric Haamer's *Eel Fishers* (1934), Voldemar Mellik's classic granite sculpture, and Ferdi Sannamees's bronze portraits and romantic marble sculptures of the thirties illustrate this turn toward traditional academism in Estonia (Narkissos 1936; Akastus 1930; *Estonian Museum* 1982). It is small wonder that several conservative-classicist Estonian artists easily adjusted to the strict requirements of Soviet socialist realism after the occupation of the country in the 1940s. Adamson-Eric's and Sannamees's works showed no change at all after 1940 (Paas 1974, 20–42, 44–56).

In Poland and Romania, where avant-garde flourished in the twenties and continued to exist, although weakened, in the thirties, a general turning back to conservative realism appeared by the late twenties and early thirties. Artistic groups such as *Rytm* (Rhythm), *Jednoróg* (Unicorn), and *Bractwo sw. Lukasza* (The guild of St. Lucas) were highly influenced by the German *Neue Sachlichkeit*, the Italian *pittura metafisica* (metaphysical painting), and by French neoclassicism. The periodical *Arkady* became a forum for realist and colorist trends between 1935 and 1939.

As in most of the other countries, a relatively older but still active and vigorous generation stepped to the forefront in Romania to reinvent connections between the nineteenth and the twentieth centuries. One of them was Demetrescu Mirea, who died in 1934 and remained "faithful to ancient formulae and recipes" (Oprescu 1935, 44). Camil Ressu's *Nude* turned back to David's classicism, whereas Jean Alexandru Steriadi's *The Whitewashers* reflected the traditions of nineteenth-century genre painting. Returned classicist realism often preserved elements of turn-of-the-century modernism, a touch of impressionism and colorism.

In returning to the past, realist propaganda wall painting played a rather important role. In St. Georges Church in Craiova, the artist Eustaţiu Stoenescu turned back to the tradition of icon painting, and the walls of the Bucharest Academy of Commerce were painted by Cecilia Cuţescu-Storck in a series of didactic stories. "Abstract art, which appeals rather to the intelligentsia . . . has found fewer disciples in our country," noted the art historian in the mid-thirties, "fewer art lovers able to understand it and fewer artists to practice it" (Oprescu 1935, 52). Romanian architecture of the period not only embodied modernist trends in modern villas at the seashore and rich family houses in Bucharest but also offered a kind of national romanticism, a "Romanian style." Meanwhile, fascist-type neoclassicist monumentalism, in buildings such as the Dalles Foundation by Horia Teodoru, appeared.

Eclecticism and the coexistence of semimodernist and traditional trends also characterized Albanian arts of the thirties. Abdurrahim Buza's portraits and still lifes combined realism with special modern light-and-color effects, but the painters Spiro Xega and Zef Kolombi represented classic nineteenth-century romantic realism.

The retreat of the avant-garde and the return to classicist academism with the associated spread of heroic and monumental romantic realism had several features in common with totalitarian arts. In cases where the fascist art trend was directly transplanted, the connection was quite direct. For example, the Hungarian government established an art academy in Rome and a scholarship to send talented young artists to Mussolini's Italy, one of the birthplaces of European art but, more importantly, the birthplace of fascist *Novecento*. This institution led to the "School of Rome," the leading Hungarian art trend of the thirties, which was a version of Italian *Novecento*. The newly established artistic order in place of the "aesthetic chaos" of the avant-garde attracted many previously avant-garde artists to the camp of official art.

Hungarian *Novecento* was the result of a dual process. On the one hand, it emerged from a seemingly spontaneous artistic movement in the twenties, but, on the other hand, it was fostered by the official cultural policy and patronage of the government. The Hungarian Academy in Rome and its grant system were the main vehicles for transplanting fascist *Novecento* to Hungary. As Tibor Gerevich, the director of the institution, stated enthusiastically in 1932, young Hungarian artists "can not only live among the great artistic remnants of the past, . . . but also inhale the air of a new Italy and its healthy aesthetic trend." *Novecento*, added Gerevich, "is the newest, most up to date and healthy modern trend of European art. . . . This new European modernity is represented by the Hungarian artists in Rome. . . . They are the followers of the same Zeitgeist and style; they are the real avant-garde of the Hungarian art today. Their merit is to safeguard Hungarian arts from the anarchy of Paris. Instead of looking to Montparnasse, they look to Rome and to the cupola of St. Peter's Basilica" (Gerevich 1932, 238–40). Gerevich invited a few talented young artists—Vilmos Aba-Novák, István Szönyi, and Károly Patkó—to the Hungarian Academy in Rome in 1928 because their high-quality classicist paintings displayed genuine similarities with the Italian *Novecento*. Aba-Novák expressed their artistic credo: "A healthy, extremely constructive, cocaine-free art" must be created "to eradicate the sham-modernism of the isms. . . . We have to work for the collectivity . . . [,] and the canvasses of the future are the walls" (Németh 1977, 72). This credo, indeed, meshed with official cultural policy, which declared, "Our heroic epoch requires that the walls of our public buildings be covered by 'textual decorations' of a new message . . . serving the higher, holy vocation of 'educating the nation'" (Németh 1977, 70).

The best representatives of the School of Rome, like those of the first waves of Italian *Novecento*, returned to figurative art by absorbing elements from the *Neue Sachlichkeit*, a trend that rejected avant-garde and yet incorporated many of its achievements. "Modern simplification, mixed with a kind of renaissance preciseness led to the general use of a visual quotation mark and an ambiguity in the works of the best representatives of the school" (Szücs 1987, 12). Hungarian *Novecento*, however, unlike its Italian model, was closely linked to the Catholic Church, the most important patron and customer of the School of Rome. Vilmos Aba-Novák's monumental historic and religious tableaus in the St. Demetrius Chapel in Szeged (1931), the Gate of the Heroes of Szeged (1936), and, most of all, the frescoes of the Stephen Mausoleum in Székesfehérvár and of the church of Városmajor in Budapest (1938–1939) most closely resemble the Italo-German trends of the thirties. Pál C. Molnár's *Credo*, dedicated to the humiliation of Hungary in the Treaty of Trianon, Pál Pátzay's *Saint Stephen*, which portrays the first Christian king of Hungary, and most of the works of the first generation of the School of Rome contained didactic political-religious content.

During the thirties, the Hungarian School of Rome became extraordinarily successful in Italy. Some 85 percent of the prizes awarded to foreigners at the Venice Biennial in 1930 went to Hungarian *Novecento* artists. One of the works of Aba-Novák, *The Little Inn*, was bought by Mussolini. In 1931, the same artist won the Gold Medal at the international ecclesiastical art exhibition in Padua.

During the second half of the decade, the second generation of the School of Rome dropped the modernist touch that had characterized the first wave of the Hungarian *Novecento* and shifted more toward Nazi artistic ideals. The 1936 exhibition of the School of Rome and the 1937 sculpture exhibition "Art of Modern Monumentality" in Budapest offered typical elements drawn from the iconographical arsenal of Nazi-fascist art. Károly Antal's and Zoltán Borbereki-Kovács's works, and the work of others, expressed monumentality, heroic will, racial power, and the cult of the saint kings in a historicized romantic manner strongly related to totalitarian art. Common topics such as *Hungarian Agriculture* by Jenö Medvecky (1937), *Hungarian Industry* by Béla Kontuly

(1936–1937), and *Miklós Horthy Leads the Soldiers* by Vilmos Aba-Novák (1934) exhibit marked parallels with German and Italian official art forms.

Jenö Medvecky's *Three Figures* (1929), nudes pointedly lacking any expression of eroticism, represents in cold classical terms the cult of the healthy body. It could have been a precursor of Nazi nude paintings. Femininity and manly strength were popular subjects of Nazi art: at the 1937 exhibition, 16 percent of the paintings illustrated such themes. A special exhibition entitled "The Wife and the Mother" was also organized. The nude, presented in classical form as healthy, nonerotic beauty, had its own important message. As F. A. Kauffman expresses in his essay *"Die Neue Deutsche Malerei"* (The new German painting) in 1941, "In nudes, the artist tries to show the healthy physical being, the biological value of the individual as a precondition of all folkish and spiritual rebirth. He concentrates on the body as nature wanted it, on perfect forms . . . on a modern and therefore palpably athletic classical ideal. . . . Our country is particularly intent on cultivating such happiness where it promises to enhance the performance of men and women in their basic duties of combat and fertility" (Hinz 1979, 78–79). The objective of such painting was highly practical. The organizers of the exhibition "The Family in Painting" called for works illustrating the "genetically sound family with a lot of children." And artists responded to this call. Erich Erler combined favorite Nazi themes in his *Blood and Soil*, where the figure of a nursing mother is placed in front of peasants, with the soil in the background. Heymann's painting *In Good Hands* is a perfect example of combining mandatory motifs: the background shows Mother Earth, and in the foreground, a mother stares intently into the distance, surrounded by her three small children; she unbuttons her blouse to nurse the smallest one.

As has been shown, Nazi art trends did not stop at the borders of Germany. The powerful forces of traditionalism—in the form of revivals of classicism, academism, and the creation of various versions of "historic monumentalism" and *Novecento*—forced "unnational," "cosmopolitan," "decadent" art out of the picture in most Central and Eastern European countries. Didactic, nationalist, propaganda art, with its heroic historical message, became directly or indirectly the servant of right-wing extremism and war preparation. Full steam ahead, the train of history barreled toward the bloodiest cataclysm in modern time.

Conclusion

The main historical, political, and economic processes in interwar Central and Eastern Europe were the elimination of the parliamentary system, the triumph of nationalist authoritarian regimes, the economic nationalism these regimes generated, extreme xenophobia, territorial revisionism, and national conflicts. Most of the area was incorporated into Hitler's large-space economy, the *Grossraumwirtschaft*, in the 1930s; this was the "first battle" of World War II—a battle that Hitler won before the war even started. All these processes paved the way for right-wing success and Nazi victory in Central and Eastern Europe. These dramatic events culminated during World War II, when the region was either occupied by Hitler or fell under the rule of his local fascist allies. The rebellion of the region's nations, which began in the peripheries of the Ottoman and the Habsburg empires and in multinational Russia, turned out to be a trap and, after a quarter of a century, shifted Central and Eastern Europe to the periphery of an emerging Nazi German Reich.

As a result of successful diplomatic preparation, assisted by the counterproductive appeasement policy of Chamberlain's Britain and Daladier's France, Hitler won the "second battle" of World War II in 1938–1939 by peacefully defeating two Central European countries of major importance. On March 14, 1938, Hitler marched into Austria and was welcomed by a euphoric crowd in Vienna. A Nazi-held referendum ensured a 99.75 percent Austrian majority for the *Anschluss*, the union with Germany. On October 1, 1938, the *Wehrmacht* entered the Sudetenland, the German-inhabited northwestern part of Czechoslovakia that was sacrificed by the Western powers to satisfy Hitler's craving for uniting all the Germans outside the Reich with the fatherland. The great robber baron mobilized small pirates who had no intention of staying passively on the sidelines: the Polish ruling military junta exploited the opportunity and occupied the Teschen (Czieszyn) area; Horthy was able to realize his twenty-year-old dream of revising the Trianon Treaty and regaining Hungary's lost territories and, as a first step, was happy to accept Hitler's offer to occupy the southern strip of Felvidék, the mostly Hungarian-inhabited southern part of Slovakia. On March 15, 1939, the Nazi-German military steamroller continued its *Drang nach Osten*, the expansion to the East: it occupied the Czech lands and made them a German "protectorate," while the one-million-strong Czechoslovak army watched passively and the Western powers remained neutral. Hitler's right-wing, populist, fascist Slovak allies, led by Father Tiso, gained their "independence" from the Führer and established their Slovak puppet state. The Nazi war-machinery continued to move: on March 23, Hitler occupied the Memel region of Lithuania and demanded Gdansk (Danzig) and the Danzig corridor from Poland.

In another skillful diplomatic maneuver, which took advantage of the lack of agreement between the Western powers and the Soviet Union, Hitler offered and signed a nonaggression pact with Stalin. In its secret clause, the pact outlined German and Russian spheres of influence in eastern areas of Central and Eastern Europe. Granting the eastern part of Poland, the entire Baltic region, Finland, and Bessarabia to Stalin, Hitler gained a free hand to incorporate Poland. A week after having signed the Molotov-Ribbentropp pact in Moscow, on September 1, 1939, at 4:45 A.M., Nazi troops, fifteen hundred airplanes, nine tank divisions, and forty-nine motorized infantry divisions launched a deadly attack against Poland. The single Polish tank brigade and twelve cavalry divisions resisted heroically but were easily defeated. In October, Hitler declared Poland a protectorate of the Reich. Stalin also cashed his check: on September 17, the Red Army occupied eastern Poland and, in mid-June 1940, the entire Baltic region. In two weeks, Bessarabia and northern Bukovina were incorporated into the Soviet Union.

The Nazi attack against Poland met with a firm Western response. On the basis of a British and French guarantee made to Poland in March 1939, Britain and France declared war against Germany on September 3, 1939. The war engulfed Europe. Yet Hitler's triumphant advance continued in Central and Eastern Europe. As a consequence, the extreme

Right gained further ground in Romania and Hungary. After it lost Bessarabia and northern Bukovina, the royal dictatorship of Romania was pushed into the corner by Hitler's Second Vienna Award, which cut Transylvania in half and gave its northern part back to Hungary. King Carol abdicated, and, together with the fascist Iron Guard, General Ion Antonescu seized power on September 4, 1940. Some seven hundred thousand German troops were allowed into Romania.

The same Second Vienna Award—a reoccupation of pre–World War I territories—strengthened the ultra-nationalist and extreme Right in Hungary. In November, Hungary, Romania, and Slovakia joined the aggressive fascist German-Italian-Japanese Tripartite Pact. In a few months, Bulgaria joined the pact. Yugoslavia's regent Prince Paul and his pro-German government urgently followed the pattern and signed the agreement as well, but in two days a military coup removed them. Hitler then changed his strategy and, on April 6, 1941, attacked Yugoslavia with the collaboration of Hungary. According to the Czechoslovak blueprint, the Nazi's separatist, fascist, Croatian, Ustasha ally was allowed to declare the "independence" of Croatia (enlarged with Bosnia-Herzegovina) on April 10, 1941. Albania was occupied by Mussolini in 1939. Greece, after the fiasco of Mussolini's independent military action, capitulated in April 1941—only a few weeks after it was attacked by Germany, with Bulgarian collaboration.

Beginning in December 1940 and continuing throughout the months of the German conquest of the Balkans, preparations were made for an attack on the Soviet Union. On June 22, 1941, General von Brauchitsch's 140 divisions launched an undeclared war against the Soviet Union. The Baltic countries and most of the European part of the Soviet Union were quickly conquered, and German forces reached the suburbs of Moscow by winter. By the end of the year, Central and Eastern Europe was virtually under Nazi-fascist control. The euphoric post–World War I national revolutions of the nations of the region met their Waterloo. The Czech lands, Poland, the Baltic region, the Serbian part of Yugoslavia, and Albania were now all occupied and governed by Nazi military administration.

The Nazis set up local quisling administrations in the occupied countries. Motivated by personal ambition, fascist ideas, belief in an Axis victory, and even a desire to assist the survival of their occupied nation, various collaborators aided the German authorities. In Serbia, General Milan Nedić formed a "national salvation" government and its military force, the Serbian State Guard. The Czech Protectorate's quisling authority worked under President Emil Hacha. The Czech cabinet and ministries, the government-militia, and the collaborating political organization of *Narodní Sourucenství* (National Cooperation) subserviently assisted their Nazi occupiers. In Italian-occupied Albania, enlarged by Kosovo and the western part of Macedonia, the collaborating government was led by Shevket Vrlaci and the military force of Balli Kombetar, and the Regency Council handled internal affairs during the German occupation after 1943. Under the Nazi *Reichskommissariat Ostland* (Reich's Commission for the Eastern Territories), which governed the occupied Baltic countries and Beloruss, various Baltic puppet governments (the so-called directorates) played a role in local administrations. The Baltic countries were slated to be incorporated into the Reich, as were Austria, western Poland, the Sudetenland, Slovenia, and a number of other territories. Alfred Rosenberg suggested to Hitler in 1941 that the suitable elements among the population must be assimilated, and the undesirable elements exterminated. Even this latter goal was assisted by Lithuanian collaborators, who launched deadly pogroms against the Jews. Collaborators assisted in governing the Italian puppet state of "independent" Montenegro. Poland was the only occupied country where a collaborating local government was not established; only a Polish "advisory committee" existed, headed by Count Roneker. The German-controlled, twenty-five-thousand-man-strong Polish police force and several civil and political organizations recruited among former German minorities, who faithfully served Nazi interests.

Hungary, Romania, Bulgaria, Slovakia, and Croatia joined Hitler's alliance and were ruled by collaborating fascist-rightist governments. These fatal steps were initiated by a continued national revolution, which, from the 1930s on, was closely linked to fascist, right-wing political trends. Newly created Slovakia and Croatia established fascist regimes and joined Hitler's war against the Soviet Union. They also rushed to participate in the annihilation of the Jews, and Ante Pavelić's Ustasha regime launched a permanent crusade against the Serbs and Tito's communist-led partisans. Although none of Hitler's other satellites in the region introduced full-fledged fascist regimes, all of them applied elements of fascism and assisted Germany in its aggression and racist practices. Local fascist movements that emerged after World War I and gained momentum during the 1930s now triumphed. Right-wing, populist, fascist revolutionaries, who were previously unable to take over their countries and were forced to accept the role of an extreme-right opposition to right-wing authoritarian regimes, now seized power.

Encouraged by consecutive territorial gains of southern Slovakia, Carpatho-Ruthenia, northern Transylvania, and Vojvodina and Muraköz from former Yugoslavia, Hungary declared war against the Soviet Union and the Western powers and continued its shift to the Right between 1941 and 1943. After a cautious attempt to split the Hitlerite alliance—when the hope of a military victory vanished under Stalingrad—German troops occupied Hungary in March 1944. The Horthy regime was still ready to collaborate and assist Hitler's Final Solution; the Hungarian gendarmerie and administration began the deportation of Hungarian Jews in the summer of 1944. Because of Horthy's continued though powerless maneuvering to distance the country from Germany's cause, Hitler removed Horthy and set up a Hungarian fascist Arrowcross government under Ferenc Szálasi on October 15, 1944. The shift toward the Right, a permanent political trend in interwar Hungary, was now concluded, and the country remained in the Axis until the final defeat.

Romania's national humiliation, with successive losses of Bessarabia, northern Transylvania, and Dobrudja at the eve of the war, was rectified by General Ion Antonescu in 1941 when he joined Hitler in attacking the Soviet Union. Antonescu's thirty divisions not only reoccupied Bessarabia and northern Bukovina but, by pushing deep into the Soviet Union, played an important role in the Crimea and Sevastopol. Consequently, as a token of Hitler's gratitude, Romania acquired large areas of "Transnistria," territories between the Dniester and Bug rivers. A firm believer in Hitler's victory, Antonescu defeated his rival Iron Guardist allies and established his own right-wing military dictatorship, ready to serve the German war effort and war economy and carry out major elements of Nazi policy in Romania by deporting and killing Bessarabian and Bukovinian Jews. The destiny of the country was closely linked to Hitler's cause.

This situation changed only in the twelfth hour, after Soviet troops entered Romanian territory in the summer of 1944. An experienced Romanian political elite acted quickly: the young King Michael invited Antonescu to the palace, had him arrested by his guard, and, with the help of loyal Romanian troops, announced an end to the war in a radio declaration on August 23. King Michael then declared war against Germany and participated in the Soviet offensive against Hungary.

Under the firm dictatorship of Tsar Boris, Bulgaria joined the Axis in 1941 and allowed German troops to use the country's territory against Greece. Motivated by great-Bulgarian nationalist aspirations, the leitmotif of interwar Bulgarian politics, Boris and his government participated in Hitler's war against Bulgaria's neighbors and acquired large territories by occupying Macedonia and Thrace. Although Bulgaria remained neutral in the anti-Soviet war and was never occupied by Germany, it served Hitler's war with subservience and introduced anti-Jewish legislation in the spring and summer of 1942. Two days after the Soviet troops entered Bulgaria, a coup removed the pro-German government and declared war against Nazi Germany on September 9, 1944. The destiny of Central and Eastern Europe, as a logical continuation of interwar rebellion against Western values and institutions, was linked to Nazism-fascism and Hitler's war until the last minutes of World War II.

Despite the general trend toward Nazi collaboration in the region, resistance against the Nazis was not uncommon. Heroic resistance significantly contributed to anti-Nazi war efforts, especially in Poland and, most of all, in Yugoslavia, Albania, and Greece, where the resistance was connected to a revival of communist rebellion against capitalism. The Polish Anders-army of the government in exile participated in the war in the near-East and Italy, and the Home Army launched partisan actions within occupied Poland. The uprising of the Warsaw Ghetto in 1943, then the Home Army's desperate Warsaw Uprising in the summer of 1944, belong to the most heroic chapters of resistance during World War II. Tito's Yugoslavian partisan army, certainly the strongest of its type with its four hundred thousand soldiers at the last stage of the war, not only resisted eleven German offensives and inflicted severe casualties on the Italian, German, and Ustasha armies, but was ultimately able to liberate Yugoslavia. Similarly, the communist-led Albanian and Greek partisan armies virtually liberated their countries, which were not on the main war routes and, consequently, were not fortified by Nazi troops as strongly as was the Central European theater at the last stage of the war. Brave acts of resistance such as the Slovak uprising in 1944 and the Prague uprising during the last days of the war, the undertakings of the Bulgarian partisans, the assassination of Nazi officials and collaborators, and other scattered resistance all over the region played an important role in reestablishing independence and defeating Nazism. Nonetheless, Nazi occupation and local collaboration were a reality in the entire region during World War II.

As we have seen, the reckless extreme nationalist rebellion that emerged during and after World War I in Central and Eastern Europe and distinguished the interwar decades ended in total failure, leading to occupation by and subordination to a most aggressive and oppressive Nazi Germany. In a similar manner, the region's revolt against West-

ern economic systems, rooted in a failed or semisuccessful modernization, led to Nazi-German economic exploitation of both the conquered
and allied countries of the area, followed by the most severe war destruction. In 1941, the Nazi journal *Berliner Börsenzeitung* openly declared the plans of the Nazis concerning these countries, stating that
South-East Europe "has to adapt itself to its natural character" and stop
industrialization, which "was contrary to the [natural] agricultural character" of the area (Hungarian Archives 1941a). The Nazi semiofficial
journal added that the economic role granted to the area in the Nazi
economic sphere, the *Grossraumwirtschaft*, was agricultural production—
most of all to supply cereal and oil seeds—supplemented by some food
processing, extraction of existing raw materials, and processing of these
materials locally into semifinished goods. As the Hungarian chargé
d'affaires in Berlin reported in 1941 to the Hungarian Ministry of Foreign Affairs, the German economic dictate sought "controlled cooperation," in other words, a "complete adjustment to the requirements of
the German market." Existing branches of industry "were to be brought
under German control, and the establishment of industrial firms in-
convenient for the Germans was to be prevented by any means" (Hungarian Archives 1941b). The economy of the occupied countries became
a part of the German war economy. The economies of Austria, the Czech
lands, and in part the Baltic countries—territories designated as an integral part of the Reich—profited from huge German investments and
the development of strategic industries and infrastructure. The Austrian
iron, steel, and engineering industries increased their employment by
nearly fivefold after the *Anschluss*. Linz developed significant coke and
steel works and chemical industries. The largest Czechoslovak industrial firms increased their employment by two- to threefold. In spite of
the decline of some civilian branches, the industrial output of the Czech
Protectorate surpassed the prewar level by nearly one-fifth at the end of
the war.

The allied countries of Romania, Hungary, Slovakia, and Bulgaria
were also incorporated into the German war economy, and 75 to 80 percent of their foreign trade was with Germany. An increasingly large portion of these deliveries from Central and Eastern Europe was "regarded
as contribution to our common war," as the German officials explicitly
stated in economic negotiations in 1942 (Hungarian Archives 1942). The
unpaid deliveries, including the supply of the German occupation
troops, reached 1 billion marks in Slovakia, 1.2 billion marks in Bulgaria,
2.5 billion marks in Hungary, and 4.6 billion marks in the Czech lands.

Nazi Germany accumulated huge amounts of debt vis-à-vis its partners and financed at least one-quarter of its war expenditures by openly exploiting its enlarged empire. Poland was plundered: together with the seven hundred thousand prisoners of war, nearly two million people were transported to Germany for forced labor, and 25 percent of the forests were mowed down and transported to the Reich.

Although German war efforts required a revision of Nazi deindustrialization plans for an agricultural south-east Europe and resulted in the development of certain strategic industrial branches in the allied countries (Slovak industrial output increased by 63 percent between 1937 and 1943, and a major Messerschmidt program built an aircraft industry in Hungary connected with the forced development of the Hungarian aluminum industry), the war's sweeping passage through these countries destroyed incomparably more than anything created by the war economy.

The five-year-long war, which mobilized twice as many people and killed nearly three times as many as World War I, led to the most severe losses in Central and Eastern Europe, the main battlefield of World War II. Occupation, deportation, expulsion, mass murder, and the planned devastation of buildings, bridges, mines, and industries of strategic importance hit some countries of the region especially hard. The war's front lines moved across these countries sometimes two, or even three times, and heavy fighting, including street fighting in some of the capital cities, particularly during the apocalyptic culmination of the war in 1944–1945, caused the most severe destruction of human life and the erosion of national wealth accumulated by several generations. Instead of achieving a successful national modernization and prosperity—the dream of the early twentieth century and the main driving force of the region's many extremist revolts—the countries of Central and Eastern Europe found themselves utterly in ruin.

The Soviet Union carried the heaviest burden of the war and suffered most of the destruction: fifteen to twenty million of its people, including many civilians, lost their lives, and twenty-five million became homeless. In contrast, Germany lost more than six million people. Nearly 90 percent of the buildings in its larger cities were destroyed or severely damaged. Millions of Europeans were uprooted, and eleven million prisoners of war and ten to fifteen million refugees were forced to start their life from scratch.

The population of Poland and Yugoslavia was decimated: nearly one and three-quarter million Yugoslavs were killed during the partisan and bloody civil war. Poland lost nearly three million lives, Hungary and Romania each suffered a half million deaths, and Czechoslovakia lost about two hundred thousand. The most severe ethnic cleansing, a culmination of intensifying interwar national hatred and xenophobia, eliminated the two largest and most characteristic minority communities from the region. The Nazi-orchestrated and locally assisted Jewish Holocaust annihilated about four million Jews, two-thirds of the total Holocaust victims in Europe, mostly in Poland, Lithuania, Romania, and Hungary. Half of the one and a half million survivors of the Holocaust emigrated from the region after World War II, and entire Jewish communities—nearly 10 percent of the Polish, 7 percent of the Lithuanian, and 5 percent of the Romanian and Hungarian populations before the war—eventually disappeared.

German communities outside of Germany—the largest minority group in Poland and Czechoslovakia, and present in significant numbers in the Baltic countries, Hungary, and Romania—were eliminated in a different way. Frightened by the advancing Red Army and the anticipated reprisals for their wartime collaboration with the Nazi occupiers, nearly eight to nine million Germans fled with the withdrawing Nazi troops before the end of the war. In addition, according to the Potsdam agreement of the victorious great powers, millions of Germans were expelled, mostly from Czechoslovakia and Poland but also from Hungary and Romania, driving out another four to five million Germans from Central and Eastern Europe after World War II.

Besides the elimination of these two minority groups, several "small" waves of ethnic cleansing engulfed the area: between two to three million Poles left the former East Polish lands beyond the Curson-line that became part of the Soviet Union. Most were resettled in the newly regained West Polish territories from which the German population had been expelled. Moreover, roughly one hundred thousand Hungarians were expelled from the southern rim of Slovakia and resettled in Hungary. Altogether about fifteen to seventeen million people of Central and Eastern Europe were displaced and resettled in other countries. Some of the multiethnic, multinational countries of the region became more homogenous: Poland's 25 percent non-Polish and non-Catholic population declined to less than 4 percent. Romania also made a major advance in romanizing Great Romania.

The Baltic area, Poland, Yugoslavia, and Hungary were ruined. The last three countries lost half of their railroad capacities and half to three-quarters of their animal stock. Warsaw became one of the most devastated capitals in Europe, with 85 percent of its buildings destroyed. More than one-quarter of the buildings of Budapest were destroyed or heavily damaged. Yugoslavia lost one-sixth of its buildings, nearly half of its telephone networks, and two-thirds of its deep-sea vessels. The countries that were in an agricultural-industrial or in a nonindustrialized state before World War II lost 25 to 35 percent of their industrial capacities. War destruction surpassed 370 and 350 percent of the 1938 gross domestic product in Yugoslavia and Poland respectively. Hungary lost twice as much as its one-year GDP, Czechoslovakia suffered a more than one-year loss of its GDP, and Romanian and Bulgarian losses reached about one-third of their 1938 GDP.

In the most seriously devastated countries, the level of transportation and communication declined to the standard of the 1870s, industrial capacities dropped to turn-of-the-century levels, and agriculture, including animal stock, declined to late-nineteenth-century standards. The modernization deficit was greater than it had been fifty years earlier. The countries that revolted against their peripheral status and relative backwardness now fell into even greater despair and a more pronounced peripheral state.

As a consequence, Central and Eastern Europe experienced a broken historical continuity: political regimes and the state apparatus collapsed, heads of state, cabinet ministers, and top officers were tried and executed as war criminals, people were uprooted and decimated, large minority groups disappeared, and entire countries were ruined. Even the map of the region was redrawn: Estonia, Latvia, and Lithuania were incorporated again into the Soviet Union, which also regained Bessarabia and northern Bukovina from Romania, Carpatho-Ukraine from Czechoslovakia, and the large, former Polish territories east of the so-called Curson-line. Czechoslovakia and Yugoslavia were reestablished by reintegrating the "independent" Slovak and Croatian states. Austria regained its independence. Hungary had to give back all the territories it acquired from Czechoslovakia, Romania, and Yugoslavia with the help of Hitler. The realized dream of Great Bulgaria vanished. Massive Soviet Army units were stationed and remained in most of these countries: German domination and occupation was replaced by Soviet rule. Small wonder that Central and Eastern Europe could not return to "normalcy" in the years to come. The pendulum moved to the other extreme; from one type of extremism emerged another, and the failure of modernization generated a new but also dictatorial modernization attempt. The interwar decades of crisis extended to the second half of the century.

Bibliography

Adanir, Fikret. 1979. "Zur 'Etatismus': Diskussion in der Türkei in der Weltwirtschaftskrise. Die Zeitschrift KADRO, 1932–1934." Working paper. Mainz: Institut für Europäische Geschichte.

Adrian, Leopold. 1937. *Oesterreich im Prisma der Idee*. Graz: Schmidt-Dengler.

Ady, Endre. 1990. "Morituri." In vol. 1 of *Helyünk Európában: Nézetek és koncepciók a 20.századi Magyarországon*, ed. Ivan T. Berend and Éva Ring. Budapest: Magvető.

——. 1973. *Összes prózai müvei*. Vol. 10. Ed. József Láng and Erzsébet Vezér. Budapest: Akadémiai Kiadó.

Ahmann, Rolf. 1989. "The German Treaties with Estonia and Latvia of 7 June 1939: Bargaining Ploy or an Alternative for German-Soviet Understanding?" *Journal of Baltic Studies* 20, no. 4 (winter).

Altman, Nathan. 1984. "Kunst der Kommune, 1918." In *Nathan Altman: Mit Beiträge von Nathan Altman und seine Zeitgenossen*, by Mark G. Etkind. Dresden: VEB Verlag der Kunst.

Amann, Klaus. 1991. "Political Attitudes and the Book Market: Special Features of the Austrian Literary Scene between 1933 and 1938." In *Austria in the Thirties: Culture and Politics*, ed. Kenneth Segar and John Warren. Riverside: Ariadne Press.

Anderson, Benedict. 1983. *Imagined Communities: Reflections on the Origin and Spread of Nationalism*. London: Verso.

Anderson, Perry. 1974. *Lineages of the Absolutist State*. London: N.L.B.

Architectura. 1949. *Architectura i Stroitelstvo*. November 4.

Arendt, Hannah. 1966. *The Origins of Totalitarianism*. Cleveland: Meridian Books.

Aspetsberger, Friedbert. 1980. *Literarisches Leben im Austrofaschismus: Der Staatspreis*. Königstein: Verlag Anton Hain.

Avtorkhanov, Abdurakham. 1953. *The Reign of Stalin*. London: Bodley Head.

Bailes, Kendall, ed. 1978. *Technology and Society under Lenin and Stalin*. Princeton: Princeton University Press.

Bairoch, Paul. 1973. "European Foreign Trade in the Nineteenth Century: The Development of the Value and Volume of Exports." *The Journal of European Economic History* no. 2.

———. 1976. "Europe's Gross National Product: 1800–1975." *The Journal of European Economic History* 5, no. 2.

Bajkay, Éva R., ed. 1979. *A konstruktivizmus: Válogatás a mozgalom dokumentumaiból*. Budapest: Gondolat.

Bálint, György. 1961. *A toronyör visszapillant*. Budapest: Gondolat.

Balogh. 1985. Balogh, Sándor, Gergely Jenö, Izsák Lajos, Jakab Sándor, Pritz Pál, and Romsics Ignác. *Magyarország a huszadik században*. Budapest: Kossuth.

Baltic History. 1974. Ed. Arvids Ziedonis, William L. Winter, and Mardi Valgemäe. Columbus: Ohio State University Press.

Baltic States. 1938. *The Baltic States: A Survey of the Political and Economic Structure and the Foreign Relations of Estonia, Latvia, and Lithuania. Royal Institute of International Affairs*. London: Oxford University Press.

Bann, Stephan, ed. 1974. *The Tradition of Constructivism*. New York: A Da Capo.

Barber, John. 1981. *Soviet Historians in Crisis, 1928–1932*. London: Macmillan.

Bartók, Béla. 1976. *Bartók Béla levelei*. Ed. János Demény. Budapest: Zenemükiadó.

Bayr, Rudolf. 1948. *Karl Heinrich Waggerl: Der Dichter und sein Werk*. Salzburg: Müller.

Bazarov, V. 1928. "Principi postroienyija perspectivovo plana." *Planovoye Hoziaystvo* 5.

Bell, J. D. 1977. *Peasants in Power: Alexander Stamboliski and the Bulgarian Agrarian National Union, 1899–1923*. Princeton: Princeton University Press.

Bender, Thomas, and Carl Schorske, eds. 1994. *Budapest and New York: Studies in Metropolitan Transformation, 1870–1930*. New York: Russel Sage Foundation.

Berend, Ivan T., and György Ránki. 1974. *Economic Development in East-Central Europe in the Nineteenth and Twentieth Centuries*. New York: Columbia University Press.

———. 1979. *Underdevelopment and Economic Growth: Studies in Hungarian Social and Economic History*. Budapest: Akadémiai Kiadó.

———. 1982. *The European Periphery and Industrialization, 1780–1914*. Cambridge: Cambridge University Press,

———. 1985. *The Hungarian Economy in the Twentieth Century*. London: Croom Helm.

Berend, Ivan T., and Knut Borchardt, eds. 1986. *The Impact of the Depression of the 1930s and Its Relevance for the Contemporary World: Comparative Studies*. Budapest: Academy Research Center of East-Central Europe.

Berény, Róbert. 1911. "Bartók esete." *Nyugat* (Budapest) 4 (June).

Berlin, Isiah. 1983. Introduction to *Roots of Revolution: A History of the Populist and Socialist Movements in Nineteenth-Century Russia*, by Franco Venturi. Chicago: University of Chicago Press.

Bernstein, Eduard. 1899. *Die Voraussetzungen des Sozialismus und die Aufgabe der Sozialdemokratie*. Stuttgart: Dietz.

Binder, Dieter A. 1991. "The Corporate State versus National Socialism: Some Aspects of Austria's Resistance." In *Austria in the Thirties: Culture and Politics*, ed. Kenneth Segar and John Warren. Riverside: Ariadne Press.

Bojtár, Endre. 1977. *A kelet-európai avantgarde irodalom*. Budapest: Akadémiai Kiadó.

Bottai, Giuseppe. 1940. *Politica fascista dell arti*. Rome: A. Signorell.

Brice, Chatrine. 1989. "G. Pagano, M. Piacentini: Un architecte 'fasciste' et un 'architecte du totalitarisme'?" In *Art et Fascisme*, ed. Pierre Milza and Fanette Roche-Pézard. Paris: Editions Complexe.

Brock, Peter. 1977. *Polish Revolutionary Populism: A Study in Agrarian Socialist Thought from the 1830s to the 1850s*. Toronto: University of Toronto Press.

Bukharin, Nikolai. 1966. *Imperialism and World Economy*. New York: H. Fertig.

———. 1971. *Economics of the Transformation Period*. New York: Bergman.

———. 1982. *Selected Writings on State and the Transition to Socialism*. Ed. Richard B. Day. Armonk, N.Y.: M. E. Sharpe.

Bulgarsko. 1972. *Bulgarsko-germanski otnosheniia i vruzki: Izsledvaniia i materiali*. 4 vols. 1972–1989. Sofia: BAN.

Butler, Rohan D'O. 1941. *The Roots of National Socialism, 1783–1933*. London: Faber and Faber.

Buzatu, Gheorgiu. 1991. *România cu și fără Antonescu: Documente, studii, reletări si comentari*. Iasi: Editura Moldova.

Carr, Edward H. 1940. *The Twenty Years Crisis*. London: Macmillan.

———. 1950–1953. *The Bolshevik Revolution, 1917–1923*. 3 vols. Baltimore: Penguin Books.

———. 1959. *Socialism in One Country, 1924–1926*. London: Macmillan.

Carr, Edward H., and R. W. Davies. 1974. *Foundations of a Planned Economy, 1926–1929*. Vol. 1. Harmondsworth: Pelican Books.

Carsten, Francis L. 1972. *Revolution in Central Europe, 1918–1919*. Berkeley: University of California Press.

———. 1979. "Interpretations of Fascism." In *Fascism, A Reader's Guide: Analyses, Interpretations, Bibliography*, ed. Walter Laqueur. Harmondsworth: Penguin Books.

Codreanu, Corneliu Zelea. 1976. *For My Legionaries (The Iron Guard)*. Madrid: Editura Libertatea.

Colonna, Bertram de. 1938. *Czecho-Slovakia Within*. London: T. Butterworth.

Conquest, Robert. 1968. *The Great Terror: Stalin's Purge of the Thirties*. New York: Macmillan.

Constantinescu, Nicolae, et al. 1960. *Contributii la Istoria Capitalului Strain in Rominia*. Bucharest: Editura Academiei.

Cresti, Carlo. 1986. *Architettura e Fascismo*. Firenze: Vallecchi Editore.

Crisp, Olga. 1972. "The Pattern of Russian Industrialization." In *Industria-*

lisation en Europe XIXe. siecle, ed. Pierre Leon, Francois Crouzet, Richard Gascon. Paris: Centre National de la Recherche Scientifique.

Czech. 1987. *Czech Functionalism, 1918–1938*. London: Architectural Association.

Davies, Norman. 1986. *Heart of Europe: A Short History of Poland*. Oxford: Oxford University Press.

Declaration. 1955. "The Declaration of the Slovak Nation." In *History of Modern Slovakia*, by Jozef Lettrich. New York: Praeger.

Declaration. 1974. "Declaration of the Council of Elders, Estonian National Council, February 24, 1918." In *Baltic History*, ed. Arvids Ziedonis, William L. Winter, and Mardi Valgemäe. Columbus: Ohio State University Press.

Deicher, Suzanne. 1988. "Die Propaganda und der Wunsch." In *Erbeutete Sinne: Nachträge zur Berliner Ausstellung "Inszenierung der Macht, ästhetische Faszination im Faschismus."* Berlin: Neue Gesellschaft für Bildende Kunst.

Deutscher, Isaak. 1967. *Stalin: A Political Biography*. New York: Oxford University Press.

Deutsches Archiv. 1934. *Deutsches Zentral Archiv Potsdam*. Auswärtiges Amt, Abt. II. Januar, 41288. German Central Archive, Ministry of Foreign Affairs.

Devitsil. 1990. *Devitsil: Czech Avant-garde Art, Architecture, and Design of the 1920s and 1930s*. Oxford: Museum of Modern Art.

Dobb, Maurice. 1966. *Soviet Economic Development since 1917*. London: Routledge.

Dragut, V., V. Florea, D. Grigorescu, and M. Mihalaci. 1977. *Romanian Painting*. Bucharest: Meridiane.

Dubnow, Seman Markovich. 1961. *History of the Jews in Russia and Poland*. Philadelphia: Jewish Publication Society of America.

Dubrovski, S. M. 1963. *Stolypinskaia zemelnaia reforma: Iz istorii selskovo hoziaistva i krestianstva Rossii v nachale XX veka*. Moscow: Izd. Akademii Nauk SSSR.

Eicholtz, Dietrich, and Kurt Grossweiler, eds. 1980. *Faschismus: Forschung. Positionen, Probleme, Polemik*. Berlin: Akademie Verlag.

Eksteins, Modris. 1989. *Rites of Spring: The Great War and the Birth of the Modern Age*. Boston: Houghton Mifflin.

Enyedi, György, and Viktoria Szirmai. 1992. *Budapest: A Central European Capital*. London: Belhaven Press.

Estonian Museum. 1982. *The State Art Museum of the Estonian SSR. Estonian and Soviet Estonian Art*. Tallin: Perioodika.

Fellner, Fritz. 1971. "The Background of Austrian Fascism." In *Native Fascism in the Successor States, 1918–1945*, ed. Peter Sugar. Santa Barbara: ABC-Clio.

Fichte, Johann Gottlieb. 1920. *Der Geschlossene Handelsstaat: Ein philosophischer Entwurf als Anhang zur Rechtslehre und Probe einer künftig zu liefernden Politik*. Jena: Gustav Fischer.

Fischer-Galati, Stephen. 1991. *Twentieth-Century Rumania*. 2d ed. New York: Columbia University Press.

Florea, Vasile. 1984. *Romanian Art: Modern and Contemporary Ages*. Bucharest: Meridiane.

Friedrich, Heinz. 1967. "Vermischte Gedanken über antiquarisches Verhalten." In *K. H. Waggerl genauer betrachtet*, ed. Lutz Besch. Salzburg: Residenz Verlag.

Futurizmus. 1967. 3d ed. Budapest: Gondolat.

Gachot, F. 1926. "Stravinsky." *Nyugat* (Budapest) 18 (March).

Galbraith, John Kenneth. 1961. *The Great Crash, 1929*. Boston: Houghton Mifflin.

———. 1964. *Economic Development*. Boston: Houghton Mifflin.

———. 1977. *The Age of Uncertainty*. Boston: Houghton Mifflin.

Gargani, A. G. 1984. "Die Verwirrungen des Zöglings Törless von Robert Musil." In *Traum und Wirklichkeit*. Vienna: Museen der Stadt Wien.

Georgescu, Vlad. 1991. *The Romanians: A History*. Columbus: Ohio State University Press.

Gerevich, Tibor. 1932. "Római magyar müvészek." *Magyar Szemle*, no. 11.

Geschichte. 1955. *Geschichte der Kommunistischen Partei Deutschlands*. Berlin: Akad. Verlag.

Getty, Arch. 1985. *Origins of the Great Purges: The Soviet Communist Party Reconsidered*. Cambridge: Cambridge University Press.

Getzler, Israel. 1992. "Soviets as Agents of Democratization." In *Revolution in Russia: Reassessment of 1917*, ed. Edith Rogavin Frankel, Jonathan Frankel, Baruch Knei-Paz. Cambridge: Cambridge University Press.

Gibbon, Edward. 1787. *The History of the Decline and Fall of the Roman Empire*. Basil: J. J. Tourneisen.

Goldinger, Walter, and Dieter A. Binder. 1992. *Geschichte der Republik Österreich, 1918–1938*. Munich: Verlag für Geschichte und Politik and Oldenbourg.

Goldstein, Eric. 1994. "Britain: The Homefront." Working paper, University of California, Berkeley.

Golomshtok, Igor. 1990. *Totalitarian Art in the Soviet Union, the Third Reich, Fascist Italy, and the People's Republic of China*. London: Collins Harvill.

Gömbös, Gyula. 1932. *A nemzeti öncélúságért! Gömbös Gyula miniszterelnök tizenkét beszéde*. Budapest: Stádium.

Good, David F. 1984. *The Economic Rise of the Habsburg Empire, 1750–1914*. Berkeley: University of California Press.

Gopenko, M. 1949. *Architectura i Stroitelstvo*, no. 11.

Gough, Hubert. 1954. *Soldiering On*. London: A. Barker.

Gray, Camilla. 1962. *The Great Experiment: Russian Art, 1863–1922*. London: Thames and Hudson.

Gregor, James A. 1969. *The Ideology of Fascism: The Rationale of Totalitarianism*. New York: Free Press.

Grois, Boris. 1992. *The Total Art of Stalinism: Avant-garde, Aesthetic, Dictatorship, and Beyond*. Princeton: Princeton University Press.

Gross, Hermann. 1938. *Die wirtschaftliche Bedeutung Südosteuropas für das Deutsche Reich*. Stuttgart.

Grünberg, Karol. 1970. *Niemcy i ich organizacje polityczne w Polsce miedzy-wojennej*. Warsaw: Wiedza Powszechna.

Gutwenger, Engelbert. 1967. "Liturgie des bäuerlichen Lebens." In *K. H. Waggerl genauer betrachtet*, ed. Lutz Besch. Salzburg: Residenz Verlag.

Haiko, Peter. 1984. "Otto Wagner: Die Postsparkasse und die Kirche am Steinhof. Des Architekten Traum und des Baukünstlers Wirklichkeit." In *Traum und Wirklichkeit*. Vienna: Museen der Stadt Wien.

Hanák, Péter, et al. 1993. *Polgárosodás és modernizáció a monarchiában*. Budapest: Hazánk Könyvkiadó.

Hanák, Péter, ed. 1984. *Zsidókérdés, asszimiláció, antiszemitizmus: Tanulmányok a zsidókérdésröl a huszadik századi Magyarországon*. Budapest: Gondolat.

Hanisch, Ernst. 1984. "Der politische Katholizismus als ideologisches Träger des 'Austrofaschismus.'" In *Austrofaschismus: Beiträge über Politik, Ökonomie und Kultur, 1934–1938*, ed. Emmerich Tálos and Wolfgang Neugebauer. Vienna: Verlag für Gesellschaftskritik.

Hauser, Arnold. 1968. *The Philosophy of Art History*. London: Routledge.

Heiden, Konrad. 1944. *Der Fuehrer: Hitler's Rise to Power*. Boston: Houghton Mifflin.

Heinen, Armin. 1986. *Die Legion Erzengel Michael in Rumänien: Soziale Bewegung und Politische Organisation*. Munich: Oldenbourg.

Herder, Johann G. 1952. *Zur Philosophie der Geschichte*. Vol. 1. Berlin: Aufbau Verlag.

Hertz, Friedrich Otto. 1947. *The Economic Problems of Danubian States: A Study in Economic Nationalism*. London: V. Gollancz.

Herzl, Theodor. 1970. *The Jewish State*. New York: Herzl Press.

Hiden, John. 1988. "From War to Peace: Britain, Germany, and the Baltic States, 1918–1921." *Journal of Baltic Studies* 19, no. 4 (winter).

Hiden, John, and Patrick Salmon. 1991. *The Baltic Nations and Europe: Estonia, Latvia, and Lithuania in the Twentieth Century*. London: Longman.

Hinz, Berthold. 1979. *Art in the Third Reich*. New York: Pantheon Books.

Hitler, Adolf. 1969. *The Speeches of Adolf Hitler, April 1922–August 1939*. Ed. N. H. Baynes. New York: H. Fertig.

Hobsbawm, Eric. 1900. *Nation and Nationalism since 1780: Program, Myth, Reality*. Cambridge: Cambridge University Press.

Hoensch, Jörg K. 1984. *A History of Modern Hungary, 1867–1986*. London: Longman.

Hoptner, Jacob, B. 1962. *Yugoslavia in Crisis, 1934–1941*. New York: Columbia University Press.

Hroch, Miroslaw. 1985. *Social Preconditions of National Revival in Europe: A Comparative Analysis of the Social Composition of Patriotic Groups among the Smaller European Nations*. Cambridge: Cambridge University Press.

Hungarian Archive. 1932. Hungarian National Archive, Kozma Iratok, fasc. 3.

Hungarian Archive. 1933. Hungarian National Archive, Ministry of Foreign Affairs, Political Department, fasc. 158, 21/7. 306. February 1.

Hungarian Archive. 1935. Hungarian National Archive, Ministry of Foreign Affairs, Department of Economic Policy, German File, no. 642, I-3-17. 391. April 6.

Hungarian Archive. 1935a. Hungarian National Archive, Ministry of Foreign

Affairs, Department of Economic Policy, German File, no. 641, I-3-A. 53070.

Hungarian Archive. 1935b. Hungarian National Archive, Ministry of Foreign Affairs, Department of Economic Policy, German File, no. 642, I-3-A. 203/4. res.

Hungarian Archive. 1935c. Hungarian National Archive, Kozma Iratok, fasc. 7.

Hungarian Archive. 1937. Hungarian National Archive, Ministry of Foreign Affairs, Department of Economic Policy, German File, no. 641, I-3-A. April 12.

Hungarian Archive. 1941a. 1941b. Hungarian National Archive, Ministry of Foreign Affairs, Department of Economic Policy, res. 466.

Hungarian Archive. 1942. Hungarian National Archive, Ministry of Foreign Affairs, Department of Economic Policy, Hungarian-German Economic Discussions.

Ioanid, Radu. 1990. *The Sword of the Archangel: Fascist Ideology in Romania.* Boulder: East European Monographs.

———. 1992. "Iorga, Nicolae and Fascism." *Journal of Contemporary History* 27, no. 3 (July).

Jacques, Edwin C. 1995. *The Albanians.* Jefferson: McFarland.

Janicki, Stanislaw. 1985. *The Polish Film: Yesterday and Today.* Warsaw: Interpress.

Janos, Andrew C. 1982. *The Politics of Backwardness in Hungary, 1825–1945.* Princeton: Princeton University Press.

Jászi, Oscar. 1918. *Magyarország jövője és a Dunai Egyesült Államok.* Budapest: Uj Magyarország Rt.

———. 1924. *Revolution and Counter-Revolution in Hungary.* London: P. S. King.

———. 1964. *The Dissolution of the Habsburg Monarchy.* Chicago: University of Chicago Press.

Jelavich, Charles, and Barbara Jelavich. 1977. *The Establishment of the Balkan National States, 1804–1920.* Seattle: University of Washington Press.

Johnson, Harry G. ed. 1967. *Economic Nationalism in Old and New States.* Chicago: University of Chicago Press.

Joll, James. 1973. *Europe since 1870.* New York: Harper and Row.

Kaiser, David. 1980. *Economic Diplomacy and the Origin of the Second World War, 1930–1939.* Princeton: Princeton University Press.

Kalnis, Bruno. 1974. "Der Rigaer Arbeiterrat 1917." In *Baltic History,* ed. Arvids Ziedonis, William L. Winter, and Mardi Valgemäe. Columbus: Ohio State University Press.

Kann, Robert. 1971. *The Multinational Empire: Nationalism and National Reform in the Habsburg Monarchy, 1848–1918.* London: Weidenfeld and Nicholson.

Kann, Robert A., and David V. Zdenek. 1984. *The Peoples of the Eastern Habsburg Lands, 1526–1918.* Seattle: University of Washington Press.

Kareva, Mariia Pavlovna. 1948. *Konstitutsiia SSSR.* Moscow: Gosudarstvenoe Uchebnopedagogicheskoe Izd.

Károlyi, Michael. 1956. *Memoirs of Michael Károlyi: Faith without Illusion.* London: Jonathan Cape.

Kaser, Michael C., and Edward A. Radice, eds. 1985. *The Economic History of Eastern Europe, 1919–1945.* Vol. 1. Oxford: Oxford University Press.

Kassák, Lajos. 1972. *Az izmusok története.* Budapest: Magvető.

Kautsky, Karl. 1914. *Der Imperialismus.* Berlin: Neue Zeit.

Kelbeceva, E. 1993. "Creation of a New National Style in Bulgarian Art After the First World War." *Bulgarian Historical Review,* no. 2–3.

Kenwood, A. G., and Alan L. Lougheed. 1971. *The Growth of the International Economy, 1820–1960.* London: Allen and Unwin.

Keynes, John Maynard. 1920. *The Economic Consequences of the Peace.* New York: Harcourt, Brace, and Howe.

Kienzl, Heinz, and Kurt Prokop, eds. 1989. *NS-Ideologie und Antisemitismus in Österreich.* Vienna: Liga der Freunde des Judentums.

Kitchen, Martin. 1980. *The Coming of Austrian Fascism.* London: Croom Helm.

Klein, Fritz. 1994. "Between Campiegne and Versailles: The Germans on the Way from a Misunderstood Defeat to an Unwanted Peace." Working paper, University of California, Berkeley.

Kluchevsky, Vasilii O. 1912. *A History of Russia.* Vol. 2. London: J. M. Dent.

Knox, Brian. 1971. *The Architecture of Poland.* New York: Praeger.

Kochanowicz, Jacek. 1989. "The Polish Economy and the Evolution of Dependency." In *The Origins of Backwardness in Eastern Europe,* ed. Daniel Chirot. Berkeley: University of California Press.

Koestler, Arthur. 1941. *Darkness at Noon.* New York: Modern Library.

Kofman, Jan. 1990. "How to Define Economic Nationalism? A Critical Review of Some Old and New Standpoints." In *Economic Nationalism in East-Central Europe and South America, 1918–1939,*ed. Henryk Szlajfer. Geneva: Librairie Droz.

Kohn, Hans. 1929. *A History of Nationalism in the East.* London: Routledge.

Kojić, Branislav. 1979. *Drustveni uslovi razvitka arhitektonske struke u Beogradu, 1920–1940 godine.* Beograd: Srpska Akademija Nauka.

Korbel, Josef. 1977. *Twentieth-Century Czechoslovakia: The Meaning of Its History.* New York: Columbia University Press.

Körner, Éva. 1963. *Magyar müvészet a két világháború között.* Budapest: Gondolat.

Korsakaite, Ingrid, Rasma Latse, and I. P. Solomykova. 1981. *Iskusstvo Pribaltiki: Sstati i issledovaniia.* Tallin: Kunst.

Kostrowicka, Irena, et al. 1966. *Historia gospodarcza Polski, XIX i XX wieku,* Warsaw: Ksiazka i Wiedza.

Kovalchenko, Ivan D. 1971. "Sootneshenia krestianskovo i pomeshchichjevo hozjajstva v zemledelskom proizvodstve kapitalisticheskoj Rossii." In *Problemi socialno-ekonomicheskoi istorii Rossii: Sbornik statej,* ed. Leonid M. Ivanov. Moscow: Nauka.

Kozlowski, Nina. 1978. *Die politischen Gruppierungen innerhalb des Piłsudski Lagers, 1926–1939.* Munich: Osteuropa Institut.

Kratka. 1965. *Kratka Istorija na Blgarskata Architektura.* Sofia: Izd. na Blgarskata Akademija Naukite.

Kreissler, Felix. 1970. *Von der Revolution zur Annexion: Österreich, 1918 bis 1938.* Vienna: Europa Verlag.

Křenek, Ernst. 1961. "Schönberg und die Atonalität." In *Századunk zenéje*, ed. Rezsö Kókai. Budapest: Zenemükiadó.

Krleža, Miroslav. 1979. *Bankett Blitvában*. Budapest: Magvetö.

Lackó, Miklós. 1966. *Nyilasok, Nemzetiszocialisták, 1935–1944*. Budapest: Kossuth.

Lampe, John R., and Marvin R. Jackson. 1982. *Balkan Economic History, 1550–1950: From Imperial Borderlands to Developing Nations*. Bloomington: Indiana University Press.

Lampert, Nicholas. 1979. *The Technical Intelligentsia and the Soviet State*. London: Macmillan.

Landau, Zbigniew, and Jerzy Tomaszewski. 1980. *Polska w Europie i Swiecie, 1918–1939*. Warszawa: Wiedza Porvszechna.

———. 1982. *Wielki Kryzys, 1930–1935*. Vol. 3 of *Gospodarka Polski miedzy-wojennej, 1918–1939*. Warsaw: Ksiakai Wiedza.

Landes, David S. 1969. *The Unbound Prometheus: Technological Change and Industrial Development in Western Europe from 1750 to the Present*. Cambridge: Cambridge University Press.

Larionov, Mikhail. 1988. "Rayonists and Futurists: A Manifesto, 1913." In *Russian Art of the Avant-Garde: Theory and Criticism*, ed. John E. Bowlt. New York: Thames and Hudson.

Lederer, Ivo J. 1969. "Nationalism and the Yugoslavs." In *Nationalism in Eastern Europe*, ed. Peter Sugar and Ivo Lederer. Seattle: University of Washington Press.

Lehmann-Haupt, Hellmut. 1954. *Art under a Dictatorship*. New York: Oxford University Press.

Lenin, Vladimir I. 1947. *Selected Works*. 2 vols. London: Lawrence and Wishart.

———. 1971. *Selected Works*. 1 vol. edition. New York: International Publishers.

Lettrich, Józef. 1955. *History of Modern Slovakia*. New York: Praeger.

Lewis, Arthur. 1949. *Economic Survey, 1919–1939*. London: Allen and Unwin.

Lissitzky, El, and Ilya Ehremburg. 1974. "The Blockade of Russia is Coming to an End." In *The Tradition of Constructivism*, Stephan Bann. New York: A Da Capo.

Loewenberg, Peter. 1985. *Decoding the Past: The Psychohistorical Approach*. Berkeley: University of California Press.

Lukács, György. 1974. *Az ész trónfosztása*. Budapest: Akadémiai Kiadó.

Lukacs, John. 1988. *Budapest, 1900: A Historical Portrait of a City and Its Culture*. New York: Weidenfeld and Nicholson.

Macartney, Almer C. 1934. *National States and National Minorities*. London: Oxford University Press.

Maddison, Angus. 1985. *Two Crises: Latin America and Asia, 1929–1938 and 1973–1983*. Paris: OECD.

———. 1994. "Monitoring the World Economy, 1820–1992." In *Convergence of Productivity*, ed. William J. Baumol, Richard R. Nelson, Edward N. Wolff. Oxford: Oxford University Press.

Malevich, Kazimir. 1959. "Suprematismo." In *Le avanguardie artistiche del Novecento*, by Mario de Micheli. Milan: Schwarz.

Malevich. 1990. Ed. Jeanne D'Andrea. Los Angeles: Armand Hammer Museum.

Mann, Thomas. 1970. *Thomas Mann Müvei: Válogatott levelek*. Budapest: Helikon.

———. 1994. "Tagebücher, 1918–1921." In "Between Campiegne and Versailles: The Germans on the Way from a Misunderstood Defeat to an Unwanted Peace," by Fritz Klein. Working paper, University of California, Berkeley.

Manoilescu, Mihail. 1931. *The Theory of Protection and International Trade*. London: P. S. King.

Marcus, Joseph. 1983. *Social and Political History of the Jews in Poland, 1919–1939*. Berlin: Mouton.

Marinetti, Filippo T. 1959. "Fondazione e Manifesto del futurismo." In *La avangardie artistiche del Novecento*, by Mario de Micheli. Milan: Schwarz.

Marković, Peda J. 1992. *Beograd i Evropa, 1918–1941*. Beograd: Savremena Administracija.

Marx, Karl. 1919. *Das Kapital: Kritik der politischen Oekonomie*. Hamburg: O. Meissner.

Marx, Karl, and Friedrich Engels. 1962. *Selected Works*. Vol. 1. Moscow: Foreign Languages Publishing House.

———. 1970. *The German Ideology*. London: Lawrence and Wishart.

Masaryk, Thomás G. 1927. *The Making of a State: Memoires and Observations, 1914–1918*. London: G. Allen and Unwin.

May, Arthur James. 1968. *The Hapsburg Monarchy, 1867–1914*. New York: Norton.

Mayer, Arno J. 1981. *The Persistence of the Old Regime: Europe to the Great War*. New York: Pantheon Books.

Medvediev, Roy A. 1989. *Let History Judge: The Origins and Consequences of Stalinism*. Oxford: Oxford University Press.

Meinecke, Friedrich. 1908. *Weltbürgertum und Nationalstaat: Studien zur Genesis des deutschen Nationalstaates*. Munich: R. Oldenbourg.

Mendelsohn, Ezra. 1983. *The Jews of East Central Europe between the World Wars*. Bloomington: Indiana University Press.

Miliukov, Paul. 1967. *Political Memoirs, 1905–1917*. Ann Arbor: University of Michigan Press.

Milosz, Czeslaw. 1981. *Native Realm: A Search for Self-Identification*. Berkeley: University of California Press.

Mirković, Mijo. 1968. *Ekonomska historija Jugoslavije*. Zagreb: Informator.

Mladek, Meda. 1975. "Central European Influences." In *Frantisek Kupka, 1871–1957: A Retrospective*. New York: Solomon R. Guggenheim Foundation.

Moholy-Nagy, László. 1979. "Vita az uj tartalom és uj forma problémájáról." In *A konstruktivizmus: Válogatás a mozgalom dokumentumaiból*, by Éva R. Bajkay. Budapest: Gondolat.

Moholy-Nagy, Sybil. 1977. "Ein Totalexperiment: Mainz und Berlin." In *Tendenzen der Zwanziger Jahre. 15.Europäischer Kunstausstellung*. Berlin: D. Reimer.

Molnár, Antal. 1912. "Schönberg Arnold." *Nyugat* (Budapest) 5 (July).

Montgomery, John Flournoy. 1947. *Hungary, the Unwilling Satellite*. New York: Bevin-Adair Co.

Moore, Barrington Jr. 1967. *Origins of Dictatorship and Democracy*, Boston: Beacon Press.

Mosse, George. 1966. *The Crisis of German Ideology: Intellectual Origins of the Third Reich*. London: Weidenfeld and Nicholson.

Nagy-Talavera, Nicholas. 1970. *The Green Shirts and the Others*. Stanford: Hoover Institution Press.

Németh, Lajos. 1973. *Minerva baglya*. Budapest: Magvetö.

———. 1977. *Modern magyar müvészet*. Budapest: Corvina.

Neumann, Friedrich. 1915. *Mitteleuropa*. Berlin: G. Reimer.

Nove, Alec. 1992. *An Economic History of the USSR, 1917–1991*. London: Penguin Books.

Nykoforov, Boris M. 1953. *Kurzer Abriss der Geschichte der Sowietischen Malerei von 1917 bis 1945*. Dresden: VEB Verlag der Kunst.

Offord, Derek. 1986. *The Russian Revolutionary Movement in the 1880s*. Cambridge: Cambridge University Press.

Oktyabr. 1936. No. 9.

Olšovský, Rudolf, et al. 1961. *Přehled hospodářského vývoje Československá v letech, 1918–1945*. Prague: Statni Nakladatelství Politické Literatury.

Oprescu, George. 1935. *Roumanian Art from 1800 to Our Days*. Malmö: Ljustrycksanstalt.

Paas, Heini. 1974. *Ferdi Sannamees, 1895–1963*. Tallin: Kirjastus "Kunst."

Pach, Zsigmond Pál. 1994. *Hungary and the European Economy in Early Modern Times*. Aldershot: Variorum.

Palairet, Michael. 1995. *Evolution without Development*. Cambridge University Press.

Palickar, Stephen Joseph. 1948. *Slovakia from Hungarian Despotism to Atheistic Czech Communism*. Cambridge, Mass.: Hampshire Press.

Passuth, Krisztina. 1985. *Moholy-Nagy*. New York: Thames and Hudson.

Pasvolsky, Leo. 1928. *Economic Nationalism of the Danubian States*. London: Macmillan.

Patrascanu, Lucretiu. 1945. *Sub Trei Dictaturi*. Bucharest: Forum.

Pauley, Bruce F. 1990. "Anti-Semitism and the Austrian Nazi Party." In *Austria in the Thirties: Culture and Politics*, ed. Kenneth Segar and John Warren. Riverside: Ariadne Press.

Pedulla, Gianfranco. 1994. *Il teatro italiano nel tempo del fascismo*. Bologna: Il Mulino.

Peiper, Tadeusz. 1986. "Kunst und Proletariat." In *Der Mensch in den Dingen: Programmtexte und Gedichte der Krakauer Avantgarde*, ed. Heinrich Olschowsky. Leipzig: Philipp Reclam.

Peters, Rita Putins. 1979. "The Baltic States and the League of Nations: A Study of Opportunities and Limitations." *Journal of Baltic Studies* 10, no. 2 (summer).

Petrosjan, Jurij A. 1977. "Die Ideen 'der Europäisierung' in dem sozialpolitischen Leben des osmanischen Reiches in der Neuzeit (Ende des 18.,

Anfang des 20. Jahrhunderts)." In *La révolution industrielle dans le sud-est Européen XIXs*. Sofia: Institut d'Études Balkaniques.

Petrovich, Mihael B. 1980. "Religion and Ethnicity in Eastern Europe." In *Ethnic Diversity and Conflict in Eastern Europe*, ed. Peter Sugar. Santa Barbara: ABC-Clio.

Pick, Frederick W. 1946. "1939: The Evidence Re-Examined." *The Baltic Review* 1, no. 4–5.

Pihlak, Evi. 1985. *Nikolai Triik: Inimese Kujatajana*. Tallin: Kirjastus "Kunst."

Piłsudski, Jósef. 1936. *Erinnerungen und Dokumente*. Vol. 4. Essen: Essener Verlagsanstalt.

Polanyi, Karl. 1964. *The Great Transformation: The Political and Economic Origins of Our Time*. Boston: Beacon Press.

Pool, James. 1979. *Who Financed Hitler: The Secret Funding of Hitler's Rise to Power, 1919–1933*. London: MacDonald.

Posse, Hans Ernst. 1934. "Möglichkeiten der Grossraumwirtschaft." In *Die Nationale Wirtschaft*, no. 2.

Pravda. 1922. July 2.

Pravda. 1924. December 12.

Pravda. 1932. April 23.

Pravda. 1934. October 31.

Pravda. 1936. January 21.

Pravda. 1936b. January 29.

Preobrazhenski, Evgeny. 1965. *The New Economics*. Oxford: Clarendon House.

Protokoll. 1923. *Protokoll des Ersten Internationalen Sozialistischen Arbeiterkongress. Hamburg, 21 bis 25 Mai 1923*. Glashütten im Taunus: Auvermann.

Protokoll. 1927. *Sozialdemokratischer Parteitag, 1927 in Kiel. Protokoll*. Glashütten im Taunus: Auvermann.

Průcha, Václav, et al., eds. 1974. *Hospodarské dejiny Ceskoslovenska v 19. a 20. století*. Bratislava: Pravda.

Rabotnicheski Vestnik, June 9, 1923.

Radnóti, Miklós. 1963. *Összes versei ès müforditàsai*. Budapest: Szépirodalmi Kiadó.

Rath, John. 1971. "Authoritarian Austria." In *Native Fascism in the Successor States, 1918–1945*, ed. Peter Sugar. Santa Barbara: ABC-Clio.

Rauch, Georg von. 1987. *The Baltic States: The Years of Independence: Estonia, Latvia, Lithuania, 1917–1940*. London: C. Hurst.

Reggel. 1935. *A Reggel* (Budapest), March 18.

Reich, Wilhelm. 1971. *Die Massenpsychologie des Faschismus*. Köln: Kiepenhauer und Witsch.

Releigh, Donald. 1992. "Political Power in the Russian Revolution: A Case Study of Saratov." In *Revolution in Russia: Reassessments of 1917*, ed. Edith Rogavin Frankel, Jonathan Frankel, and Baruch Knei-Paz. Cambridge: Cambridge University Press.

Report. 1937. *The Problem of International Investment: Report of the Royal Institute of International Affairs*. London: Oxford University Press.

Report. 1972. *Baltic States: A Study of Their Origin and National Development*;

Their Seizure and Incorporation into the USSR. Report of the Select Committee on Communist Aggression. Ed. by Igor I. Kavass and Adolph Sprudzs, House of Representatives, 83rd Congress, 2d session, 1954. Buffalo: W. S.Hein.

Robbins, Lionel. 1934. *The Great Depression.* London: Macmillan.

Rogger, Hans, and Eugen Weber, eds. 1966. *The European Right. A Historical Profile.* Berkeley: University of California Press.

Rosenberg, William G., and Marylin B. Young. 1982. *Transforming Russia and China: Revolutionary Struggle in the Twentieth Century.* New York: Oxford University Press.

Roth, Marie Louise. 1972. *Robert Musil: Ethic und Asthetic.* Munich: P. List.

Rothermund, Dietmar, ed. 1983. *Die Peripherie in der Weltwirtschaftskrise: Afrika, Asia, und Latinamerika, 1929–1939.* Paderborn: Ferdinand Schöning.

Rothschild, Joseph. 1966. *Piłsudski's Coup d'état.* New York: Columbia University Press.

———. 1977. *East Central Europe between the Two World Wars.* Seattle: University of Washington Press.

Sachslehner, Johannes. 1985. *Führerwort und Führerblick, Mirko Jelusich: Zur Strategie eines Bestsellerautors in der Dreissiger Jahren.* Königstein: Verlag Anton Hain Meisenheim.

Salvi, Sergio. 1984. "Blood and Water-Colours." In *The Water-Colours of Hitler.* Firenze: Alinari.

Schmied, Wieland. 1983. "Die österreichische Malerei in den Zwischenkriegs-jahren." In *Österreich, 1918–1938: Geschichte des Ersten Republik.* Vol. 2. Ed. Erika Weinzieler and Kurt Skalnik. Graz: Verlag Styria.

Schorske, Carl. 1980. *Fin-de-Siècle Vienna: Politics and Culture.* New York: Knopf.

Schumpeter, Joseph. 1971. "The Instability of Capitalism." In *The Economics of Technological Change,* ed. Nathan Rosenberg. Harmondsworth: Penguin Books.

———. 1976. *Capitalism, Socialism, and Democracy.* London: Allen and Unwin.

Schuschnigg, Kurt von. 1938. *Farewell Austria.* London: Cassel.

Schwarz, Boris. 1988. *Music and Music Life in Soviet Russia, 1917–1981.* Bloom-ington: Indiana University Press.

Seton-Watson, Hugh. 1964. *Nationalism and Communism: Essays, 1946–1963.* New York: Praeger.

———. 1967. *Eastern Europe between the Wars, 1918–1941.* New York: Harper Torchbooks.

Seton-Watson, Robert W. 1963. *A History of the Roumanians from Roman Times to the Completion of Union.* N.p.: Archon Books.

Silber, Michael K., ed. 1992. *Jews in the Hungarian Economy, 1760–1945.* Jeru-salem: Magnes Press.

Soffici, Ardengo. 1993. "Il fascismo e l'arte." *Gerarchia,* September 25, 1922. In *Avant-garde Florence: From Modernism to Fascism,* by Walter L. Adam-son. Cambridge, Mass.: Harvard University Press.

Speer, Albert. 1970. *Inside the Third Reich: Memoirs.* New York: Macmillan.

Spengler, Oswald. 1920. *Preussentum und Sozialismus.* Munich: Beck.

——. 1973. *The Decline of the West.* Vol. 2. New York: Knopf.

Srbska. 1973. *Srbska Architectura, 1900–1970.* Ljubljana: Archtecturni Muzej.

Stalin, I. V. 1947. *Sochinenija* (Collected works), Vol. 7, 1925. Moscow: Politicheski Literaturi.

——. 1949. *Sochinenija* (Collected works), Vol. 10, August–December 1927. Moscow: Politicheski Literaturi.

Stalin, Joseph V. 1972. *The Essential Stalin: Major Theoretical Writings, 1905–1952.* Ed. Bruce Franklin. Garden City: Doubleday.

——. 1976. *Problems of Leninism.* Peking: Foreign Language Press.

State. 1982. *The State Art Museum of the Estonian SSR: Estonian and Soviet Estonian Art.* Tallin: Perioodika.

Staundinger, Anton. 1991. "Austria—The Ideology of Austro-fascismus." In *Austria in the Thirties: Culture and Politics,* ed. Kenneth Segar and John Warren. Riverside: Ariadne Press.

Stavrianos, Leften S. 1963. *The Balkans since 1453.* New York: Holt.

Sterenberg, David. 1922. Foreword to *Erste Russische Kunstaustellung Berlin.* Berlin: Galerie van Diemen.

Sternhell, Zeev. 1979. "Fascist Ideology." In *Fascism, A Reader's Guide: Analyses, Interpretations, Bibliography,* ed. Walter Laqueur. Harmondsworth: Penguin Books.

Sugar, Peter, ed. 1971. *Native Fascism in the Successor States, 1918–1945.* Santa Barbara: ABC-Clio.

——, ed. 1980. *Ethnic Diversities and Conflict in Eastern Europe.* Santa Barbara: ABC-Clio.

Survey. 1938. *The Baltic States: Royal Institute of International Affairs.* London: Oxford University Press.

Suval, Stanley. 1974. *The Anschluss Question in the Weimar Era: A Study of Nationalism in Germany and Austria, 1918–1932.* Baltimore: John Hopkins University Press.

Szálasi, Ferenc. 1964. "Út és cél." In *Varieties of Fascism,* by Eugen Weber. Princeton: Nostrand.

Szamuely, László. 1971. *Az elsö szocialista gazdasági mechanizmusok.* Budapest: Közgazdasági Kiadó.

Szczuka, Mieczyslaw, et. al. 1974. "Editorial in 'Blok,' March 8, 1924." In *The Tradition of Constructivism,* ed. Stephan Bann. New York: A Da Capo.

Szekfü, Gyula. 1922. *A három nemzedék: Egy hanyatló kor története.* Budapest.

Szlajfer, Henryk, ed. 1990. *Economic Nationalism in East-Central Europe and South America, 1918–1939.* Geneva: Librairie Droz.

Szöllösi-Janze, Margit. 1989. *Die Pfeilkreuzlerbewegung in Ungarn.* Munich: Oldenbourg.

Szücs, Julia P. 1987. *A római iskola.* Budapest: Corvina.

Tabor, Jan, ed. 1994. *Kunst und Diktatur: Architektur, Bildhauerei, und Malerei in Österreich, Deutschland, Italien, und der Sowjetunion, 1922–1956.* Baden: Verlag Grasl.

Tatlin. 1988. Ed. Larissa A. Zhadova. New York: Rizzoli.

Teichova, Alice. 1974. *An Economic Background to Munich: International Business and Czechoslovakia, 1918–1938.* Cambridge: Cambridge University Press.

——. 1988. *The Czechoslovak Economy, 1918–1980*. London: Routledge.

Thimme, Annelise. 1957. *Gustav Stresemann: Eine politische Biographie zur Geschichte der Weimar Republik*. Hannover: O. Gödel.

Thyssen, Fritz. 1941. *I Paid Hitler*. London: Hodder and Stougton.

Tilkovszky, Loránd. 1974. *SS-toborzás Magyarországon*. Budapest: Kossuth.

Tismaneanu, Vladimir. 1995. *Fantoma lui Gherghiu-Dej*. Bucharest: Editura Univers.

Tito, Josif Broz. 1977. *The Struggle and the Development of the Communist Party of Yugoslavia between the Two Wars: Lectures in Kumrovec*. Beograd: Komunist.

Tomasevich, Jozo. 1955. *Peasants, Politics, and Economic Change in Yugoslavia*. Stanford: Stanford University Press.

Toynbee, Arnold. 1955. *A Study of History*. Vol. 1. London: Oxford University Press.

Trotsky, Lev. 1971. *The Struggle against Fascism in Germany*. New York: Pathfinder Press.

——. 1972. *Revolution Betrayed*. New York: Pathfinder Press.

Tucker, Robert C. 1990. *Stalin in Power: The Revolution from Above, 1928–1941*. New York: Norton.

Turner, Henry A., Jr. 1985. *German Big Business and the Rise of Hitler*. New York: Oxford University Press.

Tyeatr. 1938. No. 1.

Tzara, Tristan. 1959. "Manifesto Dada." In *Le avangardie artistiche del Novecento*, by Mario de Micheli. Milan: Schwarz.

Vago, Bela. 1975. *The Shadow of the Swastika: The Rise of Fascism and Anti-Semitism in the Danube Basin, 1936–1939*. Farnborough: Saxon House.

——. 1979. "Fascism in Eastern Europe" In *Fascism, A Readers Guide: Analyses, Interpretations, Bibliography*, ed. Walter Laqueur. Harmondsworth: Penguin Books.

Vardys, V. Stanley. 1978. "The Rise of Authoritarian Rule in the Baltic States." In *The Baltic States in Peace and War, 1917–1945*, ed. V. Stanley Vardys and Romual J. Misiunas. University Park: Pennsylvania State University Press.

——. 1979. "Democracy in the Baltic States, 1918–1934: The Stage and the Actors." *Journal of Baltic Studies* 10, no. 4 (winter).

Venturi, Franco. 1983. *Roots of Revolution: A History of the Populist and Socialist Movements in Nineteenth-Century Russia*. Chicago: University of Chicago Press.

Vestnik. 1920. *Vestnik rabotnikov iskustv* no. 2–3.

Vital, David. 1975. *Zionism: The Formative Years*. Oxford: Clarendon.

Vlcek, Tomás. 1990. "Art between Social Crisis and Utopia: The Czech Contribution to the Development of the Avant-garde Movement in East-Central Europe, 1910–1930." *Art Journal* 49 (spring).

Völgyes, Ivan, ed. 1971. *Hungary in Revolution, 1918–1919: Nine Essays*. Lincoln: University of Nebraska Press.

Volkogonov, Dmitrij. 1991. *Stalin: Triumph and Tragedy*. London: Weidenfeld and Nicholson.

Vörös Ujság. 1918. (Budapest) December 7.

Wade, Rex A. 1992. "The Red Guards: Spontaneity and the October Revolution." In *Revolution in Russia: Reassessments of 1917,* ed. Edith Rogavin Frankel, Jonathan Frankel, Baruch Knei-Paz. Cambridge: Cambridge University Press.

Wallerstein, Immanuel. 1974. *The Modern World System: Capitalist Agriculture and the Origins of the European World-Economy in the Sixteenth Century.* New York: Academic Press.

Wandycz, Piotr. 1962. *France and Her Eastern Allies, 1919–1925.* Minneapolis: University of Minnesota Press.

———. 1994. "The Polish Question." Working paper, University of California, Berkeley.

Weber, Eugen. 1966. "The Men of the Archangel." In *International Fascism, 1920–1945,* ed. Walter Laqueur and George Mosse. New York: Harper and Row.

———. 1979. "Revolution? Counterrevolution? What Revolution?" In *Fascism, A Reader's Guide: Analyses, Interpretations, Bibliography,* ed. Walter Laqueur. Harmondsworth: Penguin Books.

Weissenberger, R. 1984. "Arnold Schönberg Malerei." In *Traum und Wirklichkeit.* Vienna: Museen der Stadt Wien.

Wenter, Josef. 1937. *Im heiligen Land Tirol.* Graz: Verlag Styria.

Westheim, Paul. 1979. In *A konstruktivizmus,* ed. Éva R. Bajkay. Budapest: Gondolat.

Wojciechowski, Jan Stanislaw. 1984. "On the Oldest, Old, and Most Recent Monuments in Poland." *Polish Art Studies* (Wroclaw) 6.

Wynot, Edward, D. 1974. *Polish Politics in Transition.* Athens: University of Georgia Press.

Zacek, Joseph F. 1969. "Nationalism in Czechoslovakia." In *Nationalism in Eastern Europe,* ed. Peter Sugar and Ivo Lederer. Seattle: University of Washington Press.

Zádor, András. 1961. Conclusion to *Harc a Szalamandrákkal,* by Karel Capek. Budapest: Szépirodalmi Kiadó.

Zavalani, Tayor. 1969. "Albanian Nationalism." In *Nationalism in Eastern Europe,* ed. Peter Sugar and Ivo Lederer. Seattle: University of Washington Press.

Zhdanov, Andrei A. 1988. "Speech at the First All-Union Congress of Soviet Writers, 1934." In *Russian Avantgarde: Theory and Criticism, 1902–1934,* ed. John E. Bowlt. New York: Thames and Hudson.

Zinovyev, Grigory. 1921. *Zwölf Tage in Deutschland.* Petrograd: Kommunistische Internationale.

Index

Designer: Ina Clausen
Compositor: Integrated Compositon Systems, Inc.
Text: 10/13 Galliard
Display: Galliard
Printer: Data Reproductions, Inc.
Binder: Data Reproductions, Inc.